Augustine's *CITY OF GOD*

Augustine's *City of God* has profoundly influenced the course of Western political philosophy, but there are few guides to its labyrinthine argumentation that hold together the delicate interplay of religion and philosophy in Augustine's thought. The essays in this volume offer a careful examination of those themes, using the central, contested distinction between a heavenly city on earthly pilgrimage and an earthly city bound for perdition to elaborate aspects of Augustine's political and moral vision. Topics discussed include Augustine's notion of the secular, his critique of pagan virtue, his departure from classical eudaimonism, his mythology of sin, his dystopian politics, his surprising attention to female bodies, his moral psychology, his valorization of love, his critique of empire, and his conception of a Christian philosophy. Together the essays advance our understanding of Augustine's most influential work and provide a rich overview of Augustinian political theology and its philosophical implications.

JAMES WETZEL is Professor of Philosophy at Villanova University and the first permanent holder of the Augustinian Endowed Chair in the Thought of Saint Augustine. He is the author of *Augustine and the Limits of Virtue* (Cambridge, 1992) and *Augustine: A Guide for the Perplexed* (2010).

CAMBRIDGE CRITICAL GUIDES

Titles published in this series

Hegel's *Phenomenology of Spirit*
EDITED BY DEAN MOYAR AND MICHAEL QUANTE

Mill's *On Liberty*
EDITED BY C. L. TEN

Kant's *Idea for a Universal History with a Cosmopolitan Aim*
EDITED BY AMÉLIE OKSENBERG RORTY AND JAMES SCHMIDT

Kant's *Groundwork of the Metaphysics of Morals*
EDITED BY JENS TIMMERMANN

Kant's *Critique of Practical Reason*
EDITED BY ANDREWS REATH AND JENS TIMMERMANN

Wittgenstein's *Philosophical Investigations*
EDITED BY ARIF AHMED

Kierkegaard's *Concluding Unscientific Postscript*
EDITED BY RICK ANTHONY FURTAK

Plato's *Republic*
EDITED BY MARK L. MCPHERRAN

Plato's *Laws*
EDITED BY CHRISTOPHER BOBONICH

Spinoza's *Theological-Political Treatise*
EDITED BY YITZHAK Y. MELAMED AND MICHAEL A. ROSENTHAL

Aristotle's *Nicomachean Ethics*
EDITED BY JON MILLER

Kant's *Metaphysics of Morals*
EDITED BY LARA DENIS

Nietzsche's *On The Genealogy of Morality*
EDITED BY SIMON MAY

Kant's *Observations and Remarks*
EDITED BY RICHARD VELKLEY AND SUSAN MELD SHELL

Augustine's *City of God*
EDITED BY JAMES WETZEL

AUGUSTINE'S
City of God
A Critical Guide

EDITED BY
JAMES WETZEL
Villanova University

CAMBRIDGE
UNIVERSITY PRESS

CAMBRIDGE
UNIVERSITY PRESS

University Printing House, Cambridge CB2 8BS, United Kingdom

Cambridge University Press is part of the University of Cambridge.

It furthers the University's mission by disseminating knowledge in the pursuit of education, learning and research at the highest international levels of excellence.

www.cambridge.org
Information on this title: www.cambridge.org/9781107463189

© Cambridge University Press 2012

This publication is in copyright. Subject to statutory exception and to the provisions of relevant collective licensing agreements, no reproduction of any part may take place without the written permission of Cambridge University Press.

First published 2012
Reprinted 2013
First paperback edition 2014

A catalogue record for this publication is available from the British Library

Library of Congress Cataloguing in Publication data
Augustine's City of God : a critical guide / edited by James Wetzel.
  p. cm. – (Cambridge critical guides)
Includes bibliographical references (p. 245) and index.
ISBN 978-0-521-19994-0
1. Augustine, Saint, Bishop of Hippo. De civitate Dei.   2. Kingdom of God.   3. Apologetics.   I. Wetzel, James.
BR65.A65A845 2012
239′.3–dc23
               2012009104

ISBN 978-0-521-19994-0 Hardback
ISBN 978-1-107-46318-9 Paperback

Cambridge University Press has no responsibility for the persistence or accuracy of URLs for external or third-party internet websites referred to in this publication, and does not guarantee that any content on such websites is, or will remain, accurate or appropriate.

In memoriam

Robert A. Markus (1924–2010),
theorist of the saeculum

Gareth B. Matthews (1929–2011),
lover of Socratic perplexity

quid est ergo tempus? si nemo ex me quaerat, scio; si quaerenti explicare velim, nescio.
– *conf.* 11.14.17

Contents

List of contributors		*page* xi
Acknowledgements		xiii
List of abbreviations		xiv
	Introduction JAMES WETZEL	1
1	The history of the book: Augustine's *City of God* and post-Roman cultural memory MARK VESSEY	14
2	Secularity and the *saeculum* PAUL J. GRIFFITHS	33
3	Augustine's dystopia PETER IVER KAUFMAN	55
4	From rape to resurrection: sin, sexual difference, and politics MARGARET R. MILES	75
5	Ideology and solidarity in Augustine's *City of God* JOHN CAVADINI	93
6	The theater of the virtues: Augustine's critique of pagan mimesis JENNIFER HERDT	111
7	The psychology of compassion: Stoicism in *City of God* 9.5 SARAH BYERS	130
8	Augustine's rejection of eudaimonism NICHOLAS WOLTERSTORFF	149
9	Augustine on the origin of evil: myth and metaphysics JAMES WETZEL	167

10	Hell and the dilemmas of intractable alienation JOHN BOWLIN	186
11	On the nature and worth of Christian philosophy: evidence from the *City of God* JOHN RIST	205
12	Reinventing Augustine's ethics: the afterlife of *City of God* BONNIE KENT	225

Bibliography   245
Index   254

Contributors

JOHN BOWLIN is the Rimmer and Ruth de Vries Associate Professor of Reformed Theology and Public Life at Princeton Theological Seminary. He is the author of *Contingency and Fortune in Aquinas's Ethics* (Cambridge, 1999) and 'Augustine Counting Virtues,' *Augustinian Studies* (2010).

SARAH BYERS is Assistant Professor of Philosophy at Boston College. She is the author of 'Augustine and the Cognitive Cause of Stoic Preliminary Passions,' *Journal of the History of Philosophy* (2003), 'Augustine and the Philosophers,' in the *Blackwell Companion to Augustine* (2012), and *Perception, Sensibility, and Moral Motivation in Augustine* (forthcoming with Cambridge).

JOHN CAVADINI is the McGrath–Cavadini Director of the Institute for Church Life at the University of Notre Dame. He is also a member of the Department of Theology there and served as its Chair for 13 years. He is the editor of *Gregory the Great: A Symposium* (1996) and the author of numerous articles on Augustine, including 'Feeling Right: Augustine on the Passions and Sexual Desire,' *Augustinian Studies* (2005).

PAUL J. GRIFFITHS teaches theology at Duke Divinity School, where he holds the Warren Chair of Catholic Theology. His most recent books are *Song of Songs: A Commentary* (2011) and *Intellectual Appetite: A Theological Grammar* (2009).

JENNIFER HERDT is the Gilbert L. Stark Professor of Christian Ethics at the Divinity School of Yale University. She is the author of *Religion and Faction in Hume's Moral Philosophy* (Cambridge, 1997) and *Putting on Virtue: The Legacy of the Splendid Vices* (2008).

PETER IVER KAUFMAN is Professor Emeritus, University of North Carolina at Chapel Hill and – since 2008 – Charles Matthews and Virginia Brinkley Modlin Professor at the University of Richmond. He is the author of *Redeeming Politics* (1990) and *Incorrectly Political: Augustine and Thomas More* (2007).

BONNIE KENT is Professor of Philosophy at the University of California, Irvine. She is the author of *Virtues of the Will: The Transformation of Ethics in the Late Thirteenth Century* (1995), 'Augustine's Ethics,' in *The Cambridge Companion to Augustine* (Cambridge, 2001), and 'Virtue Theory,' in *The Cambridge History of Medieval Philosophy* (Cambridge, 2010).

MARGARET R. MILES is Professor of Historical Theology Emerita, The Graduate Theological Union, Berkeley. Her recent books include *Augustine and the Fundamentalist's Daughter* (2011), *A Complex Delight: The Secularization of the Breast, 1350–1750* (2008), and *The Word Made Flesh: A History of Christian Thought* (2005).

JOHN RIST is Professor of Classics and Philosophy Emeritus at the University of Toronto, Professore Incaricato at the Istituto Patristico Augustinianum in Rome, and Kurt Pritzl OP Professor of Philosophy at the Catholic University of America. He is the author of more than a dozen books on ancient philosophy, patristics, and ethics, including *Plotinus: The Road to Reality* (Cambridge, 1967), *Augustine: Ancient Thought Baptized* (Cambridge, 1994), *Real Ethics* (Cambridge, 2001), and *What is Truth? From the Academy to the Vatican* (Cambridge, 2008).

MARK VESSEY is Professor of English and Principal of Green College at the University of British Columbia. He is the co-editor (with Karla Pollmann) of *Augustine and the Disciplines: From Cassiciacum to Confessions* (2005) and editor of *A Companion to Augustine* (2012).

JAMES WETZEL is Professor of Philosophy and the Augustinian Chair in the Thought of St. Augustine at Villanova University. He is the author of *Augustine and the Limits of Virtue* (Cambridge, 1992) and *Augustine: A Guide for the Perplexed* (2010).

NICHOLAS WOLTERSTORFF is Noah Porter Professor Emeritus of Philosophical Theology at Yale University and Senior Fellow in the Institute for Advanced Studies in Culture at the University of Virginia. He is the author of *Justice: Rights and Wrongs* (2008), *Justice in Love* (2011), and *Understanding Liberal Democracy* (forthcoming).

Acknowledgements

I would like to thank Hilary Gaskin at Cambridge University Press for suggesting this project to me, and Anna Lowe, her assistant editor, for helping to shepherd it along. Over the years, I have been the beneficiary of much guidance on matters Augustinian. I would like to acknowledge in particular my friends and colleagues at the Augustinian Institute at Villanova and especially its director, Allan D. Fitzgerald, O.S.A.

Bente Polites, Special Collections Librarian for Falvey Memorial Library, Villanova University, furnished this volume with its cover image. It is taken from St. Augustine, *De civitate Dei*, Basel: Johann Amerbach, 1490 and is used with the kind permission of Special Collections.

Finally, I cannot let it pass without offering a word of explicit gratitude to R. W. Dyson, whose edition and translation of "the great and arduous work" (Cambridge, 1998) served as this volume's standard.

Abbreviations

WORKS OF AUGUSTINE

b. conjug.	*De bono conjugali*	(On the Good of Marriage)
b. vita	*De beata vita*	(On the Happy or Estimable Life)
c. Acad.	*Contra Academicos*	(Against the Skeptics)
c. ep. Man.	*Contra epistulam Manichaei quam vocant fundamenti*	(Against the "Foundation Letter" of the Manichees)
c. Faust.	*Contra Faustum Manicheum*	(Against Faustus, a Manichee)
c. Jul.	*Contra Julianum*	(Against Julian)
conf.	*Confessiones*	(Confessions)
div. qu.	*De diversis quaestionibus octoginta tribus*	(On 83 Different Questions)
doc. Chr.	*De doctrina Christiana*	(On Christian Instruction)
ench.	*Enchiridion ad Laurentium de fide spe et caritate*	(Handbook on Faith, Hope, and Love)
en. Ps.	*Enarrationes in Psalmos*	(Explications of the Psalms)
ep.	*Epistulae*	(Letters)
ep. Jo.	*In epistulam Joannis ad Parthos tractatus*	(Tractates on the First Letter of John)
f. et symb.	*De fide et symbolo*	(On Faith and the Creed)
Gn. adv. Man.	*De Genesi adversus Manicheos*	(On Genesis: Against the Manichees)
Gn. litt.	*De Genesi ad litteram*	(On Genesis: The Literal Commentary)
Jo. ev. tr.	*In Johannis evangelium tractatus*	(Tractates on the Gospel of John)

lib. arb.	*De libero arbitrio*	(On Free Choice; Free Will)
mag.	*De magistro*	(On the Teacher)
mor.	*De moribus ecclesiae catholicae et de moribus Manichaeorum*	(On the Catholic and the Manichean Ways of Life)
nat. et gr.	*De natura et gratia*	(On Nature and Grace)
ord.	*De ordine*	(On Order)
perf. just.	*De perfectione justitiae hominis*	(On the Perfection of Human Righteousness)
praed. sanc.	*De praedestinatione sanctorum*	(On the Predestination of the Saints)
retr.	*Retractationes*	(Retractations; Reconsiderations)
s.	*Sermones*	(Sermons)
Simpl.	*De diversis quaestionibus ad Simplicianum*	(To Simplician, Various Questions)
sol.	*Soliloquia*	(Soliloquies)
spir. et litt.	*De spiritu et littera*	(On the Spirit and the Letter)
Trin.	*De trinitate*	(On the Trinity)
util. cred.	*De utilitate credendi*	(On the Advantage of Believing)
vera rel.	*De vera religione*	(On True Religion)

Note: For the most part, abbreviations and title translations of Augustine's works conform to the listing in Fitzgerald 1999: xxxv–xlii.

OTHER AUTHORS

Apuleius

deo Soc.	*De deo Socratis*	(The God of Socrates)

Aquinas

Disp. qu. de virtutibus	*Disputatae quaestiones: de virtutibus in communi*	(Disputed Questions: On the Virtues, in General)
ST	*Summa theologiae*	(The Sum of Theology)

Aristotle

eth. Nic. (Nicomachean Ethics)

Aulus Gellius

NA   *Noctes Atticae*   (Attic Nights)

Cicero

leg.   *De legibus*   (On the Laws)
rep.   *De re publica*   (On the Republic)
Tusc.   *Tusculanae disputationes*   (Tusculan Disputations)

Diogenes Laertius

DL   (Lives of the Eminent Philosophers)

Epictetus

ench.   *Enchiridion*   (Handbook)
disc.   (Discourses)

Peter Lombard

sent.   *Sententiae*   (Sentences)

Origen

c. Cels.   *Contra Celsum*   (Against Celsus)

Plotinus

enn.   *Enneads*

Possidius

v. Aug.	*Vita Sancta Augustini*	(The Saintly Life of Augustine)

Seneca

clem.	*De clementia*	(On Clemency)
ira	*De ira*	(On Anger)
otio	*De otio*	(On the Private Life)
prov.	*De providentia*	(On Providence)

Virgil

Aen.	*Aeneid*

Biblical sources

1 Cor.	Paul's First Letter to the Church at Corinth
Ecclus.	Ecclesiasticus
Eph.	Ephesians
Exod.	Exodus
Gen.	Genesis
Is.	Isaiah
Jer.	Jeremiah
Matt.	Matthew
1 Pet.	1 Peter
Phil.	Philippians
Ps.	Psalms
Rom.	Paul's Letter to the Church at Rome
1 Tim.	Paul's First Letter to Timothy

Latin source collections

PL	*Patrologiae Cursus Completus, Series Latina*	(Migne's Latin Church Fathers)
CCSL	*Corpus Christianorum Series Latina*	(Latin Patristics, Brepols)

CSEL	*Corpus Christianorum Ecclesiasticorum Latinorum*	(Latin Patristics, Austrian Academy of Sciences)
BA	*Bibliothèque Augustinienne, Oeuvres de Saint Augustin*	(Augustine's Works, Études Augustiniennes)

Reference works

AL	*Augustinus Lexicon*	(Augustine Encyclopedia, C. Mayer et al., eds., Schwabe AG)

Introduction

James Wetzel

> *In this world, the two cities are indeed entangled and mingled with one another; and they will remain so until the last judgment shall separate them.*
>
> – *civ. Dei* 1.35

In his *Retractations* (*retr.* 2.43.2; cf. *ep.* 1A*.1), Augustine suggests that there are basically two ways, not in his mind opposed, of reading *City of God*: as a defense of Christianity's superiority over paganism, and as a treatise on the two cities – one that "most glorious" city (*civ. Dei* pref.) of which the Psalmist sings (Ps. 87:3), the other the heavenly city's earthly antithesis. The latter Augustine mostly refers to as the "earthly city" (*terrena civitas*), but he also calls the city "diabolical" (*diaboli*), "demon-revering" (*daemonicola*), "death-bound" (*mortalium*), "ungodly" (*impia*), and "of the age" (*huius saeculi*).[1]

The more damning designations are reminders that the earthly city has its roots in hell, where fallen angels, having become demons, are doomed to reside. Members of the earthly city bind themselves through sin to a demonic love – a profound, soul-defining love, but a love so thoroughly perverted that it has become both impossible to satisfy and an endless source of suffering. Meanwhile, members of the heavenly city on earth, who through grace are being made fit company for angels, endure the purgation that rids their love of its demonic propensities. They are part of a city on pilgrimage (*peregrinatur in mundo*; *civ. Dei* 1.35). Having to share an earthly politics with their dispirited alter-egos is undoubtedly part of their spiritual adventure. But Augustine realizes that it is far from a simple matter to translate the messy antipathies of historical beings into an antithesis between two, all-encompassing cities, each defined by an unseen end, that of heaven or hell. In *City of God*, pagan Rome and the earthly city keep close company, but for the most part Augustine keeps them conceptually

---

[1] See Van Oort 1990: 116, 130 for references and further elaboration.

distinct. Analogously, Christian Rome and the heavenly city on pilgrimage have close ties, but they are not identical. For while it is inconceivable to Augustine that redemption would come to human beings other than through Christ, he does not assume that church membership is enough; there are some who take the sacraments without benefit (*civ. Dei* 1.35).

The first ten books of *City of God* most naturally read as Augustine's critique of classically Roman paganism. It divides into two parts: a critique of pagan claims that the gods provide happiness to those who revere them (Books 1–5), and a critique of pagan claims that the gods do so, not necessarily in this life, but certainly in the life to come (Books 6–10). This lengthy polemic, which he began writing in 413 and finished by 417, didn't just come out of the blue.[2] In August of 410 the Visigoths under the command of Alaric pillaged and bloodied the city of Rome for three long days, sending shaken refugees to places like Roman North Africa, where their presence fueled old order resentment over 'Christian times' (*tempora Christiana*).[3] Augustine tells us that he felt compelled to answer the complaints of pagan sophisticates who were missing their gods and blaspheming against "the true God" (*deum verum*) more than usual (*retr.* 2.43.1).

Ten books of relentless assault against the worship of false gods certainly sets up an ample stage for reintroducing true worship and its benefits. And indeed Augustine does say that the next twelve books of *City of God*, written over a markedly longer stretch of time, 417 to 426, can be read as his positive case for the Christian religion. But they can also be read, he adds, as a tripartite treatise on the two cities: four books on their respective origins, four books on their joint concourse through history, and four books on their ultimate – and radically divergent – ends.

It is hardly surprising, given the firmness of Augustine's belief in the superiority of the Christian faith over rival pieties, that he would have failed to make much of the difference between a positive apologetic and a meditation on the two cities. But, to be frank, if there were not much of a difference, if the two-cities meditation were more of a rhetorical flourish than a substantive transformation of apologetic discourse, then *City of God* would be a long footnote in the history of religious chauvinism and not the work of abiding fascination that it is and deserves to be. As a work of Christian apologetics, *City of God* is quick to turn an antiquated paganism into the standard-bearer of a

---

[2] For the composition history of *City of God*, see O'Daly 1999a: 27–36.
[3] The phrase connotes the ascendency of the Christian religion to imperial favor, particularly under the emperor Theodosius (d. 395), whose favoritism included a campaign against the old paganism. Augustine's sense of the providential value of this ascendency will have changed significantly by the time he begins writing *City of God*. See Markus 1988: 22–44.

debased desire – a "lust for mastery" (*libido dominandi*; *civ. Dei* pref.) – and to grant Christians living in a Christian empire the benefit of their professed humility. As a reflection on the two cities, *City of God* acknowledges an eschatological gap between Christians and their virtues, one that leaves Christ alone the master of humility. His students will have to relearn humility in all the contexts where worldly necessities and spiritual imperatives have yet to be sorted out. And perhaps needn't be: Augustine contends that the two cities, while remaining antithetical in their ultimate aims, both value earthly peace in the interim – no civil war, no domestic violence, public civility, a common and orderly use of temporal goods (*civ. Dei* 19.17; cf. 19.14).

The two-cities framework presses the question of the secular upon Augustine's Christian apologetic. If Christians do not fully own their virtues, nor pagans their vices, then what would it mean for them, in the time before their self-formations fix, to mingle? Partly it means that it is possible for a pagan to convert to Christianity and for a Christian, living in a once pagan empire, to revert to the old reverences. But when set within the two-cities framework, conversion and reversion mask a more basic rigidity of identity: the pagan who converts never was not a member of the heavenly city on pilgrimage, bound for life in the celestial city; the Christian who reverts never was not a member of the earthly city, doomed, despite the occasional show of virtue, to sink into an untenable love. The implications of this extraordinary framing are, to say the least, far from obvious.

It is tempting for a modern reader of *City of God*, especially a liberally inclined one, to downplay Augustine's association of a pagan form of reverence with a demonic perversion and leave the alternative to Christianity less tendentiously described.[4] In that way the eschatological framing lends itself to a more neutral conception of the secular: where no one knows the ultimate disposition of souls, it is possible for religious rivals to put aside disputes over ultimates and concentrate on basics – the terms for peaceful co-existence within a worldly order of finite goods (the earthly city, but here no longer demonized). This is the line interpretation advanced by Robert Markus, whose pivotal study of the two-cities framework shaped more than four decades of *City of God* debate.[5] Markus

---

[4] For Augustine, paganism and Judaism are Christianity's primary rivals (leaving aside the issue of competing versions of Christianity). His attitude towards Judaism differs markedly from his stance against paganism. He is far less tempted either to demonize or to evangelize the Jews. The story of Augustine's relation to Judaism is in Fredriksen 2008.
[5] Markus 1970; rev. ed. 1988. Markus revisits his reading of Augustine in his Blessed Pope John XXIII lectures on the Christian roots of secularism. To my mind, his reading remains fundamentally the same. See Markus 2006; cf. Wetzel 2007.

reads Augustine as having founded his theology of the *saeculum*, of worldliness, on the indiscernibility of the two cities in historical time. The result, Markus contends, is a secularization of political life that requires, even if it does not outrightly announce, "a pluralistic, religiously neutral civil community."[6]

The readings of Augustine in this volume, all of which touch upon the complexity of the two-cities distinction, are in significant ways post Markus. I mean by this basically two things. The dominant critical response to Markus has been to accept his emphasis on eschatology but veer from his insistence on the historical invisibility of the two cities.[7] Pagan Rome may not be identical to the debased earthly city, but surely for Augustine it can be seen to be closer to that city than, for all its imperfections, the Roman Church is? Given the influence of Markus and the tradition of critique that his reading of Augustine has inspired, it is very hard to write about *City of God* from within Augustinian studies and make Augustine out to be either some Eusebian-style theocrat, ready to bless a Christian empire, or a post Vatican II Catholic liberal, ready to celebrate the diversity of faiths. But if Augustine's thinking does not obviously incline him towards either option, how does he think about the intersection between temporary and ultimate realities?

This brings me to the other, broader way in which the essays in this volume are post Markus. *Saeculum* came out in 1970, a boon time for religious liberalism. In the decades to follow, the book would fascinate largely due to its stunning suggestion that secular liberalism, with its dream of an urbane and cosmopolitan peace, could take its inspiration from a religiously conservative source, from the doctor of sin and grace himself. But now that we are well into the second decade of the fractious twenty-first century, with its resurgent fundamentalisms, it seems increasingly unlikely that secular liberalism will find within itself the conceptual resources for framing and really illuminating the global debate over religion. The Augustine of most interest to our cultural moment is the one who weds his philosophical ambitions to his cultic identity, but without entirely conflating the two. This Augustine, if we can find him, may give us some reason to think that a religious philosophy is something other than an impossible compromise between a skeptical liberalism and a dogmatic faith.

---

[6] Markus 1988: 173.
[7] I think especially of Williams 1987, Milbank 1990 (rev. ed. 2006), O'Donovan 2004, and Dodaro 2004.

I am not claiming that the contributors to this volume would frame the cultural moment the way that I do, or even that they have a similar view of Augustinian studies and of the influence that Markus has had on readings of *City of God*. What I am willing to claim is that it is no accident that the most fruitful new forays into that massive text tend not to read a neutral secularity into the space of the "mingled cities" (*permixtae civitates*; civ. Dei 1.35). Nor do they adopt a secularity of this sort into their respective analytical perspectives. The historians of this volume are too historicist to favor the (modernist) imposition; the theologians and the philosophers, who are often also the historians, favor a more fluid, less fixed engagement between reason and faith. They collectively give us a *City of God* with the potential to reshape a philosophical landscape.

I turn now to a synopsis of the individual offerings.

The volume begins with Mark Vessey's essay, "The history of the book." Take that reference to "the book" in at least two ways. Vessey means to refer, unsurprisingly, to *City of God*, but he embeds that reference within a nod to the readerly technology that *City of God* so effectively exploits. The literary high culture of Virgil's day stored its poems, oratory, and historical writings on scrolls; the papyrus or parchment codex, the ancestral form of the book (pages bound between two covers), became widely available in imperial times. Christian writers, unconcerned with culturally pagan precedent, readily used the codex for their most cherished literary productions. The codex, more than the scroll, is a technology that facilitates synopsis – a view of the whole set within the compass of readily surveyable parts or, in this case, pages. For most of his essay, Vessey works to give us some sense of the synoptic ambitions of *City of God*. It is a book that attempts to situate all of human history within a Christian reading of the Bible (yet another meaning of "the book"), and it offers to its non-Christian readers especially terms for rendering themselves foreign to their own self-descriptions. Vessey calls *City of God* "Augustine's greatest work of writerly and 'bookish' coercion."

The next two essays, by Paul Griffiths and Peter Kaufman respectively, are the ones that deal most directly with the problematic of history. Augustine endorses a thickly providential reading of history in *City of God*, but he also claims that no one, not even a bona fide heavenly pilgrim on earth, is able to read divine purposes off historical events. With providence being so hidden, how are we not consigned in practice to an unstable order of agonistically imposed human purposes, the world of a God-vacated secularity?

In "Secularity and the *saeculum*," Griffiths works methodically to differentiate Augustine's use of the Latin term "*saeculum*" from the meaning of the etymologically related English term "secular." His ultimate aim is to assess whether an Augustinian secularity, properly delineated, has any normative purchase on the modern conception. He proceeds on the assumption that Markus exaggerates the difference between the eschatological and the empirical, turning a distinction into a disparity. To a significant degree, it is possible for the faithful to detect and convey the signs of a divinely governed order, but only if they look through the lens of the Biblical witness and only if they have learned to use the language of this witness within a properly liturgical context. The Augustine that Griffiths uncovers has predictably little to say to secularists still intent on secular fundamentalism, but perhaps quite a bit to those who can see in religious integrity something other than a political threat or a philosophical non-starter.

Now turning to Kaufman: in "Augustine's dystopia," he entertains the idea that the earthly city – or what he punningly calls, "the city of gaud" – is dystopian. There is a long tradition of darkly pessimistic readings of *City of God*, where Augustine is made out to be a world-blackener, a preacher of life's unrelenting miseries. In the midst of such a dystopia, all hope is insignificant – there is literally no sign of it. Kaufman's reading of *City of God* is a corrective to the pessimistic tradition, as well as to its kissing cousin, the tradition of "things are not so bad" optimism. Both traditions bring too limited a conception of dystopia to the table. To call a society "dystopian" is not necessarily to claim that it has realized its worst possibilities of chaos and oppression; the adjective can also be applied, notes Kaufman, to societies that are perpetually on the verge of becoming hells. Kaufman charts with great care Augustine's sense of the limits of Christian politics. What is the best that the Church can do for the World? Not bring it closer to heaven, for it has always been too late for that, but perhaps keep it another day from hell, the one it is so intent on becoming. That may seem to describe a dystopian scenario, in the extended sense of dystopia, but Kaufman ends his essay with a provocative suggestion: that the *City of God* itself, in its insistence on two divergently oriented cities, has become the greatest consolation of all – the one in regard to which none of the others matter. For the dystopian coincidence of the two cities on earth is also, in the framework of Augustine's eschatology, the symbolism of human redemption.

The next two essays, by Margaret R. Miles and John Cavadini respectively, take up the question of the good of the body, or more precisely, the value of an incarnate life. If there is serious doubt about the possibility of history being an arena in which irreducibly particular agents labor for their share in the good that is greater, perhaps infinitely so, than themselves, then the question of whether it is good for me to have my particular body and history, or you yours, is sure to follow. As theologians, Miles and Cavadini share the same sense of the Christian doctrine of the resurrection: that it is an affirmation not just of bodily life in general, but also of the irreducible goodness of all the particular bodily lives that have been. Augustine has a reputation both for disdaining the life of the body, particularly in its sexual expression, and for idealizing, à la Platonism, the life of the disembodied soul. We get quite a different Augustine from Miles and Cavadini.

In "From rape to resurrection," Miles proposes to treat *City of God* as a history of bodies – suffering, sexual, gloried – and not simply a compendium of ideas, and she underscores the striking and rather surprising attention that Augustine devotes to the female body. Her main contention is that the female body functions in *City of God* as "the normative body." In its dramatic transfiguration from object of use to object of "useless" but still fully female beauty, it best discloses the meaning of pilgrimage.

In "Ideology and solidarity in Augustine's *City of God*," Cavadini explores the critical edge of Augustine's incarnational ethic and theology. Philosophers who see nothing of wonder or beauty in the linking of soul to body are, for Augustine, more than just aesthetically impaired; the ones who belittle that linkage and elevate the life of the soul to some vacant and immobile abstraction are not just making an intellectual mistake. To ignore or deny the value of an incarnation – God's or anyone else's – is to invite the reduction of the body, and the life conjoined it, to an object of exploitation. Empires typically exploit embodied subjects and their abilities for the glory of empire. Cavadini argues that Platonists in *City of God* come off as ideologues of Empire, not because they are overt apologists, but because their disincarnate spirituality leaves the field wide open for exploitive conceptions of an embodied life. He also develops Augustine's notion of solidarity, the contrast to ideology, based on what Augustine has to say about the quality of the bonds in the pilgrim city. (It is ironic that only the city whose love is on the move is solid.)

The next three essays are centrally concerned with Augustine's critique of pagan (heroic) virtue and classical conceptions of the good life. In *City of God* 19.25, Augustine condemns as vices virtues that lack appropriate reference to God; that leaves condemned, by his previous reckoning, every school of philosophy that could have come out of a pagan animus (and apparently there are 288 of them; *civ. Dei* 19.1). *City of God* 19.25 has been a *locus classicus* for scholars looking to authenticate the break between classicism and Christianity and Augustine's role in bringing that break about. The great temptation, when filling out the picture, has been to downplay the two-cities framework of Augustine's critique and interpret that chapter's reference to God as an invocation of supernatural power. Pagans, having false or non-existent gods, or better, gods that never enter into their ethical theories, get to be the naturalists; that leaves Augustine to call upon higher power. But Augustine does not vilify pagan Roman virtue for its lack of power; he can admire, to a point, the extraordinary courage of a Regulus (*civ. Dei* 1.15); he worries more about misconception, or virtue that proves to have its origins, all theatrics to the contrary aside, in self-love. His pagan philosophers are certainly not the only exponents of earthly city wisdom, but they are dangerously good at making it seem noble, and even self-sacrificing. Once their self-deception is exposed, Augustine can more properly address the fraught issue of divine power: the only access to it is through humility, and humility is the form, as well as the prerequisite, of whatever power is received.

In "The theater of the virtues," Jennifer Herdt links Augustine's critique of pagan virtue to his critique of pagan worship, and she reminds us that, for Augustine, worship always draws deeply from the power of spectacle. Think of Dido weeping over Aeneas, who has left her for good, much against his private desires, in order to fight battles, serve the gods, and found a new city. It is not obvious that all the dramas that feed the piously pagan imagination are at bottom exultations of self over God. Herdt affirms what is usually claimed about Augustine's critique – that it is "fundamentally a critique of pride" – but she sees Augustine's alternative to pride not as willful self-abasement but as openness to the true spectacle of humility: God in the flesh and on a cross. As that is an openness that already requires humility, it is not a power that can be cultivated. The conceptual summit of pagan virtue, which remains, at heart, a cultivation of personal power, is virtue that is pursued for its own sake and not for love of praise or glory. For Herdt's Augustine, this is virtue that is still caught up in the spectacle of a self curved in on itself (*curvatus in se*) and averting divine compassion.

In an essay that pairs well with Herdt's, Sarah Byers offers a close reading of *City of God* 9.5, where Augustine faults Stoics for failing to find the virtue in compassion (*misericordia*). He has been in the previous chapter musing on the small drama that Aulus Gellius recounts in *Attic Nights* (*civ. Dei* 9.4; cf. *NA* 19.1): "a distinguished Stoic philosopher" pales and shudders when the ship he is aboard seems about to go down in a storm; when the storm subsides, "a wealthy and pleasure-loving Asiatic" teases him for not being very Stoic; the philosopher repays his critic with ridicule in kind, but then goes on to explain to Aulus Gellius why involuntary responses to a fearful situation are, in a wise man, no indications of real fear. Augustine is less preoccupied with the plausibility of the proffered explanation than he is struck by the Stoic's hard-heartedness (*civ. Dei* 9.5): "But how much more honorable it would have been if the Stoic in Aulus Gellius's story had been disturbed by compassion for a fellow man, in order comfort him, rather than by fear of shipwreck." In his more developed critique, not just of one Stoic, but of Stoicism itself, Augustine does not content himself with a rant against cold and unfeeling self-control. As Byers is careful to argue, Augustine never confuses the Stoic ideal of *apatheia* – freedom from passion – with a total shutdown of affective receptivity. His critique of Stoic lack of compassion is both particular and subtle, and, as Byers sets it out, it rests on two key assertions. First, in wishing not to be grieved by the suffering of those who suffer from real evils, the Stoics are unreasonably privileging their own virtues (they are curving in on themselves); by their own lights they should simply be valuing virtue. Second, their privatization of virtue, having no clearly Stoic motive, speaks to their unacknowledged fear of having to feel the pain of another's pain (in this they are closet Epicureans). The philosopher who emerges from Augustine's critique is not dead to compassion, but subconsciously is trying to be.

It is hard not to get the impression, given his sweeping critique of philosophical ethics in *City of God* 19, that Augustine thinks of pagan luminaries as ideologists of the earthly city. They may not be charter members of that city, and yet they all seem to be finding subtle and interesting ways of promoting its campaign of self-love. But consider that, for Augustine, this is a campaign to promote not just any kind of self-love, but a boundlessly self-aggrandizing form, really a kind of madness. The ancient schools were hardly calling for that, certainly not explicitly. Their predominant ethical paradigm was eudaimonist. As an ethical paradigm, eudaimonism is self-regarding but not narrowly egoistic. I can be a eudaimonist and still consistently act out of concern for the well-being of others, albeit on this proviso: that another person's well-being be either a means to my own or an actual constituent of it.

In his essay, "Augustine's rejection of eudaimonism," Nicholas Wolterstorff calls this "the agent-wellbeing proviso." The proviso admits of different elaborations – e.g., Stoic, Peripatetic – but it is basic to eudaimonism. Most interpreters of Augustine have assumed that when he is criticizing pagan eudaimonists for failing to refer their virtues to God, he is criticizing them for their lack of piety and not for their eudaimonism. Theirs is an Augustine who holds fast to the possibility of a *Christian* eudaimonism and indeed is himself a Christian eudaimonist. Wolterstorff makes a strong case for thinking that the real Augustine breaks with eudaimonism. It is a break that begins to appear in the 390s, especially with the *Confessions*, and is on full display in *City of God*. If Wolterstorff is right, then the eudaimonist philosophies that come under assault in Book 19 are not halfway houses between debased self-love and Christian temperance; they are, for Augustine, formulas for evading compassion, and followed diligently they will drive love mad. There simply is no eudaimonist way to love God "to the point of self-contempt" (*usque ad contemptum sui*; *civ. Dei* 14.28).

The next two essays are closely related in theme and point of view. They are both concerned with, and are troubled by, Augustine's metaphysics of the will. On the face of it, Augustine looks to be a libertarian (the metaphysical kind). Consider Adam in the garden, faced with a fateful choice: obey God, or join the woman. To keep things simple, let's just stipulate that choosing to obey is good; choosing not to obey not so good. "Libertarian" Adam chooses to disobey, but being free, he might have chosen otherwise. Because he retains the ability not to sin while sinning (*posse non peccare*), Adam is, by Augustine's reckoning, justly liable to be punished. The same logic applies to those strange angels who tire of divine light and freely choose to embrace (or create) an inner darkness within themselves; they are culpable for their demonization. But now add two complications. Augustine apparently thinks it possible for "libertarian" freedom to be lost. For unless they are given the appropriate grace, Adam's heirs, all born into sin, make Adam's choice. They choose something over God; they are not, Augustine insists, able not to sin (*non posse non peccare*). Demons have it even worse. There is no grace for them. They have no further possibility of not choosing their darkness. So complication one: it is possible to sin but not be free not to sin. What about redemption? Augustine does not claim that divine grace has the effect of restoring to human beings their original Adamic freedom. It does better than that. It makes it so that saints in Christ, sealed in the Spirit, have no ability (because they have *absolutely* no desire) to break again from God; they are remade so as not to be able to sin (*non posse peccare*). So complication two: there is a freedom that is better than the freedom not to sin. Dwell on these complications, and it will seem increasingly less likely that Augustine was ever talking about libertarian freedom. The freedom that originally makes for culpability – the freedom to sin – ends up a pathology to be cured. It is hard to say what kind of freedom he has been talking about.

In my essay on the origin of evil, subtitled "Myth and metaphysics," I focus on Augustine's story of how the two cities came into being. It is principally a tale of angels, light and dark, and it turns out to be not much of a story – high stakes, but no drama. I am not questioning Augustine's ability to dramatize; my point is that his fallen angels, who create the *civitas diaboli*, have no motive for falling, and so there is no drama to convey. They have an abstractly metaphysical freedom to choose God or nothing, and they choose nothing. After that choice, Augustine shuts the door on such "freedom"; no angel in heaven is ever again going to choose privation over fullness, and no demon in hell is ever going to stop lacking. The two cities are fixed in their eternal division. When Augustine turns his attention to the human part of the story – the creation of *terrena civitas*, the earthly city – he has the option of likening Adam to an angel who is liable to fall. When Adam sins, it will be for no reason beyond a drop-in metaphysical freedom that disappears the moment that it is exercised. But Augustine also has the option not to "angelize" Adam. The human part to the two-cities story has, at its inception, a vein of dramatic possibility that the angelic part lacks. Adam faces a choice, not between God and nothing, but between his heavenly father and his partner in the flesh. While Adam has a clear motive for choosing flesh over spirit (the flesh of his flesh is good), he apparently has none at all for choosing nothing (sheer privation) over God (plenitude). For most of my essay, I discuss the implications of Augustine's two options for framing Adam's choice.

In his essay, "Hell and the dilemmas of intractable alienation," John Bowlin ponders the end of the earthly city – its slip into hell – and whether the end fits with the beginning. In the beginning, Adam sins; in the end, his ungraced descendants end up perpetually warring against the good in themselves, with no hope of respite. They were living like this on earth, of course, but now that they are in hell, they know that there is no hope. Do they deserve such a hopeless fate? If the question is really, How is it fair that they are being punished for their ancestral father's sin?, then we are heading into the murky waters of vicarious guilt and original sin. Bowlin is prepared to talk about original sin, but not about its transmission. That seems reasonable. If Adam's sin, upon analysis, proves to be either unintelligible or far from hell-worthy, then it will not, however it is being transmitted to his descendants, do much to explain their hellish fate. Bowlin argues that Augustine saddles himself with a number of dilemmas when he tries to make too much of Adam's original will. The central dilemma is this: if Adam's sin is to be bad enough to be hell-worthy, then his will has to have been perverse – wholly God-alienated; if Adam's sin is to be redeemable (as it must be in his *graced* descendants), then his will has to have been less than perverse, or just voluntary – not wholly God-alienated but distracted.

To situate Adam's descendants between heaven and hell, in the indeterminate arena of the mingled cities, Augustine needs Adam's will to have been both perverse and voluntary. But that is not possible.

In the penultimate essay in the volume, John Rist looks into the very idea of Christian philosophy and how *City of God* comports with it. He distinguishes between two ways of proceeding philosophically, both of which can be found in Augustine, early and late. There is the use of reason alone to arrive at truth, or, if not quite that, then the use of reason whose extra-rational application is restricted to non-religious assumptions; Rist calls philosophy thus dedicated "General Philosophy." There is alternatively the use of reason that begins in faith and leads ultimately to faith's vindication, in the form of understanding (the profoundest possibilities of it); Rist refers to faith-invested philosophy as "Advanced Philosophy." Augustine is no position to learn what is advanced about Advanced Philosophy until he has first pursued a general program of truth-seeking and come to see its limitations. General Philosophy enables him to defeat skepticism, secure an intelligible domain of mathematics and logic, and touch upon a mind that is markedly greater than the human, but this form of philosophy is incapable of taking him much beyond his self-obsessions. There is no revelation of God there, but at best a promissory note, requiring humility. When Rist turns to see how *City of God* advances Augustine's practice of Advanced Philosophy, he finds, in the mix of metaphysics and history, an aspiration to know particulars – events and persons – and not just kinds of particulars (an exercise in abstraction). It is the great particular, the life of God in Christ, that limits the general ambitions of any philosophy to know and not to have to love.

The last essay in the volume, Bonnie Kent's look at the historical, and especially the medieval, reception of Augustine's two-loves ethic, speaks to (and against) our modern tendency to medievalize Augustine. The medievals themselves, whose access to copies of Augustine's works was often limited and easily compromised by a growing pseudo-Augustinian corpus, read *City of God* selectively, if at all, and within an idiom of moral psychology quite different from Augustine's own. It is not until the fourteenth century that *City of God* begins to enjoy something like canonical status, but more for its literary qualities and knowledge of the ancient Roman world than for its political theology and critique of heroic virtue. Kent's analysis of texts and lines of transmission cuts against a grand modern narrative of Western moral thought, the one that begins with ancient Greek ethicists espousing natural forms of virtue, pauses at Augustine's degradation of all such forms in *City of God* 19, and continues on to the *Summa theologiae* of Thomas Aquinas, the great reconciler of the ancient (Aristotelian) thesis and the Augustinian antithesis. In Kent's more historically informed picture, Thomas has little interest in conveying, much less contesting, Augustine's antithetical cities and their radically opposed loves; when he holds to the legitimacy of natural, albeit imperfect, virtues, and defends the possibility of dual citizenship – earthly and heavenly – he is aware of Augustine's point of view, but he is not actively seeking to oppose it. He is simply working through a problematic of nature and supernature that belongs to his own time.

Kent's essay on Augustine's dubiously medieval status and Vessey's on his late antique originality together suggest the need for philosophical periodization that is less at home with the distinction between classics and patristics and more willing, in keeping with other forms of historicism, to accord to late antiquity an interest and integrity of its own. However variable the boundaries of this period may prove to be, Augustine is sure to end up in the thick of it – being, in no small way, the motivation for a newly bounded time. For he is neither a philosopher of the ancient world nor a proto-medieval thinker. Nor is he a Christian whose Christianity is neatly detachable from his philosophical engagements. He is a philosophically Christian thinker whose famous but yet to be deciphered antitheses – two cities, two loves, two ends – can still challenge the parodies that we would make of them.

CHAPTER 1

The history of the book: Augustine's City of God *and post-Roman cultural memory*

Mark Vessey

1 MEMORY AND EXPECTATION

Unlike Horace's ideal epic poet, who hurried his readers "into the midst of things" (*ars poetica* 149), Augustine had a way of beginning at the beginning, then beginning again. In his other great narrative work, and his closest engagement with Roman epic outside *City of God*, he began the story of himself, if not *ab ovo* then at his mother's breast (*conf.* 1.6.7). Ten books later, this long story told (*conf.* 11.1.1), he began again, as if where he had meant to begin all along, in order to (re)tell a greater story *ab usque principio*, "from the beginning in which you [God] made heaven and earth" (11.2.3). That greater story, extrapolated from Gen. 1:1–2:3, made a further triad of books, indeed a Christian trinity.[1] Roughly two decades later, *c.* 417, upon completing another ten books in which he had reviewed the history of the *civitas Romana* from its beginnings (*ab origine sua*; *civ. Dei* 2.2) and "refute[d] the objections of the ungodly, who prefer[red] their own gods to the Founder of the Holy City of which [he had] undertaken to speak" (*civ. Dei* 10.32), Augustine renewed his undertaking in the preface to another supplementary triad, this time of four-book units, in which he would relate the "origin, progress and merited ends of the two cities," one heavenly and the other earthly. The curious symmetry between *Confessions* and *City of God* was already recognized by Augustine's first biographer, Possidius, who, embarking upon a "Life" that could not simply summarize the subject's own account of himself in ten books, announced that he would narrate the latter's "origin, career and appointed end."[2] In Augustinian narratology, as in evolutionary biology, ontogeny recapitulates phylogeny.

Although only half the length of the sentence addressed to Marcellinus at the beginning of *City of God*, whose sinuosity once deceived Henri-Irénée

---

[1] O'Donnell 1992: 3.251.   [2] Possidius, *Vita Sancti Augustini*, pref.

Marrou into declaring Augustine to be a poor stylist,³ the first sentence of Book 11 is just as enveloping (*civ. Dei* 11.1; Dyson 449):

The City of God of which we speak is that to which the Scriptures bear witness: the Scriptures which, excelling all the writings of all the nations in their divine authority, have brought under their sway every kind of human genius, not by a chance motion of the soul, but clearly by the supreme disposition of providence.

Almost all English translations stumble in their rendering of this pronouncement. Its first trick is to begin with the "City of God" as the subject and reiterated title of Augustine's work, and then to begin again immediately with the "scriptures" – or rather the singular *scriptura* – that are (is) the grammatical subject of the main clause, and to which all writings and works of human genius, Augustine's included, are said to have been subjected by divine providence. Dyson's pluralizing of the noun and expansion of the syntax ("the Scriptures ... the Scriptures") instructively ruin one of Augustine's more calculated compositional effects. The force of this second opening of *City of God* derives from the strict opposition that it establishes between the perfect singularity of God's attributes (in the order of the Latin: *civitas Dei, scriptura excellens, dispositio providentiae, divina auctoritas*) and the plurality of each of the attributes of a fatally divided and distracted humankind (*motus animorum, omnes gentes, omnes litterae, omnia genera ingeniorum humanorum*). "The City of God of which we speak is one attested by that scripture ... which, in its divine authority, excels all the writings (*litteras*) of all the nations." More literally: "The City of God of which we speak is one attested by that writing which, in its divine authority, excels all the literary resources of all the nations." "Literary" in this context should not be taken to imply the existence of any "literature" in the modern, post-Romantic sense of a more or less clearly delimited universe of mainly imaginative, aesthetically ambitious artifacts. *Litterae* in its extended, classical and post-classical Latin applications meant something like the written resources – both "archival" and "canonical" – of a human culture; the textual reserve and repertoire of a people's "cultural memory."⁴ Augustine's *City of God* is a manifesto for the people or nation whose cultural memory – of past, present, and future – would be primarily encoded in the biblical–canonical books from Genesis to Revelation.

Like other Latin speakers and writers of his time, Augustine habitually spoke and wrote of the Christian biblical canon as *scripturae* ("writings").

---

³ Marrou 1938: 66–67; but cf. Marrou 1949: 668–70, with Vessey 1999: 13–15.
⁴ For a model of the operations of "cultural memory" between "archive" or "reference memory" and "canon" or "working memory," see Assmann 2008.

To understand how much depends on the singular *scriptura* of the beginning of Book 11 of *City of God*, we must turn back to the final chapter of Book 10. In his work *On the Return of the Soul* the philosopher Porphyry claimed to have been unable to discover any "universal way of the soul's deliverance," despite his extensive researches into the traditions of various nations, which had included a process described by Augustine as "historical inquiry" (*historialis cognitio*). Augustine shows that Porphyry's comparative and historical inquiries were incomplete. The universal way of the soul's deliverance could in fact be discerned both in the historical records and in the contemporary practices of a particular people, the Hebrews or Jews, "whose commonwealth (*res publica*) was in a certain sense consecrated to foreshadow and herald, by its tabernacles and temple and priesthood and sacrifices, the City of God which was to be gathered in from all the nations (*ex omnibus gentibus*)."[5] The conceptual and narrative relationship here sketched between the cultural institutions of a particular people and the promise of a universal way of salvation already points towards a resolution of the dialectic of the "all" and the "one" inscribed at the beginning of Book 11. Without yet mentioning the key notion of "scripture(s)," Augustine articulates two others essential to it, namely "history" and "authority" (*civ. Dei* 10.32):

> Porphyry says that the universal way of the soul's deliverance has never come to his knowledge through historical inquiry. But what more illustrious history can be found than that which has taken possession of the whole world (*universum orbem . . . obtinuit*) because its authority is so eminent? Or what history could be more faithful than that which narrates past events and foretells future ones, so many of the predictions of which have been fulfilled that we are enabled to believe without doubt that the rest will be fulfilled also?

"History" in this use of the word stands for a narrative and cognitive unity rendered through writing. As surely as *this* history has taken possession of the world, the full mental possession of it is the soul's assurance of eternal life.

Augustine's mature conception of the Jewish–Christian scripture/s was the product of complex processes in his intellectual life and environment, but probably no single factor was more important than his response to Manicheism. For this ex-Manichee, saving God's justice and saving human freedom – that is, saving the two of them together – meant saving the overall unity of the scriptures by then held as canonical in the "catholic" church. In

---

[5] For Augustine's thinking on this subject, and much of what follows in the next three paragraphs, see Fredriksen 2008.

the first place, the writings of St. Paul (crucially, his Letter to the Romans) and the writings traditionally attributed to Moses (crucially, his account of Adam's sin in Genesis) had to be shown to explicate each other. The Apostle had coordinated Adam's original fault with the current condition of humankind and, through the person of Christ, with its future prospects. He had done so scripturally, by referring to the written history of God's past dealings with the Jews and extrapolating from it, in the light of the "gospel," to his present and future dealings with other nations. From Paul, Augustine derived two guiding principles: first, that God's long-term purposes for humankind were securely encoded in the texts of his prophets, apostles, and evangelists; second, that in this life those purposes – and hence those texts – were indecipherable beyond a certain point (Rom. 11:33). The history that mattered was plotted in divine scripture; scripture was partly opaque; the clarity and opacity of scripture defined the human condition as, for the time being, a "textual" one.

Other Christian exegetes and theologians, working with the same or similar materials, had appealed before Augustine to the marvelous unity of the scriptural dispensation. None, however, had tackled the task of biblical interpretation with the same urgent desire to locate the predicament of the individual human being within a narrative of the origin, descent, and future of the species. Absent evolutionary biology, Augustine's theological notions of the relation between human ontogeny and human phylogeny were worked out on the basis of the books that came to be known in the Middle Ages as "The Bible." The Bible was his genetic code, his book of the generations and of the history of nations, the narrative structure in reference to which all other histories or stories, collective and individual, would make whatever sense they could ultimately bear.

Vital encouragement for the "historical" biblicist that Augustine would become by the time he composed *City of God* was supplied by the *Book of Rules* of Tyconius, a fellow North African writer and former Donatist whose work was in his hands by the early 390s. The *Liber regularum* furnished Augustine with the means for an anti-Manichean reading of Paul: "By insisting that the dynamics of Law and faith, will and grace were constant across nations, times, and individuals, from Abraham to Jacob to David to the apostles and on into the present life of the church, Tyconius disclosed in the entire double canon of scripture a continuous and consistent record of God's saving acts in history."[6] It was partly on the strength of the guidance provided by Tyconius that Augustine conceived the project of

---

[6] Fredriksen 2008: 163.

De doctrina Christiana ("On Christian Instruction"), a work in which he intended to set out the principles for an effective exegesis of the "holy scriptures."[7] Like other works of his begun in the early and mid 390s, this one was abandoned incomplete.[8] Not until the late 420s, around the time he finished the *City of God* and as he was reviewing his entire published output for the *Retractations* (*retr.*), did Augustine pick up his hermeneutical treatise again in the middle of Book 3 and relaunch it with an annotated digest of Tyconius's *Liber regularum*. In the meantime, he had made a fresh assault on the problem of discerning and expounding God's saving acts in history, with direct reference to his own case, in *Confessions*.

Augustine divided the *Confessions* as a whole between Books 10 and 11, describing the first decade as "about me" and the final triad as "about the holy scriptures" (*retr.* 2.6). The work can usefully be seen as a set of transactions between three kinds of memory: the natural memory of an individual human mind (Book 10); the prosthetic memory of a life humanly transcribed (Books 1–9); and the providential memory divinely encoded in the Bible as a whole and, on Augustine's reading, already epitomized in the Genesis narrative of the seven days of creation (Books 11–13).[9] To complete this analysis, while also extending it on the one hand to *Christian Instruction* and on the other to *City of God*, we should allow for a further repository of accumulated knowledge: the collective or social memory transmitted in the texts and practices of a given culture and acquired by individuals in the course of their education and wider experience ("cultural memory"). Augustine had traversed the "places" of such a cultural memory, in its late "classical" Graeco-Roman form, in Book 2 of *Christian Instruction* (*doc. Chr.* 19.29–42.63). He would review them again, according to a different taxonomy and with a sharper polemical intent, in Books 1–10 of *City of God*. In the interim, in *Confessions*, he narrated a process by which the inherited and assimilated resources of this same "classical" culture, now his own, were exposed to the radical critique of a biblical counter-memory.[10] "Not in vain have you willed so many pages to be written, pages deep in shadow, obscure in their secrets," Augustine assured himself, addressing God as usual (*conf.* 11.2.3, Boulding). His prayer for access to the scriptures echoes the idioms of his earlier exploration of the recesses of his own memory (*conf.* 10) and those of the prologue to Tyconius' *Book of Rules* (quoted at *doc. Chr.* 3.30.43). "Let me confess to you," he went on,

---

[7] Pollmann 1996.   [8] See O'Donnell 1992: xlii–xlv.   [9] Stock 1996: 207–12.
[10] The expression "counter-memory" is used here in a sense nearly opposite to the Nietzschean one for which it was coined by Foucault 1977.

"all I have found in your books (*quidquid invenero in libris tuis*) ... from the beginning when you made heaven and earth to that everlasting reign when we shall be with you in your holy city."

The last three books of *Confessions* model a process of "finding" (*invenire*) and of "proclaiming" (*proferre*) the sense of the scriptures, which Augustine had lately theorized (*doc. Chr.* 1.1.1). The exegetical–confessional text becomes a medium between God's understanding of all things, as selectively imparted in the books of his appointed authors, and the understandings of Augustine's present and future readers. Like the other confessions that make up the *Confessions*, Augustine's act of confessing what he knows and does not know about God's "law" in the scriptures (*conf.* 11.2.2) is essentially an act of recollection. It is a making-present, in the extended "now" of a humanly composed text, of things previously discovered by the author in other texts that had been humanly composed but divinely disposed (cf. *doc. Chr.* 2.2.3). From the providential memory of the scriptures those things pass via the natural memory of Augustine to the prosthetic memory of his text and so to the natural memories of his readers. Those "things," as the above-quoted passage from *conf.* 11.2.3 already suggests, were identical with the history of the "city of God" hymned by the psalmist. Another poem, Ambrose's hymn *Deus creator omnium* ("God, creator of all things"), gave the cue for the famous analogy by which, later in Book 11, Augustine would attempt to account for the general human experience of life in time (*conf.* 11.28.38):

Suppose I have to recite a poem I know by heart. Before I begin, my expectation is directed to the whole psalm, but once I have begun, whatever I plucked away from the domain of expectation and tossed behind me to the past becomes the business of my memory, and the vital energy of what I am doing is in tension between the two of them ... What is true of the poem as a whole is true equally of its individual parts and syllables. The same is true of the whole long performance, in which the poem may be a single item. The same thing happens in the entirety of a person's life, of which all his or her actions are parts; and the same in the entire sweep of human history (*in toto saeculo*), the parts of which are individual human lives.

God's knowledge of "all past and all future things," Augustine ventured, might be comparable with a human being's knowledge of a single poem, due allowance made for the critical fact that the mind of God, being outside time, could never be pulled between memory and expectation as human beings were in the *saeculum* or "historical time."[11]

---

[11] Marrou 1950; Markus 1988; Markus 2006: 31–48.

That predicament of suspense (*distentio*), emblematized in *Confessions* by the experience of reciting a memorized text, would for Augustine be a defining trait of the "city" or community of God in its earthly wayfaring. It is strikingly enacted in the first sentence of *City of God*, which mimics by its own drawn-out periodic structure the processes of deferral and distraction that are natural to human life "in the course of these succeeding times", (*in hoc temporum cursu*; *civ. Dei* 1.1.1). No less than all other human beings, the godly are forever being pitched *in medias res*, even when beginning again with their eyes set on that "most glorious City of God." The pathos of Augustine's prayer for entry into the hidden sense of God's scriptures stems from a recognition that those inscribed places of divine mind held out rare opportunities of stability, self-collectedness, and "continence" (cf. *conf.* 10.9.16, 29.40) in the midst of a world set whirling by the same God: "Yours is the day, yours the night, a sign from you sends minutes speeding by; spare in their fleeting course a space for us to ponder the hidden wonders of your law" (11.2.3). If the Psalms were a primary inspiration for both *Confessions* and *City of God*, that was no doubt partly because, as readily memorizable lyric texts of impressive narrative compass, they had the power not only to represent but also to relieve a secular and textual condition of life whose highest felicity could – on scriptural authority – be identified with meditation on the scriptures (Ps. 1:1–2).

2 THE WRITINGS OF ALL THE NATIONS

2.1 *Varro's pen*

Immense as it is, *City of God* is held together by a tissue of actual or implied cross-references, many of them turning on individual figures from biblical or Roman history. One such figure is that of Rome's second king after Romulus, Numa Pompilius. It was thanks to Numa, Augustine reports midway through the synoptic–historical Book 18, that Rome acquired many of its (false) gods – so many, indeed, that apparently there was no space left in heaven for Numa himself, who unlike Romulus was not deified after his death (*civ. Dei* 18.24). Numa's role in establishing Roman religious rites (*sacra*) is signaled early on and frequently underlined (*civ. Dei* 2.16, 3.9, 3.12, 4.23). The main treatment of it is reserved for a prominent passage at the end of Book 7, as Augustine wraps up his critique of the demonic religious practices current in the more popular forms of Roman culture, both "poetic" and "civic," and prepares to engage with the "natural" theology of the philosophers in Book 8 (following a triple division of *theologia* that he took from Varro; *civ. Dei* 4.27, 6.5). In his *De cultu deorum* ("On the Worship of the Gods"), Varro (116–27 BC) had specified a class of "select gods" whose functions he identified with aspects of the natural world. Augustine rejects out of hand Varro's "naturalistic" defense of the core elements of the pagan pantheon. These supposed deities of nature, like the deities popularly worshipped in place of long-dead human beings, were merely the imposture of demons (fallen angels) who liked to be taken for gods (*civ. Dei* 7.33). The example of Numa Pompilius clinches the argument (7.34–35).

Augustine inferred from Varro that Numa had communed with demons who had revealed to him the origins of the rites of Roman religion. Afraid to disclose what he had learned, yet not wishing to offend his informants, Numa had committed these mysteries to books that, after his death, were buried with him on the Janiculum at Rome. Years later, by Varro's account, a farmer accidentally turned up Numa's secret books with his plow, and took them to the praetor. The praetor referred them to the Senate, and leading senators read far enough to appreciate why Numa had acted as he did, whereupon they ordered the books burnt. Augustine assumes that Numa must have discovered how execrable were the demons whom the Romans mistakenly venerated as gods, or else that all the reputed "gods of the nations" were merely dead human beings. Either way, Augustine's case was made. But he does not rest it there. Varro's story of Numa's books was evidence, for the author of *City of God*, not only of the demonic nature of traditional Roman religion but also of the sublime workings of divine providence: the demons had not been permitted to warn Numa that he should burn his books before he died, "nor could they prevent them becoming known by resisting either the plow that uncovered them or the pen of Varro (*stilo Varronis*) through which the record of these events has come down to our time" (*in nostram memoriam pervenerunt*; *civ. Dei* 7.35).

Augustine's mention of the providential disclosure of Numa's books by the farmer's plow and Varro's pen is matched by his emphasis a few pages earlier, in a passage that exceeds the requirements of its immediate argumentative context, upon the providential preservation and worldwide dissemination of Jewish writings prophesying "the eternal salvation which was to come through Christ" (*civ. Dei* 7.32). That passage is a prelude to the elaboration, between Books 10 and 11, of Augustine's main argument for the supreme importance of the Jewish scriptures, understood in a Christian sense, as revelation to all nations of the soul's deliverance (see Section 1 above). There is thus in view at this point of *City of God* a double dispensation in writing: on the one hand, a set of texts that, right down to the details of Jewish worship, ceremonies "and whatever else pertains to that service which is due to God and properly called *latreia*," symbolize those things which "the faithful in Christ . . . believe to be fulfilled, or which we see in the course of fulfilment, or the fulfilment of which we trustingly wait"; on the other, the ultimately illegible, non-extant but conjecturally recoverable records of a religious cult erroneously rendered to demons. Varro's story of Numa's sacrilegious books would have been attractive to Augustine for the opportunity it afforded him of drawing negative inferences about the bases of Roman religion. Its prominence in *City of God* owes at least as much to his desire to enhance the authority of God's special textual provision for *his* people, now embracing all nations, by juxtaposing it with the written records of the *gens populi Romani*, "the nation of the Roman people" (the title-phrase of one of the works of Varro that he relied upon for his representation of traditional Roman religious observance).

While Augustine might claim that divine scripture outranked the literary resources (*litterae*) of *all* the nations, the only comparison that he was competent and concerned to pursue in any detail was with the "letters" or writings belonging to the Roman nation and the Latin language. The four main curricular authors of the Latin grammatical and rhetorical schools – Virgil, Cicero, Sallust, and Terence – are all to the fore in *City of God* and play vital roles in defining its polemical targets. None of them, however, competes in eminence with Varro.[12] These other authors all excelled in their respective genres or disciplines. Varro was the great Roman polymath, hailed by one poet as "a man most learned in all domains" (quoted by Augustine, 6.2). He was the author of the encyclopaedic *Libri disciplinarum* that Augustine had once meant to transpose into a Christian key.[13] More significantly, for *City of God*, he was an outstanding researcher of Rome's antiquities and tireless compiler of the records of her "culture" in the widest sense of that term. "When we were wandering and roaming like strangers in our own city," Cicero had written of Varro in the *Academica*, "it was as though your books led us back to our home" (quoted by Augustine, *civ. Dei* 6.2).[14] Cicero's allusion here to Varro's books (*tui libri*) is doubled and expanded in the phrase with which Augustine introduces the quotation, which refers to the same author's *litteraria opera* – not "literary" works in the modern sense but "written works" intended for publication in the form of

---

[12] O'Daly 1999a: 236–38 itemizes Augustine's recourse to Varro in the *City of God*.
[13] Shanzer 2005.
[14] The passage is highlighted by Clark 2007 in the course of a valuable discussion of the "bookishness" of the *City of God*: Varro, according to Cicero, had made accessible the "'societal archive' of history and religion" that was constituted by the "buildings and monuments" of Rome (127).

books (i.e., papyrus book-rolls, in Varro's time). A few lines later, Varro's efforts to preserve the memory of the Roman gods are recalled from a passage *in eo ipso opere litterarum suarum*, "from that same work of his writings/letters." These are not ordinary locutions. The materiality of Varro's texts has ideological value for Augustine. Associated with their extent and durability, it is an aspect of their still commanding authority. A little later on, the Varronian oeuvre is designated, even more unusually, as *omnis vestra litteratura*, "all your writing" (*civ. Dei* 6.6). Here the word *litteratura* is as good as synonymous with *scriptura*. Almost from the start, and uniquely among the Latin authors cited by Augustine in *City of God*, Varro cuts the figure of a *writer* in the most literal sense, one who sets things down in a written form that will stand the test of time. (Augustine would have relished the irony that most of what now survives of the works of Varro quoted by him in *City of God* does so only through his quotations.)

After a fleeting appearance at *civ. Dei* 3.4, Varro is formally introduced at 4.1. Augustine looks back on his summary of Roman history in Books 1–3: "I have drawn partly upon my own recent memory ... and partly upon the writings (*conscripta*) of those who have left accounts of these matters to posterity." He adds: "Varro, who is esteemed among our adversaries as a most learned man (*vir doctissimus*) and the weightiest of authorities, is a case in point. He compiled separate books (*dispertitos faceret libros*) concerning things human and divine, assigning some books to the human and some to the divine, according to the dignity of each." Varro's sense of the boundaries between divine and human things will be disputed in *City of God*. What is perhaps most noteworthy in this formulation, however, is the precision of Augustine's sense of Varro as a redactor of Roman cultural memory, organizing his material by means of a division between sets of book-rolls. The use of the verb *conscribere* (literally, "gather up, compile in writing," "write or copy out in full"), here and elsewhere, with respect to Varro (cf. 6.2–3), points in the same direction. Even when it serves merely for rhetorical variation and rhythmical effect, the frequent substitution of *scribere* by *conscribere* with reference to Roman texts in *City of God* emphasizes the material solidity of the cultural archive that Augustine was aiming to represent in its most imposing form, in order then to invalidate it. In Varro's case, that solidity is quickly dismissed as a distraction. His forty-two books of *Antiquitates*, twenty-five devoted to "things human" and sixteen to "things divine," were a wonder to contemplate: "But in this whole series of distributions and distinctions," observes Augustine, "it is vain to seek eternal life" (*civ. Dei* 6.4). Watching Augustine wander the imaginary library of Roman culture in *City of God* is like watching him investigate the places of his own memory in Book 10 of *Confessions*, this time secure in the knowledge not only that he will not be able to find what he is looking for but also that the thing in question is nowhere there to be found.

2.2 Comparative "literature"

Augustine's turn to Varro at the beginning of Book 4 is echoed by his return to him at the beginning of Book 18. Again, the accent is on written delivery. Augustine had "promised to write (*me scripturum esse promisi*) of the origin, progress, and proper ends of the two cities" (*civ. Dei* 18.1). The unfolding of the promised contents of his own writing in *City of God* becomes a theme almost as insistent as the fulfilment of the prophecies of Jewish–Christian scripture. At the beginning of this new book, but not for the first or last time, he inventories the contents of the entire work, Varro-like in his care to apportion his subject matter into its respective containers. In Book 15 the stories of the two cities down to Abraham had run concurrently "in [Augustine's] writing as in real time" (*sicut in temporibus, ita et in nostris litteris*). Then, in Books 16 and 17, the city of God had taken its course alone in his text (*in meo stilo*). Now it was time to put this other city back in the picture, so that the fortunes of both could be held together for comparison "in the overall view of readers" (*consideratione legentium*; *civ. Dei* 18.1). Book 18 will provide a synoptic history of the two cities from the time of Abraham to the time of Christ, beginning with a synchronism between Abraham's birth and the accession of Ninus as king of Assyria, which Augustine found in the *Chronicle* of Eusebius of Caesarea, as translated into Latin and expanded by Jerome, c. 380.[15] Straightaway he coordinates those data with a pre-Roman chronology supplied by Varro – hailed again as "most learned in all domains" – in his *De gente populi Romani* (*civ. Dei* 18.2). Only Assyria/Babylon could bear comparison with Rome as an empire, and, since the rise of the latter began around the time of the eclipse of the former, the combined history of these two powers would properly constitute the main axis of any narrative of the earthly city. Yet Augustine will have little to say about the Assyrians. The culture of another people (or confederation of peoples) claimed his interest instead, namely that of the Greeks, and not only because of their closer historical relationship with Rome. As representatives of the earthly city, the Athenians in particular punched far above their weight, and for a reason already given by Sallust: the "genius of their

---

[15] For an introduction to the *Chronicle* in Jerome's version, see Burgess 2002, and on the work as "literary history," Vessey 2010. For the Latin text, see Helm (1984).

writers" (*scriptorum magna ingenia*) had made this people famous "throughout the world" (*civ. Dei* 18.2). The renown that Athens had acquired "from its learning [i.e., as committed to and transmitted by writing] and from its philosophers (*ex litteris et philosophis*)" ranked it with Rome for the purposes of the present comparison of the histories of the earthly and heavenly cities (*propter comparationem civitatis utriusque*; *civ. Dei* 18.2).

From the outset, then, the main section of Augustine's parallel narrative of the two cities (Book 18) is organized partly as a comparison between two "literary" histories, one relating to the authors and texts of the "scriptural" dispensation, the other to those of "classical" Greek culture (or, speaking somewhat anachronistically, "literature") as it had been assimilated by the Romans. The focus on textual canon-formation as a dimension of culture was all but dictated to him by his primary historical source, the comparative chronological tables (*Chronici canones* or *Chronicle*) of Eusebius–Jerome. Eusebius had followed earlier Greek chronographers in including notices on eminent Greek poets, philosophers, orators, and historians amid the records of political history. In a preface, moreover, he had made much of the fact that, on his dating, Moses not only came before Homer and Hesiod but even before the so-called "theological poets," Linus, Musaeus, and Orpheus. And since Homer came long before Thales and the other "Seven Sages" (*sophoi*, *sapientes*), who in turn preceded Pythagoras, Socrates, Plato, and their fellow self-styled "philosophers," the priority of Hebrew over Greek cultural tradition was assured; the tabulation of the *Chronicle*, which presented the records of the various "nations" in parallel columns, was designed to make that assurance visible. In Book 18 Augustine faithfully rehearses the Eusebian comparative cultural chronology (*civ. Dei* 18.14, 18.24–25, 18.37, 18.39), reconciling it where possible with information from Varro's *De gente populi Romani*. At the same time, he adds his own flourishes. Thus he makes a pointed distinction between the myths purveyed by Greek poets about their gods and the things that can truly be ascribed to "history" (*civ. Dei* 18.8, 18.12–13, 18.16); recalls with relish how Athens, "the mother or nurse of liberal studies and of so many great philosophers," owed its name to a trick of the demons (*civ. Dei* 18.9); and throws up his hands in dismay at the irreconcilable differences between the philosophical schools that flourished in that "demon-worshipping city" (*civ. Dei* 18.41; see further Book 19). To the false fictions and discordant doctrines of such a demonically possessed culture, he naturally opposes the unified and historically reliable divine discourse of the Jewish–Christian textual dispensation (*civ. Dei* 18.40–41 and *passim*).

At no point in this critical–comparative review of cultural traditions are the material media of textual transmission far from the surface of Augustine's own text. The legend of the invention of writing (*litteras*) by Io, daughter of Inachus, also venerated as Isis, is skeptically rehearsed early on (*civ. Dei* 18.3), to be revived some chapters later in rebuttal of the claim that Egypt could have had wise men in pre-Abrahamic times (*civ. Dei* 18.37). For this and other synchronisms, Augustine never tires of observing, we are reliant on the texts of those who "have committed these ancient things to writing," the *scriptores historiae*, as already laid under contribution by "our own people who have written chronicles – first Eusebius and afterwards Jerome" (*civ. Dei* 18.8; cf. 23). Varro, in this perspective, does not merely tell a story, he "inserts [it] into his writings" (*suis litteris inserit; civ. Dei* 18.10), just as Lactantius "inserts" certain Sibylline prophecies "into his work" (*civ. Dei* 18.23). Other facts and fictions are said to be "published in writing," "committed to writing," and so on. The event of the Fall of Troy is common knowledge "because of both its own magnitude and the outstanding skill of the authors who recorded it" (*civ. Dei* 18.16). The Seven Sages "did not leave behind them any memorials, at least not in writing" (*quod ad litteras adtinet; civ. Dei* 18.25). The Hebrew prophets, by contrast, can often be dated on the basis of their own texts (*litterae, volumina, scriptura, scripta; civ. Dei* 18.27, 18.29, 18.31, 18.33). Israel had had prophets in earlier times too but "those prophets who, not only in speech, but also *in their writings* bore witness to [Christ]," belonged to the period of Rome's rise. As Rome was the second Babylon and future ruler of many nations, so from the moment of her foundation (*ab urbe condita*) the countervailing textual resources of the City of God were providentially reinforced by the "founding of a writing that prophesied more openly" (*scriptura manifestius prophetica condebatur; civ. Dei* 18.27). The synchronism is later repeated with a poetic twist: it was during the reign of Romulus that "the river of prophecy burst forth from its source in Israel, embodied in those texts (*in eis litteris*) which were to spread throughout the world (*toto orbe*)" (*civ. Dei* 18.37).

Divinely not demonically inspired, manifesting a doctrinal unity that put the "philosophers" to shame, diffused as wide in the world as Rome's empire, predating at their origins the earliest of the Greek or Egyptian sages – the "holy writings called canonical" by Christians (*civ. Dei* 18.36) are characterized in Book 18 of *City of God* chiefly by their capacity to match and exceed the most that could be claimed for the writings of the "nations."

At a critical juncture, however, Augustine's argument for the supremacy of the Jewish–Christian scriptures goes beyond the literary–comparative frame that he has constructed for it on the basis of Eusebius–Jerome.

Among Jerome's most salient additions to the *Chronicle* was a record, for the year 283 BC, of the commissioning of the "Septuagint" (Greek translation of the Hebrew Bible) by King Ptolemy Philadelphus. Jerome's notice concluded: "And these divine scriptures [the king] held in the Alexandrian library that he had procured for himself out of every kind of writing (*ex omni genere litteraturae*)." The translation of the Septuagint, which Augustine, unlike Jerome, was inclined to regard as a miracle (cf. *doc. Chr.* 2.15.22), provides the climax of the literary–historical narrative of Book 18 and at the same time marks the limit of the comparative model underlying it. Though included by Ptolemy in his universal library, the Septuagint is to be seen as *sui generis*, beyond comparison, an exorbitant textual universe unto itself. The inspired consensus of its translators ensured that "the authority of those scriptures was commended not as human, but as divine (which it was), for the benefit of the nations who were to come to believe in Christ" (*civ. Dei* 18.42). Unified by the spirit, dictated at a single sitting, disseminated far and wide, the Septuagint instantiated the idea of a perfectly singular scripture of divine dispensation (*civ. Dei* 11.1, Section 1 above). Not even Jerome's impressively 'literate labor' (*tam litteratum laborem*) as translator of the Old Testament from Hebrew could undermine its authority (*civ. Dei* 18.43). In promoting the Septuagint, Augustine was careful, nonetheless, not to lower the status of the Hebrew books. In his imagination, the latter were as likely as any Greek version to be in the hands of the wandering Jews whose continuing possession of scripture was the Christians' most practical guarantee of the reliability of the source-texts for *their* narrative of the City of God (*civ. Dei* 18.43, 18.46–47).

3 HISTORY AND THE BOOKS

A certain Firmus was so enthralled by Book 18 of *City of God* when he heard it recited over three successive afternoons, in Augustine's presence, that he immediately asked the author for a copy of the complete work in twenty-two books (*ep.* 1A*.1; cf. 2*.3). Nearly every one of the other twenty-one books could have been recited comfortably in a single afternoon. But Book 18 was a monster, accounting for an eighth of the whole. It had to be that long; it is the nearest Augustine came to writing a "very short history" of the world, and also the clearest account he ever gave of the temporal and textual dispensation under which Christians held their scriptures. It is at once a self-contained historical epitome and an opening into the larger synoptic history of the two cities presented by Books 15 to 18, and by the *City of God* as a whole.

We have seen how, in Book 11 of *Confessions*, Augustine toyed with the idea that God's comprehension of all reality might be analogous to a human being's perfect mastery of the text of a single poem, only timeless. Poems in the classical world were traditionally imagined as sung or spoken aloud, even when they were written. When Virgil appeared with a scroll in late classical art, it was usually rolled up; the poet's performance did not depend upon a script.[16] Owing no allegiance to such traditions of high "literary" culture, Christians as a collectivity were no more obliged to keep their texts scrolled than they were to keep them all singable. In practice, they preferred the spine-hinged book or *codex*.[17] Codex technology was mainstream book technology under the Roman Empire, relied upon by traders, lawyers, teachers, soldiers, civil servants, and by anyone else with a useful occupation requiring ready and secure access to written data. Although scrolls or rolls were in daily practical use too, those of the fancier, more polished, and calligraphic kind were mainly reserved for a niche market of leisured consumers of poetry, history, oratory, and philosophy – and, on somewhat different terms, for the sacred texts of the Jews.[18] Augustine used the words *liber* and *volumen* with the same freedom as other Latin authors, in senses ranging from "book as object" through "unit of text" to "literary work." However, when he wanted to focus attention on the bodily and cognitive–affective relationship between a reader and the book that he or she took in hand or held in sight, *codex* was generally the word he chose.[19] The distinctive functionality of the codex, as both a highly capacious container for text and as a device for bringing the complex relationships between textually represented phenomena into a unified and cognitively impactful view, is exploited to special advantage in *City of God*.

Gillian Clark has noted that "Augustine was particularly aware of *City of God* as a book, a physical object used by readers."[20] We know that by the time he began to dictate this work, in the year 413, he was already planning the general review of his literary output that would become the *Retractations*. We know, because he mentioned the project in a letter of the previous year to the same Marcellinus who would receive the dedication of *City of God* (*ep.* 143). More intently and with better reason than any previous Christian author, Augustine was by then contemplating the

---

[16] See further Vessey 2002: 59–64, 67–71.
[17] Hurtado 2006: 43–93 surveys evidence and interpretations for the earliest period.
[18] Augustine, however, imagined the Jews of his time carrying their scriptures in *codices*; Petitmengin in *AL* 1: 1029–30.
[19] See especially Jager 2000: 33–38, with Holtz 1989, and Petitmengin in *AL* 1: 1022–32.
[20] Clark 2007: 120.

ultimate dimensions of his own published oeuvre and anticipating the judgments that it would incur in the sight of future readers.[21] *City of God* is not only a late work in the Christian apologetic tradition, one that summons its readers to act as judges in a forensic case.[22] It is also a late work of its author, one that demands to be read from beginning to end, in order to be apprehended and appreciated as a whole – like the text of the poem that Augustine had used in *Confessions* as a paradigm for the entire life of a human being or the entire course of human history. Whatever the external impulses for its inception, *City of God* has the distinction of being one of the three truly monumental works that Augustine produced on his own terms, and over which he intermittently spent many years – the two others being *De trinitate* ("On the Trinity") and *De Genesi ad litteram* ("On the Literal Sense of Genesis"). Although its germ is already visible in *Confessions*, *City of God* was by more than a decade the last of the three to be undertaken, and it is also the most architectonic in design. Augustine had measured his task carefully. Even if this *opus magnum* turned out in the end to be far longer than he had expected, its overall proportions remained as envisaged in his original plan (*ratio operis*; *civ. Dei* 1.pref.).

The very first sentence of the work, as we have seen (Section 1 above), is already mimetic of the compulsive logic of the twenty-two books. *City of God* is Augustine's greatest work of writerly and "bookish" coercion. In a letter to Firmus (*ep.* 2*.2–3), he barely concealed his irritation that his correspondent, having pressured him to send the whole, showed no sign yet of having read for himself beyond the first ten books (*libri*). He reminded him, as he would remind readers of the *Retractations* (*retr.* 2.43), that these first ten "books" and the subsequent twelve belonged inseparably together, the two parts of the work completing, interpreting, and reinforcing each other. Already when dispatching the exemplar from which Firmus was to have further copies made, Augustine explained how the component sections of this huge artifact ought to be bound up (*ep.* 1A*.1). A single papyrus or parchment codex could if necessary hold considerably more text than a single papyrus roll, which beyond a certain length would become unwieldy and fragile. Still, Augustine recognized that the *City of God* would probably be too big to fit manageably in one codex. The first ten *libri*, he suggested to Firmus, might conveniently be combined in one codex, and the last twelve in another. Or, for greater portability, Part One (Books 1–10) could be divided after Book 5, where there was a break in the argument, while Part Two could be split into three codices of four books

---

[21] For the wider context in his thought and writing, see Vessey 1997. [22] Tornau 2006.

each; the first comprising the origins of the two cities (11–14), the second their historical development (15–18), the third their appointed ends (19–22).

The simultaneously authorial and bibliological sensibility on display in Augustine's correspondence with Firmus is something of a novelty with respect to classical literary or textual culture. What we find Augustine doing here is of a different order from a Roman historian's division of his narrative into ten-book packets ("decades": Livy) or a Greek philosopher's (or his editor's) arrangement of his work into sets of nine chapters ("enneads": Plotinus). Those were routine devices of ancient bookmaking as *tomology*, the slicing of literary compositions to fit convenient lengths of papyrus roll. They were procedures of publishing, rather than principles of composition. By contrast, Augustine's *codicology* in *City of God* made publishing and composition aspects of each other. We have seen him review Varro's procedure of dividing his "human" and "divine" subject matter between different sets of "books" (*dispertitos faceret libros*; *civ. Dei* 4.1). Varro would not have considered the codex as a possible container for each of these groupings, for the simple reason that in his time and milieu codices were generally not used for the calligraphically transcribed "works" or "monuments" of higher intellectual culture, the category to which his *Antiquitates* was clearly meant to belong. Augustine's bibliological horizon was different from Varro's. The increasing visibility, in the period now known as late antiquity, of Christian biblical and non-biblical religious texts in codex form – along with the many legal, administrative, technical, and professional works that conventionally also used that format – led to a situation in which the scroll or roll form of book (in Latin, *volumen*) was no longer felt to be obligatory even for reputed works of higher, "literary" culture (poetry, philosophy, oratory, history). The tendency of Christian writers to disparage such works in order to exalt the "holy scriptures" will have contributed further to the weakening of the ideological link between those genres and the roll format that had traditionally been used for them. It is telling that the Latin Christian text from late antiquity that most exhaustively contrasts the respective material–textual resources of classical Graeco-Roman and biblical Jewish–Christian culture – Augustine's *City of God* – is also the first one for which we have the author's exact instructions to the copyist for its presentation in codex form.

Late in his life and in his career as a Christian author, Augustine had conceived of a large-scale written work whose overall unity would be both articulated and apprehended according to the techno-logic of the codex as text-container. It has been astutely conjectured that Augustine "never saw a bible."[23] That is to say, he is unlikely ever to have set eyes on a "pandect" or single-codex exemplar of the canonical scriptures that contained, as he would have said, the whole story of the two cities. He did, however, have direct knowledge of a codex that presented the history of all kingdoms of the "known" world from the time of Abraham and Ninus down to the present, in a tabular form that highlighted synchronisms and graphically revealed the chronological succession of powers from ancient Assyria/Babylon to the Roman Empire under its Christian leaders. He had that book open before him as he composed Book 18 of *City of God*. The revolutionary cognitive–epistemological force of Eusebius's *Chronicle* as an instance of codex-making has been demonstrated by Anthony Grafton.[24] It was Jerome, as translator and expander of the Eusebian *Chronicle*, who imparted that force to Latin readers in late antiquity, and Augustine who first felt it in a way that we can still register today.

The layout of the *Chronicle* absolutely required the codex format, and Jerome in his preface admonished future copyists to respect the special logic of its *mise-en-page*, including the use of different colors of ink to distinguish adjacently tabulated world powers. These visual effects, he explained, had been contrived not merely to delight the eye but in order to clarify the "order of reading" (*legendi ordinem*).[25] Augustine's stated concern at the beginning of Book 18 to set the histories of the heavenly and earthly cities within a single frame, "so that the two may be compared with each other in the overall view of readers (*consideratione legentium*)," is the clearest sign of his indebtedness to the codex-dependent optics of the *Chronicle*.[26] In an essay that claims Augustine's *Confessions* as prototype of one of the four dominant forms of "prose fiction" in western "book literature," the Canadian literary critic and theorist Northrop Frye once described the spine-hinged book as "a mechanical device for bringing an entire artistic structure under the interpretive control of a single person," namely the reader.[27] Augustine anticipates this insight in Book 20 of *City of God*, when he interprets the "book of life" of Revelation 20:12 as signifying "a certain divine power, by which it will be made possible for every man to recall to memory all his own works, both good and evil, and for the mind to review them all with miraculous speed, so that each man's knowledge will accuse or excuse his conscience" (20.14). As Eric Jager has pointed out, "the same

---

[23] O'Donnell 1999: 99. [24] Grafton and Williams 2006: 133–77.
[25] Jerome, *Chron.* pref. (ed. Helm) 5; Grafton and Williams 2006: 199.
[26] Feeney 2007: 229, n. 110, cites this passage from *civ. Dei* 18.1 as evidence of Augustine's "profound understanding of the mechanisms and implications of synchronism."
[27] Frye 1957: 248; cf. 307.

principle informs the *Confessions*"²⁸ – just as it informs Augustine's review of his life's "literary" works in the *Retractations*, and the text-based synopsis of the collective "life" of humanity (cf. *conf.* 11.28.38) that he urged upon Firmus for the eternal good of the latter's soul. It was for the sake of a reader thus mechanically empowered to appreciate and respond to the supreme non-fiction of God's ordering of universal history that Augustine designed his books of the *City of God*.

---

²⁸ Jager 2000: 43.

CHAPTER 2

Secularity and the saeculum

Paul J. Griffiths

The first task is to get clear about what Augustine means by *saeculum* in *City of God* and consequently to make some suggestions about how the word and its kin might be rendered into English. The second task is to see what his understanding of the *saeculum* has to do with our understandings of the secular – for the Latin word and the English are etymologically intimate and are sometimes, because of this, taken to have conceptual and practical affinities as well. Addressing the *saeculum*/secular relation requires comment on some of the many ways in which Augustine draws the distinction between the two cities that together constitute the *saeculum* and its politics. And the third task is to engage Augustine normatively and constructively on the question of what use his thought on these matters might be to those who want to think about politics and the political sixteen centuries after the entry into Rome of Alaric and his Goths in 410, the event that prompted Augustine to compose the *City*.

I SAECULUM

For Augustine in the *City*, and for the most part elsewhere, the noun *saeculum* has as its core meaning a period of time with a beginning. There are two such periods to which the name is applied. One, *hoc saeculum*, has an end as well as a beginning: it begins with God's creation of the world and all that is in it out of nothing, and ends with the last things, to which the return of Christ is central. The second, *saeculum futurum*, has a beginning but no end: it begins with the end of *hoc saeculum* and never ends, stretching *in aeternum*, into eternity. The compound form, *saecula saeculorum*, designates only the second *saeculum*, the one without end. And the adjectival form, *saecularis*, is applied only to things or events that belong to the first *saeculum*. No other cognates or derivatives occur in the *City*.

How then to translate? Most translators find it impossible, exactly because of this range of meanings, to render *saeculum–saecularis* with an

English noun–adjective pair that preserves the intimacy of the Latin pair. And even in the case of *saeculum* alone, it is normal in English to find a wide range of renderings within a single version of a single text: "world," "age," and "time" are all common, and promiscuously mixed. The matter is made more complex by the fact that there is a rich vocabulary of time in Augustine (*tempus*, *aetas*, and so on) that has no formal or etymological connection with *saeculum*.[1] Is it possible to do better? Probably not much. I adopt "age" for *saeculum*, which yields "in this age" for *in hoc saeculo*, "the future age" for *saeculum futurum*, and "belonging to this age" for *saecularis*. This has at least the benefit of preserving in English the relation in Latin between *saeculum* and *saecularis*; it indicates, too, the dependence of *saeculum* and *saecularis* on *aiôn* and *aiônion*. In Augustine's view, then, all learning about matters belonging to this age can be called *saecularis*, and the promise of the land to Abraham extends to the end of this age, an end that marks the beginning of the future age. Also the scriptural phrase *saecula saeculorum* comes out literally as "ages of ages," embracing thereby both this age and the future one, and meaning, as a result, "for ever."

This age (*hoc saeculum*) is constituted exhaustively by the set of events that begins with the creation out of nothing of the cosmos as a beautifully ordered whole (*civ. Dei* 11.3–6) and ends with the last judgment that definitively and irreversibly separates the Lord's city from the human city (20.1, 20.14–30). Within it occurs all human history as well as the coming to be and passing away of every non-human creature. This age is the container for everything temporal, and, considered simply as such, it is beautiful, ordered, and a gift of the triune Lord who freely decides to bring it into being. It is also disordered and thereby ugly: that disorder and ugliness came into being with the fall, and thereafter the story is one of increasing and spreading decay and violence, coupled with, at first in a small way and then in an increasingly visible one, God's action to make this systemic violence peaceful and thus to return the cosmos to the beauty and tranquility of order. That action hinges around Jesus; his coming is prepared for by the call of Abraham and has its principal visible effect in the presence of the Church in the world; it culminates in the final healing of the cosmos by the removal of violence from it, which is depicted scripturally and by Augustine as a new, or second, creation, which is to say the making of a new heaven and a new earth.

---

[1] On the difference between *saeculum* and *aetas*, see the use of *saecularis* in *civ. Dei* 6.2 and the use of *aetas* in the quotation from Cicero in that same chapter.

2 SAECULUM AND THE SECULAR

If "secular" in English is taken to have "ecclesial" as its antonym, as it is when the process of secularization is depicted as the gradual reduction of the influence of particular churches upon the laws, norms, and customs of particular societies,[2] then there is a very limited sense in which Augustine's understanding of the *saeculum* is like it. For him, the Church as a visible institutional form, a human society with laws and practices and buildings and boundaries, is prepared for by the Jewish *societas hominum* with its visible laws and forms and then begins to become visibly itself in response to Jesus' earthly life and to the sending of the Holy Spirit. Outside these two *societates* – the Jewish and the Christian – there is no Church, no *ecclesia*, no visible community called out from the mass of humanity to serve as vanguard and representation of its healing. It follows from this that there was no visible ecclesial presence before the call of Abraham, or after that call where there are no Jews or Christians. Assyria–Babylon and Egypt fall under this heading for Augustine, at least until they come to have contact with Jews; and so does Rome before its contact with Jews and Christians. Aeneas may serve as type here: his flight from Troy after the fall of that city and his eventual founding of Rome, as depicted by Virgil (which is largely how Augustine knows the story), is the story of two secular cities (*civitates saeculares*), both in the sense that they belong to this age (that is true of Jerusalem as well), but also in the modern sense that they are cities without churches, cities whose public life lacks response to institutional forms and laws directly ordained by God. The events in the garden that precede the fall and those that occur between the fall and the call of Abraham are also secular in the modern sense in play here, as well as events of this age in the Augustinian sense; they are thus *saecularis* for him as well.

There is a second modern sense of "secular" as applied to the principles and practices ordering the life of particular societies. Here the idea is that there are society-ordering principles – laws and other norms – capable of assent both by those who are members of particular churches and those who are not; and that a society is secular to the extent that it is ordered by such norms rather than by ones assent to which requires active membership in a particular church. Translated into Augustine's terms, this is to say that there are mixed societies, comprising pagans and Christians and Jews – such was Augustine's Rome; and that some of the laws and norms that order such societies can and should be assented to as right and proper by all those who

---

[2] On the various senses of "secular," see Markus 2006: 4–8; and, *in extenso*, Taylor 2007.

live within them; from which it follows that there are societal laws and norms properly capable of assent by both Christians and pagans.

On this, Augustine has things to say both for and against; and his interpreters, ancient and modern, are divided correspondingly, according to what they wish to emphasize. Augustine says, for instance, that the Romans ruled, for a time, as well as humans can, and that the principal difference between the rule of a pagan emperor and a Christian one lies in their understandings of what it is they do rather than in their judgments about what needs to be done. Pagans tend to understand what they do when they rule or in some other way exercise political power as exhaustively explicable by appeal to temporal power and other realities of this age; Christian emperors and administrators understand (or ought to) what they do in terms of constraining damage and giving glory to God (*civ. Dei* 5.20) – and in any case as not exhaustively explicable or comprehensible in terms of what belongs to this age. Augustine also praises quite extravagantly the virtues of particular pagan Romans, for example Marcus Regulus (1.15), whose sacrifice of his own life in the interests of justice impresses him. The implication of these and other similar statements is that some of what Christians and pagans undertake as rulers and subjects and citizens is substantively the same even when it is understood and explained differently. In the particular case of such judicial acts as using torture to extract confessions, the difference between the pagan and the Christian judge is not that the former does such things and the latter does not; it is rather that the latter laments that he must do them, using the words of Psalm 24:17, "Deliver me from my necessities!" (*de necessitatibus meis erue me; civ. Dei* 19.6), while the former is unlikely to do so. Both the pagan and the Christian emperor, therefore, might agree that this or that tax needs to be written into law, this or that road needs to be built, this or that man needs to be imprisoned, this or that military campaign needs to be fought; and Augustine is explicit that both the pagan and the Christian judge can agree that this or that prisoner needs to be interrogated by torture. This gives some support to the view that Augustine does think that there are secular society-ordering principles, if by that is meant that some such can be assented to by both pagans and Christians, even if under different descriptions and analyses.

None of this, however, is to say that there are societal laws and norms which are theologically neutral. A theologically neutral law or norm would have no claims about God among its truth (or meaning) conditions; it could thus be fully understood, engaged, explained, defended, explored, and justified without raising any questions about God or God's action in the world. Those who think there are laws and norms of this kind and who apply the term "secular" to them are employing a third sense of the word "secular."³

This third sense of the word is in every significant respect unlike Augustine's use of *saeculum* and *saecularis*, and he does not explicitly entertain the thought that there might be such laws and norms. For him, it is axiomatic that every good of whatever kind has what goodness it has by way of its participation in God. A good law or norm, one that, for instance, supports the *tranquillitas ordinis* (*civ. Dei* 19.13) necessary for the Church to do what it does, is good because and to the extent that it participates in the principles ordained by God for human flourishing. Any account of such a law or norm's goodness that prescinds from God, therefore, is incomplete exactly to the extent that it does so. Any account of the principles that do or should order the public life of a society that pretends theological neutrality is, Augustine thinks, confused just to the extent that it pretends so. Those who establish and implement public policy on the assumption that such policy can be secular in this sense are certain to do so with violent, domineering, and self-aggrandizing ends in view; and serving those ends inevitably affects both what is thought politically desirable and how what is thought desirable is put into practice. A judge who laments the necessity of judicial torture will prescribe it not only with less relish but also probably less frequency than one who, equally committed to its necessity, sees nothing to regret in it; and Christians charged with undertaking torture are, because they lament what they have to do, likely to be less energetically excessive in the art of pain-infliction than pagan torturers who enjoy their job.

Societal norms and laws can, therefore, in Augustine's view, be secular in the first sense: there can be *societates hominum* or *civitates saeculares* in which there is no visible ecclesial presence, but which nevertheless have, in different ways and to differing degrees, laws and the public order that accompanies them. Such norms and laws can also be, to a limited extent, secular in the second sense, which is to say that they can be assented to and acted upon by pagans and Christians alike. There are, however, no norms or laws secular in the third sense, the sense of being fully accountable and justifiable independently of speaking to and about God, independently, that is, of acknowledging the participation of good laws and norms in their giver. And this fact explains, from Augustine's point of view, the limits of secularity in the second sense: while it is certainly true that pagans and Christians may together agree to and actively support a particular law or

---

³ For an ideal–typical instance of the third sense of "secular," see Rawls 1993.

norm, the fact that they inevitably understand, explain, and justify their support differently limits both what they can agree to and how they implement what they can agree to.

3 THE POLITICAL CONSTITUTION OF THE *SAECULUM*

If this present age embraces everything that has happened, is happening, and will happen, from the beginning of temporal change at the creation to its ending at the eschaton (*civ. Dei* 13.1), then it also embraces all creatures, material, immaterial, rational, and irrational. All places, as well as all times, belong to *hoc saeculum*: there is nothing outside this age other than God and those creatures who have, in one way or another, left this age and entered into the *saeculum futurum* in which they enjoy eternal life or suffer eternal death (of a metaphorical sort). But not everything in this age is political, if by that we mean, as etymology suggests, what has to do with the city, which is to say the ordered social life of potentially, and occasionally actually, rational creatures. To ask about the political constitution of this age, then, is not to ask about its physical constitution or about the lives of its non-human creatures. It is to ask only about the ordering principles, the constitutive practices, the history, and the ends of human *societates*.

Augustine's principal term of art for these matters is *civitas*, "city"; this occurs hundreds of times in *City* and provides the work's title. The city for him is a *concors hominum multitudo* (*civ. Dei* 1.15), a concordant or harmonious crowd of people; or, slightly more expansively, it is *hominum multitudo aliquo societatis vinculo conligata* (15.8), a particular crowd of people tied together by a social bond. It is more briefly and frequently called a *societas hominum* (e.g., 14.1), by which Augustine means, usually, a group of people who ordinarily live in spatial contiguity and under a single body of laws and norms. The members of a city are *cives*, citizens; and what they do and think and say in so far as they are citizens may be called "civil" or "civic" (*civilis, civicus*). Consider the following passage for one aspect of Augustine's city–citizen–civic–civil talk (*civ. Dei* 19.16):

> A man's household, then, ought to be the beginning, or a little part of the city (*civitas*); and every beginning has reference to some end proper to itself, and every part has reference to the integrity of the whole of which it is a part. From this, it appears clearly enough that domestic peace has reference to civic peace: that is, that the ordered concord of domestic rule and obedience has reference to the ordered concord of civic rule and obedience. Thus, it is fitting that the father of a family should draw his own precepts from the law of the city, and rule his household in such a way that it is brought into harmony with the city's peace.

Being a citizen is a matter of law and of the command and obedience that belong to law. Those who live together in the same house are as much citizens of that household as Roman citizens are of Rome; and the small peace of one, effected by command and obedience, participates in the larger peace of the other. This aspect of the grammar of Augustine's city-thought is descriptive: according to it, all that is needed for there to be a city with citizens is a sufficient degree of ordered concord that life together occurs, at least for a time, without degenerating into chaos or unrestricted violence. This might be true of a family under the command of a tyrannical paterfamilias, as well as of one ordered by benevolently democratic principles. It might also be true of a dictatorship as well as of a state ordered by Confucian or Islamic principles. There is also no distinction as to size: a *civitas* might be as small as a single biological family or as large as the fifth-century Roman Empire.

But there is more to Augustine's civic grammar. The city is not only, and perhaps not even most fundamentally, a society ordered by law and command and obedience, even though it is always at least that. It is also a society ordered by love. Consider the following passage from *civ. Dei* 15.3, where Augustine is discussing the symbolic significance of the birth of Isaac to Sarah and Ishmael to Hagar:

Isaac, then, who was born of a promise, is rightly interpreted as signifying the children of grace, the citizens of the redeemed city, the companions in eternal peace, among whom there is no love of a will that is proprietary, which is to say in a sense private, but rather a love that rejoices in that very good which is common and changeless. Such a love makes one heart out of many because it is the perfectly concordant obedience of charity.

Here, the citizens of the free city, identical with the city of God, are characterized by a particular kind of *amor*, or love. It is a love that, positively, directs them toward a good that is *communis*, or common, which is to say a good open to all, freely and identically given to all who wish to receive it. This common or public good is *immutabilis*: it does not change in any way, which is to say that by definition it does not belong to this age, to *hoc saeculum*. It is, of course, God, the triune Lord to whom all citizens of the city of God turn, first and last, in love. That they do so together, loving a public good, is what makes them a city: they participate in a particular form, the ideal form, of concordance. The shared love that constitutes Isaac and his descendants as citizens of God's city is contrasted here with the love that belongs to the citizens of another city, and those contrasts will be taken up in more detail below. Here it is sufficient to note that the loves that belong to the other city are private in the sense that they are directed by each citizen to what is his or hers, to the nurture of an individual will that is the individual's own freehold possession. Where the citizens of the city of God have a shared love, a love of the commons, those of the other city have privately proprietary loves, each enclosing a piece of the commons for him or herself.

For Augustine, then, to belong to a city is to belong to a community ordered by law and other norms and at the same time to be a lover of a certain kind, one whose desires and will are ordered to a particular end. The balance between these two – between love and law, desire and obedience – is not always the same: there may be cities principally ordered around obedience and threat and command; and there may be cities, *liberae civitates*, principally ordered around freely given love. But here below, *in hoc saeculo*, every city will contain elements of both.

Much of all this can be applied directly to Augustine's other main term of art for the political, which is to say *res publica*, which means literally the (or a) public thing. In *civ. Dei* 2.21 he opens a discussion of the definition of the *res publica* found in the second book of Cicero's *De republica*, a discussion he promises to return to later in the *City*. He eventually does so in *civ. Dei* 19.21, perhaps a quarter of a million words later. This is not to say that the term occurs nowhere else in the *City*: it does, dozens of times. But these are the main places in which he gives definitional attention to it. Cicero's definition of the *res publica* (voiced through Scipio) speaks of it as ideally consisting of harmony-concord (the analogy is musical) among its citizens, which yields security; a necessary condition for all this is *iustitia*, justice. The public thing, then, is ideal–typically a group of people living together in secure and harmonious concord, their common life justly ordered, and with agreement, therefore, both about what the laws should prescribe and proscribe and about what is in their common interest (*civ. Dei* 2.21). Not just any group of people meets this criterion: the gang of robbers does not (their laws are not just); neither does the city in civil war (it has no consensus about interest or purpose).

It is difficult to know how to translate *res publica*. "Republic" is the calque, but it is a false friend, much more specific in meaning than Augustine's (and Cicero's) *res publica* and therefore incapable of being used as a kind-term under which every law-governed society might be included. "Commonwealth" is much used (for example by Dyson) as a rendering for *res publica*, and it has the advantage of preserving the public element of the sense of *res publica*; but it is now archaic in English in most of its senses and etymologically too intimate with ideas about the common good, which emphatically do not belong to *res publica*, which is, for Augustine, a value-neutral term of a highly abstract kind: there are just and unjust *res publicae*. And then there is "state," the most generic modern term for the institutional forms that provide and constitute government. Of the three, this is the most possible; but it is a quintessentially modern term and conjures, for most contemporary users of English, the apparatus of government (legislatures, judiciaries) and their documentary and institutional affines (constitutions, courts, prisons), all of which is, again, more specific than what Augustine intends by *res publica*. It is also important to find a rendering capable of preserving Augustine's play with *res publica* and *res populi*: what belongs to the public, its *res* or thing, is also what belongs to the people. In order to preserve this, and also in order to make Augustine seem stranger than he is often made to seem, I will use "people's thing" for *res populi*, and "public thing" for *res publica*. The "thing" in question is everything that binds a particular public–people together: their laws, if they have any; their norms of custom; their habits of language and gesture and dress and diet – everything, in fact, that makes them a people. On this understanding of *res publica*, it approaches what we mean by culture; it is certainly broader than what we mean by politics or the state.

Augustine says, after discussing Cicero's definition of the public thing, which is the same as the people's thing, the *res populi*, that he will now try to show that there never was a public thing of that sort because there has been none with true justice (*vera iustitia*; *civ. Dei* 2.21). But he at once goes on to modify this dramatic claim: there have of course been public things in a less exalted sense, some of them better (more just) than others. Ancient Rome, for instance, was better ordered than Rome of more recent vintage. And so although true justice is found only in that public thing "whose founder and leader is Christ" (2.21), there are and have been all sorts of cities, *res publicae*, some of which are more just – and thus more properly cities – than others. To say that true justice is not to be had in cities other than those explicit in their allegiance to Christ is not to say that all those more-or-less pagan cities are on a par with respect to injustice. Or, better put, Augustine is sometimes concerned to explain what all pagan cities have in common, and in that way to place them on a par; and sometimes concerned to discriminate one pagan city from another in terms of the degree to which the perfectly concordant obedience and love of the city of God is evident in it. The two enterprises are not contradictory; but Augustine sometimes veers alarmingly quickly from one to the other.[4]

---

[4] I draw in the last several paragraphs from Curbelié 2004: 405–77.

We now have Augustine's political vocabulary before us. Central to it, indeed largely constitutive of it, are *civitas* and its cognates, together with *res publica* and its glosses. We can now ask again: how is the *saeculum*, this present age, constituted politically? The answer needs to be divided into two parts. The first has to do with citizens, *cives*, which is to say with city-inhabitants or city-members; and the second with communities, *societates hominum*.

Citizens are those individual human beings whose life together constitutes the life of cities. Eschatologically speaking, in terms of final and unchanging citizenship, every human being has citizenship in exactly one of the two cities, the *civitas Dei*, or city of God, and the *civitas terrena*, or earthly city. (Each of these cities is given other names, but these are by far the most common, each occurring hundreds of times in the *City*.) In every case that final citizenship is known to God; but living people typically do not know it with anything approaching clarity or certainty about themselves, and much less about others with whom they have to do; and even in the case of dead people it is the exception rather than the rule that their citizenship is known to those yet living. Even when it is known, it is known only with respect to the citizens of God's city: there is a list of saints, which is exactly a list of those known to have such citizenship; but there is no corresponding list of the damned, the permanent members of the earthly city. Augustine is sure that there are many of these latter (*civ. Dei* 20.4–6, 21.17–27); but, unlike Dante, he is chary of providing their names, and in this he is at one with the usual practice of the Church.[5] This eschatological understanding of citizenship is skeptical exactly because it is eschatological: no particular visible city in this age, not the Church and not Rome, has an unmixed citizenry. Every particular visible city has among its citizens some who are, or will finally be, citizens of the *civitas Dei*, and some who are or will finally be citizens of the *civitas terrena*.

Since the fall of Eve and Adam, every human being is born as one marked for eternal citizenship in the *civitas terrena*, which is to say for damnation (*civ. Dei* 15.1):

When those two cities began to run through their course of birth and death, the first to be born [i.e., Cain] was a citizen of this age, and the second [i.e., Abel] was a pilgrim in this age, belonging to the City of God. The latter was predestined by grace and chosen by grace; by grace he was a pilgrim below, and by grace he was a

---

[5] Augustine does often call one person or another a citizen of the *civitas terrena*: for example, Cain in *civ. Dei* 15.1. I take him here not to mean that he is certain of Cain's eternal destiny, but rather that he understands Cain's murder of Abel to be archetypical of what citizens of the earthly city do.

citizen above ... for in every case, as I have said already, man is first reprobate. But though it is of necessity that we begin in this way, we do not of necessity remain thus; for later comes the noble state towards which we may advance, and in which we may abide when we have attained it. Hence, though not every bad man will become good, it is nonetheless true that no one will be good who was not originally bad.

Speaking eschatologically, citizenship is given (predestined); speaking in terms of this age, there is the possibility of a change of citizenship, and for all who are (will finally be) citizens of God's city, such a change is unavoidable. Augustine here, as often elsewhere in the *City*, combines two rhetorical and logical registers. The first is *sub specie aeternitatis*, according to which you will always have been a citizen of whichever city you are finally a citizen of; and the second is *sub specie saecularitatis*, according to which there is real change in citizenship.

So much for the question of individual citizenship in this age. This is a genuine element in the political constitution of this age, but because final political allegiance in this sense is not knowable, Augustine's talk about it in the *City* serves principally as a check on facile identifications of the members of one or another particular visible city (Rome, Babylon, the Church, the United States) with the members of one or another of the two fundamental and eternal cities, the *civitas terrena* and the *civitas Dei*.

What then of the *societates hominum*, the particular human societies of this age? Augustine categorizes these also by way of the distinction between the city of God and the earthly city. But he never identifies any particular human society with either of the two. Or, more exactly, when he does (see, e.g., *civ. Dei* 8.24, where *civitas Dei* is identified in passing with *sancta ecclesia*), he typically qualifies the identification by saying that of course the two fundamental and final cities are inextricably mixed and intertwined,[6] both in the sense that citizens of each final city are to be found within every visible city, and in the sense that what is done in the name of any particular city of this age exhibits always and necessarily both some features of the city of God as it will finally be, and some features of the earthly city as it will finally be. Within any actual society, then, there is a mixed population: some will finally be (and always have been) citizens of the *civitas Dei*; and some will finally be (and always have been) citizens of the *civitas terrena*. Actual human societies are therefore not discriminated one from another by

---

[6] Augustine's vocabulary for the mixed nature of actual human societies is variegated and beautiful: *permixta, perplexa, commixta*, and many other terms. See *civ. Dei* 1.35 for a programmatic statement.

assessing what proportion of their citizens will at the end turn out to have belonged to one or other of the two fundamental cities.

Instead, actual human societies are discriminated one from another and categorized as bearing affinity to and tending toward one or other of the two fundamental cities by examination and description of their fundamental and constitutive practices. And about our capacity to discern and describe what these are, Augustine thinks, we do not have to be as skeptical as we must be about our capacity to know the final citizenship of particular individuals. What actual cities do is nakedly available to the eye, whether of the historian (a very great deal of the *City* is historiographic) or of the contemporary observer, and discussion of it need therefore not be constrained by eschatological skepticism.[7] In much of the *City*, Augustine describes and contrasts incompatible patterns of social practice, along with their associated (though usually implicit) norms. He then judges one set of practices good, and as belonging, in its pure, ideal–typical form (never actual), to the city of God; the other, with all the same qualifications, he judges bad, and as belonging to the earthly city. The practices in question belong to various spheres of human social practice: shedding blood; seeking power; offering worship; using the body; pursuing peace; taking life; performing punishment; and so on. In all these, and more, there is a spectrum: at one end there is what Babylon, the city of confusion, whose founder among men born of women is Cain, ideal–typically recommends and does; at the other there is what the Church, whose founder among men born of women is Jesus, ideal–typically recommends and does. Babylon is also Rome (an identification Augustine often repeats: e.g., *civ. Dei* 16.17, 18.2, 18.22), and the relation between those two particular visible cities is in many formal ways like that between the people of Israel and the Church: the one foreshadows the other, and its fundamental and constitutive practices find their fulfilment in those of the latter. In the case of Babylon–Rome, those fundamental and constitutive practices are bloody, idolatrous, and constituted by self-reference as their final good; in the case of Israel–Church they are worshipfully and beautifully peaceful, constituted by reference to God as their final good. It is not, once again, that everything Babylon–Rome does is of that ideal–typical kind; neither is it that everything Israel–Church does belongs to that ideal–typical kind. Rather, it is that

---

[7] Markus 1988: 151 is much too decided when he says that eschatological categories are invisible in historical realities. If this were so, it would have to be the case that the celebration of the Eucharist and the gladiatorial games were identically opaque to the eschatological reality of the *civitas Dei*. Augustine certainly does not think that.

when each of these political societies comes to a full understanding of itself and finds itself purged of every element that contradicts its identity, it will stand forth exactly as the *civitas terrena* in the former case, and the *civitas Dei* in the latter. The distinction between what the earthly city does and what the city of God does *in hoc saeculo* is not, however, only eschatological: the peace of the heavenly city and the violence of the earthly one are already evident, even if in chiaroscuro, in the patterns of action they commend and perform here and now.

Augustine's method in discerning which practices and norms belong to the city of God and which to the earthly city is from beginning to end theological, and also to a considerable extent exegetical, which is to say based upon and justified by a particular reading of Scripture. He discriminates the political good from its opposite by appeal to an understanding of what God is like and how God intends humans to order their lives together. The theological nature of Augustine's politics is most evident in the fundamental contrast he draws between the political order of Babylon–Rome and that of Israel–Church: the former is constitutively idolatrous, he says, while the latter is ordered around the worship of the one God. This matched pair (*idololatreia* || *veri Dei latreia*) is not a distinction that belongs to secular reasoning in any of our contemporary senses. It does in a sense belong to Augustine's understanding of the *saecularis*: both kinds of *latreia* occur *in hoc saeculo*. But the distinction is still thoroughly theological: a *societas hominum*, he says in one of his more excitable moments, which is not ordered around the worship of the one God, is ipso facto incapable of being truly just (*civ. Dei* 19.21), and there can scarcely be a more theological way of judging the justice of particular polities.

The question about the political constitution of the present age as Augustine sees it in the *City* can now be answered more fully and precisely. There is a very large number of actual political entities, actual *societates hominum* ordered by law and norm and aspiration and custom, found in this present age; each of them has among its *cohabitantes* some individuals who belong to the city of God and some who belong to the earthly city; and each commends and performs some political activities that belong properly (finally) to the human city, and others that belong properly (finally) to the divine city. In all those senses, the particular polities of this age are on a par: the formal analysis just given applies identically to each. Particular societies are discriminated one from another, then, according to their degree of corruption, which is to say the distance between what they commend and do and what the city of God commends and does. This abstract characterization cries out for instances; and to those, to contrasts between particular practices proper to Babylon–Rome and those proper to Israel–Church, I now turn.

4 BABYLON–ROME AND ISRAEL–CHURCH

On the one hand there are polities ordered around the worship, the *cultus*, of false gods; on the other there are those ordered around the true worship (*verax cultus*) of the true God, the one God of Jesus Christ. This distinction, between idolatry (*idololatreia*) and *latreia* simpliciter (Augustine finds the Greek words unavoidable; *civ. Dei* 10.1), marks the deepest divide between Babylon and the Church, each a visible city of this age. From it all other distinctions flow, and with it all other distinctions are intertwined (*civ. Dei* 11.1):

> The citizens of the earthly city prefer their own gods to the Founder of the holy city, for they do not know that he is the God of gods. Not of false gods, however, who are impious and proud, and who, deprived of His immutable light in which all may share, are thereby reduced to a kind of destitute power: who strive after certain personal privileges of their own, and who seek divine honours from their misguided subjects. Rather, He is the God of pious and holy gods, who take delight rather in submitting themselves to One than in subjecting many to themselves, and in worshipping God than in being worshipped in place of God.

This is couched in terms of the relation between the one God and the many gods, but the points it makes about that apply more or less directly to human citizens of the polities of this age: the impious gods are what the citizens of the earthly city worship, and the axiom that worshippers conform themselves to what they worship means that what is said about the impious gods applies also to their worshippers. There is the distinction between private and public we have already seen: what the ideal–typical citizens of the earthly city seek is something *privatus*, something of their own, something they can own without remainder. What they especially seek is power (*potestas, potentia*) that can be held and exercised without reference to any other power: the ideal type of that power is held by the one God, and in seeking private mastery the earthly city attempts to become like him. This attempt fails. The power attained by the earthly city is destitute or indigent (*egena*): there is an echo here, probably, of the needs of the prodigal son who, having consumed and exhausted the substance his father has given him, began to suffer need (*coepit egere*; Luke 15:14). Indigent power is an oxymoron that indicates a simulacrum: it is what you get when you seek private power, power that is yours without remainder. It is the kind of power yielded by idolatry, and, therefore, the kind of power that belongs, ideal–typically, to Babylon–Rome. It is the self-cancelling political outflow of misdirected worship.

Those who worship the one God, in contrast to idolaters, understand themselves to be constituted as citizens of the particular polities they inhabit, including the Church, by their response to God's action upon them; no polity, therefore, is taken to be self-constituted, self-explanatory, or exhaustively explicable in terms given by this age. Worshippers of the one God understand, too, that the constitutive practices of their particular polities *in hoc saeculo* point beyond themselves and will either cease or be radically transformed when this age is folded into the future age. These understandings yield a particular mode of political existence, for which Augustine's favored term is *peregrinatio*, wandering or pilgrimage (*civ. Dei* 15.1, citing Gen. 4:17):

It is written, then, that Cain founded a city, whereas Abel, a pilgrim, did not found one. For the City of the Saints is on high, although it produces citizens here below, in whose persons it is a pilgrim until the time of its kingdom shall come.

The extent to which a polity's constitutive practices are idolatrous is tightly indexed to the extent to which it understands itself as an enduring city with a firm location here below. By contrast, wanderers in this age know themselves to be wanderers because they are worshippers of the one God: they cannot rest in the citizenships of this age (not even in ecclesial citizenship) because they know that those citizenships have only temporary significance (which is not to say that they have none), and because they know it to be characteristic of the constitutive practices of those polities that participate most fully in the earthly city precisely to imply the denial of this by presenting what is local and temporary and partial as if it were otherwise. The polities of this age that participate most fully in the city of God have constitutive practices that enshrine, dramatize, and represent their own incompleteness, constantly pointing to the fact that they are what they are by gift rather than possession, and that even what they are will, eventually, be brought to nothing or radically transformed. Those practices are liturgical: it is in the explicit sacramental worship of the one God undertaken by the body of Christ, that the Church shows itself to be, in its politics – the practices that order its common life as a polity, a city – the fullest possible participant in the city of God.

At the end of the fourteenth book of the *City*, Augustine treats at length the distinction between the two *genera humanae* (the one belonging to the city of God and the other to the earthly city), and then writes, by way of summary (*civ. Dei* 14.28):

> Two cities, then, have been created by two loves: that is, the earthly by love of self extending even to contempt of God, and the heavenly by love of God, extending to contempt of self. The one, therefore, glories in itself, the other in the Lord; the one seeks glory from men, the other finds its highest glory in God, the Witness of our conscience. The one lifts up its head in its own glory; the other says to its God, 'Thou art my glory, and the lifter up of mine head' [Psalm 3:4, Vulgate]. In the Earthly City, princes are as much mastered by the lust for mastery as the nations which they subdue are by them; in the Heavenly, all serve one another in charity, rulers by their counsel and subjects by their obedience.

The love typical of and proper to the earthly city is, in origin and end, self-love: what the citizens of that city do, and what visible cities whose laws and norms participate in those of the earthly city require of their citizens and enshrine in their laws, is love and glorify themselves as their own proper end. "Glory," for Augustine, as for Scripture, is a technical term: it belongs to God and is to be returned to him. Self-glorying, therefore, is an idolatrous act by definition, with all the deleterious consequences of such acts. Among these consequences is a desire for domination that can find no terminus: it proliferates without end, and makes those who dance to its tune by attempting to subordinate others to their will themselves subject to (not masters of) their desire. To have the *libido dominandi* is to seek *dominatio*, which is, in turn, to seek to be a *dominus*. *Dominus* is the Latin rendering of the Tetragrammaton, the unsayable four-lettered name of God, a fact of which Augustine is much aware. When he writes of the *libido dominandi* as characteristic of the earthly city, then, he is depicting a desire to be God: idolatry again, in an elegantly lexical key, and again an explicitly theological account of what constitutes the politics of the earthly city.

In practice, the proliferative nature of the *libido dominandi* makes it recognizable. It can be seen most clearly in attempts to bring in all those not (yet) citizens of Babylon–Rome, typically by force, with death as the other option. The extent to which a particular visible city performs actions like this is the extent to which (what we would call) its foreign policy participates in the desires proper to the earthly city. Augustine takes as an instance of *libido dominandi* in this sense the Roman Republic's destruction of Carthage, its principle economic and military rival, in the Third Punic War (*civ. Dei* 3.16–29). Rome's *libido dominandi*, as Augustine depicts it, made it impossible for it to tolerate the continued existence of any rival; and so Carthage had to be destroyed, which it was, its people slaughtered, its buildings razed, and its ground salted (methods that Rome would later use on Jerusalem itself). From this destruction, Augustine says, came violence and suffering of much greater magnitude than would have occurred had Carthage been permitted to remain in being as a check upon Roman passions (3.22). It is also what distinguishes it from the violence deployed by visible cities whose laws and norms participate more fully in those of the city of God. The violence of those cities is restricted, lamented, and defensively protective (3.10); the violence of Babylon–Rome is in every way the other thing, and it is so because it is something the earthly city is itself dominated by.

Service in loving-kindness (*servitium in caritate*; *civ. Dei* 14.28) is the heavenly city's version of *libido dominandi*. Internally, such service relates the sovereign of that city to its subjects; externally, it relates sovereign and subjects to those outside, whether enemies or neutrals or friends. The model here is the love of God for his people: God's bringing into being of the cosmos is his first act of loving-kindness; his election of a people his second; and his third the incarnation and passion of Christ. These are gifts and offerings of peace, without a trace of violence. They are, however, accompanied by divine judgments upon those who do not receive the offered gifts with gratitude. Those acts of judgment Augustine typically describes under the heading of punishment (the central category of Book 21), and he is detailed and enthusiastic in his depictions of it. The visible Church, in its internal economy, participates in and represents this combination of service and judgment; this explains the violence it uses.[8] Any violence there is in the visible cities that participate in the city of God is, however, limited and responsive to the violence already present in the world's fabric because of the fall. The heavenly city has no interest in it for its own sake, whereas the earthly city is defined by its tendency toward the unrestricted use of violence.

The unrestricted violence of the earthly city's politics, and its contrast with the limited violence of the heavenly city, is matched in Augustine's thought by a contrast between the norms of the two cities with respect to suicide. Augustine thinks it clear that the fifth commandment's ban against killing extends to self-killing (*civ. Dei* 1.20), and that there are no conceivable circumstances that justify that act (1.22–24). He is concerned about the case of Christian women who might (or in some cases did), following the example of the Sabines, kill themselves as a result of being raped, or in order to avoid an imminent rape. To the first case he says that there is no sin in

---

[8] For example, in Augustine's reluctant use of Roman military and judicial power against the Donatists in North Africa in the early years of the fifth century.

being raped, and indeed no real loss, not even of virginity properly understood. From this he takes it to follow that killing oneself because one has been raped is both an excessive and a sinful response. And to the second case he says that even if there were sin in being raped, the idea that one should sin by committing suicide in order to avoid sin is absurd. It would lead, if pressed, to the conclusion that Christians should commit suicide immediately upon being baptized (1.27), for that would guarantee no future sin; and that is a *reductio ad absurdum* of the position.

Suicide, then, does not belong to the city of God. The earthly city, by contrast, not only tolerates suicide but also in some circumstances is required by its own logic to embrace and advocate it. If, as the norms of the earthly city suggest, the fully happy life (*vita beata*) can be had here below, in this age, by such things as the cultivation and control of virtue and the carefully ordered enjoyment of local and temporal goods; and if, too, those goods and joys can be removed by violence and other calamities, as they obviously can, then suicide is the proper (and perhaps the only proper) response to the imminent and unavoidable threat of such removal. This kind of argument has special purchase on Stoic views, and Augustine probably has in mind famous instances of Stoic suicide, such as that of Seneca. But Augustine generalizes it to all those who think that happiness can be found *in hoc saeculo* (there are strong words about this view in *civ. Dei* 19.4–5). The *civitas terrena* is, in his view, necessarily necrophiliac because it does not acknowledge its own insufficiency, while necessarily acknowledging the presence of violent contingency. The suicide's gesture, on this view, is one of control over contingency; in this it is like the earthly city's attempt to erase all those who refuse subjection to it; and both gestures flow from the earthly city's attempt to live consistently *secundum carnem* and not *secundum spiritum*.

Israel–Church rejects suicide, which is of course not to say that none of its members perform that act; but it affirms martyrdom, which is its approximate functional equivalent of Babylon–Rome's endorsement of suicide. Augustine has a lot to say about the martyrs in the *City*: he discusses the proper and improper forms of veneration directed toward them (*civ. Dei* 8.27); he depicts them as Christian heroes (10.21), serving a function for Israel–Church analogous to that performed by Hector and Priam for Romans; and he is very interested in (and for the most part endorses) stories of miracles resulting from prayer at the shrines of martyrs (22.8 at length, and elsewhere). But most importantly, martyrs are those who willingly accept death at the hands of pagans as a mode of witness to the truth. By that act they are *coronati*, crowned; and it is that act which constitutes the ideal death for Christians (18.52, 20.13, 21.26, and elsewhere). The bodily marks of martyrdom – the wounds – are sufficiently important as witnesses to who they are and what they have done that Augustine thinks they will remain upon their resurrected bodies in order to give delight to the saints (22.19; he hastens to add that if a martyr has lost limbs or head, those will be restored in the resurrection). Martyrs are not suicides because they do not seek death but rather accept it when given. Augustine is aware that this is a difficult line to draw, especially because the literary accounts of the deaths of martyrs, the *passiones martyrum*, which were very popular among Christians in the North Africa of his time, and for two centuries before, sometimes depict particular martyrs as dying in ways that approach uncomfortably close to Augustine's understanding of suicide. But it is a line he consistently affirms as normatively important, and his arguments for it are one of the roots of the Church's later categorization of suicide as a mortal sin. The martyr–suicide distinction encapsulates, therefore, one of the distinctive differences between the norms of the two cities with respect to death.

5 AN AUGUSTINIAN SECULARITY

Augustine's understanding of the political constitution of the *saeculum* is essentially theological. This is true of his eschatology, according to which there are only sheep and goats, only, eventually, citizens of God's city and of the earthly city, the saved and the damned. It is true, too, of his assessment of the laws and norms and customs of visible polities, visible public things: these laws and norms are divided and categorized according to a theological and scriptural–exegetical understanding of the political activities that belong, ideal-typically, to each of the two cities. His politics is most fundamentally one of longing for what is not,[9] which is to say a truly public thing where love and peace are harmoniously and indefectibly shared by all those who are intimate with God. It is also, and correspondingly, a politics of lament for what is *in hoc saeculo*: bloody violence in the service of a self-defeating, nihilist, and necrophiliac self-love. And there is, threaded through his historical account of the rise and fall of particular, visible, public things (Assyria, Babylon, Egypt, Rome), occasional delightedly surprised recognition of the *vestigia*, the traces, of God's city even where there are only pagans, or where Israel–Church and Babylon–Rome cohabit. It is not (quite) all lament.

[9] I draw here from Von Heyking 2001.

For Christians, Augustine does provide properly political guidance, mostly by giving the lexicon and syntax of a Christian account of the public thing, and by illustrating that grammar historically. This grammar has *peregrinatio* as its central term of art. To say that Christians are wanderers *in hoc saeculo* is, first, to restrict the kind and intensity of love and loyalty that may properly be directed toward any visible public thing that is not the Church. Even in the case of the Church, a distinction must be drawn between the Church visible, the *corpus permixtum* that embraces both kinds of citizen among its members, and that is perplexingly intertwined with pagan public things; and the Church as she will finally be. The love for the Church that Augustine commends to Christians is different (more intense, less hedged, vastly more intimate) from the love for other public things because Christians know that the visible Church shows, in the activities definitive and constitutive of itself – that is, liturgical acts – the fullest and most beautiful foreshadowing in this age of what the resurrected life of the city of God will be *in futuro saeculo*. But Christian love for the visible Church is nonetheless constrained to some degree by the knowledge that some of what is done in the Church's name is contradictory to what she is – or, as Augustine would prefer to say, it rends her rather than builds her up. In the hierarchy of loves for particular visible political things, the Church stands at the top; but love for her is not lament-free.

Emphasizing *peregrinatio* also requires the judgment that political perfectionism (the view that we can, in this age, get our politics right) and most kinds of political progressivism (the view that we can, in this age, significantly improve our politics) are utopian and may never be endorsed by Christians. The particulars of perfectionist and progressivist programs, whether broad-scope (the worldwide establishment of Sharia law; the spread of international socialism; the Great Leap Forward; the colonization of the Americas; making the world safe for democracy) or local (privately financed prison systems; regressive taxation; proportional representation; this candidate for office or that one) may or may not be capable of endorsement or support by Christians. But the progressivist or perfectionist claims with which commendations of these particulars are associated and in terms of which they are justified – this will make the world perfect; this will make the world better – are never acceptable.

This implication of *peregrinatio* suggests a kind of political quietism, not with respect to recommendation of political particulars, but with respect to concern for their outcome.[10] That outcome will always be, in a formal sense,

---

[10] On quietism, see Griffiths 2009.

exactly the same: an unpredictable blend of the good and the dreadful, and a blend that has much less to do with the intentions of the agents advocating political change than with other things. A useful illustration of this limited quietism can be found in Augustine's twin claims that it doesn't matter how long you live so long as you live well and are resurrected to eternal life rather than to eternal death (*civ. Dei* 1.11), and that it doesn't matter by whom you're ruled so long as they don't force you to do what is impious and iniquitous (5.17). On this view, the principal significance of the laws and norms of the public thing, whether it is pagan or mixed or inhabited entirely by Christians (the last possibility is not one that Augustine imagines clearly), is negative: they are on a par one with another so long as they don't order you to do what contradicts God's intentions. Suppose they do? Suppose a Christian is faced with a public law that requires just such an action? That is straightforward enough: Christians are not to obey such laws, and must joyously suffer the penalty for refusing to do so (19.17). Martyrdom is the proper and delightful end of that practice, when circumstance requires.

There is, however, one positive thing to say about the politics of the public thing for Christians, a thing in addition to the negatives just mentioned. It is that earthly peace is a good (a preliminary good, but still a good) that Christians should seek, support, and celebrate (with qualifications) when it occurs. This requires them to obey and to support the laws that provide such peace. For example (*civ. Dei* 19.26):

> ... while the two cities are intermingled, we also make use of the peace of Babylon. We do so even though the people of God is delivered from Babylon by faith, so that it is only for a while that we are pilgrims in her midst. It is for this reason, therefore, that the Apostle admonishes the Church to pray for kings and for all that are in authority, adding these words: 'that we may live a quiet and tranquil life in all godliness and love' [1 Tim. 2:2]. Again, when the prophet Jeremiah foretold the captivity which was to befall the ancient People of God, he bade them, by divine command, to go obediently into Babylon, thereby serving God even by their patient endurance; and he himself admonished them to pray for Babylon, saying: 'In the peace thereof shall ye have peace' [Jer. 29:7]: the temporal peace which is for the time being shared by the good and the wicked alike.

Peace in this age, the tranquility of order (*civ. Dei* 19.13; cf. 14.9, on the *tranquillitas caritatis*), is to be loved by the Church for what it is: a breathing-space, a short pause in the shedding of blood; and those who provide it prayed for and supported in their provision of it. Such prayer, however, occurs always with the warning, as in the passage just quoted, that what is prayed for will not last, and that those prayed for may well be evil and evildoers. Prayer for the rulers of Babylon–Rome is therefore always to be accompanied by lament (Ps. 137:1, often quoted by Augustine). Just so with the work Christians may properly do in making and administering the laws and norms of a particular visible public thing. There can, for a fully Augustinian view of the secular, be Christian presidents or elected representatives or judges or police or soldiers; but any who do not lament their necessities as such are misunderstanding what they do. The stance of lament, implying as it does an accurate (as Augustine sees it) understanding of what the laws and norms of visible public things can do, may lead to less bloody and damaging political judgments than would be made by those who do not occupy it; but there is no guarantee of that.[11]

So much for the political guidance Augustine gives to Christians *in hoc saeculo*. The principal guidance he provides for pagans is as an illustration of the grammar of one variety of Christian thought about human social life. Absent the theology that frames and supports Augustine's views on that matter, nothing is left but *disjecta membra*. Those have often been taken up; but when they are, Augustine is left far behind. Augustine's yield for political theory in our secular sense of that term is also very small, in large part because he has no interest in the theoretical questions central to the discipline. One element in the *City* may, however, be of considerable current relevance, and this provides, perhaps, a partial explanation of the recent flood of publication on Augustine and Augustinian politics. It is the idea that the *saeculum* is not and cannot be a political space neutral to and capable of framing, accounting for, and explaining the Church.[12] That element in secular political theory has less and less purchase on our political life. Its four-century or so prominence for us is waning; and so Augustine, for whom it would have seemed ludicrous, may be of increasing interest to us as a theorist of the *saeculum*, if not of the secular.

---

[11] On the question of the Christian statesman's virtues, not extensively explored in *City of God*, see *ep.* 155, to Macedonius. There are hints here as to how the Church might positively transform the *res publica*; for the most part, Augustine is properly pessimistic both about the possibility that this might happen and about the likelihood in particular cases of our knowing that it has. See Kaufman 2007.

[12] Following O'Donovan 2004 and against the general line of interpretation in Markus 1988.

CHAPTER 3

Augustine's dystopia

Peter Iver Kaufman

I BAD NEWS

The news from North Africa was bad. The infection had spread long before Augustine proffered a diagnosis and before Rome's capitulations along the empire's borders – before Emperor Honorius had been chased from Rome and the city sacked in 410. Indeed, humanity had been infected even before those multiple enslavements and emancipations reported in the Hebrews' sacred texts, which had become sacred as well for Christians. The apostle Paul's take on the disobedience and disgrace recorded in the first chapters of Genesis (Rom. 5:12) was instrumental in convincing Augustine that humanity's parents had sinned so gravely that all their children lived wretchedly – and, for shame, there could be no returning to the *status quo ante*. Therapies, plausibly, but no complete cures, no way out from the sins and suffering in time (*civ. Dei* 22.24). Envy inexorably led to violence from the time Cain murdered Abel into the fifth century, and violence littered the shrinking empire with conflicts' unburied casualties (*civ. Dei* 1.2). Nature was far from neutral. Storms, earthquakes, rabid animals took a terrible toll. Lives were lost or wrecked. The jeopardy afflicted all with anxiety. Yet all were villains as well as victims. Scratch the ostensibly blameless, and one finds hatred, escalating ambition, and pride, with flattery, adultery, and other forms of deceit, along with cruelty and treachery – in intent and often enough in act as well (*civ. Dei* 22.22).

Christianity and the empire's political culture had become partners nearly a century before Augustine started writing *City of God*. Although a few Christians thought – and others now think – piety and politics mismatched, many of the faithful in the fourth and early fifth centuries trusted that the partnership between their relatively new religion and old Rome would yield tremendous benefits for both. Augustine conceived some good coming from the coupling – especially when its more extreme, puritanical critics in Africa turned militant – yet he was convinced that

Christianity could not redeem terrestrial cities. Life in time was a Gulag or – in current coin – a Gitmo, a detention camp. Christians were fortunate to be passing through to a better place, yet their here and now would always be a dreadfully sad place and time. "The human race's present condition is a punishment" for its parents' sin – for and among the sins that followed (*civ. Dei* 22.24). All are oppressed; their shared miseries defy description, Augustine lamented, while describing many that came to mind (*civ. Dei* 22.22).[1]

Yet the news from North Africa was not all bad. The steadfastly faithful could look forward to the celestial city as they passed through their terrestrial city as pilgrims, Augustine explained, and, looking around, they would also discover that this world was loaded with "consolations." Humans were alive, rational, creative, and procreative. *Non in eo tamen penitus extincta est*: a spark within them, an image of God flickering in their reason, had not been entirely doused by the environing evil (*civ. Dei* 22.24). And even their material or corporeal presence – their intricate networks of arteries, veins, and organs – impressed, as did their inventiveness. Augustine's *City of God*, one might say, finds humanity punching well beyond its weight. The text inventories the results that range from culinary cleverness, advances in navigation, and healthcare improvements to greater efficiency in waging wars. By shuttling between hygiene and combat, vocations in which humans had become especially effective – respectively, preserving and terminating life – Augustine seems mischievous. Arguably, he was apprehensive rather than altogether appreciative, particularly about humanity's belligerence, but the important point here is that he did identify a number of *damnatorum solacia*, consolations for those condemned to live in time – for a time. They were, above all, "blessings" or gifts from God and only secondarily the outcomes of human industry (*civ. Dei* 22.24). Appeals to prelates, saints, and relics have no prompt payoff, for example, but the faithful now pray for – and should be consoled by – benefits they would have when this wicked world's evil no longer played havoc with the good (*civ. Dei* 22.22).

Among the "blessings" and "consolations" in time, God deposited virtues, though only faith and properly oriented hope gave pilgrims' virtues traction in the terrestrial city. But even with that traction, the challenges of cohabitation seemed to unsettle "children of the promise and of the kingdom." Augustine appeared to be discouraged by the way some of those "children" were meeting the challenge of living as pilgrims among

---

[1] Tornau 2006: 152.

pagans. Early in his pontificate, he had been asked to sift several related difficulties. Most commercial transactions depended, in part, on oaths. Were Christians complicit in idolatry when they witnessed and benefited from infidels swearing to their gods to uphold the bargains they made? Did Christians at public baths, where their idolatrous neighbors burned incense during feast days, inhale idolatry with the polluted air after those neighbors were long gone? No, Augustine replied, humorlessly dispelling exaggerated fears of contamination. Relying in business transactions on an idolater's oaths did not make Christians idolaters; smoke from pagans' sacrifices could not corrupt Christians, who, on other occasions, applauded the destruction of infidels' idols and thus made their abhorrence of idolatry clear. The faithful need not withhold their credit; they need not hold their breath (*ep.* 47.2–3). True, to some extent, one could distance oneself from amoral and immoral fellow travelers and from the temptation to fall in with (and to fall with) them – nonetheless, the pilgrims must travel through time with unpleasant company and mark time until their emancipation and everlasting felicity in the celestial city (*civ. Dei* 22.23).

As pastor, Augustine tried to resolve problems posed by traveling through time in mixed company. Business and bathing raised questions for ordinary Christians, yet by far the prickliest problems their prelates faced related to leadership. Should their church's lay leaders or, for that matter, its bishops be ruthless policing this wicked world? Could they coerce others, ostracize or incarcerate, *ut non dormiat disciplina*, "to keep discipline from nodding off" and to prevent the spread of evil? (*s.* 164.11). Might influential Christians accept public office, negotiate hairpin turns around the familiar obstacles to achieving just results in the late Roman empire (corruptible colleagues and corrupt courts), and punish offenders with sufficient severity to deter subsequent offenses while remaining faithful to their religion's principles? Surely those principles would not sanction political paralysis! Consolations could be found, *City of God* suggests, if Christian magistrates badger themselves before bludgeoning fellow citizens. For, with God's help, those magistrates, much as ordinary Christians, can be somewhat – yet never completely – successful struggling against "forces of darkness to which they were born subject," forces that infected and enfeebled them (*civ. Dei* 22.22). So the bad news holds, and although any Christian appointed to a position of authority *in hoc saeculo maligno*, "in this wicked world" (*civ. Dei* 18.49), can make a difference, that difference amounts to little more than damage control in dystopia.

2 DYSTOPIA?

By discussing several of the issues that complicated the Christian's cohabitation and political participation in "this wicked world," as Augustine saw them, the remainder of this contribution will garrison the ground we have gained collecting the bad news he conveyed in his *City*. We shall inquire whether the assorted "consolations" he enumerated compensated for the corruption. And we shall consider one reason he might have had for composing his tome as a massive disorienting device. Of course, certainty about authorial intent is impossible to pocket, yet one can make the case that Augustine dropped *City of God* into the post-410 conversation about empires, conquest, glory, and cupidity to put such ephemera in perspective. Might he have wanted to give pause to colleagues who too readily acquiesced in the hot pursuit of trifles in their terrestrial cities? Before attempting to answer, we ought to ask if "dystopia" is the right term to characterize Augustine's city where trifles and the desire to possess them dominated the practice of politics – a city of gaud – or, to be precise, to characterize his depictions of his terribly flawed and "wicked world."

Readers familiar with dystopian fiction will likely conjure up terrifyingly oppressive societies. To take the best examples of the worst conditions: Ray Bradbury's *Fahrenheit 451*, Aldous Huxley's *Brave New World*, George Orwell's *1984*, and Anatole France's *Penguin Island* offer few, if any, consolations as they describe with memorable flourishes the wretched societies their protagonists protest. Yet the adjective "dystopian" has also been applied to a particular environmental or economic imbalance that has not yet tipped an entire society into chaos or tyranny. If, let's say, the principal architects or overseers of a society's crime-fighting apparatus deliberately misinform the law-abiding and perpetuate their fear of the lawless solely to justify a policing agency's budget or its very being, the situation or predicament could be called dystopian. Or, to cite cinema's frightening tribute to our justifications for overkill, "Dr Strangelove," recall General Turgidson's fondness for unanswerable first-strike capabilities and his flirtation with disaster.

By contrast, if one places *City of God*'s inventory of the city of gaud's various "consolations" alongside Augustine's concessions that Christians so inclined could participate in public life, this wicked world seems only mildly dystopian. And, arguably, Augustine's indomitable rectitude, breaking into the text's passages on greed, envy, lust, and larceny, made this world look much more wicked than it usually seemed to him. Perhaps, yet consider the alternative: after surveying the political cultures of the ancient Near East, republican and imperial Rome, and the new, improved, yet relatively diminished Christian empire, the *City* concludes with all that bad news simply because "this wicked world" looked to Augustine to be utterly, irredeemably dysfunctional and dystopian.

One short chapter can be taken to support both of these alternatives. It recycles the then familiar story of a pirate who had been captured by Alexander the Great. When the captive was scolded for terrorizing travelers, he explained he had only done what the great Alexander was doing. When done with one vessel, it was called piracy, pirates and their captains were called rogues, and no effort was spared to hunt them down. When fleets or armies terrorized settled populations as well as travelers, the devastation was dignified – called conquest – and the captain of it all called "great" (*civ. Dei* 4.4). The ablative absolute, *remota justitia*, in the story's preamble is critical. The phrase can be translated either "once justice is removed" or "remote from justice." So Augustine could have been asking hyperbolically, "once [or when] justice is removed, what are kingdoms but great bands of robbers" or, descriptively, "remote from justice, what are kingdoms are but great bands of robbers?" If the removal of justice had been hypothetical and hyperbolic or, one could say, rhetorical, Augustine could have been warning a sickly, profligate society of a coronary-to-come, if it did not mend its ways. If the prevailing injustices were temporary, stiffening resistance and strenuous criticism might just bring society back from the brink. Customs were not hopelessly corrupt; government was not buccaneering by other means. But if *remota justitia* was an inescapable characteristic of political leadership as well as larceny, what passed for justice in the city of gaud, this terrestrial city, would appear to be vastly overrated. Matters were doomed to proceed from bad to worse. After Adam and Eve fell from grace, humans lost too much altitude to clear the obstacles to good government that their own infected selves and histories placed in their way.[2]

Corruption was common; behind it, cupidity. A promising start to end both had been made in Jerusalem with Jesus' preaching repentance. Faith was then so "fired up" that many of the converted sold what they possessed, gave the proceeds to the poor, and prepared to endure the enmity of the unconverted as well as destitution. Augustine, with help from the biblical narrative, remembers the earliest Christians' enthusiasm that way (*civ. Dei* 18.54) and defies Christian readers, dispossessed by invading Goths and Vandals more than three centuries after that promising start, to consider their material losses as spiritual gains. One could stretch his recollection and

---

[2] Horn 2007: 61–64; Kaufman 2007: 229–30.

argue that his *City* also urged its readers who had yet lost little to become less attached to what they had, less eager for more, and less corrupt in their quest for increase. Fair enough, yet a comparison is in order, a comparison between Augustine and the moralist whose lessons from Rome's humiliation fueled a more ferocious indictment of the Romans' corruption and greed, Salvian of Marseilles.

Salvian registered his complaints several decades after Augustine completed *City of God*. Corrupt officials were then shamelessly auctioning off their influence. The bidders were complicit, Salvian said, yet he seemed most concerned with corruption's casualties, commoners who were overtaxed to pay for the elite's excesses.[3] Had Augustine lived to read Salvian's screed, however, he might have called it something of an understatement. For Augustine was well acquainted with the predatory character of public life. Before conscience and Christianity thwarted his maneuvering for political preferment, he was not above indulging in fraud and flattery to get results.[4] But in Milan, in the mid 380s, Augustine decided to abandon his promising political career and thereafter, on occasion, characterized political practice as a set of snares. He gently mocked correspondents who could not (or would not) see it as such. Yet the tone of his *City*'s assessment is different. That tome sometimes displays Salvian's distemper. It recalls how impressively – and for centuries – moral philosophers reprimanded the greedy. The philosophers-turned-critics avoided language that did not invite immediate comprehension; that is, they thundered or "pealed" as prophets, specifying concrete abuses instead of formulating abstract ideas that few could apply to everyday choices (*civ. Dei* 2.19). But little good that did, Augustine pointed out; Christians were destined to pass through their fifth century harassed and scandalized by corrupt government officials and by the gusting corruption in their churches.

Yet did he wink at corruption or – worse – willingly participate, as some scholars allege?[5] One episode in 411 has been regularly rehearsed to support that allegation. It began with Valerius Pinianus' visit to Hippo. Pinianus, a distinguished philanthropist, was a prize for any parish, and, if an irritable correspondent's accusations can be trusted, Augustine schemed with several parishioners to detain and ordain their guest. Pinianus' plans did not include a long stay; still, he must have known that abductions of prominent persons were not unprecedented, that, twenty years earlier, Augustine was detained and ordained, to good effect, one could argue, although his assets

---

[3] Salvian 1930: 4.4.4–6. [4] Lepelley 1987: 99–117.
[5] MacMullen 1990: 152–53; Lancel 2002: 313; Lepelley 2006: 205–6.

were different from those Pinianus would have delivered. As for the locals' scheming, Augustine insisted that he neither coached them nor connived with them. But he did excuse them after suggesting he helped their prey get away. True, his excuse for the locals seems lame; they were not after money, he said, but wanted to keep Pinianus where his contempt for wealth and his generosity would inspire others. Was Augustine being disingenuous, or should his reply be read as evidence of his embarrassment? Probably he was resigned to his prodigiously opportunistic parishioners' desires for a windfall – and possibly he was covering for it; he looks to have been covering up his embarrassment, not his complicity (*ep.* 126).

Augustine's resignation to corruption rather than his approval of it appears to have influenced his comments on influence peddling in the government's courts. The clerks had their palms up, he noticed, but he was more outraged by the courts' higher authorities who accepted bribes and by the attorneys who paid them. The practice of paying clerks to expedite a case's progress through the courts looked less reprehensible. Corruptible clerks were cogs in a dystopian system. Bribing (or tipping) them was less repulsive than paying for perjury, which, Augustine reported, usually went undetected. He deplored the "culture" in provincial, municipal, and manorial courts that encouraged malicious litigants with ample resources to pour buckets of trouble over their less well-connected and under-funded neighbors. He stridently objected to what he considered to be the more monstrous abuses of power, letting lesser offenses pass with a slap, but not with a shrug. He loathed exploitation yet let corrupt clerks follow custom, urging them graciously to share their ill-gotten gain with the poor (*ep.* 153.10, 153.24–26).

Still, for all their imperfections, the courts played a crucial part in maintaining some semblance of order. What there was of peace on earth would disintegrate without courts, clerks, and magistrates. *City of God* concedes as much. "Peace possessed in faith" – and in anticipation of everlasting peace – Augustine explained, consoled citizens of the celestial city during its pilgrimage in time (*civ. Dei* 19.17). Gone from a world without secular laws and courts – hence, without peace – were the props that braced Christians' hopes for their wholly and holy alternative future. And the courts and governments in this wicked world, staggeringly flawed as they were, still helped the pilgrim citizens of the celestial city cope with the wretchedness of their city of gaud. Bishops helped as well, of course, and their assistance will concern us soon, yet what is important here is that Augustine was reluctant to intervene and agitate for government reforms. He once tried but was humiliated (*s.* 302.17). He seems to have preferred to refer his and parishioners' complaints about corruption to municipal ombudsmen, people's "defenders," who were authorized by law to protect the powerless from the powerful and predatory. As local notables, "defenders" were unlikely to be cold-shouldered by the influential, their social equals. Ombudsmen's integrity and ingenuity (*sollertia*), therefore, gave victims a route toward a remedy (*ep.* 22*.3–4). Still Augustine sees no safety in the streets. Enemies are everywhere. "This mortal condition" is an ordeal; the larger the city, the more crime, contention, lawsuits, and corruption. And whenever some serenity is achieved, the serene are still troubled by thoughts of renewed distress around the next turn (*civ. Dei* 19.5).

Hence, to persevere was to live in fear that the sinful and irrational within will occasionally, if not often, break the restraints that citizens and their societies had devised. *City of God* acknowledges that humans are right to worry about themselves – and not just about others. Furthermore, when the pilgrim citizens of the celestial city worry about others, they should also try to relieve others' distress. They are righteous as well as right, that is, to experience "a serene fear," the "fear that love has." It is both serene and loving because resignation to the inevitability of corruption does not preclude compassion. The apathy Augustine deplored was a wholly inappropriate response to corruption; that and the exploitation of the poor struck him as "disturbance worthy," according to Nicholas Wolterstorff, although many of the bishop's admirers have turned his disturbance into something progressive and astonishingly "populist."[6]

Claude Lepelley is among the more cautious, on this count. He has Augustine campaigning for tenants' rights, yet without directly (and recklessly) challenging socio-economic structures that favored proprietors, permitted forms of fraud and slavery, and ensured Africa would always have an exploitable underclass. But Lepelley's man stood up to scurrilous landlords and slave traders. Jean-Marie Salamito's Augustine is also an aggressive advocate of "the downtrodden" whose goodwill and *plébéisme* never seemed to congeal into a program for social reform. Yet Salamito contrasts his protagonist with Pelagians and stipulates the former's zero tolerance for the latter's – and for all elites' – arrogance. Finally, Eric Gregory's reconstruction of Augustine's "morally robust civic liberalism" argues that it "democratizes and publicizes love through a theological (and political) populism."[7] Somewhat surprisingly, the interpreters in this small stampede to make Augustine an ardent social reformer either forget or dismiss (as fraying

---

[6] Wolterstorff 2008: 194–98.
[7] Lepelley 2006: 211–13; Salamito 2005: 265, 296–98; Gregory 2008: 355.

pessimism) the bad news from North Africa which introduced this paper. They forget or question the seriousness of Augustine's warnings that practicing politics supersized sin. His analysis was unlike that of Lord Acton. For the bishop, power does not corrupt. Corruption came before power. The desire to acquire power and to use it – even to reform one's dystopian surrounds – amplifies corruption. So Augustine thought it better to "bring vice indoors," as John Parrish puts it, to "internalize the conceived location of moral action" without battling – and possibly undermining – entrenched social custom and popular political rituals.[8]

Social customs, political practice – which includes strategic bullying – and rituals celebrating order while attempting to generate solidarity generally kept the peace which, as we noted, made it possible for pilgrims to cope with their terrestrial travail and to hope for their celestial rewards. But *City of God* stresses the greater importance of the peace pious pilgrims endeavor to win within. Souls must care for, yet bridle their bodies, much as all horsemen groom, ride, and restrain their mounts (*civ. Dei* 19.3). Reason must govern the vices, and both soul and reason – to be comprehensively effective – must subject themselves to God (*civ. Dei* 19.25). Betrayed by their rebellious bodies – a betrayal they endure, Augustine proposed, as fitting punishment for their first parents' disobedience or rebellion – they fail, and the failures account for this wicked world's wickedness and inefficiencies – and for the fact that whatever peace is achieved is partial, provisional, and far less than what the righteous crave. Still, a modicum of equanimity is available to the faithful, should they practice "Christian self-control" in a world where contention and corruption rule.[9]

Evidence suggests that the apostle Paul believed that extra effort at such self-control paid personal – if not social and political – dividends. But he also specified that their purchasing power, so to speak, was limited. The faithful would remain, in some measure, slaves to sin. Their insensitivity to neighbors' interests would be particularly problematic for a new religion that preached compassion. The apostle instructed that when Christians quarreled among each other they ought to avoid airing grievances in government courts. Centuries later, Augustine said so as well (*en. Ps.* 118.24.3). By then, Christians possessed their own courts. Bishops were meant to preside. Augustine obliged – but unenthusiastically. He might have approved on the grounds that the church courts or "audiences," as they were called, which Emperor Constantine decreed into existence in 318 to

---

[8] Parrish 2007: 95. [9] Tornau 2006: 337–38.

give Christians the fair hearing they were unlikely to get before pagan judges, had done precisely what was intended. Augustine might also have approved the bishops' new roles, supposing that the clerical magistrates might be less tempted to sell verdicts. But he knew better and took a different tack. He confided that church courts invited belligerence into the bishops' chambers and put the prelates in a terribly delicate position. Either they must alienate one parishioner by finding in favor of another or, reckoning reconciliation more important than justly assessing reparations, they must turn a blind eye to the truth; they must slight rather than sift certain complainants' claims (*en. Ps.* 25.2.13). "Audiences," moreover, seemed to have turned bishops into consultants or, as Augustine pejoratively insinuated, into co-conspirators. He was appalled to learn from having been asked that parishioners, trusting their bishops had discovered while arbitrating how to distinguish the provable from the preposterous, approached them for advice on how to outfox adversaries and influence other justices (*s.* 137.4).

He had different things to teach parishioners. He was uninterested in giving them an edge in litigation. The biblical passages that studded his sermons had everything to do with love and little to say about lawsuits, save that they brought shame on all participants and forfeited the higher ground that Christianity staked in its sacred texts. Nonetheless, custom required him to convene his court, to listen to the faithful complain about their coreligionists, and to referee. He recoiled from it all. His audience was an unwelcome, dystopian drip into his career.

3 CAREERS

But Augustine had no alternative. He had to preside and arbitrate, though we catch a glimpse of what might have been, had he been able to reinvent procedures for arbitration. We see him trying to reach an out-of-court settlement when a local landlord accosted one of his tenants. That tenant, Faventius, claimed sanctuary, the protection of the church, for thirty days to put his affairs in order before answering the summons to a provincial court. The landlord was impatient and had a constable snatch Faventius from sanctuary, at which point Augustine intervened. The bishop did not suggest a change of venue. In his version of the tale – the only one we have – he presumed that resolution and reconciliation would have been forthcoming, had Faventius been permitted to remain in sanctuary for the month allowed in such instances and had he – Augustine – undertaken a form of shuttle diplomacy (*ep.* 115). A chapter of his *City* written long afterward may give us a clue to what he might have said to the litigants. Those passages amount to a brief against the acquisitive individualism which he blamed for most of the contention in this wicked world. People who invest their energy and egos accumulating or protecting property risk "vanishing into vanity," he said, quoting what passed in sacred literature as the Wisdom of Solomon. Solomon's statements offered a panoramic view of the city of gaud while categorically declaring that, given "the calamities and errors of this life . . . nothing [is] solid and nothing . . . remains stable" (*civ. Dei* 20.13). May we surmise that Augustine's out-of-court negotiations would have contained a dollop of criticism of both litigants, criticism that fit comfortably in the slipstream of Solomon's celebrity and counsel?

Elsewhere in *City of God*, Solomon nudged Augustine to remind Christians plotting their careers as pilgrims that their preeminent concern should be the celestial city, which was held together by passion – by suffering – not by prudence or jurisprudence. Solomon was undeniably shrewd – an exemplary, incorruptible judge – although his tenure as king "ended badly." The Christian church respected his wisdom yet was not united to him as it was to Jesus Christ, Augustine confirmed, emphasizing that such unity was accomplished by taking the savior's suffering and sacrifice as the church's legacy and by recycling both in its sacrament of solidarity and in pilgrims' self-effacement, respectively (*civ. Dei* 17.20). A pilgrim's soul burns as a sacrifice with a love for God, and that fire consumes desires for this world's rewards (*civ. Dei* 10.6). Laws and courts do not inspire pilgrims' passion ("fire") and discipline as infallibly as the examples of their savior's selflessness. Justice – aimed at or administered – does not show that fire and discipline as dramatically as acts of mercy that "pay forward" God's love for the celestial city in its citizens' compassion, a sacrifice that *City of God* rates as most agreeable to God (*civ. Dei* 20.24). But careers as Christians and pilgrims begin with contrition, which is kindled by prayer and by what Luigi Alici describes as "a spiritual reconnaissance" or self-inventory (*autoriconoscimento spirituale*), introspection which restructures and stabilizes desire. The result, a desire to share the celestial city as well as God's love with other pilgrims, fortifies faith, enabling the faithful resourcefully to encounter the "calamities and errors of this life" – the many uncertainties of history.[10]

Calamities carpeted life *in saeculo maligno* and challenged agile officials to maintain order. Laws, courts, and constables, as noted, served that purpose, but, notably, when Augustine protested slave traffickers who had kidnapped

---

[10] Alici 1994: 87–90.

North Africans and sold them on the Mediterranean's other shores, he forwarded his complaints to fellow prelates, not to emperors, governors, and municipal or manorial magistrates (*ep.* 10*.2). He does not appear to have been suggesting that bishops brew and implement remedies in their audiences or that they organize opposition to slavery. Perhaps he thought slavery, much as corruption, was as ineradicable as the lust to dominate. Slavery joined court corruption, domination, and the fascination with the garish or gaudy as symptoms of the sin within everyone. Be that as it may, historians who consider Augustine a judicial activist, who was looking to expand the jurisdiction of the church's courts, have gotten him wrong. True, he inquired about the status of slaves as if he were preparing to tackle related issues in his audience. (Could parents sell their children into perpetual servitude? Was a child of a free woman and a slave free?) But there is no proof that his inquiries constituted the early stages of a campaign to emancipate slaves. He simply seems to have been scratching for information that would make him a more knowledgeable umpire (*ep.* 24*): "we must endure hearing litigants' petitions and must learn this world's laws affecting the temporal conditions of persons." Augustine may have wanted to rid his world of slavery, yet Clifford Ando is surely right to conclude that the courts gave him little reason to think that, in chambers, any morally questionable customs could be changed, and he rejected the conceit that laws and courts would transform a community (or a church) into "the supreme arena for the exercise of human virtue." Ando adds that Augustine's rejection "could not be more stark."[11]

Yet there was work for magistrates in Augustine's *City*. Their challenge, as we learned, was damage control, although, given the nature of government in a fallen world, efforts at damage control ordinarily involved doing damage. Torture, for instance, often was used to get to the truth; witnesses and accusers were not spared. *City of God* refers to it as "a miserable necessity," a reference that amounts to a grudging endorsement of torture, which accompanies advice to Christians whose careers as justices implicated them in the brutality and suggested to onlookers that faith had not put down roots in their characters. Augustine told magistrates to fret about the inconsistency between their piety and their practice and to pray for deliverance from their distress (*civ. Dei* 19.6). "Deliverance," in this application, did not mean early retirement. Christian magistrates were told to pray for sufficient distance from their unpleasant obligations, for distance that

---

[11] Compare Ando 2006: 143–44, Lepelley 2001: 365–66, and Kaufman 2003 with Raikas 1997: 476–78, Uhalde 2007: 66–67, and Kuhn 2007: 103–4.

delivered some peace of mind to the prayerful who performed disagreeable duties ("necessities") to ensure a modicum of peace "in this wicked world" (*civ. Dei* 18.49).

Prayer itself was a deliverance of sorts. It lifted prayerful pious magistrates' hearts above "miserable necessities." To abridge John Milbank's apt description of the prayers responding to priests' *Sursum Corda* at Mass, prayer "suspend[ed] presence in favor of ... expectation."[12] During the course of their careers, the Christian magistrates measured out compassion according to the laws they enforced. They could be charitable, to a point. Augustine was known to encourage Christians in government to stretch that point, yet, to repeat, he seems to have had no brief for judicial activism, as we define it, which is to say that he was uninterested in the evangelization of the late Roman justice system. In prayer, he preached, there should be no limit to love. Quite the contrary, the prayerful and faithful ought to ration their devotion to laws and courts but love God limitlessly, as such love requires (*amandi deum modus est sine modo*; *s.* 2.9).[13]

Municipal magistrates would not have had abundant time for prayer. Historians once believed that they were little more than the local executors of others' policies, but Claude Lepelley's research shows that African authorities were more independent and versatile – and that civic virtues were highly prized.[14] Indeed, pagan Nectarius thought there was no need to persuade Augustine that public service was divinely prescribed and divinely rewarded, that officials who kept their cities safe and solvent "will live closer to God" (*ep.* 103.1–2). Augustine replied (*ep.* 104), correcting his correspondent, who was writing in 408 to ask for the bishop's help. Excessive patriotism was particularly offensive, Augustine noted, when it inspired services that made citizens secure in – and tenaciously attached to – their possessions. Hence, he would not assist Nectarius in saving the citizens of Calama who feared poverty because punitive damages were about to be assessed. They had attacked Christians in that city – thirty or so miles from Augustine's home – and burned the church there in 408, and he predictably commented on the severity of their offense. But he also seized the chance to scold Nectarius for having linked civic virtue with celestial rewards and for having failed to render greater service to the Calama community. To avoid what Nectarius had called destitution might appear admirable, but, as Augustine explained to his correspondent, he could be much more useful to his clients by urging them to repent their crime, accept their punishment,

---

[12] Milbank 2009: 134.   [13] Dolbeau 1996: 64.   [14] Lepelley 2001: 105–7; Lepelley 2002: 283–85.

and learn that security, solvency, and civic pride were nothing next to God's goodwill (*ep.* 104.5–6, 104.12, 104.16).

Obsessions with possessions did not please God, Nectarius was informed, and, years later, Augustine said so again, in *City of God*, for the benefit of Christians and pagans who believed one of their most precious "possessions," Rome, had been terribly scuffed. The text named Cain as the fratricidal founder of this world's order. The implication was obvious, but that did not deter Augustine from elaborating: "Cain begat Enoch and built a city in his name: that is, the earthly city, which is not a pilgrim in this world." By trotting out an odd etymology, the bishop pressed his point and discredited efforts to gauge God's (or the gods') favor and disfavor by Rome's or the empire's fortune and misfortune. "Now the name Cain means possession. And Enoch," *City of God* adds (*civ. Dei* 15.17), "means dedication; for the earthly city is dedicated here, where it is built, since the end of what it strives after is here." Careers here are advanced by desires to acquire. The successful engage in a single-minded pursuit of this world's rewards – fame, funds, and power – and pilgrims who work among them must cling to eternity in hope and prayer (*civ. Dei* 21.9).[15]

Cain's kin have choices. True, they are unrighteous and lust for power. Much as Cain had, they despise the relative righteousness of others. *City of God*, however, draws on Pauline observations and exhortations to suggest that repentance is a route to conversion and that conversion gives individuals some "mastery" over their sins. A few may cross to a redoubtably devout life. They might overcome some temptations and resist reaching for what others have. Yet envy retains some hold on everyone in time and, sadly, tightens its hold on this wicked world and its governments. Envy held Cain captive. It drove him to murder. Conduct and competition in the city of gaud only occasionally erupted in murderous ways, yet envy was a constant (*civ. Dei* 15.7).

Citizens of the celestial city on pilgrimage in time among the contemptibly envious and impious, yet also in positions of authority among or over them, had their instructions from Augustine. He issued them in *City of God* but also in his correspondence, and no letter is more explicit and telling than the one he wrote to a military tribune who was contemplating a change in career (*ep.* 189). He thought of becoming a monk. Augustine was not about to have the gifts of a good soldier closeted or cloistered while barbarians were at the gate, notwithstanding his own trademark devaluation of worldly security. He told the tribune that his desire to live *cum solis sanctis* – "with

---

[15] Curbelié 2004: 432–3.

only the holy" – was praiseworthy yet untimely. Only God determines the proper time for such a withdrawal, and all could see that, with the faithful in jeopardy, it was inopportune for a competent soldier, with a celebrated winning streak, to stand down. *Agendo et orando*, "by acting and praying," the tribune in the field could meet the challenges of both the times and his faith (*ep.* 189.8).

What applied to the Christian soldier in combat applied as well to the Christian magistrate in court, and it is quite possible that Augustine commended prayers-in-place rather than retirement to both at roughly the same time. The prayers were spiritual exit strategies that kept the prayerful, materially, at their tasks. Charles Mathewes adroitly summarizes Augustine's approach: advocating prayer, humility, and duty, the bishop reminded those who "inhabit authority" that they ought to "undertake that inhabitation in fear and trembling" and to "signal to others that [they] recognize the differences between the office [they] occupy and the person[s they are]."[16]

4 DIFFERENCES

Or was Augustine hesitantly optimistic? When he barked "we are not yet perfect" at the Pelagians, who, to his mind, had infuriatingly overestimated the faithful's abilities to suppress sin, was he looking forward to a time – in time – when Christians "inhabiting authority," could rehabilitate government (*perf. just.* 8.19)? One passage in *City of God* would appear to suggest as much (*civ. Dei* 15.4):

> If the higher goods are neglected, which belong to the City on high, where victory will be secure in the enjoyment of eternal and supreme peace: if these are neglected and those other goods [terrestrial peace and prosperity] desired so much that they are thought to be the only goods or loved more than the goods which are believed to be higher [*meliora*], then misery of necessity will follow, and present misery will be increased by it.

The conditional clause seems to press Christian magistrates to bring out the good crystal, make a display of their devotion to "higher goods," and somehow improve public administration. But typically Augustine characterized both political routine and political intrigue as an unsavory and cursedly unstoppable chase after lower and lesser "goods." Hence, the passage just cited looks to be referring to damage control, not to an end

---

[16] Mathewes 2007: 186.

of misery but to the avoidance of its "increase." Grief was inevitable this side of the grave. Its "increase" could conceivably be averted, but misery kept humanity company because concupiscence afflicted the human will as the punishment for humanity's original sin of disobedience. That is the theme of the four books immediately preceding the *City*'s "if the higher goods are neglected," and a quick thumb-through of the four is sufficient to discover that, for Augustine, the political was just an extension of the personal – that factions in government normalized disharmony.[17]

From those telling books that reflect on the origin of sin and evil, Luigi Alici infers that their author believed everything that "fills time" had been infected, that an *inestirpabile insediamente* – an ineradicable parasite – left creation permanently disabled. That point was not lost on R. W. Dyson, who wrote, more relevantly to our discussion of dystopia, that "the state," in *City of God*, was "an enduring witness to the moral disfigurement of the world."[18] Christians, as pilgrims, even in the best of times and with coreligionists in positions of leadership, could never be at home in that "state." Sermons he preached while composing *City of God*, moreover, exhibit Augustine's awareness of the practical difficulties posed for pilgrims by the state of that "state." For the temporal order, to which cultivated Romans had grown accustomed, was passing, and authorities looked for scapegoats. Faithful Christians were excellent candidates inasmuch as they "love[d] not the world" and were, in theory at least, reconciled to its passing (*s*. 96.7–8). Much in *City of God* was written for them, to urge them to beware of this world's charms (*blandimenta*) and to concentrate on their celestial rewards. Augustine paused occasionally to remind them of the differences between the two (*civ. Dei* 5.18, 18.1).

The celestial was beyond the power of superlatives to describe; genuine justice and spiritual satisfactions awaited pilgrims at their celestial destination. Identifying the courts and commerce in terrestrial cities as particularly problematic, Augustine's sermons depict this world as "a land of lies" (*s*. 180.3). Churches were parts of that land, but many bishops in Africa, whose parishes composed the *pars Donati*, aspired to perfection. They touted the courage and moral superiority of their forebears. They claimed numerical superiority in the region. Augustine caught a whiff of arrogance in their perfectionism, exaggerating it and prolifically arguing that neither their history nor their numbers proved their claims about themselves and about the cowardice and contamination of the "catholic" churches.[19]

---

[17] Wu 2007: 24–25.   [18] Dyson 2005: 54–55; Alici 1994: 90.
[19] Frend 1985: 227–43; Brown 2000: 207–21; Kaufman 2007: 71–98.

He assumed that significant portions of the celestial city on pilgrimage could be found in all churches – even outside them, which is not to argue choice of church was unimportant. According to Augustine, pilgrims who lived among the unregenerate, uncharitable, and contentious made the right choice, tolerating, to an extent, the tawdry and imperfect in this city of gaud. Carping and uncompromising, Donatists, who resisted reconciliation with their rivals, created atmospheric conditions that made it difficult for pilgrims in their churches to pay forward God's love in their love for the purportedly less fortunate – less fastidious and discriminating – and climb toward the celestial city. But the pilgrimage, as Augustine appropriated it narratively, was most critical and helped the faithful mark the differences between Christian piety and civic piety – and be patient.[20]

When he marked those differences, Augustine sounded patronizing about civic piety and patriotism. His correspondence with Nectarius clearly condescends. As for his sentiments about public service, they ranged from icy indifference to tepid approval. The latter – lukewarm approval – was accompanied, in *City of God*, by a call to prayer stipulating that prayerful public servants ask for strength to remain detached from their duties and free from the lust to dominate that motivated politically ambitious and assiduous – and yet religiously remiss – colleagues.

That much we have learned, but *City of God*'s last word on political virtues came early in the text and came coated with skepticism as Augustine assessed the earnestness with which the old Roman heroes had achieved impressive results. In the fifth book, he turned scorekeeper (*civ. Dei* 5.15):

> The Romans held their own private interests in low esteem for the sake of the common good, that is, for the commonwealth. For the sake of its treasury they resisted avarice, and they took counsel for the good of their fatherland with unfettered minds; nor were they guilty of any offense against its laws, or of any unwholesome desires. By all these arts did they seek honor and power and glory, as by a true way. They were honored among almost all the nations; they imposed the laws of their empire upon many races; and they were glorious among almost all peoples to this day, in literature and in history. They have no reason to complain of the justice of the highest and true God: they have received their reward.

The final line about the sufficiency of the reward echoes the gospel of Matthew, which refers to hypocrites who boast of the alms they grudgingly give "that they may have the glory of men" (Matt. 6:2). Augustine editorialized, and knowledgeable Christians likely caught his contempt. It is impossible to know how many would also have known that Livy had helped

---

[20] Van Oort 1990: 159–63; Alici 1994: 95–96.

him with the history and that Sallust as well as their sacred texts had spurred him to moralize and to put Rome's glory in perspective, a comparative perspective. *City of God* exploits just that comparison to mark the contrast between "the reward of the saints who in this life suffer reproaches for the sake of the city of God" and the rewards of citizens who "so greatly love[d] Rome" and who cultivated what pilgrims should recognize as specious virtues to grow an empire "for the sake of merely human glory" (*civ. Dei* 5.16).[21]

No nostalgia here! Glory and possessions – not God and piety – had been the Romans' preoccupations, and, from a Christian perspective, they were inconsequential. To insist otherwise was to ensure that there could be no genuine justice in this wicked world, insofar as such insistence stole glory from God (*civ. Dei* 19.21): "Are we to call a man unjust if he takes a piece of property away from one who bought it and hands it over to someone who has no right to it" – or, one must add, keeps it for himself? Nearer the start of *City of God*, Augustine summoned Cicero to offer an arresting, luminous response to precisely this question. In his *Republic* (*rep.* 3), Cicero had staged a conversation about the necessity of justice, asking whether and why it was indispensable for "state-making." He had an interlocutor argue that "injustice is advantageous and justice useless" in government, a position that surely qualifies as dystopian and that appears to have struck Augustine as a plausible counter to the proposition that good government – a commonwealth – depended on social harmony, which, in turn, depended on a just distribution of goods and services. Yet the bishop elected to follow Cicero, who adapted the second alternative to serve the evaluation inscribed in the first. In other words, Cicero confirmed the constitutive role of justice in good government but denied that either was present in his time. Augustine went his source one better – or, to be precise – one worse. "True justice," he says, "does not exist other than in that commonwealth whose Founder and Ruler is Christ ... There is true justice in that City of which [the psalmist] says 'glorious things are spoken of thee, O City of God'" (*civ. Dei* 2.21; Ps. 87:3).

How well did that notion sell? We know that the celestial city fascinated religious theorists from that time forward, many of whom identified it with the church, despite the disclaimers Augustine deposited in his anti-Donatist treatises. We know of bishops who continued to struggle for something approximating genuine justice in their terrestrial cities, and we can now see that their efforts were quite compatible with Augustine's counsel in *City of*

---

[21] See Harding 2008: 47–83 for the Sallustian overtones of Augustine's political skepticism.

God and in his correspondence. Bishops, he said, should promote the "wellbeing of those under [them]." He appreciated that his colleagues were often local celebrities yet advised that it would be a mistake for them to relish their star wattage, to become self-important. "A bishop who takes delight in ruling rather than in doing good is no true bishop" (*civ. Dei* 19.20). There was nothing unusual about a bishop becoming a power-broker, resorting to "the threat of human judgment" to move misbehaving parishioners to relent and repent. And that worked, one suspects, only as long as that bishop had enough leverage to make good on his threats. "Emphatically and always," however, bishops must "use the threat of divine judgment," Augustine wrote, explaining why the second strategy was preferable in a letter to a local official whose agents had apparently misappropriated taxes collected from his tenants (*ep.* 153.21). The view was widespread that all tax collectors were tyrants, and Augustine's correspondent seems to have been playing the part, demanding that the tenants pay again the sums lost to or by the collectors. But, for our purpose, the implication of Augustine's letter is more important than the details of the scam, for the bishop suggested that those victims could not expect remedies from this world's courts. He did not "threaten" his correspondent or the scurrilous agents with "human judgment" or introduce the possibility of transferring the case to the church's court. Instead, to get the official to rescind his regrettable orders, Augustine reminded him that God was just. The taxpayers were not to be pitied, he continued, because their rewards for enduring inequity in this wicked world would come in the next – as would the punishment for tyrants making inequitable demands (*ep.* 247.4).[22]

Augustine wrote to save his correspondent as well as the overtaxed taxpayers. Impressing his correspondent, "emphatically," with the prospect of God's unfavorable judgment should have served both ends, though troubled times inclined the possessive tenaciously to cling to their possessions. And *City of God*, along with most of Augustine's letters, was written in and for troubled times. The pillars that pagans thought sturdy – Romans' legions, Romans' virtues, and Rome itself – were proving undependable. The Christian empire, which Constantine's conversion and his sons' support extended many miles inland from the Mediterranean's shores, looked terribly precarious. Historian Peter Brown, therefore, is no doubt right to put one challenge near the top of Augustine's to-do list: "creating new loyalty to a yet greater, invisible empire of God." To associate that loyalty with an invisible, celestial city required an agile mind, for, although

---

[22] On tyrannical taxmen, see Loseby 2009: 145–46.

it was true that "Augustine wielded a weight of authority that was so formidable in theory," the "social and moral constraints" were such, Brown says, that the bishop's authority was "far from overpowering in practice." The world was "confidently profane."[23] The unprincipled (*improbi*) ruled, and they were shameless. There is nothing, for example, to indicate that the fellow who so cruelly trawled for taxes ever reconsidered as a result of Augustine's threats. In this wicked world, exploitation, servitude, and corruption reigned, and there was no sign the *improbi* could be "deprived of their freedom to do wrong" (*civ. Dei* 19.21).

The bad news reported at the onset seems to have gotten worse. Augustine's compendious *City* numbered several consolations, but none bear on the text's having developed into the most comforting consolation of all. The world mired in mediocrity turns out not to be the final word. That world transformed into many words reads as an occasion for piety, an opportunity to underscore the differences between the terrestrial city and its "opposite" (*civ. Dei* 18.1), the city of gaud and the city of God: unlike the former, which made gods (or idols) of power and possessions, the latter, on pilgrimage in time, is "to be [God's] true sacrifice. Both cities . . . make use of good things or are afflicted with the evils of this temporal state, but they do so," Augustine wrote, "with a different faith, a different hope, and a different love" (*civ. Dei* 18.54). And marking the differences, which has the effect of making *City of God* a comfort and consolation, makes all the difference. For the convergence of terrestrial and celestial cities remains dystopian. "Evils of this temporal state" invariably stain every attempt to politicize or institutionalize what the virtues of good pilgrims inspire. But their different faith, hope, and love are portals through which Augustine permits another reality to make itself known.

---

[23] Brown 2000: 491–92.

CHAPTER 4

From rape to resurrection: sin, sexual difference, and politics

Margaret R. Miles

I INTRODUCTION

Fewer than twenty years after the Roman Empire became Christian under Theodosius I, Rome was conquered and pillaged by the Goths, led by their commander, a former Roman general, Alaric. Jerome, in Jerusalem, summarized pagan reactions: "If Rome hasn't been saved by its guardian deities, it's because they are no longer there; for as long as they were present, they preserved the city."[1] Augustine heard eyewitness reports of the 410 CE sack (*vastatio*) of Rome from refugees who fled to North Africa. Almost immediately he began to address the allegation that the Roman gods that for eight hundred years had protected Rome had permitted the fall of *Roma eterna* because they were now neglected. The first three books of his epic were made public in 413 as the event was still vivid in the minds and bodies of his readers.

Augustine's rebuttal consisted of a detailed demonstration that the suffering presently endured by the Roman people was not unique but merely the last stage of a long history of disasters and misfortunes, both natural and man-made. He believed that suffering is simply endemic to postlapsarian human existence, requiring no special explanation. However, Augustine's broader agenda in *The City of God* consisted of a strikingly original interpretation of the saga of the human race from creation to the resurrection of bodies.

Augustine enlisted the research assistance of a young Spanish priest; he asked Orosius to provide him with a list of Rome's past misfortunes, including "war, disease, famine, and natural disasters" to support his interpretation.[2] But Orosius had another agenda. He wanted to demonstrate that because of Christianity, the present suffering was relatively mild;

[1] Jerome, *Commentary on Ezekiel*, Pref. to Book 1; as quoted by Heather 2006: 511, n. 1.
[2] Rohrbacher 2002: 138–39.

75

misfortunes of all kinds, he said, had been much worse in the past. For example, the Gallic invasion of 390 BCE was far more destructive than the 410 CE sack of Rome. In the Gallic invasion, the city was almost completely burned to the ground, while Alaric and the Visigoths burned only the old Senate House and a few surrounding buildings near the Salarian gate. "The vast majority of the city's monuments and buildings remained intact."[3]

Orosius, writing within five years of the sack, sought to show that, while the suffering caused by the sack was just punishment for the many sins of the Empire and its people, God's mercy was visible in the "comparatively mild effects of the invasions" and the speedy rebuilding of the city.[4] Indeed, ancient chroniclers and modern historians agree that in the sack of Rome the killing and destruction were mild compared to most ancient warfare.[5] There was "relatively little rape," and "not a particularly violent looting." In short, it was "one of the most civilized sacks of a city ever witnessed."[6]

Why? For the first time in an ancient war, sanctuary was granted for the sake of a people's God; Alaric's Goths were Arian Christians who respected the sanctuary provided by churches. St. Peter's and St. Paul's, the largest and most richly appointed churches in Rome, were declared sanctuaries, and even the portable liturgical vessels remained in place. Refugees to North Africa reported with amazement that the Goths even transported several wealthy women to sanctuary before looting their homes. Indeed, Alaric was reluctant to loot the city at all. Looting occurred only because "Alaric needed to compensate his followers for their loyalty."[7]

Augustine did not share Orosius's triumphal agenda. He did not minimize the damages and destruction caused by three days of rape and looting (begun 24 August 410). Rome was no longer the capital of the Empire (the capital having been moved to Ravenna in 402), but it was still a powerful symbol of Empire. Augustine allowed himself to feel the full symbolic weight, as well as the physical distress and pain caused by the sack. For a population repeatedly assailed for the prior two hundred years by waves of military attack, famine, and disease, the devastation was not to be underestimated.

Although Augustine addressed *City of God* to pagans, he also strongly sought to reassure and encourage Christians. Augustine wanted to provide arguments that would support many Christians' faltering faith and their anxiety that pagan accusations might be correct. To do so, he presented a

---

[3] Heather 2006: 232.   [4] Rohrbacher 2002: 147.   [5] Gaddis 2005: 156.   [6] Heather 2006: 227.
[7] Heather 2006: 232.

thoroughgoing revision of human history from creation to a point beyond time, the resurrection of body. *City of God* is a history of bodies – suffering bodies, sexual bodies, and glorified bodies – no less than ideas. His interest in female bodies is especially noteworthy.[8] From Book 1, in which he considered in detail the rape of Christian women that had occurred in the sack of Rome, to his insistence in Book 22 that female bodies will not become male in the resurrection, the topic of female bodies bookends his massive epic. Female bodies became a paradigm of the experience of the human race, from rape to resurrection, from abjection to perfection.

Augustine's limitations as a man endeavoring to *imagine* the experience of that other body, are evident in his discussion of rape, sex, and politics, but his awareness that the history of humanity is a history of bodies prepares the ground for his hypothetical description of resurrected bodies. Augustine *imagined* the perfect unity of the human person, a body completely permeated by spirit. His passionate speculation can begin to correct one of the most unquestioned assumptions of Christian theology and philosophy from antiquity to the present, namely that persons are composed of components that are in inevitable and irreducible disequilibrium – body and soul (spirit, or mind). Augustine could not imagine that an intelligent body, one entity, could be a present possibility, but I will consider, later in this essay, whether perhaps we can.

There must have been more written about *City of God* than any other historical text. It is not the purpose of this essay to describe this voluminous work, or even to summarize its primary themes. I seek, rather, to identify Augustine's thought about sin, sexual/gender difference, and politics through an analysis of his surprising attention to female bodies, especially in Books 1, 19, and 22.

2 AUGUSTINE AS RAPE CRISIS COUNSELOR

The perfection of human integrity that Augustine imagined in Book 22 is remote from his discussion of pillage and rape in Book 1. Although it may seem that "you can't get there from here," we must respect the structure of

---

[8] A preliminary note: I avoid the phrase "the body" because it implies that there is such a thing as a generic, genderless body, unmarked by race, sexual orientation, age, and myriad other factors – a body, in brief, that no one has ever seen or touched. Bodies are always marked by health or illness, skin color, age, sex, and ethnicity, to name only a few of bodies' variables. Or, "the body" indicated might be the traditionally normative male body. Both of these conceptions of "the body" are erroneous and misleading.

Augustine's authorial decisions and begin by considering the formidable Augustine as a rape crisis counselor.[9]

Augustine accused the Roman people of the pervasive sin of *libido dominandi*, lust for mastery (*civ. Dei* 1.30). When Rome was sacked and a military society's pride unceremoniously damaged, Augustine observed that the Roman refugees who fled to Africa became avid for entertainment. While the rest of the world wept in sympathy, Romans flocked to the theater: "a warlike people ... suddenly developed an effeminate enthusiasm for stage plays," which Augustine called "disgraceful spectacles of licentious vanity" (*civ. Dei* 1.32; Dyson, emended). Over against Roman pride, Augustine advocated, not entertainment, but humility. He extolled the power of humility in his Preface to *City of God*. Immediately after introducing his agenda of addressing pagan accusations, his opening salvo includes a recommendation of humility (*civ. Dei* 1.pref.):

I know, however, what efforts are needed to persuade the proud how great is that virtue of humility which, not by dint of any human loftiness, but by divine grace bestowed from on high, raises it above all the earthly pinnacles which sway in this inconstant age. For the King and Founder of this City of which we are resolved to speak has revealed a maxim of the divine law in the Scriptures of His people, where it is said [James 4:6; 1 Pet. 5:5]: "God resists the proud but gives grace unto the humble."

Throughout his career humility was one of Augustine's most treasured values. He said in a letter (*ep.* 118): "The way is first humility, second humility, third humility."[10] In an image used repeatedly, he juxtaposed swelling pride (*inflatus superbis*) and humility (*humilitatis*). It will be important to recall the importance of humility for Augustine, especially as we examine his discussion of rape.

Augustine's reader can imagine him greeting his congregation at the door of the basilica in Hippo, besieged by their anguished queries and struggling to find satisfying answers. For example, why were both good and bad punished by God and made to suffer in the sack of Rome (*civ. Dei* 1.9)? Even the good, Augustine replied, were probably flawed by love of this life

---

[9] Although rape is commonly considered one of the perennial and universal effects of male aggression, Sheets-Johnstone (1994: 138) has shown that from the perspective of "our own primate biological order ... we find rape only in our own human case." Peggy Sanday's cross-cultural studies of rape revealed that in forty percent of the societies she studied, rape is absent or rare; see Sanday 1981: 41.

[10] *ep.* 118, written to Dioscorus in 410–11, continues: "[H]owever often you should ask me I would say the same, not because there are not other precepts to be explained, but, if humility does not precede and accompany and follow every good work we do, and if it is not set before us to look upon, and beside us to lean upon, and behind us to fence us in, pride will wrest from our hand any good deed we do while we are in the very act of taking pleasure in it." Trans. Parsons 1953: 282.

(*civ. Dei* 1.10). Perhaps they were tortured to force them to hand over their goods to the enemy; or perhaps they were tortured because they secretly desired wealth, and the enemy did not believe that they had none. Even starvation, the plague of late antiquity, borne with patience and faith, carried the lesson that (if the sufferer survived), he should live more moderately and fast more assiduously.

Augustine dealt with questions surrounding the sack of Rome by arguing that it is not the misfortune that matters, but the response of the sufferer. Although the suffering may be the same, sufferers differ: "when one and the same force falls upon the good and the wicked, the former are purged and purified, but the latter are damned, ruined, and destroyed" (*civ. Dei* 1.8). Augustine's rationalizations may seem to trivialize suffering, or even to blame the victim. But he did not – as a Platonist would – claim that the soul of a good man is able to detach from his body so completely that he could maintain a pleasant disposition while being burned alive in the Bull of Phalaris.[11] Instead, Augustine acknowledged that bodies and their sufferings belong to the core of human being; bodies are "not an adornment, or an external aid; rather, they belong to the very nature of humans" (*naturam hominis*; *civ. Dei* 1.13). Where he remained thoroughly Platonist, however, was in his assumption that the *really* good have nothing to fear and cannot be harmed in life or death (*civ. Dei* 1.10): "Again, some good and Christian men were subjected to torture in order to make them surrender their goods to the enemy. But these could neither betray nor lose that good by which they were themselves made good."

In wars and religious persecutions of antiquity, violence against consecrated virgins was a common practice. "Female virgins were regularly singled out for particularly degrading treatment" – sometimes rape; sometimes public stripping.[12] In *civ. Dei* 1.16, Augustine turned specifically to the suffering of Christian women, both virgins and married women, raped in the three-day sack of the city. He states and affirms the following principle:

[T]hat the virtue by which life is lived rightly has its seat in the soul; that it directs the members of the body from there; that the body is made holy by the exercise of a holy will; and that, while this will remains unshaken and steadfast, nothing that another does with the body, or in the body, that the sufferer has no power to avert without sinning in turn, is the fault of the sufferer.

---

[11] The legendary bull of Phalaris was described by Cicero in his *Verrine Orations* (4.73). Phalaris, tyrant of Acragas (in Sicily) from 570 to 554 BCE, is said to have had an iron oven in the shape of a bull in which he burned dissidents.
[12] Gaddis 2005: 84, esp. n. 48.

Augustine's attempt to offer *consolationem*, however, is undermined in the same paragraph by his suggestion that, even in the face of the victim's utmost resolution to maintain purity, a raped woman is likely to feel shame because "some will think" that "an act which, perhaps, could not have been undergone without some bodily pleasure occurred with the consent of the mind also" (*cum mentis etiam voluntate*). Here, as elsewhere, Augustine's assumption that male sexual experience is normative for women is blatantly evident. Certainly male arousal is necessary if rape is to occur, but according to all reports, rape is the opposite of pleasurable for the raped woman.[13] Indeed, rape harms both body and soul. "The actual trauma [of rape]," writes Maxine Sheets-Johnstone, "is so extreme as to destroy the implicit foundations of trust upon which a raped woman has heretofore lived her life."[14]

Augustine's trivializing treatment of rape is remarkable for another reason. It ignores a prominent Christian value, with a long history, and still powerful. Augustine did not seem to think that the insult to a consecrated virgin's body symbolized anything more than personal suffering. In Christian literature of his time, however, "[t]he virgin's body was commonly taken to stand for the imagined body of the entire church, both being symbolically understood as the bride of Christ." Church buildings also carried bodily symbolism, "so that violation either of the virgin or of the sanctuary constituted both assault and insult ... against the very body of Christ."[15] Moreover, "the virgin's undefiled body symbolized the promise of resurrection ... for women martyrs and ascetics, holiness demanded an extreme emphasis on maintaining chastity."[16]

Augustine has not finished with the topic of rape, but he expands it to consider whether it is permissible for women to commit suicide, either because of the shame of having been raped, or to avoid rape. Some women killed themselves, Augustine admits, and despite his opposition to suicide, he comes close to excusing them (*civ. Dei* 1.17): "what person of feeling would refuse to forgive those women who for this reason slew themselves rather than suffer in such a way?" Ambrose, the young Augustine's mentor, following traditional Roman morality, had allowed raped women to commit suicide, but Augustine brought the force of his rhetorical skill to persuading raped women not to do so.[17]

---

[13] Zillmann writes: "[P]enile erection may accompany numerous aggressive and nonaggressive actions in nonsexual contexts. Erection has been observed during anxiety, surprise, appeasement, anger, and aggressive behavior as well as during greeting, joy, and elation," as quoted by Sheets-Johnstone 1994: 150.
[14] Sheets-Johnstone 1994: 132.   [15] Gaddis 2005: 85.   [16] Gaddis 2005: 168.
[17] Ambrose, *On Virgins* 3.7.33, as quoted by Gaddis 2005: 168.

He insisted that Lucretia, the usual Roman example of a woman outraged by rape who committed suicide, far from being an example for Christian women in the same plight, was guilty of the crime of gratuitous self-murder. He snidely suggested that perhaps Lucretia actually killed herself because she was aware that she was guilty of enjoying her rape. He also speculated that she may have been "excessively eager for honor." Christian women's continuing chastity in God's eyes should sufficiently reassure raped women that that they should continue to live. Those who did not commit suicide "did not avenge another's crime upon themselves; and it was because they feared adding to the crime of others a crime of their own that they did not do so" (*civ. Dei* 1.19).

Segueing into a more general consideration of whether there are grounds for suicide under any conditions, Augustine asserts that there are not. However, some circumstances override the commandment: Do not kill. For example, it should not apply to plants, "for these have no sensation"; nor does it apply to animals which "fly, swim, walk, or crawl, for these do not share the use of reason with us." Because animals are not within the community of rational minds, "both their life and death are subject to our needs" (*civ. Dei* 1.20). There are even circumstances in which it is acceptable to kill another human being – Augustine cites those who act on God's direct command, magistrates who impose the death penalty for criminal action, and those who wage wars on God's authority (1.21). Yet as regards suicide, God's law is unambiguous: suicide is wicked (*nefas;* 1.27). Book 1, chapters 19–27 reiterate Augustine's prohibition of suicide at length. His carefully worded suggestion that it would be difficult for a person of feeling *not* to forgive a woman who avoided rape by suicide, is striking in the context of his extended and repetitious condemnation of self-murder. Clearly he did not trivialize the horror of rape, and yet other values and theological commitments undermined his sympathy for victims of rape. He worried at greater textual length about victims' possible occasions for sin than for their suffering.

Augustine had two ways of dealing with the question of why God permits suffering, and he used his method to address every kind of suffering, whether loss of wealth, rape, disease, or slavery. He believed that when God "subjects me to adversity, it is either to test my merits or to chastise my sins" (*civ. Dei* 1.29). So he asked first what possible sin the sufferer may have committed to deserve the punishment of suffering; in other words, he blames the victim. Second, he seeks to identify the good that may be inherent in the suffering.

Returning to the plight of women who have been raped, Augustine relentlessly searched for possible sins even when victims behaved flawlessly and were confident that they did not consent mentally: "Perhaps you have been too puffed up by the good of maidenhood or chastity, or purity, and [perhaps you suffered rape] lest you take such delight in human praise that you have indeed begrudged others this great good." Even if victims had no pride in their chastity, they might still have had "some latent infirmity which might have swollen into the arrogance of pride had they escaped this humiliation during the sack, and this, then, is why they suffered the violation of their flesh by the enemy." In case women who bore their humiliation bravely might feel some pride in this, Augustine reminds them that their strength was not their own, but "divine assistance was added to divine grace, lest grace be lost" (*civ. Dei* 1.28).

Finally, just as he had found benefit in other evils attendant on the sack – loss of wealth and property, starvation – Augustine concludes his discussion by finding some good in raped women's experience: "their chastity was not diminished, but their *humility strengthened*" (my emphasis; *civ. Dei* 1.28). Augustine did not distinguish in this discussion, though he does elsewhere, between humility and humiliation. Rape makes a woman humble, and humility is, for Augustine, the greatest theological virtue, overriding all others. Recall that Augustine prefaced his great work, *De civitate Dei*, with an exhortation to humility.[18]

Augustine's whole treatment of rape as a crime is contained in a single sentence in which he declined to judge the perpetrators of rape. "For it may be that some of the heaviest loads of guilty lust are overlooked by the hidden judgment of God at present, yet reserved to a last and visible judgment" (*civ. Dei* 1.28). Invoking his standard assumption, he reiterated that God, in his great wisdom, permits calamities (like rape) either "to test [Christian women's] merits or chastise [their] sins" (*civ. Dei* 1.29).

Scholars have not sufficiently remarked that it is in his discussions of suffering that some of the most body-denying statements of Augustine's entire corpus appear. Recall that his agenda was to offer *consolationem* to victims of rape, and he does so by denying that harm done to bodies intimately affects the whole person – and this, in spite of his initial affirmation of the centrality of body to human being. It cannot be denied that his discussion is hopelessly conflicted and should not be smoothed out by interpretations that notice only his denial, or only his affirmation, of suffering bodies.

---

[18] Lacking all evidence, I cannot resist suggesting that Augustine, like myself, might have made a practice of writing prefaces to his many books *after* he had written the whole work and when he knew what he needed to introduce. If so he might have been admonishing himself against pride in his voluminous and brilliant work.

Readers of later books of *City of God* will notice that a similar rhetorical method governs his discussion of slavery in *civ. Dei* 19.15. God, he says, "did not intend that his rational creature, made in his own image, should have lordship over any but irrational creatures: not man over man, but man over the beasts." Slavery is wrong, but he goes on to deny that slavery is unambiguously harmful. Indeed, he trivializes slaves' mental and physical pain: "Clearly, it is a happier lot to be the slave of a man than of a lust." We are on familiar ground here. Augustine says that slaves are slaves because of "the judgment of God" who alone "knows how to distribute different punishments according to the merits of the offenders" – he blames the victim. He ends his discussion by saying that slavery, by punishing its victim's sin, preserves "the order of nature" (*naturalem ordinem*; *civ. Dei* 19.15). "God's in his heaven; all's right with the world."[19] He then proceeds to find the good in slavery, happily concluding that "*in that order of peace* which prevails among men when some are placed under others, humility is as profitable to those who serve as pride is harmful to those who rule" (*pacis ordine*; my emphasis). Like rape, slavery makes its victim humble; it can't be all bad.[20]

3 SEXED AND GENDERED BODIES IN PRIVATE AND PUBLIC

Modern readers of Augustine must be reminded, against the popular assumption that all lust (*libido*) is sexual, that Augustine used the word more broadly (*civ. Dei* 14.15):

Lust is the general name for desire of every kind ... There is lust for vengeance, called anger. There is lust for money, called avarice; the lust for victory at any price, called obstinacy; the lust for glory, called vanity [and, last but not least] lust for mastery (*libido dominandi*).

But it is "lust that arouses the impure parts of the body" that is Augustine's paradigm for all other lusts (*civ. Dei* 14.16):

When the emotion of the mind is united with the craving of the flesh, it convulses the whole man, so that there follows a pleasure greater than any other: a bodily pleasure so great that, at the moment of time when he achieves his climax, the alertness and, so to speak, vigilance of a man's mind is almost completely overwhelmed.

---

[19] From Robert Browning's 1841 poem "Pippa's Song."
[20] For an account of slaves' physical vulnerability to abuse of all kinds, rape, and murder, see Glancy 2002.

Aristotle's objection to sexual activity was that when one is thus engaged, it is almost impossible to *think*. Augustine's objection was different: sexual lust (*concupiscentia carnis*) is involuntary; it is not governed by *will*. "The will is so much at odds with the passions, and the passions with the will, that their hostility cannot be ended by the victory of either." Surprisingly, however, Augustine was as concerned with impotence as with sexual intercourse: "Sometimes the urge arises unwanted; sometimes, on the other hand, it forsakes the eager lover, and desire grows cold in the body, even while burning in the mind."

In an ideal world, Augustine said, lust-free procreation could occur; the sexual organs would "act at the command of his will, and not because incited by the urging of lust" (*civ. Dei* 14.16). Indeed, before sin, there was no lust, and the sexual organs "would have been the obedient servants of humankind" (14.23). However, after the sin of Adam and Eve, the genital organs became the private property of lust (14.19). Augustine attempts to picture procreation without lust: "the man would have poured his seed into his wife's womb in tranquility of mind and without any corruption of her body's integrity." Similarly, giving birth would have been a peaceful experience "without any moans of pain" (14.26). But the peaceable part of procreation has been damnably lost (14.20):

> Lust, in fact, is not only unruly; it is also itself decisive evidence of original sin. For the disobedient nature of this lust, which has entirely subdued the organs of generation to its own urges and snatched them from the power of the will, is enough to show what retribution has been visited upon humans for that first disobedience. And it was fitting that this retribution should appear especially in that part of the body which brings about the generation of that very nature that was changed for the worse through that first and great sin.

What troubled Augustine about *concupiscentia carnis*, then, was not sexual desire itself, but its proven capacity for creating disorder. Augustine was profoundly (and at great textual length) disturbed by rape, not primarily because it caused suffering, but because it created social chaos, abjection. According to Julia Kristeva's definition: "It is not lack of cleanness or health that causes abjection but what disturbs identity, system, *order*" (my emphasis).[21] Whether it leads to sexual activity or fails to arouse, lust in Augustine's experience notoriously evades the will's control, causing personal and public confusion (*civ. Dei* 22.17).

---

[21] Kristeva 1982: 4.

Theologically and philosophically, Augustine worked with a full set of interlocking, mutually defining, hierarchically arranged, pairs. Beginning with body and soul/mind: "The soul is superior to the body," he wrote in *Letter* 118, "something it would be extremely foolish to deny." Will, the energy of the soul/mind, should then govern body. Sin occurs when it does not do so. Starting at the bottom of the hierarchy of components that defines Augustine's idea of the human person, he writes (*civ. Dei* 19.13; my emphasis):

> The peace of the body ... lies in the balanced *ordering* of its parts; the peace of the irrational soul lies in the rightly *ordered* disposition of the appetites; the peace of the rational soul lies in the rightly *ordered* relationship of cognition and action; the peace of body and soul lies in the rightly *ordered* life and health of a living creature.

Body and soul, for Augustine, seemed to him so distinguishable as to be separable. They even have different deaths. Body is moribund, having "no life of its own" apart from soul. But body's death was not for Augustine, as it was for earlier classical and Christian authors, a blessed release; the separation of body and soul is a harsh and unnatural experience; "it is a good to no one" (*civ. Dei* 13.6).

After his extensive discussion of the right order of body and soul in relation to death (Book 13) and lust (Book 14), Augustine continued (in Book 19) to analyze the right order of the household, the city, and the heavenly city on the model of body and soul. He concludes (*civ. Dei* 19.13; my emphasis): "The peace of all things lies in the tranquility of order; *and order is the disposition of equal and unequal things in such a way as to give to each its proper place.*" In the household, for example, peace consists of "an ordered concord with respect to command and obedience among those who dwell together." The order of command is "husband to wife, parents to children, masters to slaves" (19.14).

Augustine attempted to correct the possible/probable abuses of this order by insisting that the commander of each pair must not be motivated by *libido dominandi* but rather by "dutiful concern for others." Thus, "those who give orders are, in fact, slaves (*servi*) of those they order" (*civ. Dei* 9.14; Dyson, emended) – a rationalization no medieval tyrant failed to cite. By substituting attention to *ordo* for attention to *potestas*, Augustine evaded the issue of power and its abuses. In his account of social arrangements, family, slavery, and the state mirror one another. According to Augustine, it is not power but order that is at stake. Social order reflects cosmic order, the "order of nature," in the earthly city (*civ. Dei* 19.15).

It is frequently fruitful to check Augustine's quotations, quoted (presumably) from memory. He frequently "remembers" the quotation in a way that slightly enhances the point he wishes to make. For example, in *On True Religion*, he wrote (*vera rel.* 41.77): "As the apostle says, 'All order is of God' (*omnis ordo a deo est*)," misquoting Rom. 13:1: "There is no power but of God." He "remembered" *potestas* as *ordo*, subtly but surely denying the centrality of power to the maintenance of order. Many years later, in writing his *Retractations*, he discovered his error in the quotation, but he explained and excused it by adding that the text goes on to say (*retr.* 1.12.8): "All that is, is ordered by God" (*quae autem sunt, a deo ordinate sunt*). Robert Markus comments: "The first thing that came to his mind when thinking of political authority (which is what *potestas* refers to) was the idea of order."[22]

Augustine placed a very high value – almost the highest – on order. In *On Order*, he wrote of order that it is "that which, if we follow it in our lives, will lead us to God" (*ord.* 1.9.27). But order is itself instrumental to the production of peace, a value easily understood in the context of a society that had recently experienced the pillage of Rome. Even earthly peace, however, is not an end in itself; it too is instrumental, being useful to citizens of the heavenly city (*civ. Dei* 19.26): "For the time being ... it is advantageous to us that this people should have such peace in this life; for, while the two cities are intermingled, we also make use of the peace of Babylon." Markus finds that for Augustine there could be no Christian politics, for coercive power, masked as natural and God-given order, is the only possible politics. Augustine gave up the ancient dream of a polis. All earthly peace is instrumental.

To understand Augustine's criticism of the earthly city, it would be useful to read *City of God* backwards. It is only when we understand his vision of the completion and perfection of human life that we grasp accurately his pervasive sense of the *wrongness* of present life. He ends Book 19 with a "preview of coming attractions" (*civ. Dei* 19.27):

In that final peace ... our nature will be healed by immortality and incorruption. Then, it will have no vices, and nothing at all, in ourselves or any other, will be in conflict with any one of us. Thus, there will be no need for reason to govern the vices, because there will be no vices. Rather, God will rule humans, and the soul will rule the body; and the delight and effortlessness with which we obey in that final peace will be as great as our happiness in living and reigning.

[22] Markus 1988: 76.

4 FEMALE BODIES IN *CITY OF GOD*

Augustine devoted a chapter in the last book of *City of God* to refuting "not a few people [who] believe that women will not be resurrected as female in sex, but that all are to be men, because God made only man from earth, and the woman from man" (*civ. Dei* 22.17). God created the sexes, he wrote, because God had foreknowledge that the Fall would occur, bringing the punishment of death to humans. Death and reproduction are intimately related: without death, reproduction would be disastrous, quickly overpopulating the world; without reproduction, death would end the human race. Lust – sexual desire uncontrolled by the will – is part of the punishment for sin, as we have noticed, but it does carry the fringe benefit of rather effectively assuring that reproduction will occur. Augustine's list of the goods of mortal life begins with the miracle of reproduction (*civ. Dei* 22.24). But sex "as we knew it," as well as reproduction, will no longer be needed in the resurrection. So why will sexual differentiation continue in the resurrection?

Greek patristic authors contemporary with Augustine did not share his insistence on the existence of female bodies in the resurrection. They believed and taught that, although God created prelapsarian women and men, he did so because he foresaw the Fall of humanity. Sexual differentiation was part of a fallen nature that would not continue into eschatological existence.[23] Augustine disagreed strongly. Even when, in the next chapter, he is considering the meaning of Paul's statement that the church and its members would become "perfect man" in the resurrection, Augustine wonders (*civ. Dei* 22.18): "what is to prevent us from understanding the word 'man,' here used instead of 'person,' as applying to the woman also?" His inclination for sexually differentiated resurrection bodies he already made clear (*civ. Dei* 22.17):

Defect (*vitium*) will be taken away from those bodies, and nature preserved.[24] And the sex of a woman is not a defect, but nature. They will then be exempt from sexual intercourse and childbearing, but the female parts will nonetheless remain in being, accommodated, not to the old uses, but to a new beauty (*decori novo*).

---

[23] For example, Gregory of Nyssa understood sexual differentiation as part of human's present physical nature, but he did not, as Karas puts it (2006: 365), "believe sexual differentiation to be a necessary and eternal aspect of human existence."

[24] Dyson translates *vitium* as "vice," but this goes too far, signifying that Augustine protests against the idea that there is something wicked or evil about female bodies. *Vitium* indicates, rather, Tertullian's description of *vitium originalis* as flaw or weakness in human nature. Augustine is responsible for the sterner doctrine of *peccatum originalis*, carrying both condition and guilt of sin.

Why was Augustine so adamant, even against scripture that seems to suggest that women will become men (Rom. 12:2), that female bodies will be preserved in the resurrection? The answer depends upon his distinction between "use" and "beauty." Female bodies with their vulnerability to rape, their domestic vulnerability to unwanted or forced sex, and the discomfort and pain of childbearing, were Augustine's paradigm of the "used" body, the instrumental body that will be transformed in the resurrection to a body whose beauty is enjoyed "for itself alone" (*civ. Dei* 22.24).[25] The female body is Augustine's normative body – on pilgrimage, in life, and on the pages of *The City of God* – from rape to resurrection.

5 GLORIFIED BODIES

Augustine acknowledged that his detailed conjectures about resurrection bodies were fantasies. Indeed, neither experience nor scripture supported the more exotic of his suggestions (about aborted fetuses, cannibals, and the resurrected body's size; *civ. Dei* 22.19–20). It was indeed, he admitted, "rash to offer any description of a spiritual body" (*civ. Dei* 22.21). However, never one to shrink from a challenge, and "unable to remain silent," he did his best to conjecture. His vision of the resurrected body begins at *civ. Dei* 22.29; since it has been discussed elsewhere, I will focus, not on the details Augustine imagined, but on the infrastructure of his glorified bodies.[26]

Augustine thought, and repeatedly reiterated, that persons are composed of components – body and irrational and rational soul/mind. This model originated in Orphic and Pythagorean philosophy and was fully articulated in Plato's *Phaedo*. It became a commonplace ideology in the West, before and after Augustine. Its modern expression is the philosophical dualism Descartes described in his identification of the person as an entity that thinks: "I think, therefore I am" (*cogito ergo sum*).[27] Having found this statement indubitable, however, Descartes found it difficult to explain how body was attached to this thinking entity. He was forced to hypothesize an odd quasi-physical thing called "the pineal gland" that exists solely to link body and mind. Descartes' body, much like Augustine's mortal body, is an

---

[25] For a discussion of the development of Augustine's thinking on the bodily resurrection from his early to his later writings, see Miles 2005: 315.
[26] For example, Miles 2005 and 2007. See also the essay by Cavadini in this volume.
[27] Descartes, *Principles of Philosophy*, Part I, article 7. The French phrase, "je pense, donc je suis," predates the Latin formulation and can be found in *Discourse on Method*, Part IV.

object. It is mechanical, it is soul's possession, and, lacking the animating energy of soul, it is a corpse.[28]

But while Descartes sought a quasi-physical explanation to the question of how a thinking thing and a material thing can be joined, Augustine sought a metaphysical explanation. God "brings about that wondrous combination and union of an incorporeal and a corporeal nature, with the former in command, and the latter subject to it, by which a living being is made" (*civ. Dei* 22.24). Within Christianity, this understanding of human persons was extended. Sacraments and doctrines assume and *must have* two entities: spirit and matter; divinity and humanity; soul and body. These entities must be brought as close together as possible in order to achieve the *frisson* of transcending and uniting them, yet without mixing them. For accompanying these dualities was a horror of mixture. The contents of the Roman sewer were called *mixtus*. Conceptualizing an irreducible, unanalyzable blending of soul and body, spirit and matter – producing a third thing – was not acceptable.

But this is precisely what Augustine imagined, *not in present bodies*, but on the day of resurrection. Resurrected bodies, according to Augustine, will overcome the conceptual habit of thinking in pairs, hierarchically arranged. The primary characteristic of resurrected bodies, he speculated, will be the intimate fusion of body and soul: "The bodily eyes shall see God, and God will be all in all." Augustine insisted that what he (following Paul) called a "spiritual body" is a real body permeated throughout with spirit. Quoting Job 19:26: "And in my flesh, I shall see God," Augustine wrote: God will be seen "in every body by means of bodies, wherever the eyes of the spiritual body are directed with their penetrating gaze" (*civ. Dei* 22.29).

In short, Augustine's imaginative description of the bodily resurrection in Book 22 suggests a different model of the human person than the hierarchically ordered components he – and virtually all philosophers and theologians to our own time – have assumed. The relationship of body and soul was at the foundation of his thinking about the earthly city, repetitively reiterated throughout not only *City of God* but the rest of his oeuvre as well. Except when he imagined the resurrection. His excited and lyrical hypothetical description of resurrected bodies is profoundly counter-experiential, counter-cultural, and beautiful.

Augustine's extended discussion of the present beauty of bodies reinforces his point that, even though they will be transformed in the resurrection, mortal bodies are to be substantively continuous with

---

[28] Sheets-Johnstone 2009: 215.

resurrected bodies. "Nothing will perish at the resurrection ... for every part of the body's substance will be restored to it" (*civ. Dei* 22.19).

Clearly a great deal of human experience is forfeited in Augustine's resurrection of body, but he insisted that Christians will lose only what we don't like anyway. Augustine's list reads: evil, inactivity and idleness, toil, constraint, decay, necessity, and hidden agenda.[29] Defects, deformities, and ugliness will also disappear, as well as weakness, sluggishness, and corruption. No longer for use, resurrected bodies, according to Augustine, will be characterized by their beauty; his examples are the internal organs, men's beards and nipples (which already have no use), and women's reproductive organs.

He worked out the "picture suggested to [his] mind" by beginning with present bodies and subtracting their encumbrances (*civ. Dei* 22.30), thus emphasizing the continuity of present and resurrected bodies. Yet simultaneously, he created a picture of radical discontinuity, even *enantiadromia* or conversion to the opposite. The scripture verse Augustine quoted more frequently than any other throughout his oeuvre is woven through his lyrical description of resurrected bodies (1 Cor. 13:12): "We see now through a glass darkly; then, however, face to face" (*Videmus nunc per speculum in aenigmate; tunc autem, facie ad faciem*). The syncrisis "*nunc ... tunc*" both connects and contrasts present and future experience. This device creates a textual tension that jars the reader's mind to imagine a body that is both intimately experienced (flesh, bones, internal organs, sexual differentiation) and wholly unknown (invulnerable, weightless, and with an incredible capacity for effortless movement and penetrating vision).

The importance to Augustine of sharply distinguishing resurrected bodies from present bodies, even as he insisted on their continuity, is demonstrated by his failure to suggest that Christians work to remedy the ills of the earthly city. His vision of the city of God came to an abrupt stop at the point at which he might have advocated the ways by which the peace and happiness of that city might be preemptively practiced. If he believed that we are to enjoy one another in the heavenly city, not for use, but for each other's beauty alone, why not practice now? If we are to see one another with full transparency – *facie ad faciem* – why not practice now? If present social arrangements are unjust (gender assumptions and arrangements, slavery), why not work to fix them now? If sexual lust creates chaos and misery – forced prostitution, disease, overpopulation – why not work

---

[29] Miles 2005: 319. Augustine's *Sermon* 242A adds fear, poverty, weariness, and clumsiness: "none of these things will be there, but the body will be."

now toward "just good sex"?³⁰ Can we extend Augustine's conception of resurrected bodies into our thinking about present bodies? I digress in order to consider this question.

Philosopher Maxine Sheets-Johnstone proposes a conceptualization of "person" that she calls the "first-person body," or the "intelligent body." According to this model, body is not an epiphenomenon of mind, nor is person composed of a body that holds brain a "captive audience," as contemporary neurophysiologists argue.³¹ The first-person body, Sheets-Johnstone writes, "is the body that we know directly in the context or process of being alive." It is

> the body with which we came into the world prior to technology or science telling us what we are made of, how we are put together, how that togetherness works. The body that emerges from the womb alive and kicking is the primordial one. From the moment of birth that body is the center and origin of our being in the world. It is, in fact, our first world and reality. The first-person body is not a body that we outgrow, or even can outgrow; it is only one we can choose to deny or deprecate. It is a body not lacking biological reality, but a body whose biological reality is neither separable from, nor a third-person dimension of its lived and living presence.³²

According to Sheets-Johnstone, when we analyze a human being according to components, *no matter how we stack the components, we have already lost the person*. For a person is an irreducible, non-negotiable intelligent body. "It is not that 'they' [body and mind/soul] are inseparable, but that 'they' do not exist."³³ Surely this is what Christians hope for in the resurrection body: "Head and body together, made up of all the members" (*caput et corpus constant omnibus membris*; civ. Dei 22.18).

Can Augustine's speculative description of resurrected bodies provide a strengthened view of the person both *nunc* and *tunc*? I suggest that the doctrine of the resurrection of body, though Christians profess to believe it every time we recite the Apostles' Creed, tests our credulity as it tested Augustine's imagination. In fact, it places new urgency on considering what it *means* to believe. If we insist that belief is something done by the rational mind, the doctrine of the resurrection of body places an immense, if not impossible, demand on twenty-first-century Christians. But intelligent bodies believe in a different way than do rational minds. For intelligent bodies, to believe this doctrine is to commit oneself to living *toward* it. We need to think of ourselves as bodies permeated at every point by Christian commitment. In fact, to seek, *in the present and day by day*, to live out into

---

³⁰ Hunt 2001: 158–73. ³¹ See, for example, Damasio 1999. ³² Sheets-Johnstone 2009: 20.
³³ Sheets-Johnstone 2009: 20.

the resurrection body, seems both a more realistic and a more demanding definition of belief than that of the rational mind's assent.

Again: can we have the resurrected body *now*? I think Augustine could agree that there is an important sense in which we *do* presently practice the integrated wholeness characteristic of the resurrection as he imagined it. The *practices* of Christian communities assume and engage intelligent bodies – from catechesis to sacraments. For at least the first thousand years of the history of Christianity, adult Christians were baptized naked in the full congregation. What stronger statement could there possibly be that it is not something labeled "the soul," nor yet something labeled "the body," but only the "intelligent body" that can pledge commitment to the religion of the Word made flesh? Moreover, the doctrines of creation and Incarnation, as well as the resurrection of bodies, pointedly and emphatically identify intelligent bodies as both location and symbol of Christian faith.

Clearly, Augustine would not have been happy with a collapse into immediacy of his syncrisis, the contrast between *nunc* and *tunc*. Indeed, some fundamental features of the resurrected body –for example, immortality, invulnerability, etc. – cannot be imagined in the present. But his model of human beings prevented his ability to see even the sense I have proposed in which resurrected bodies can be – and are – practiced *now*. Prompted by Augustine's vision of resurrected bodies, I have sought an understanding of humans not posited on an arrangement of components.

For as long as Christians think of ourselves, "our souls and bodies," as stacked components, we do not have the *person*, the intelligent body required for religious commitment. Our ancient habit of thinking of the person as dissectible makes it very difficult for us to think of the whole person as irreducible, not subject to analysis. But it is this model, I believe, that makes the history of the Christian movement pop into the eye in all its rich diversity: passionately committed beliefs, liturgies designed to attract and stimulate the senses, and intercorporeal communities.

CHAPTER 5

Ideology and solidarity in Augustine's City of God

John Cavadini

The closing chapters of Augustine's *City of God* display before the reader a panoramic vista. Almost as though he had never put aside the question that animated his conversation with Monica, recorded in Book 9 of the *Confessions*, Augustine invites the reader to reflect on what the eternal life of the saints might be like. It will consist in the vision of God, as Augustine and his mother realized. And because it is the peace of God, it will surpass all understanding (Phil. 4:7). So far so good – he and his mother had concluded, with the prophet Isaiah, that it is something eye has not seen nor ear heard nor human heart conceived (Is. 64:4, 1 Cor. 2:9–10), as they just touched the edge of this vision, as a kind of promissory note for another day.[1] But at the end of the long and arduous pilgrimage that is the *City of God*, as he brings us readers to the brink of the vision of the promised land of eternity, the original question is now more specific. It is not only about what the eternal life of the saints will be like, but "what the saints will be doing when they are clothed in immortal and spiritual bodies" (*civ. Dei* 22.29). What it means for the vision we will then have to surpass understanding is also intensified and specified by the focus on the *embodied* eternal life of the saints.

Augustine opens for the reader a more dramatic and perhaps even unsettling view as he entertains the possibility that we might actually be able to see God with our bodily eyes. Although the resurrection body is a "spiritual" body, it is still a body, and the eyes may be enough like our eyes that we will be able to open and close them (*civ. Dei* 22.29):

And so I say that the saints will see God in the body; but whether they will see Him by means of the body's eyes, as we now see the sun, moon, stars, sea and earth and all the things of the earth: that is no small question. On the one hand, it is hard to

---

[1] See *conf.* 9.10.23, where he speaks of his conversation with his mother at Ostia on the Tiber, "We inquired between ourselves ... as to what the eternal life of the saints would be like, which *eye has not seen nor ear heard nor human heart conceived.*" Translation from Boulding 1997 (emended).

say that the saints will have bodies of such a kind that they will not be able to close and open their eyes at will; but, on the other hand, it is still harder to say that someone will then not be able to see God simply because he closes his eyes.

Significantly, Augustine does not choose to use Is. 64:4, "eye has not seen . . . ," in his evocation of the lives of the saints in this text, though it figured prominently in the *Confessions* passage cited above. Perhaps this is because the very question is what the eyes will be able to see, and how it compares to what we can see now. That bodily eyes might be able to see something immaterial directly is the astonishing possibility that Augustine holds out for our consideration. Will these bodily eyes, when open, be able to see "that incorporeal nature which is not contained in any place, but which is everywhere entire" (22.29; Dyson, emended)? This puts the question in the starkest terms possible, so we do not miss how striking it is. It is a possibility, not a certainty. We are not required by the Scriptures to hold this view. Augustine examines Job 42:5 ("but now my eyes see you"); Luke 3:6 ("All flesh will see the salvation of God"); and Job 19:26 ("and in my flesh I shall see God"), for example, and finds that, though tempting, they are not conclusive evidence for vision of the immaterial with the eyes of the resurrection body. And yet the Scriptures do not foreclose this possibility, either. It is at least suggested by Scripture, insofar as Scripture reveals the promise of the resurrection of the body, and at the same time the vision of God as our highest Good. The *City of God* closes with this, the ultimate limit of the imagination and challenge to the imagination laid out for us, the possibility that we might, with our bodily eyes, see God.

I RATIOCINATION AND RESURRECTION: IDEOLOGY

There is bound to be a spoilsport in this play of the imagination, and not unsurprisingly the "reasoning of the philosophers" (*ratiocinatio philosophorum*; *civ. Dei* 22.29) arrives just in time to play that role, arguing that intelligible things are seen by the gaze of the mind alone and sensible or corporeal things by bodily senses. Augustine concedes that, "if we could establish this reasoning as entirely certain," then we would have to conclude that "God could not be seen by the eye even of a spiritual body." But "true reason" (*vera ratio*) and "prophetic authority" (*prophetica auctoritas*) easily offer counter-examples that mock this line of reasoning (*istam ratiocinationem*). Note that *istam* is a rhetorical gesture of contempt and that *ratiocinatio* is thus negatively contrasted with *ratio*, implying that the *ratiocinatio* of the philosophers is at best incomplete and

Ideology and solidarity

at worst a distortion of true reasoning. Augustine goes on to comment (still 22.29):

> It may well be, then – indeed, this is entirely credible (*valdeque credibile*) – that, in the world to come, we shall see the bodily forms of the new heaven and the new earth in such a way as to perceive God with total clarity and distinctiveness, everywhere present and governing all things, both material and spiritual. In this life, we understand the invisible things of God by the things which are made, and we see Him darkly and in part, as in a glass, and by faith rather than by perceiving corporeal appearances with our bodily eyes. In the life to come, however, it may well be that we shall see Him by means of the bodies which we shall then wear, and wherever we shall turn our eyes ... It may be, therefore, that God will be seen in this way because the eyes will then have some excellence similar to that of the mind, by which they will be able to discern incorporeal natures.

Augustine is aware that he has pushed the reader to the brink of the imagination; even as he tenders this interpretation to the imagination of his readers, he offers another possible interpretation of the prophetic claims of Scripture, which, he says, is "easier to understand" (*ad intellegendum facilius*). But even if the claim that the eyes of the resurrection body will be able to see immaterial reality cannot be proven from Scripture, it is not ruled out. Simply in opening up the question as a serious question, prophetic authority has brought the reader past the artificial limits set on reason and, we could say, the imagination, by the ratiocination of the philosophers, freeing reason to stretch to the true limits of the imagination, a corporeal seeing of incorporeal reality.

The closing chapters are not the first instance in Book 22 where the philosophers, especially the Platonists, are held responsible for premature foreclosure of the imagination. Book 22 has as its object "a discussion of the eternal bliss of the city of God" (*civ. Dei* 22.1), and Augustine keeps emphasizing that, whatever else this bliss (*beatitudo*) may be, it is an embodied bliss. This embodied bliss in a new heaven and a new earth has been foretold by the prophets, including Isaiah (26:19, 65:17ff.) and Daniel (12:1f., 7:18, 7:27). Some of the oracles of Scripture have already come true, for example, the promise made to Abraham that in his seed all nations will be blessed (Gen. 22:18), which for Augustine has been fulfilled in Christ and the Church. In Augustine's opinion (*civ. Dei* 22.3), that should prompt a readiness to accept the prophecies that have not yet been fulfilled. In his rehearsal of the objections of the philosophers, Augustine presents a picture of intellectual complacency, a contemptuous refusal to expand the imagination beyond received wisdom, and a prideful reluctance to follow where the imaginations of the masses of believers have led (*civ. Dei* 22.4):

But there are certain learned and wise men who oppose the might of that great authority which, in fulfilment of what was foretold so long ago, has now converted all the nations of men to believe and hope in its promises. For they seem to themselves to be arguing acutely against the resurrection of the body when they remind us of what Cicero has to say in the third book of his *De republica*. For while asserting that Hercules and Romulus were human beings made into gods, he says (*rep.* 3.28.30): "Their bodies were not taken up into heaven, for Nature would not suffer that which comes from earth to do anything other than remain on earth."

"This, then, is the impressive reasoning of the wise," Augustine drily remarks, "but," he adds, citing Ps. 94:11, "God knows their thoughts, how futile they are" (*civ. Dei* 22.4). He then invites the reader into a thought experiment: what if we were non-embodied spirits in heaven, who knew nothing of earthly creatures, and someone were to suggest to us that we ourselves would someday "be joined to earthly bodies by some wondrous bond, to animate them." Perhaps, Augustine suggests, we would argue that "nature does not permit an incorporeal substance to be bound by a corporeal bond." But such argument would serve only to demonstrate our complacency and unwillingness to imagine anything but what we have experienced, since the world is full of such creatures, souls connected to and bound up with bodies in what Augustine calls a "wondrous fashion" (*miro modo*).

It also serves to analyze Platonist refusal to believe in the resurrection of the body. The major problem for the Platonists, as Augustine sees it, is really embodiment itself, considered as a constitutive and permanent feature of human life and indeed as a constitutive feature of life on earth. If we were thinking rightly, Augustine remarks, it is actually much less incredible that, at the appropriate time as decreed by God, corporeal reality should be exalted to heavenly abodes that are, nevertheless, themselves corporeal, than that an inherently superior element, the immaterial soul, should be intimately linked to or even bound by inferior, material reality. This is inherently "far more wondrous" (*molto mirabilius*), this conjunction of opposites, but we have become complacent because it is so commonplace, and we have come to disregard the wonder that we are (*hoc sumus*). But "sober reason" (*sobria ratione*) – that is, reason unaffected by whatever jades common sense and contributes to the philosophical complacency that underwrites it –without doubt shows which is the greater wonder. Be that as it may, "the whole world now believes that the earthly body of Christ was received up into heaven" (*civ. Dei* 22.5); this, Augustine adds, has been believed by both learned and unlearned alike.

Book 22 continues on as a book of wonders and miracles, all centered on the body and the renewal of the body. The resurrection and ascension of Christ himself, preached by the unlikely ministrations of uneducated fishermen, have been believed so widely, supported by miraculous signs of healing, that if one were to find these miracles too incredible, then one is left with "one great miracle" (*unum grande miraculum*; *civ. Dei* 22.5), namely, that these uneducated preachers were believed without any miracles to support them.[2] Augustine depicts a community of new vision, of possibility, of imagination, straining forward, with Augustine, to imagine the life to come, both bodily and eternal. The martyrs were informed by this new vision, and were able to suffer torture and death for it (*civ. Dei* 22.7, 22.11). Their persistence in the face of persecution is itself a wonder, founded as it is on faith and hope in something that seems incredible. Even now, miracles of bodily healing are attested and recorded in witness to the faith that proclaims "Christ risen in the flesh and ascended with His flesh into heaven" (*civ. Dei* 22.9). The long list of accounts of contemporary bodily miracles is meant to stretch the imagination of the readers regarding what is possible, in God's providence, for the body.

Returning to the objections of the Platonist *ratiocinatores*, Augustine recounts another argument of theirs against "God's great gift" of the resurrection (*civ. Dei* 22.11). The extended argument of the philosophers is based on the order and level of elements in the universe, in other words, on a fixed order of nature that, because of considerations of weight, does not permit the ascension of the body and its dwelling in the heavens. Although the philosophers (i.e., the Platonists) believe in the true, transcendent God, Augustine notes that this "ratiocination" of theirs amounts to nothing more than an interested line of reasoning that ignores common violations of the so-called fixed order. These include flies and birds, which manage very well in the air, and also lead, which, if properly formed, can float on water. It ignores the placement of air between waters above and waters below, as well as fire – the lightest element – that is under the earth. But most of all what it ignores, once again and most especially, is the conjunction of body and soul itself (*civ. Dei* 22.11):

For if that order is such that earth is first, water second, air third and heaven fourth, then the soul is above them all. For Aristotle says that the soul is a fifth kind of

---

[2] This is contrasted in *civ. Dei* 22.6 with the belief that Romulus was a god, something with no intrinsic credibility were it not for the chauvinism, it is implied, of the early Romans.

body, and Plato says that it is not a body at all. If it were a fifth kind of body, then certainly it would be above the rest; and if it is not a body at all, then so much the more does it rise above everything else.

Ratiocinating on the basis of the "order of the elements," the Platonists place undue limits on the power of the God they supposedly know (*civ. Dei* 22.11): "they therefore infer nothing from the weights and order of the elements which shows that Almighty God cannot make our bodies such that they can dwell in the heavens."

Augustine then takes up, one by one, particular objections brought forward, all of them underwritten in some way by the limitation on the imagination in which he has shown Platonism to be invested. By his own flight of the imagination, he shows, one by one, that these objections proceed from a premature foreclosure of imaginative possibilities. It is not so difficult, for example, to imagine God restoring what was lost by decay or dissolution or reassigning what was eaten by cannibalism, completing what was cut off by premature death, making up for what was lost by premature death or abortion, and even preserving intact the gender of the body, for both women and men (*civ. Dei* 22.12–20). It is only if you have lost all wonder at your own being in the first place, lost a sense of the original amazing wonder of *yourself* as constituted by the link between body and soul, that you would believe its preservation and perfection beyond imagining.

Augustine is aware of the provisional character of what he imagines, namely, that we will all have the height and vigor we had, or would have had, in the prime of life, that is, at age thirty, the age at which Christ died (*civ. Dei* 22.15). It is essentially an image of wholeness, defined by the attainment of the stature of the perfect maturity of Christ mentioned in Eph. 4:13. This also involves the healing of all deformities (*civ. Dei* 22.20), though the wounds of the martyrs, like the wounds of Christ himself, will remain at least in the form of glorious scars, so that our affection for them can be continually kindled (*civ. Dei* 22.19). From this it seems fair to infer that any physical mark of one's witness to Christ – essentially, one's whole identity insofar as it was a witness to faith in the body – will remain in some way visible.[3]

---

[3] In *civ. Dei* 13.4 Augustine tells us that, though death is an evil and not a good, the faith of the martyrs enables them to put death to a good use. On closer examination of what the evil is that the martyrs put to good use, Augustine notes, at *civ. Dei* 13.9, that it is not death itself but the suffering associated with death, that is, dying, and thus it is a particular kind of living that is put to a good use. The wounds of the martyrs are the mark of their having put dying – or mortal living – to a good use; there is no reason that other marks of witness in the flesh should not be subject to the same economy. On *civ. Dei* 13, see Cavadini 1999.

Despite the provisional character of his imaginings about what it means to attain to the full stature of Christ, Augustine provides the passage from Ephesians with a further reference, beyond the individual resurrection body, a reference which contextualizes Augustine's imaginative theological work about the individual resurrection body and is less provisional, that is, a reference to the maturity and perfection of the Body of Christ, the Church. As his discussion develops (*civ. Dei* 22.15–18), Augustine quotes Eph. 4:10–16, supplementing it with 1 Cor. 12:27 and 10:17. He emphasizes that the stature of the perfect maturity of Christ is not only a reference to the individual resurrection body, but also to the Church, perfectly "built up" in charity, so that it is the fully grown up Body of Christ the Head (*civ. Dei* 22.18).

Augustine presents us here with an image of solidarity in love. It is a solidarity that is the product of a long process of "re-formation," to use the terminology of Rom. 12:2, which Augustine had cited just a little earlier, "Be not conformed to this world, but be reformed in the renewing of your mind" (*civ. Dei* 22.16). Augustine explores what it means to attain to the stature of the perfect maturity of Christ with the help of both Rom. 12:2 and Rom. 8:29. Attaining the stature of the full maturity of Christ will mean being contoured or "conformed to the image of God's Son" (Rom. 8:29). This will include a dimension of inwardness, the "interior *homo*," expressed by Rom. 12:2 in terms of the mind. It will also include a dimension of body. Augustine is exploring the different levels of what it might mean to have attained the perfect stature of Christ, or to be conformed to His image as the Son of God. Attaining to immortality is not simply realizing in an eternal existence a state the soul had all along. It is being conformed to *Christ* and to *His* immortality. Augustine puts this in a striking way (*civ. Dei* 22.16): "as Christ was conformed to us by mortality, so shall we be conformed in Him by immortality." Immortality is integration: our whole being will be integrated according to the love by which Christ became incarnate. This individual re-formation will be at the same time our perfect incorporation as members of each other in the one Body of Christ – the body that defines bodiliness.

Significantly, it is in this context that Augustine remarks that women will retain their sex in the resurrected body. Being conformed to the image of God's Son does not mean being made into a man, since "the sex of a woman is not a vice, but nature" (*civ. Dei* 22.17). Women retain their sex in the resurrected body because the gendered reality of the body is part of the original wonder of embodiment. Augustine comments that there will be no lust present in that life, so that looking upon the naked bodies of women (and men) will not arouse lust but praise of God for His wisdom and mercy (*civ. Dei* 22.17; cf. 22.24). The wonder of embodied life will be freed of the fetters of the imagination imposed by lust, and the prophetic significance of the gendered body will leap forth in clarity. The creation of Eve from Adam is an indication not that the woman is less of a creature of God than the man, or less eligible to be conformed to the likeness of Christ, but rather to indicate what a strong bond of unity should exist between spouses and so offers a prophetic foreshadowing of the unity of Christ and the Church. The sleep of Adam foreshadows the death of Christ, who hung lifeless on the Cross as his side was pierced by the lance (*civ. Dei* 22.17): "from ... there flowed forth water and blood, which we know to be the sacraments by which the Church is built up." This prophetic foreshadowing is represented and recalled by the bodies of men and women *as* men and women; gender carries an indication of the self-giving love of Christ that prompted the Incarnation and built up the Church.[4] If we could look upon the naked bodies of men and women without lust, we would see this love, for this is what gender signifies. The re-formation of the Church away from conformation to the world is thus a re-formation in the love that is continuous from the creation; in a mysterious way this love fulfills the original meaning of the body.

Most significantly, from the perspective gained in this re-forming according to the love of Christ, one begins to see not only the next world but also this one here and now with renewed vision. One can see the sadness and misery of the fallen world and recognize it for what it is (*civ. Dei* 22.22–23) and yet also retain a sense of its still stunning beauty. Augustine provides a catalog of wonders, of the sea with its many colors, "the plenteousness of light and its wondrous quality," the astonishing activities of ants and bees and of the countless forms and species of living things – and, what is most marvelous of all, the presupposition of all this life, namely, the union of immaterial soul and material body (*civ. Dei* 22.24):

> This is a work so great and marvelous as to astonish the mind that considers it well, and to call forth praise to the Creator. And this is true not only in the case of man, who is a rational being and therefore more excellent and outstanding than any other creature on earth, but in the case of the tiniest fly.

In Christ we are re-formed away from the complacency of the world and the Platonist philosophy which underwrites it, into a renewed sense of awe and

---

[4] Augustine only adumbrates here what we can find more fully exposited in his preaching. See Cavadini 2008.

wonder at the gift of the original creation, and so we have the wherewithal and warrant to imagine something even more wondrous as the new heaven and earth that includes bodies raised for eternal life. The solidarity of the new society, bound by the re-forming power of Christ's love, is the basis for reimagining our world as it is now as well as what it will become, when we will be occupied in the perfect worship of God (*civ. Dei* 22.30).

2 EUCHARISTIC LIFE AND TRUE WORSHIP: SOLIDARITY

The discussion of the Church as Christ's Body in Book 22 recalls a more in-depth discussion of this matter earlier in Book 10, where the question under consideration was specifically what constitutes true worship of God. More specifically, Augustine engages in Book 10 in a polemic against Platonist (and in particular, Porphyry's) endorsement or toleration of the worship of gods. Augustine had established as early as Book 8 that Plato and his philosophical descendants knew the one true God (*civ. Dei* 8.1):

> They confess a God Who is above all that belongs to the nature of the soul. They confess a God Who made not only this visible world, which is often called heaven and earth, but also every soul whatever, and Who makes the rational and the intellectual soul, of which kind is that of human beings, blessed by participation in His unchangeable and incorporeal light.

For Augustine, the problem with Platonism, however, was always a fundamental inconsistency, which he found perfectly summed up by Rom. 1:21–22 (*civ. Dei* 8.10): 'Knowing God, they glorified Him not as God; neither were they thankful ... Professing themselves to be wise, they became fools, and changed the glory of the incorruptible God into the likeness of the image of corruptible man, and of birds, and fourfooted beasts, and creeping things." In other words, although they recognized the true God, they refused to worship him properly and continued instead to tolerate or endorse polytheistic worship.

It is this fundamental inconsistency, consistent only in its universality among Platonist philosophers, that is Augustine's primary criticism of them. It is a special unseemliness to have recognized and known the true God and yet to countenance worship of other gods, and it is the sort of inconsistency that prompts Augustine to search for the vested interest it reflects.

The desire to analyze and repudiate this inconsistency brings Augustine in Book 10, the central, hinge book of the *City of God*, to ask what constitutes true worship of God, the worship that will make the worshipper truly happy. The worship or service that is uniquely to be rendered to God and to no one else, Augustine says, is that designated by the Greek term *latreia* (*civ. Dei* 10.1). After examining the matter further, Augustine concludes that the essence of *latreia* is sacrifice, for no one would argue that sacrifice is to be rendered to any being not divine (*civ. Dei* 10.4). But true worship of God is a matter of the heart, and external acts of sacrifice are signs or sacraments of the heart's sacrifice, which, says Augustine, is the "mercy" or "compassion" (*misericordia*) that is shown to ourselves or our neighbors and directed towards God (*civ. Dei* 10.6).

Anticipating the passages we have examined from Book 22, Augustine uses Rom. 12:1–2 to indicate the integration of the whole human being, body and soul, by way of true sacrifice (*civ. Dei* 10.6):

Thus the apostle has exhorted us to present our bodies as a living sacrifice, holy, acceptable to God, our reasonable service, and not to be con-formed to this world, but to be re-formed in the renewing of our mind, that we might prove what is that good, and acceptable, and perfect will of God, that is, the true sacrifice of ourselves.

"Acts of compassion" or "works of mercy," depending on how you translate *opera misericordiae*, are meant to help us lose "the form of worldly desire" (*formam concupiscentiae saecularis*) and be re-formed by submission to God.

This is not as easy as it may seem. As Augustine had pointed out in the very first Book, in the Preface to the whole *City of God*, the city of this world, that is, the fellowship of human beings and angels defined by worldly desire and most visibly represented in worldly Empire, boasts precisely of *mercy* as its greatest accomplishment (*civ. Dei* 1.pref.):

For the King and Founder of this City of which we are resolved to speak has revealed a maxim of the divine law in the Scriptures of His people, where it is said, "God resists the proud but gives grace to the humble" (James 4:6). But the swollen fancy of the proud-spirited envies even this utterance, which belongs to God, and loves to hear the following words spoken in its own praise: "To spare the conquered and subdue the proud" (*Aen.* 6.853).

The form of worldly desire is pride (*superbia*), and it reveals itself in the desire for praise.[5] The perversion of works of mercy into self-glorification is in fact the special work of Empire, so that what is the very best act a human being can perform, revealing the human being at his or her most generous, free and loving state, fails to achieve its true end in glorifying God, the Creator of this human being, and instead is turned toward the glorification of the Empire,

---

[5] The constitutive feature of the Roman imperial character is the love of praise (*cupiditas gloriae, laudis aviditas, cupiditas laudis*), as Augustine analyzes it in *civ. Dei* 5.

which "spares the conquered" in dramatic acts of mercy only to solidify its grasp on the imaginations of oppressed and oppressor. This perversion of compassion is the primal blight on the imagination. That which would reflect in human beings the beauty of God's form and so offer praise to God is reduced to a moment in a project of self-glorification, of the quest for prestige, until there seems to be nothing left than the quest for praise and prestige and no greater purpose for human beings to serve than to contribute their personal prestige to the glory of the Empire and to receive personal prestige in turn. The Empire comes to define the scope of human excellence (*virtus*) by co-opting the very worship of God, compassion, for itself. Under this regime, an actual, pure work of compassion done for the sake of God, that is, for no ulterior motive (as we might say today) is unimaginable, because it would seem to be done for absolutely nothing, an unimaginably deep sacrifice, undertaken without hope of any benefit whatsoever.

That, of course, is a precise description of the sacrifice of Christ in his Incarnation and passion. It is an unimaginable act of mercy or compassion in which the Word, through whom all things were made, became flesh and dwelt among us as a pure act of mercy, without any benefit to himself whatsoever (*civ. Dei* 10.24; cf. John 1:3, 14). The Church comes into being by this most precious sacrifice and is "built up" by the sacraments signified by the blood and water flowing from Christ's pierced side. The Church is a fellowship or *societas* defined by God's compassion in Christ, conformed and configured to it, and in that conformation, undergoing purification from the form of worldly love mentioned in Rom. 12.2. In other words, the sacrifice of Christ creates a community whose very existence is formed by non-worldly love, by the humility of God the Word in assuming human nature, by the humility represented and enacted in human nature by Jesus Christ's death on the Cross, and by the continuing presence of that sacrifice in the Eucharistic bonds of mutual love formed among the members of the Church, his Body. The Body of Christ *is* the compassion of Christ present as a fellowship in transformation, in renovation, in re-formation. This solidarity-in-transformation is sacramentally represented and enacted in the Eucharist (*civ. Dei* 10.20):

> Thus, He is both the priest who offers and the sacrifice which is offered; and He intended that there should be a daily sign of this in the sacrament of the Church's sacrifice. For the Church, being the body of which He is the Head, is taught to offer herself through Him.

Again, making use of the language of Rom. 12:3–4:

> 'For, as we have many members in one body, and all members have not the same office, so we, being many, are one body in Christ, and every one members of

one another, having gifts differing according to the grace that is given to us.' This is the sacrifice of Christians: 'we, being many, are one body in Christ.' And this also, as the faithful know, is the sacrifice which the Church continually celebrates in the sacrament of the altar, by which she demonstrates that she herself is offered in the offering that she makes to God.

The Church is a "congregation and fellowship" (*congregatio societasque*) offered to God as a universal sacrifice through the great Priest that "we might be the body of so great a Head" (*civ. Dei* 10.6). We are not purified by our own power or excellence (*virtus*), but by the mercy or compassion of God, which defines us and which conforms our works, our poor little allotment of virtue, to that mercy. We don't have to fall back on the narrow mercy of our own hearts. We don't have to fall back on whatever speck of excellence we might muster up, hoping all the while to put it on our personal résumés to ensure it will go down in history in the archives of magnificent compassion. The perfect worship of God is the Eucharistic life, the continual offering of Christ to us and for us, the continual formation of a *societas* whose loves and works are being transformed in Christ's compassion and configured to it. Here is a solidarity which is an alternative to Empire, not as a political entity, not as a worldly city, but as a fellowship of love available to people of any nation or city, and it provides immediate perspective on the imperial project, shows it up for the limited enterprise it truly is, for the shocking limitation of vision and imagination that it has always been.

The fact that this solidarity is not an alternative state or earthly city is what is captured in the metaphor Augustine uses frequently in the text, especially in the latter books, that of pilgrimage (e.g., *civ. Dei* 19.17, 19.26). If there is anything that has a claim to being the just society on earth, it is this pilgrim people, precisely not as another worldly entity or power, as yet another settled perfection claiming praise for itself, but a fellowship founded in the humility of Christ, aware of its own imperfection and its continual need for re-formation (*civ. Dei* 19.27).[6] It is a justice that breeds longing and not complacency. We can usefully observe that this idea of pilgrimage is an inversion of a Platonic metaphor. The Neoplatonic soul is on an odyssey or

---

[6] Dodaro 2004 shows that Augustine's dispute is not only with Roman religion and pagan philosophy, but also with Pelagian conceptions of virtue. Dodaro does not seem to say unequivocally that the Church *is* the just society, as far as we can have such a thing on earth, as I would like to say, but he comes close to saying this in his discussion of the *totus Christus* (p. 107): "Christ's justifying prayer becomes the oration of the just society, of the church (*vox ecclesiae*), whereby Christ speaks through the suffering members of his body." This can sound like the Church is defined *only* in relation to Christ, as many individuals all related to Christ, whereas for Augustine, for whom love of neighbor and love of God are intrinsically related, the web of interconnectedness is the locus of the sacrifice by which we are being reformed.

pilgrimage in this world of bodies, from which it hopes to ascend to a contemplative union with God apart from the world of bodies.[7] Augustine's heavenly fellowship, by contrast, is on pilgrimage through what Augustine calls the "earthly city," not the world of bodies, which, in fact, it will never leave. The earthly city, Augustine remarks, is "a kind of fellowship (*societas*) of common nature, even though each section of mankind pursued devices and desires of its own" (*civ. Dei* 18.2). This generates a situation where human society is divided against itself and one part always oppresses another, and it has been divided into a great number of empires. The city of God has existed throughout history as a people formed by a different kind of solidarity, emerging as being re-formed away from the form of worldly love, and conformed to the humility of God which was to be fully revealed in Christ.

This community, before the advent of Christ, was localized mainly in the Israelite people, defined by God's favor and grace. Augustine says that the universal way of salvation sought unsuccessfully by Porphyry was foretold by the holy prophets (*civ. Dei* 10.32):

They did this by certain manifest pronouncements and by many veiled ones, especially in the Hebrew nation, whose commonwealth (*res publica*) was in a certain sense consecrated to foreshadow and herald, by its tabernacles and temple and priesthood and sacrifices, the city of God which was to be gathered in from all the nations.

In general, *civ. Dei* 10.32 contrasts the success of prophetic revelation in forming a community in a solidarity that eventually transcends national differences with the philosophical failure to inspire any such community or even to notice it once it has come into being. Augustine attributes Porphyry's failure to notice it first to pride (*civ. Dei* 10.29) – he would have had to embrace embodied existence as a fundamental constituent of human being and accept dependence upon the Incarnate Word as necessary for his salvation – and then to fear (*civ. Dei* 10.32), for he knew the Christians were being persecuted and thought they would eventually be rubbed out. In his fear, he defers to the Roman *imperium*, just as the colonized worshippers of Romulus did long ago. His philosophy

---

[7] In *City of God* this idea is especially associated with Porphyry, whom Augustine repeatedly charges with teaching that in order for the soul to be happy, it must be completely free of body (e.g., *civ. Dei* 10.29, 13.19). On Augustine and Porphyry, see Bochet 2010. Augustine remarks that Plato does teach that human souls will return to bodies, but also that this return will be problematic, similar to what is the case at present; there is in Plato no real doctrine of a resurrection in which the body is perfected and glorified (*civ. Dei* 22.26–27). In both Porphyry and Plato, as Augustine interprets them, the soul is better off apart from the body.

underwrites the splintering of human community fostered by the permission it gives for polytheistic worship such as that endorsed by the Empire. And, though there can be times when Augustine's appeal to the prophets' vision of Christ's coming can seem artificial to us, the visionary power of prophecy is really the new possibility for vision and imagination that is generated by solidarity in the humility of God, which is already, even in advance, solidarity in the sacrifice of Christ. Prophecy is the forward-looking vision of people whose imaginations have been unfettered by faith in God's revelation.

Platonism, by contrast, is in Augustine's *City of God* the ideology of Empire, the philosophy that permits the vision of the true God and the worship of the true God to be subverted into the complacency, the stasis, the immobility of the fellowship of this earth, which can achieve a semblance of solidarity only through domination. The image of pilgrimage is thus not simply an image of movement, but also an image of stasis. The city of God, continually constituted out of the Church as it is purified and conformed to Christ's love, progresses by being re-formed from what by contrast is static and stagnant, the city of this world, the form of worldly love, which perpetually generates community that is no community. The city of God, in the mortality it shares with the city of this earth, is on pilgrimage through this other city, denominated "Babylon" (*civ. Dei* 18.2, 18.22) as an image of captivity, and not through the world of bodies.

To return to Book 10, Augustine argues that Porphyry and the other Platonists refuse to accept the Incarnation because they are proud. In order to accept the Incarnation and to submit to its purifying power in the Church, they would have first to admit that the link between body and soul is something wondrous, marvelous, and humbling, rather than finally something to be left behind. Augustine comments that it is actually less wondrous that one spirit should assume another, that is, that the Word of God, even though eternal, should assume another immaterial nature, the soul of a human being, than that the soul, an immaterial being, should be linked to a body (*civ. Dei* 10.29). It is the doctrine that final happiness involves an escape from all bodies that has allowed our own being, body and soul, to lapse into cheap familiarity, something that can be overlooked as insignificant. The body is that to be avoided, to be left behind – naturally, since the body is that which belies any *mythos* or pretence of self-sufficiency. The body is that which gives the lie to pride because it is so obviously needy and fleeting. Platonism nurtures pride by imaging salvation as fleeing from the body, that is, as something I, not being in any essential way linked to the body, can do on my own. The body can perish, and I can, as Rom. 1:22 says,

Ideology and solidarity

claim to be wise and accept praise for my wisdom. This relieves me of any embarrassing need for gratitude. It also divides humanity into the dominating few, the wise, and the rest, who are not wise, and who therefore must resort to some kind of appeal to the gods in order to purify the soul of its attachment to the body at least to some degree. Addressing Porphyry, Augustine observes (*civ. Dei* 10.27):

> You raise yourself above these divine revelations by the intellectual character of your life, which, it seems, has no need of the cleansings effected by the theurgic arts; for these are not at all necessary to the philosopher. Because you wish to reward your teachers, however, you recommend such arts to others, who, not being philosophers, are seduced into using what you admit is useless to yourself, who are capable of higher things. Thus, those who are remote from the power of philosophy, which is too arduous for all save the few, may, with your encouragement, seek purification at the hands of theurgists: purification not, indeed, of the intellectual, but of the spiritual part of the soul. Now since those incapable of philosophy form incomparably the greater part of the multitude of mankind, more may be compelled to resort to these secret and illicit teachers of yours than to the Platonic schools.

Platonism has a vested interest in continuing to tolerate or even to endorse polytheism. Insofar as it is a philosophy of self-purgation available only to the few, based on the purgation of the soul from any connection to the body, the Platonists can glory in their wisdom and appeal to the pride of those less talented by providing access to sacrificial rites that will in effect make them, too, the principles of their own purification, simply by enacting the rites and so forcing the hand of the gods. Here is reproduced the community that is no community, the community continually degenerating into self-serving domination and subordination, splintered and splintering.

In Book 4 of *City of God*, Augustine offers a parody of the pantheon of gods worshipped by the Romans. Here he describes (though in exaggerated form) the set of deities in charge of the countryside, the mountains, hills, valleys, and farmland. After listing them all, he remarks (*civ. Dei* 4.8):

> I do not mention them all ... I have, however, said these few things in order to make it understood that the Romans certainly do not venture to assert that it was these deities who established, increased and preserved their empire. For each of these deities was so busy with his own duties (*officiis*) that no one thing was ascribed as a whole to any one of them. How could Segetia care for the empire when she was not allowed to take care of the corn and the trees at the same time? How could Cunina think of arms when she was not permitted to go beyond the care of the little ones? How could Nodotus help in war when he was concerned, not even with the sheath of the ear, but only with the nodes of the joints?

A skillful parody, but the subject of the parody is not only the pantheon of gods but also the imperial bureaucracy. The gods are pictured as an extension of the bureaucracy, a kind of projection onto nature of the body politic. It is no wonder that nature has lost its wonder and been cheapened by familiarity, when it has been, as it were, politicized, subsumed under the imperial project, reflecting back as in a mirror not the glory of the Creator, as Rom. 1.20 says it should, but the glory of the Empire, reducing nature to what will be later and more prosaically described as a hierarchy of utility (*ordo usus*; *civ. Dei* 11.16.) Nature is reduced to the status of the commonplace, subsumed under the realm of the commonwealth, where it will not be a competitor against the Empire for glory. The pantheon is nothing but the Empire writ large, divinized, and thus we recognize in the parody the accusation that the Roman religion represented nothing but the apotheosis of the Empire itself, which amounts to the sin of self-worship, or pride. This is an image of a society that has lost all self-perspective. It has lost any vantage point from which to have self-perspective. It is at a standstill. The beauty of the physical world is referred not to the glory of God, but to the Empire.

The Platonist refusal to see the link between body and soul as the wondrous work of God empties the bodily world of its reference to God (its wonder) and leaves it to the mercy of the Empire to define. The Platonist refusal to stand in awe at the link between body and soul denigrates human being as such, and so leaves any of its accomplishments in the realm of the body equally to the Empire to define. Platonist refusal to see the divine miracle of the link between body and soul blinds them to true compassion, that is, to the Incarnation, and so they can no longer imagine anything so wonderful. This leaves the true worship of God, which is compassion, itself available for redefinition by the Empire. Once the true worship of God, compassion, is redirected towards the glory not of God but of the Empire, one has eliminated the only adequate basis for true solidarity and the renewal of vision, the recovery of perspective, and the opening of the imagination, which comes with it.

Augustine's analysis of the stagnation of Roman society and culture is prosecuted in full in Book 5 of *City of God*, where the subject of analysis is now not the physical world but the world of human excellence (*virtus*). Augustine analyzes the incredible growth and extension of the Roman Empire, not as a function of mythological fate or destiny but rather as an achievement of the Roman imperial character, defined, as we have already noted, as the "lust for praise." Augustine goes on to offer a catalogue of excellence – accomplishments of valor, loyalty, and temperance on the part of the Romans – and he repeatedly draws attention to this excellence as "wondrous" (*civ. Dei* 5.12, 5.13). Who cannot admire the excellence of Cincinnatus, Marcus Regulus, and all those Romans who preferred to suffer death or poverty in order to seek glory for Rome? Since such people sought praise in the eyes of "enlightened judges" (*bene iudicantibus*; *civ. Dei* 5.19), evidently Platonic or Stoic philosophers,[8] they worked to deserve such praise by seeking to achieve a commonwealth genuinely characterized by excellence and in particular, justice, and thus deservedly gained an empire.

But, if cultural excellence is simply a function of the desire for praise, which is nothing more than a form of opinion, then it becomes a virtue not to rise above opinion (even when that opinion is one's own). If excellence is simply a function of opinion, then the society has reached a level of complacency in which excellence consists in not rising above prevailing imperial opinion. Thus the very best a human being has to offer, the human being at his most wonderful, precisely the point at which he should most irresistibly reflect the glory of God the Creator, is made rather to refract the wondrous glory of the Empire. Wonder is thus completely correlate to the glory of the body politic, which becomes the ultimate locus of wonder, not to God or to the human being as the image of God. Since the martyrs, however, though their deeds are truly glorious, do not ascribe their excellence to themselves, but to the grace of God (*civ. Dei* 5.14), they make it so the glory of human being recovers its proper referent, God, the Creator, and so they serve to refresh the vista available to reason, sparking the mind beyond the complacency of the imperial imagination.[9]

We have seen that Platonism in Augustine's *City of God* is analyzed as underwriting this complacency by assuring that no one at the very highest levels of culture will make the mistake of thinking that our own being, our own self, composed of body and soul, is anything to wonder at or to feel grateful for. Recognition of the source of this wonder and the object for such gratitude would threaten the whole imperial project of the hegemony

---

[8] At any rate, not the Epicureans; Augustine aligns himself with the Stoic critique of the Epicureans in *civ. Dei* 5.20, making the point that just as pleasure is obviously not the proper motivation for excellence, even though it can indeed motivate one to prudence, justice, courage and temperance, so love of praise is not the proper motivation for excellence.

[9] The perspective that the martyrs afford also, Augustine hopes, will enable Christians to use the wonderful stories of pagan Roman excellence as a warning to be humble, since the heroes of such stories accomplished extraordinary feats of virtue without the benefit of a heavenly goal to strive for. If Christians are able to be modest about their own excellence in ascetical achievements, giving the glory to God, then they will avoid making grist for a glory that would render Christian excellence just a form of the old Roman triumphalism redivivus. It is clear from *civ. Dei* 5.18 that the force of Augustine's imperial critique in *City of God* is directed as much, if not more, against the triumphalist pretensions of the Christian empire as it is of the older pagan version.

of meaning. Platonism, as Augustine portrays it, is an enabler of Empire, selling us out to the tender mercies of *imperium* and the lust for domination which creates it. In that sense, Platonism is an ideology of empire, pitting a distorted and static contemplative vision against the forward-looking prophetic spirit that in every age has seen through the arrogance of all the kingdoms of this world.[10]

---

[10] The Platonic vision of God is indeed a vision of the fatherland to which we tend, but it is a vision at a great distance, and distorted as by a cataract of intellectual vision, a dim obscurity of the imagination. See *civ. Dei* 10.29, to the Platonists: "You see after a fashion, although at a distance, and with clouded vision, the country in which we should abide; but you do not hold fast to the way that leads to it."

CHAPTER 6

The theater of the virtues: Augustine's critique of pagan mimesis

Jennifer Herdt

For Augustine, both pagan and Christian worship are best construed as spectacle, as the authoritative public presentation of attractive exemplars before the eyes of a collected assembly. Augustine's critique of pagan virtue must, then, be interpreted through the lens of his critique of pagan worship. Attending to the power of spectacle, we are reminded of the receptive character of our agency, reminded that our possibilities for action are fundamentally determined by what and how we see. Those held up by pagan culture as shining models are finally examples of a pride that closes sinful humanity in on itself rather than opening it up to the love of God and neighbor. There is, though, nothing obviously repulsive about pagan heroes. Quite the contrary, there is about them a kind of splendor, borrowed from the good which they imitate, however perversely, that invites admiration and imitation. These "virtues" are enacted in theatrical spectacles and performed in pagan worship in ways that present them attractively and inscribe them authoritatively. Pagan worship blinds viewers to the goodness and beauty of God and renders them unable to recognize that we return to our divine exemplar not by imitating glorious heroes or self-sufficient philosophers, but only by accepting the love shown to us in Christ's self-emptying humility. Our eyes opened to see the true exemplarity of Christ's humility, we are freed from our desire for independence, freed to reach out with God's compassionate love to those around us, and freed humbly to take our place in the common worship of God.

Augustine's critique of pagan virtue is fundamentally a critique of pride. But only the humble can recognize God in the offensive spectacle of Christ's humiliation on the cross. And this humility is itself Christ's gift. Recognizing the ever-prevenient character of grace ought, then, to chasten both Augustine's critique of pagan virtue and our own predilections for mapping "pagan" onto "secular."

I THE FORMATIVE POWER OF PAGAN SPECTACLE

The burden of Book 2 of *City of God* is to demonstrate that the fall of Rome cannot be blamed on Christians, since in fact the moral corruption of Rome, and so its true fall, happened prior to the dawning of Christianity. The primary cause of this corruption is here identified as pagan worship, which directed the attention of worshippers toward examples of avarice, ambition, and lust in the persons of the gods themselves. Nor can any dividing line be drawn between the rites of the gods and the theatrical games, spectacles, and festivals associated with these, such that the former could be exonerated of vice and the latter dismissed as mere entertainment. For it was the gods themselves who ordered that the public games and theatrical shows be introduced into their worship in order to avert a plague (*civ. Dei* 1.32). If the gods indeed commanded the incorporation of obscene theatrical performances into their worship, they are convicted of corrupting their own worshippers; if in fact the Roman leaders did this on their own initiative in order to distract the people from the ravages of the plague, then the gods are convicted of having failed to avenge their slander (*civ. Dei* 2.8). The upshot is that the gods are in fact demonic, powerless, or fictive.

Augustine is rehearsing what is by his time a standard Christian trope, which assimilates a wide range of public performances under the category of "spectacle": athletic competitions, executions in the arena and amphitheater, gladiatorial contexts, military reenactments, and comedies, tragedies, and mimes in the theater.[1] From Athenagoras, Tatian, and Minucius Felix to John Chrysostom, Lactantius, and perhaps most obviously Tertullian in *De spectaculis*, Christian writers cautioned against the seductive power of Roman spectacle while at the same time, in a kind of subversive mimesis, presenting Christian liturgy and most especially Christian martyrdom as holy spectacle.[2] Christians rejected these spectacles as powerful illusions that turn the spectator away from goodness and truth and feed cruelty, concupiscence, and idolatry. In recent decades, scholars have analyzed the arena, the games, and other forms of Roman spectacle and have argued that these phenomena must be read as performances that inscribed the logic of imperial power: "staged as ritual performance and as public entertainment, the arena's spectacles were simultaneously acts of raw violence, gestures

---

[1] Castelli 2004: 107.
[2] See David Potter 1993. I borrow the term "subversive mimesis" from Morrison 1982: 83, who applies the term in the first place to Paul and then to Augustine.

toward collective catharsis, and enactments of public power."³ The prominence that Augustine gives to the phenomenon of pagan spectacles in his account of the City of Man indicates his own grasp of this logic of *imperium*.

Augustine's distinctive appropriation of the tropes of perverse and holy spectacle in *City of God* places greatest emphasis on spectacle as liturgy, as public worship.⁴ Within that context, it is lust for sex and power (as the perversions of love for divine beauty and divine glory, respectively), rather than violence, which receive the lion's share of attention.⁵ Key to the corrupting power of this theatrical pagan worship were three factors. First, it was culturally authoritative; even if the plays themselves were of human invention and the performers human, they were cloaked with divine authority. Viewers are given an authoritative pattern for their own shameful conduct (*civ. Dei* 2.7). Even those who considered the spectacles to be merely fictional inventions regarded them nevertheless as pleasing to the gods and thus as legitimate examples for human conduct (*civ. Dei* 2.25). Second, it was public; these were "shows" and "spectacles" presented before the people assembled together, of all strata of society (*civ. Dei* 2.26). Pagan worship was thus formative of the people as a whole. This contrasts both with the secret rites of the mystery religions and with the elite teachings of philosophers (*civ. Dei* 2.6–7). In pagan society, "shameful things are furnished with a public stage and the praiseworthy are concealed," as if decency ought to be veiled from sight. This was a divide-and-conquer strategy: "the secret teaching is intended to ensnare honest men, who are scarce, and the public exhibition of wickedness to keep the many, who are wholly base, from improvement" (*civ. Dei* 2.26). Lastly, pagan worship was attractive, appealing to basic human desires, if in a perverse way. This Augustine knows from his own experience; "I myself, when a young man, used to come to their sacrilegious spectacles and games ... and enjoy the most disgraceful exhibitions which were enacted in honour of the gods and goddesses" (*civ. Dei* 2.4).

These are for Augustine features of true worship as well: if we ask "where the wretched people received the instruction of the gods concerning the restraint of avarice, the subduing of ambition, and the curbing of luxury," or

---

³ Castelli 2004: 111; she offers a brief overview of this scholarship, pp. 108–11.
⁴ Thus my account complements that of Robert Dodaro, who notes Augustine's critique of the corrupt examples offered by pagan theater and religious cult and develops a powerful account of the way in which the soul is drawn to God through the divine rhetoric of liturgical and biblical sacraments, but does not attend to the fact that Augustine explicitly presents Christian worship as holy spectacle. See Dodaro 2004: 42–47, 50, 124–25.
⁵ Although Augustine does of course analyze Alypius' passion for gladiatorial shows in *conf.* 6.7–8.

"in what places those precepts of the gods who taught them were wont to be recited and frequently heard by the peoples who worshipped them," Christians can point to their churches (*civ. Dei* 2.6). Augustine repeatedly stresses authoritative proclamation and assembly of the people. Even scripture is treated in this emphatically liturgical way: "let our adversaries read our many commandments against avarice and luxury, found in the prophets, in the holy Gospel, in the Acts of the Apostles and in the Epistles, which are everywhere read to the people who assemble to hear them" (*civ. Dei* 2.19). Earlier Christian thinkers such as Tertullian and Origen had focused primarily on the theatrical character of martyrdom.[6] The public spaces of pagan justice, worship, and entertainment were all subverted and taken up into a divine theater in which God has assigned pagan magistrates their roles and is directing the performance – humiliating death is rescripted as glorified entrance into new life.[7] For Augustine, in contrast, the liturgy itself was the primary holy spectacle. The *age* of martyrs has given way to the *cult* of the martyrs, which is integrated into that liturgical theater.[8] This turns out to be important to Augustine's understanding of what proper viewing of the spectacle of martyrdom requires, as we shall see.

2 TEARS FOR DIDO: THE PROBLEM OF COMPASSION

Augustine's autobiographical reference to Roman spectacles in *City of God* refers us back to the *Confessions* and his exploration there of his own youthful passion for stage plays. These passages are sometimes seen as evidence that Augustine remained attracted to a Stoic critique of the passions or to a Neoplatonic ascent of love which has ultimately no room for human love of particular human others for their own sake. But in fact Augustine reclaims the emotions in general and compassionate love for others in particular. The target of his critique is illusion and the false mimesis that it feeds. In the *Confessions*, the issue of false worship is not in the foreground, but the imitation of bad exemplars is already key. From Terence Augustine learned of the adulteries of the god of thunder, "and so sham thunder is made to legitimize and play pander to real adultery" (*conf.* 1.16.25).[9] Augustine's classical education required him not simply to read and watch the sinful antics of the gods but to reenact them rhetorically; he was required, for instance, to "declaim the words uttered by Juno in her rage and grief when she could not keep the Trojan prince from coming to

---

[6] Castelli 2004: 118–21.   [7] Bowersock 1995: 52.   [8] Brown 1981.
[9] English translations are taken from Sheed 1993 (1st edn 1942).

God that is centered in the participatory spectacle of Christian worship. Christians are summoned away from the imitation of appearance as it appears to fallen human perception to the imitation of reality as it has been revealed in Christ, to assemble where "no foul or disgraceful spectacle or example is ever presented when the teachings of the true God are expounded" (*civ. Dei* 2.28).

Real as his admiration for Platonic philosophy is, Augustine's criticism is directed at just this point: even while possessing an intuition of the Trinity, and acknowledging rightly a process of corrective reversion of copy to primordial divine exemplar, the Platonists fail to see that this takes place most fully in the liturgical mimesis of the people assembled, not in philosophical contemplation. They privilege a path available only to the philosophical elite. The people, meanwhile, are left with popular pagan religion and its perverted exemplarity. Augustine develops this point at length in Book 10 of *City of God*, where his focus is on Porphyry's support for theurgy. Porphyry is shown to be both inconsistent and deceptive; with other Platonists, he comes close to the truth in holding that only the *principia*, i.e., the Platonic trinity, can purify us (*civ. Dei* 10.23). Despite this, he also promises that a certain sort of purification of the soul is available via theurgic practices. These cannot purify the highest, intellectual part of the soul, but only the spiritual part, which apprehends the images of material things (*civ. Dei* 10.9, 10.27). But Augustine points out that Porphyry cannot consistently claim that theurgy offers even a partial form of purification while also insisting elsewhere, as he does, that theurgic practices "are not the work of powers which assist us in the attainment of the blessed life, but pertain rather to deceitful demons" (*civ. Dei* 10.11). Porphyry rightly advises that the angels who reveal the truth about the Father are not to be worshiped but rather imitated (*civ. Dei* 10.26), and yet he does not confidently reject the worship of many gods and the theurgic invocation of spirits whose wickedness is revealed by their participation in human evil-doing.

Why don't Platonists like Porphyry take seriously their own self-contradictions on this score? Because ultimately they consider themselves superior to such practices and endorse them only in order to satisfy the rabble. "You recommend such arts to others, who, not being philosophers, are seduced into using what you admit is useless to yourself, who are capable of higher things" (*civ. Dei* 10.27). They are willing to contemplate a split between public worship and philosophical contemplation because they are ultimately concerned only for their own salvation. Augustine notes that they have failed to offer a "universal way of the soul's deliverance," since this

3 PLATONIC MIMESIS AND THE PROBLEM OF PRIDE

symptom of a deeper problem, the human tendency to declare independence from God, to seek in ourselves and in the world what we can only find in God.

Importantly, though, imitation of God is itself good and integral to the corrective reversion of created reality to divine exemplar.[12] In a twisted way, sinners in fact testify to the glory of God, since "by the mere fact of their imitation, they declare that You are the creator of all that is, and that there is nowhere for them to go where You are not" (*conf.* 2.6.14). In many respects, Augustine adopts a Platonic understanding of mimesis. Nature is itself mimetic for Plato; it issues forth from a transcendent order of archetypes. Corrective reversion requires ascending from transitory, unreal material images through intellectual images of reality to a perception of the transcendent Forms that are that ultimate reality. Augustine, too, envisions an ascent from carnal images to the discernment of the eternal patterns or *rationes* present within created reality, to the divine truths grasped through faith.[13] But while Augustine declares his approval of Plato's banishment of the artists from his ideal republic, he does not share Plato's suspicion of artistic mimesis. Plato makes a distinction between a form of imitation that copies reality "as it is" and a form that imitates "appearance as it appears."[14] Poets copy "appearance as it appears," reinforcing the delusions of public opinion.[15] They offer images twice removed from the truth of the Forms; a copy of a copy of reality. Thus, they compete with the work of philosophers, who arrive at true knowledge of reality as it is.[16] Only philosophers properly recollect the Forms and thus open the way to a proper mimetic reconversion to those paradigms. Even given his distinction between these two forms of mimesis, and thus the theoretical possibility of a poetry that would complement rather than compete with philosophy, Plato himself would rather banish than reform the arts.

Augustine represents Plato as sharing his own concern with the power of vicious theatrical fiction: "he could not bear to see base injury done to the gods, and he refused to have the souls of his citizens tainted and corrupted by falsehood" (*civ. Dei* 2.14). Poets are enemies to the truth because they slander the gods. But Augustine, in contrast, celebrates the holy mimesis of

---

other's sinfulness and separation from God and is thus a failure of compassion. But learning to love all things in God is learning to love as God loves, with a love of creation that marks the importance of worldly losses and injustices by standing in solidarity with those who suffer from them.

[12] Morrison 1982: 6–10. [13] Morrison 1982: 93.
[14] Plato, *Republic*, 598b, trans. Hamilton and Cairns 1961: 823.
[15] *Republic* 10.601–606, 3.394–399. [16] Halliwell 2002; Griswold 1981: 141; Janaway 1995: 5–6.

viewing to action. Second, in order to be genuine, pity must feel for the objective losses and sufferings of others, not simply their subjective experiences of suffering. Augustine notes that now, in contrast, "I have more pity for the sinner getting enjoyment from his sin than when he suffers torment from the loss of pleasure which is ultimately destructive." Pity for others "takes its rise in that stream of friendship" (*illa vena amicitiae*; *conf.* 3.2.3) which Augustine has just been exploring in Book 2's reflection on the stolen pears (see *conf.* 2.4.9 to 2.8.16). Genuine friendship, like genuine pity, is a great good, yet one that can be perverted (*conf.* 3.2.3): "by some inclination in itself friendship is twisted and torn away from its heavenly cleanness." So the goodness of the human capacity to feel with the sufferings of others is here warped into a tool for the inflaming of sinful lusts. Those whose loves are already misdirected are incapable of correctly perceiving the joys and sufferings of others and so are incapable of true pity.

It is the illusory character of this pity, both in terms of its detachment from action and its association with vicious desire, that is Augustine's real focus here, not the puzzle of pleasure in dramatic fiction; Augustine is not, after all, developing a reception aesthetics, and false pity is not confined to the theater but crops up in real life as well. Strikingly, Augustine's wanderings become more vivid and powerful for us through his own linking of them with the wanderings of Aeneas, and his lack of tears for his own fallen state more poignant juxtaposed with his tears for Dido. Pity for fictional tragedy serves here essentially as a stand-in for perverted friendship and, in fact, as a stand-in for the mystery of human sinfulness more generally. For, as Augustine writes in trying to understand how he could love his rather unmotivated act of theft, "the soul is guilty of fornication when she turns from You and seeks from any other source what she will nowhere find pure and without taint unless she returns to You" (*conf.* 2.6.14). It is not love of creation or of other human beings, or compassion for their sorrows, that constitutes this "fornication," but seeking from created reality what we can finally find only in God. At the heart of this fornication stands a perverse act of imitation; we seek to be independent of God and thus to be God: "thus even those who go from You and stand up against You are still perversely imitating You." So at one level Augustine's tears for Dido are false compassion because they are tears for a fictional character. At a deeper level they represent a compassion that is false because it fails to grasp the genuine needs of others.[11] And this failure of compassion is itself a

---

[11] Nor are the genuine needs of others purely otherworldly, as Martha Nussbaum argues. From her perspective, Nussbaum 2001: 552, Augustinian love "is committed to denying the importance of the worldly losses and injustices to which my neighbor may attach importance"; it is focused solely on

Italy" (*conf.* 1.17.27). "It was no wonder," he muses (*conf.* 1.18.28), "that I fell away into vanity and went so far from Thee, my God, seeing that men were held up as models for my imitation who were coved in shame if, in relating some act of theirs in no way evil, they fell into some barbarism or grammatical solecism." This critique of false exemplars is paired with a critique of false compassion.

It can in fact seem as though Augustine is counseling care for one's own soul over concern for others: "I was forced . . . to weep for the death of Dido who killed herself for love, while bearing dry-eyed my own pitiful state" (*conf.* 1.13.20). And it is true that Augustine mourns the fact that he was blind to the pitiful state of his soul. But this is neither a critique of compassion as such nor a counsel to place concern for the self before concern for others. The broader theme here is forgetfulness and illusion – forgetfulness of self that is also a forgetfulness of God and of real finite others, and illusions that aid in this forgetfulness.[10] It is not that these illusions feed passions that should rightly not exist, but that they misdirect our passions, they pervert our loves, so that we are unable properly to love God, or self, or neighbor. Augustine's education in rhetoric did this in presenting as authoritative not just gods who gloried in adultery but also rhetoricians who are more ashamed should they drop the *h* in *hominem* than should they hate a human being (*conf.* 1.18.29). In his tears for Dido he forgot to weep for the death he himself was suffering "through not loving You, O God, Light of my heart, Bread of my soul" (*conf.* 1.13.21).

When in Book 3 Augustine turns to the puzzle of why spectators take pleasure in tragic drama, he calls it lunacy that we want to feel the sorrow that comes from being moved by the sight of tragic suffering on stage. Rather than suggesting either that pity is in itself a form of weakness or that pity for fictional suffering can bring about a cleansing catharsis, Augustine argues that this is not properly pity at all (*conf.* 3.2.2): "How can the unreal sufferings of the stage possibly move pity? The spectator is not moved to aid the sufferer but merely to be sorry for him." Genuine compassion, on the other hand, is "by no means" to be shunned (*conf.* 3.2.3): "the sorrows of others must move our love." Why, then, is this not genuine pity or compassion? Obviously, in some sense it is not genuine because it is pity for the fictional suffering of fictional characters. But this does not yet really get at what is at stake here. Rather, Augustine points beyond this to two other factors. First, this pity is truncated from action; it exhausts itself in feeling rather than playing its proper role in moving the spectator from

[10] Gregory 2008: 280–83.

must be "that by which all souls universally are redeemed, and without which, therefore, no soul is redeemed" (*civ. Dei* 10.32). Instead, they offer one way for the elite, and another, which is actually either only a partial liberation or in fact a form of enslavement to evil, for the rest. They take up a paternalistic stance that countenances deception.

The elitism of Platonic philosophy is rooted in its pridefulness. The Platonists are proud of their superiority to the common people. Ultimately, they trust for their salvation in themselves and their own philosophic virtue (*civ. Dei* 10.27). Hence it is no surprise that they are unable to identify Jesus Christ with the "principle" that they speak of as the Son. Blinded by pride, they despise the notion of God appearing in humble flesh and dying on a cross. "It was because of his pride that Porphyry did not understand this great mystery: the pride which our true and gracious redeemer brought low by His own humility when He revealed Himself to mortal men clothed in the mortality which he assumed" (*civ. Dei* 10.24). They are repulsed by the notion of God in flesh because they are repulsed by humility itself. They cannot grasp that divinity could be revealed in an act of compassionate solidarity with what is most weak and lowly, in stretching out a hand "to the fallen and helpless" (*civ. Dei* 10.24). They can make sense of principles to be grasped by contemplation or spirits to be manipulated by theurgic practices, but not of the humiliation of the incarnation. For the Platonists, mimetic reversion to the Divine requires that the soul ascetically strip "itself of finite reason, of temperament and emotion, and of concern with material things and of ties to finite historical situations."[17]

Christianity, in contrast, does offer a universal way for the liberation of the soul, that is, a way by which all souls may be liberated. It is a way that purifies the whole person, not separating the intellectual from the spiritual soul or the soul from the body (*civ. Dei* 10.32). And it is a way that does not differentiate the wise and educated from the simple. It is folly to those who think themselves wise and strong by their own achievement, since it is a path of admitting one's inability and accepting assistance: "this is the grace which heals the weak, who do not proudly boast a false blessedness of their own, but rather humbly confess their own true wretchedness" (*civ. Dei* 10.28). In worship, Christians assemble together to rehearse the humility of God incarnate, human copy returning to divine exemplar through divine love, not human achievement.[18]

---

[17] Morrison 1982: 28.
[18] On the centrality of humility in Augustine's theology, see Rist 1994: 190 and Dodaro 2004: 72–114.

4 PREACHING HUMILITY

As John Cavadini has shown, the sermons of Augustine are a powerful instantiation of this humility. In contrast to difficult works like *The Trinity* (*Trin.*), in which Augustine's rhetorical virtuosity is clearly evident, in his sermons we see Augustine using a simple homiletic style specially designed to reach a heterogeneous audience. In a culture in which rhetorical prowess was the sign of membership in an educated noble elite and a way of expressing social distance from the masses, "Augustine's renunciation of the intricate, jeweled rhetorical style ... was itself a kind of social statement."[19] His key move is to position himself not as authoritative master but as fellow student, fellow inquirer, fellow listener to Scripture. All may partake in a common *quest* for understanding; inquiry rather than understanding becomes key. Even the uneducated may participate in a kind of "exotericized" Neoplatonic quest for spiritual vision. This is possible not because the listeners somehow acquire the culture of the elite, but because they inquire in faith, and "faith is the indwelling of Christ, who is the loftiness of God made lowly."[20] Augustine thus rhetorically humbles himself in imitation of the humility of Christ in order to enable his hearers humbly to accept the humble Christ in whom the glory of a compassionate God is revealed. Here, too, Augustine praises the insight of Neoplatonic ascent while stripping it of its elitism and thus radically transforming its basic shape; because God is revealed in Christ as compassionate and self-humbling, God is to be found not via philosophical achievement but via an imitation of divine compassion and humility.[21]

It should, then, come as no surprise that the theme of the theatrical character of the liturgy is also quite marked in Augustine's sermons. The sermons rhetorically embody Christ's humility even as they urge the people assembled together, elites and masses, literate and illiterate, humbly to receive the grace that is the universal way of salvation. In his sermons Augustine often returns to the theme of the perverse mimesis of pagan theater in contrast to the holy mimesis of Christian liturgy. The juxtaposition is particularly vivid in sermons preached in honor of the martyrs or on the occasion of martyr passions. Again and again Augustine speaks of what it means to watch, to be a spectator. To be a spectator is not, for Augustine, to be detached or uninvolved. Rather, what Augustine emphasizes is that the spectator is in a receptive position, determined first by what he or she *sees* rather than by what he or she

---

[19] Cavadini 2004: 69. [20] Cavadini 2004: 79. [21] Dodaro 2004: 31.

*does.*²² In priding themselves on their own abilities, the Platonists have failed to grasp the dependent character of their own achievements; they are blind to the fact that it is what they have seen that has determined their agency. The spectator is powerfully remade by what is seen and felt (*s.* 301a): "Compare with this holy spectacle the pleasures and delights of the theater; there the eyes are defiled, here the heart is purified; here spectators are to be praised, if they become imitators, while there the spectator is base, and the imitator infamous."²³ Augustine chides his hearers for failing to see that they cannot attend the pagan spectacles and remain untouched by them; they will be drawn in and reformed after the image of the exemplars before their eyes. To think that one is immune from this perverse influence is another form of pride, that mysterious sinfulness that seeks to declare independence from God. Thus Augustine's good friend, Alypius, thinking that he had conquered his own passion for gladiatorial games and could witness them without danger, "opened his eyes and was stricken with a deeper wound in the soul than the man whom he had opened his eyes to see got in the body... [His soul's] courage had so far been only audaciousness, and it was weak because it had relied upon itself when it should have trusted only in You" (*conf.* 6.8.13). It is because we resist dependence on God that we are capable of preferring perverse over truly good exemplars and of becoming increasingly blind to the beauty of the good. The Christian should, then, immerse herself in holy spectacles that constantly nourish this vision and love of the God who "condescends to dwell in the union of all and in each person," in order "to see him as he can be seen and to cleave to him." In response to this condescending God, "we offer to him, on the altar of the heart, the sacrifice of humility and praise, and the flame on the altar is the burning fire of charity" (*civ. Dei* 10.3).

If watching violent death in the gladiatorial arena poses such dire danger to the soul, how is it that holy spectacles that bring the violent deaths of the martyrs before the eyes of Christians can be cleansing to the soul? Tertullian had celebrated the glory available to Christians through a difficult public death, with public infamy winning divine fame. Appropriating the Roman valorization of heroic suicide, he cast Christian martyrs as exceeding these heroes by dying for truth rather than falsehood. As G. W. Bowersock starkly

---

²² A preoccupation with the gaze was another common feature of Christian critiques of pagan spectacle. See Castelli 2004: 114–16 and Leyerle 1993, whose feminist analysis turns Chrysostom's critique of voyeurism back on himself.
²³ Trans. Hill 1994.

puts it, "Tertullian's position is that of an old Roman pagan."[24] It is thus hardly surprising that Tertullian can glory in the spectacle of Christian martyrdom. Augustine, in contrast, emphatically repudiates voluntary martyrdom and the ethic of glory that animates it. His subversion of pagan spectacle must be subtler and more radical than that of Tertullian.

What Augustine does is to set up a contrast between the eyes of the body and the eyes of the mind, the materially minded and the spiritually minded (*s.* 51.2; trans. Hill):

> The materially-minded look on, and think how wretched and unfortunate those martyrs are, thrown to wild beasts, beheaded, burned with fire, and they are filled with detestation and horror. Others, however, look on, as do the holy angels also, and don't fix their attention on the mangling of bodies, but instead marvel at the completeness of faith. A splendid spectacle offered to the eyes of the mind is a spirit whole and unbroken while the body is torn to pieces. That is what you people gaze on with pleasure when the accounts of such things are read in church. After all, if you didn't form some sort of picture of what happened, it would mean you weren't listening at all.[25]

In one sense, of course, all are now "viewing" the sufferings for the martyrs with the eyes of the mind, since Augustine's hearers have now to do with accounts of martyr passions rather than the actual events themselves. Yet even when it comes to liturgical recollections of martyrdom, Augustine distinguishes between materially minded and spiritually minded viewers. The materially minded in this instance don't glory in bloodlust, as do spectators at gladiatorial games, but they fail to see what is exemplary in that which is set before their mental gaze. The spiritually minded are those who have ascended from carnal images of cruelty and suffering to the hidden spiritual reality of complete faith and unbroken spirit. They grasp in the passion of the martyrs what in truth is offered for their imitation, and they respond with pleasure, a pleasure that initiates the process of their own conformity to exemplary faith and fidelity. This is once again Augustine's appropriation of Platonic corrective reversion from material images to inner *rationes* to spiritual Forms, but the eyes of the mind are now the eyes of faith; spiritual vision is made possible by humbly receiving the gift of faith and is therefore available also to the humble, not just to philosophers.

---

[24] Bowersock 1995: 63
[25] Trans. Hill 1991; discussed in Castelli 2004: 105, 124–25. See also *s.* 280.2, in celebration of the birthdays of the martyrs Perpetua and Felicity.

5 PAGAN EXEMPLARITY

When it comes to pagan virtue, many interpreters emphasize what seems to be the bottom line for Augustine: that the apparent virtues of those who are ignorant of the true God are in fact vices rather than virtues (*civ. Dei* 19.25). Others, such as John Rist, qualify this conclusion, noting that Augustine "seems to recoil from condemning them outright as vicious," considering pagan virtues "sterile," and "hence not good, but not explicitly bad either." Whereas Cato and Lucretia turn out on Augustine's account to have had viciously mixed motives, "at least Regulus emerges from the text as a hero." Hence, Rist concludes that "there are indeed pagan virtues – perfect of their kind but rare – but as a rule pagans are both unjust and unjustified."[26] Does Regulus really emerge from *City of God* as a hero? As we shall see, it is indeed possible to answer in the affirmative, but only by recognizing that heroism is itself problematized. Robert Dodaro rightly points out that when Augustine sets up the contrast between true and false virtue, he is following Cicero in thinking of virtue primarily in terms of courage; *virtus* is manliness, *vir*-tus.[27] Seeing this allows us to see just how provocative it is for Augustine to insist that true virtue – true courage – is humility. In the absence of humility, "virtue" can only be an illusion of order created by one vice assuming control over other vices; not true courage which accepts the most humiliating of deaths but a kind of bravado that seeks glory in death. Yet one of the most fascinating aspects of Augustine's account of pagan virtue is his affirmation that that these splendid vices can nevertheless offer a positive example for Christians. This stands in striking contrast to Augustine's treatment of pagan theater, where his counsel to Christians is *not* to look, *not* to become spectators, because to look is to become open to having one's loves contaminated and reoriented. Augustine treats the glory of the Roman empire and of Roman heroes, in contrast, as serving the citizens of the Eternal City according to God's purposes, so that they, "in the days of their pilgrimage, should fix their eyes steadily and soberly on those examples and observe what love they should have towards the City on high, in view of life eternal, if the earthly city had received such devotion from her citizens, in their hope of glory in the sight of men" (*civ. Dei* 5.16). Here it seems that Christian love for the City of God is to *surpass* and *outdo* pagan love for the earthly city, such that pagan examples become a legitimate object of spectation and emulation even if not a perfect exemplar. In order to reconcile this with Augustine's critique of the splendid

---

[26] Rist 1994: 172. [27] Dodaro 2004: 55.

vices, we must dig into the details of Augustine's accounts of Regulus, Cato, and others.

Augustine's account of Regulus comes in the middle of Book 1, in the context of a discussion of persecutions endured by Christians. Regulus offers a parallel pagan example, a "noble instance of the willing endurance of captivity for the sake of religion" (*civ. Dei* 1.15). Having taken an oath to return to captivity in Carthage if he failed in a mission to persuade the Romans to return Carthaginian prisoners, he first deliberately thwarted that mission and then voluntarily returned to Carthage in fulfillment of his oath, whereupon he was tortured to death. This is persecution and death endured "for the sake of religion" because an oath is a promise witnessed by the gods; the one who promises invites divine punishment should she break her oath. Augustine certainly treats Regulus' actions as praiseworthy. "Rightly indeed," he notes, "do the Romans praise a virtue greater than such misfortune." And in a later chapter, he adds that "among all their praiseworthy and illustrious men of outstanding virtue, the Romans offer no one better than this man" (*civ. Dei* 1.24). Yet at the same time he contrasts Regulus' courage with true virtue.

Significantly, the overall point of the Book 1 discussion is not to offer an assessment of Regulus nor of pagan virtue as such, but to undermine the logic of pagan criticisms of Christians. If the gods are worshipped in order to secure prosperity in this life, the case of Regulus shows how groundless such a hope is; if the gods are instead worshipped for the sake of prosperity in the next life, not because they assist their devotees in avoiding disaster in this life, then it makes no sense to claim that disaster has come upon Rome because Christians have abandoned pagan worship. Embedded within this is a defense of the exemplarity of Christian saints together with an exhortation to Christians to refrain from the crime of suicide. The example of Regulus serves this purpose too; over against Cato, Regulus refused suicide and so showed truer courage. The key question lurking here is not just what enables a person to stand firm in the face of death, but, more significantly, what allows a person to stand firm in the face of humiliation and dishonor. By committing suicide, "heroes" like Cato reveal the fact that they have not in fact overcome their fear. As Dodaro writes, "while appearing courageous, Roman heroes fear death in the guise of defeat or dishonor."[28] To die dishonorably was to forfeit the immortality available through glory. And it was finally this glory that lent Roman heroes their courage, their manly virtue.

---

[28] Dodaro 2004: 56.

The example of Regulus, then, together with that of other pagan heroes who refused to commit suicide when conquered, can spur Christians on (*civ. Dei* 1.24): "if the bravest and most distinguished men, defenders of an earthly fatherland and of their gods – false gods, certainly; but they were not false worshippers, for they indeed kept their oaths most faithfully: if these could ... when conquered by their enemies, refuse to smite themselves ... then how much more will Christians, worshippers of the true God, who aspire to a supernal fatherland, abstain from this crime!" If even pagans can avoid the temptation to commit suicide, all the more so should Christians be able to do so. This is a striking form of mimesis, which works in part through contrast and in part through assimilation. As we saw above, the verbal and liturgical mediation of martyrdom fostered, even if did not ensure, spiritually rather than materially minded viewing of the sufferings of the martyrs. So here as well, the fact that pagan examples are set before Christian eyes by Augustine's text is crucial to the possibility of grasping what is in fact exemplary in them rather than becoming trapped in the carnal images perceived by the outer eye. For the outer eye is easily deceived and led astray; Alypius thought he was immune from the bloodlust of the arena, but opened his eyes to his immediate downfall. What Augustine offers is a sight that comes from words, almost a kind of *ekphrasis*. As his words emerge from faith, so they carry with them something of the spiritual vision of faith; Augustine is able to single out those aspects of pagan heroism that are truly exemplary and to distinguish these from the dross that might otherwise confuse and mislead.

6 LOVE OF GLORY

When Augustine returns in Book 5 to the theme of pagan virtue, he does so in the context of a discussion of the merits by which the ancient Romans deserved, God permitting, the expansion of their empire. Drawing especially on Sallust and Virgil, Augustine argues that the ancient Romans were driven by a desire for Roman glory (*civ. Dei* 5.12): "in short, because they deemed it ignoble for their fatherland to serve and glorious for it to rule and command, the first object of all their desire was freedom, and the second mastery." This love of liberty was later displaced by the love of domination and then, as wealth led to enervation and public spiritedness gave way to a focus on private interest, by love of luxury. At times Augustine writes as though it is the love of domination which is most especially to be equated with the desire for glory, as when he says (still 5.12) that "once they had achieved freedom, however, so great a desire for glory then arose that liberty seemed to them too little by itself, unless they also sought dominion over others." This is not, though, a shift from love of liberty to love of glory, but rather a further expression of the same love of glory; having achieved liberty, the desire for glory was no longer satisfied with freedom from servitude but sought a fuller expression in domination. And the desire for private glory remained the driving force even as wealth fed avarice and luxury, only that in this context many sought honor and glory by fraud and deceit, rather than through deeds of valor and courage. For Sallust, as Augustine notes, the key contrast between men of virtue and the base is that the former seek glory and honor "the true way," by "good arts," rather than deceitfully. Expanding on this, Augustine writes that "good and base men alike desire [honor, glory, and power]; but the former – the good man, that is – strives after them by the true way. This way is virtue, by which he endeavours to possess what he seeks: that is, glory, honour, and power." Virtue here – and we should be reminding ourselves that this is Ciceronian virtue, manly courage – is not an end in itself but a means, a way to what is truly prized and sought. Cato, though, seems to transcend this, in that Sallust says of him that "the less he sought glory, the more it followed him." This, then, seems to be the pinnacle of pagan virtue – not simply through the love of praise to overcome other vices, but to perceive that the love of praise itself is a vice. Augustine seems to credit at least Cato and Horace with this realization (*civ. Dei* 5.13). For the most part, though, the Romans – as did Cicero, for instance – saw nothing amiss in the desire for glory, and indeed sought to arouse it in order to motivate others to set aside their private interests and perform courageous deeds in service of the commonwealth.

What, then, of Cato, who rightly discounted the judgment of other men and rested in his own consciousness of *deserving* that honor, or of Regulus, who accepted an ignominious death? Were they truly virtuous? Even if we bracket the matter of Cato's suicide, which shows that he feared a death that signaled defeat, we are left with a point that Augustine drives home most clearly in Book 19 (*civ. Dei* 19.25): "Some, indeed, suppose that the virtues are true and honourable even when they have reference only to themselves and are sought for no other end. Then, however, they are puffed up and proud, and so are to be adjudged vices rather than virtues." While Augustine appears to be saying here that choosing virtue for its own sake is prideful and vicious, in fact the claim being made is that even when virtue is sought *with reference only to the agent him or herself*, rather than for the sake of winning praise and glory from others, it is nevertheless corrupt. It is in fact only a further exacerbation of the way in which fallen human beings are curved in on themselves, *curvatus in se*. Cato and Regulus were in fact still pursuing glory, although glory in their own eyes rather than those of others. Regulus, for instance, grasped that in fact breaking his oath would be a greater dishonor than dying at the hands of his enemies, even if he could not trust that his countrymen would recognize that fact. That which allowed even these pinnacles of pagan virtue to act as they did was their consciousness of their own virtue, their sense of self, their pride.

This pride-supported courage in the face of death stands in contrast with the example of the apostles and martyrs. In preaching Christ they were met with low esteem, hatred, persecution, and torture, but this did not deter them. Nor was it self-esteem, the consciousness of their own courage, which made them strong in the face of these trials. In fact the apostles and martyrs were honored by the Church, but they did not act as they did for the sake of winning that glory – here Augustine subverts not simply pagan heroism but also Tertullian's reading of Christian martyrdom. Instead, Augustine writes (*civ. Dei* 5.14): "they did not rest in that glory as if it were the virtue which they sought as their end. Rather, they referred that glory itself to the glory of God, by Whose grace they were what they were." It was God's grace, not their own strength, which made the martyrs capable of holding fast to the faith in the face of humiliating death.[29] In accepting and acknowledging this grace, they were not turned in upon themselves in pride but opened up to the love of God and others. The glory they receive was passed on to God to whom it was properly due, not kept as a private possession. Likewise, the love with which they loved God was passed along to others (*civ. Dei* 5.14): "And with that same spark they kindled the hearts of those in their care, so that they also burned with the love of Him Who, again, had made them what they were."

In the theater of liturgy Christians are made participants in a holy mimesis of God, together with the apostles and martyrs imitating the divine humility and compassion. Turned toward God, the love at the heart of our being works to reunite copy with exemplar. True virtue, then, must be directed toward our true final end, and this is not our own glory but rather God (*civ. Dei* 5.12): "For no virtue is truly such unless it is directed towards that end in which man's good – the good than which nothing better exists – is found." But as we saw above in considering Augustine's affirmation of compassion, to be turned toward God is not to be turned away from the world or away from other people. Rather, we learn to love the world as God's beloved creation; loving God, we love as God loves, in the self-emptying love that we witness in the incarnation. "His position grew like a

[29] Dodaro 2004: 29.

pearl around his central, granular insight: we are part of the world, and we are in a way the vehicles of God's love for the world, vessels of the world's redemption... In terms of marriage and human sexuality, in terms of the mixed nature of the church – in case after case, Augustine encouraged Christians to move towards deeper commitment to 'worldly' affairs, and to distinguish themselves from those who would seek to escape this condition."[30] This is not a love that turns away from this world and its sufferings and losses, but which inhabits and embraces it.

7 CONCLUSION

Augustine, then, finds pagan sages and heroes finally incapable of recognizing their own radical dependency on God in a way that opens them up to compassionate love of the world. In denigrating the humility of the incarnation, they close themselves to the grace that would allow them to recognize the dependent character of their own agency and reach out to lift up the needs and cares of dependent others. But in closing, we might ask, how is it then ever possible to receive the humility of faith? How, in the face of the powerful sway of corrupt pagan loves, can the holy spectacle of Christian worship lure human desire toward the truly good? After all, "more are lovers of the evil blandishments of vice than of austere virtue" (*civ. Dei* 2.19), even if Augustine also claims that "so great is the force of probity and chastity that the whole, or nearly the whole, of humankind is moved to praise them" (*civ. Dei* 2.26). Dodaro comments: "it is through their faith in this mystery [of the incarnation] that believers receive Christ's gift of humility." But a few sentences later it appears that humility is itself a prerequisite for accepting the truth of the incarnation: "Augustine insists that humility is required for submission to the truth of the incarnation."[31] Despair might conclude this to be a vicious circle that renders faith and humility equally inaccessible. In fact, though, it is yet another respect in which human pride is chastened in its desire to control and define the workings of grace. Augustine's *Confessions* witnesses to the priority of grace, at work in him long before his conversion and baptism; as James Wetzel has shown, only in retrospect does Augustine find it possible to trace the beginnings of faith.[32] There is indeed a world of difference between the glittering pagan virtues which rely on the self to create order in the soul and transcend the limitations of finitude and the true if struggling virtue that relies on God and compassionately embraces suffering. But there is finally

---

[30] Mathewes 2007: 90.   [31] Dodaro 2004: 97.   [32] Wetzel 1992: 168.

no bright line to mark off graced from ungraced, even if Augustine gave way at times to the temptation to try to provide one. Hence, we should not map the divide between splendid vice and true virtue onto a contemporary distinction between Christian and non-Christian or Christian and secular. In the end, Augustine not only holds up pagan heroes for corrective Christian emulation, but – despite his own dismissal of the possibility of true pagan virtue – gives us grounds to keep looking for pagans who do after all see the beauty of a self-emptying compassion, who do recognize in some form the dependent character of their own agency, just as Christians continue to recognize their own sinful pride. That the unbaptized, the faithless might after all be capable of humility and compassion means not that independent human agency is, after all, able to achieve some measure of either faith or virtue. Rather, it means that grace is already at work in them, preparing the ground for the conversion of perverse to holy mimesis.

CHAPTER 7

The psychology of compassion: Stoicism in City of God 9.5

Sarah Byers

Questions about the role of compassion in civic life, and especially in legal contexts, seem particularly germane to us at the beginning of the twenty-first century. Yet as Martha Nussbaum has reminded us, analysis of the issues involved goes back to the ancient world, with Seneca in particular offering a somewhat sophisticated distinction between mercy and compassion, and seeking to foreground mercy in an account of the worthiness of those who receive it.

Augustine famously attacks the Stoic denigration of compassion in *City of God* 9.5, and this comes as part of his larger engagement with the Stoic theory of affectivity in *City of God* 8.17, 9.4–5, and 14.8–9. But it is rather difficult to tell just where he stands in relation to the Stoics, given that he employs Stoic criteria for evaluating emotions, as well as Stoic distinctions and definitions, while chastising the Stoics.

In the particular case of compassion, the fact is that Augustine has a nuanced account which is sensitive to the distinctions and concerns that inform the Stoic position. A close examination of *City of God* 9.5 and of Seneca's *On Clemency*, in conjunction with Augustine's statements about compassion, affectivity and dignity in other works, will allow us to track his appropriation and rejection of various elements in the Stoic account, and to identify his reasons for doing so. That in turn will make it possible for us to address the question of whether his account has anything important to offer that is lacking to the Senecan mercy ethic.[1]

---

[1] The Stoics consistently call compassion (*ho eleos, misericordia*) a morally bad emotion (*DL* 7.123; *Tusc.* 3.9.20). Seneca agrees, in keeping with this tradition, but he adds that there is a virtue called mercy (*clementia*), which is not the same as compassion. See below on Seneca.

I *CITY OF GOD* 9.5 AT FIRST GLANCE, AND UNDER CLOSER SCRUTINY

Augustine claims in *City of God* that his endorsement of compassion (*misericordia*) is the distinctive feature of his ethics as compared to Stoicism, which regarded compassion as a morally bad species of emotion (*civ. Dei* 9.5):

> Within our [Christian] discipline, then, we do not so much ask whether a pious soul is angry, as why he is angry; not whether he is sad, but whence comes his sadness; not whether he is afraid, but what he fears. For I do not think that any right-minded person would condemn anger directed at a sinner in order to correct him; or sadness on behalf of one who is afflicted in order to liberate him, or fear for one in peril, lest he perish. The Stoics, indeed, are wont to reproach even compassion; but how much more honorable it would have been for the Stoic in Aulus Gellius' story [*NA* 19.1] to be moved by compassion for a man in order to liberate him, than by [preliminary[2]] fear of shipwreck.

The beginning of this passage sounds, *prima facie*, like a mischaracterization of the Stoic account. When Augustine says that in the system *he* subscribes to, emotions are classified as good and bad based on what makes them arise (*quare, unde esse*), he seems to cast the Stoic theory as one which fails to distinguish emotions by their objects. That would be wrong, given that the Stoics distinguish emotions in just that way, as we shall see momentarily. The passage also makes the reader wonder whether Augustine is proposing an ethic of altruism rather than a desire–satisfaction model of classical eudaimonism, when he contrasts compassion and fear for another with fear for oneself. And generally this looks like an unreflective and undefended dismissal of Stoic concerns about "compassion."

However, the fact that this work is apologetic means that there is more here than meets the eye. As Runia has noted in another context, Augustine only selectively acknowledges his indebtedness to earlier authors and schools of thought.[3] It is not uncommon in late antiquity that the names of authors or schools are omitted when being drawn upon positively. Apparently the rationale for this is that it allows the raw truth of the ideas to stand out, rather than appearing parochial, as the mere opinions of one particular school or individual philosopher. In contrast, names are named when there is a perceived need to warn the reader about errors. So although

---

[2] On Augustine's use and understanding of the Stoic category of preliminary passion (with responses to Sorabji), see Byers 2003.
[3] Runia 1993: 322–23; cf. Runia 1995: 120–21, 125.

Augustine is clearly critical of something in the Stoic account, we would be ill-advised to assume that he is rejecting it *tout court*.

Indeed, when we look more closely at this statement of Augustine's in the context of *City of God*, we notice a few things which require us to revise our initial impression. First, it no longer appears that Augustine has misunderstood the Stoic picture. He is not mistakenly accusing the Stoics of failing to distinguish between emotions caused by different objects. He refers to the Stoics' distinction between two kinds of sadness, of desire and of joy – morally good versions of these and morally bad ones (*civ. Dei* 14.8, referring to the *eupatheiai* and *pathē*) – and shows that he not only understands but also adopts the Stoic definition of the latter in *City of God* 8.17, when alluding to the *daemones* of Apuleius: they are, he notes, subject to passions (*passiones, turbationes mentis*; *deo Soc.* 13). He proceeds to define passion according to Zeno of Citium's definition of *pathos* as it appears in Cicero: a movement of the rational soul or mind that is contrary to right reason.

The Stoic distinction of emotions by their objects is described at some length in the *Tusculan Disputations* (*Tusc.*),[4] which Augustine uses as his touchstone for talking about affectivity in *City of God*. In the Stoic theory, which has been much discussed because it is formally similar to the cognitive model of emotional therapy found to be clinically effective today, fear is caused by the judgment that something bad will happen; grief, by the judgment that something bad has happened. Desire results from the belief that something good is to be attained in the future; joy is caused by the judgment that something good has happened. (These four emotions are genera, and each has its own species-emotions, which are about specific kinds of circumstances and objects.) What makes emotions good or bad is the truth or falsity of the judgments. Since the Stoics held, in Socratic fashion, that only moral goods are true goods, because only virtue makes humans happy, the paradigmatic wise person feels precaution at the prospect of doing something morally wrong, because this is a true evil, rational desire at the prospect of doing a virtuous act in the future, joy reflecting on the attainment of some virtue or the completion of some virtuous act. These are the only kinds of emotions the sage has (though these, again, are genera encompassing a number of species); there is no grief for the paradigmatic sage – and thus no compassion, a species of grief – because a wise person, being wise, never commits moral evil. In contrast, failure to train one's thoughts in the truth results in morally bad emotions caused by rash and erroneous judgments that loss of a job, the death of relatives, winning the lottery, getting a promotion, and so on are important

---

[4] See *Tusc.* 3.11.24–25, 4.6.11–4.7.14.

for happiness. Emotions caused by these false beliefs are craven fear, exhilaration about frivolous matters, a kind of lust for accidentals, and a grief that hysterically overreacts to things which are really irrelevant to happiness.

The Stoics labeled the two kinds of emotion, and also each particular emotion, in order to avoid confusion. Emotions caused by false judgments are given the technical name "passions" (*pathē*; Cicero: *perturbationes*, Seneca: *affectus*). Those caused by true judgments are the "good emotions" (the *eupatheiai*; Cicero: *constantiae*). To the *pathos* that is fear they gave a different name from the *eupatheia* that is fear (*phobos* vs. *eulabeia*), and so on. In Cicero's doxography of the Stoic account in the *Tusculan Disputations*, he did the same in Latin.[5]

So Augustine's references to *pathos* and to *eupatheia* in the *City of God* indicate that he is familiar with this division of emotions according to cause. Moreover, he makes clear that the whole purpose of his bringing it up in *City of God* 14.8 is to show that although scripture uses different terminology, it respects a conceptual distinction between emotions that are morally good because they conform to right reason, and those which do not. The works of secular literature, which also imply a conceptual distinction without following the Ciceronian–Stoic terminology, are brought in as a way of lending prestige to the colloquial usage of the scriptures.

Second, upon closer inspection of the passage about compassion in *City of God* 9.5, it becomes clear that Augustine is not presenting a dichotomy between altruism and self-interest when he commends compassion and fearing for someone else, rather than fearing for one's own life. He speaks of compassion in order to "liberate" and fear lest someone "perish." But a parallel passage in *City of God* 14.9 also speaks of "liberation" and "perishing," and the words have a moral sense: liberating from vice, perishing through sin. The surrounding context is one in which virtue and vice are the intentional objects of emotions[6] when Augustine says: "But they [the citizens of the city of God] are moved by these emotions not only on their own account but also on account of those whom they desire to be liberated and for whom they fear lest they perish. They grieve if these do perish, and rejoice if they are liberated." So here in *City of God* 9.5, he is

---

[5] The *pathē/perturbationes* are: undue exultation = *hēdonē/laetitia*; irrational desire = *epithumia/libido*; craven fear = *phobos/metus*; grief = *lupē/aegritudo*. The *eupatheiai/constantiae* are: joy = *chara/gaudium*; rational desire = *boulēsis/voluntas*; fear of doing wrong = *eulabeia/cautio*. See DL 7.110–14, 7.116; *Tusc.* 3.11.24–25, 4.6.11–4.7.14.

[6] See before and after the quote, in *civ. Dei* 14.9: joy in good works, fear of being tempted, desire to persevere in virtue, grief over sins committed by oneself and by others, desiring to make others virtuous, fearing that others might be led astray from holiness, grieving at others' lack of righteousness.

saying that it would have been better, and consistent with the Stoic concern for virtue over everything else, had the Stoic in Gellius' story been concerned with saving others from vice,[7] rather than having preliminary fear for his own physical life: "But how much more honorable it would have been for the Stoic in Aulus Gellius' story to be moved by compassion for a man in order to liberate him, than by fear of shipwreck." His point is that the former is a true good, the latter an "indifferent" according to the Stoics. He is not advocating that we supplant care for ourselves with care for others, but pointing out that virtue and vice per se, regardless of whose they are, are proper objects for good emotions: we should be moved by these emotions not only on our own account but also (*non solum verum etiam*) on account of others.

But this last point does seem to signal a substantive disagreement with the Stoics. He implies that the Stoics, by their proscription of compassion, show that they are not concerned about virtue per se; they hold instead to an arbitrary distinction between the virtue of others and the virtue that is one's own. Compassion is a species of grief for the Stoics, grief over another's perceived subjection to evil, but the Stoics do not want the sage to grieve even when others are in *true* evils. Given their definitions of *pathos*, *eupatheia*, and grief, they would need to provide some further reason for concluding that the sage should not have compassion for someone else's moral failings; this reason seems to be lacking.

Does the Stoic circumscription of affective involvement to the case of oneself lack philosophical justification? In order to assess the fairness of this charge, we need to explore in greater detail the third *prima facie* plausible interpretation of *City of God* 9.5 that we noted above. Does Augustine unreflectively dismiss the Stoics' concerns about compassion (*misericordia*)? They think that they have good ethical reasons for saying that compassion is an ethical failure. Does Augustine make an attempt to understand those reasons, and does his advocacy of compassion adequately respond to them?

2 SENECAN CLEMENCY, AUGUSTINE'S APPROPRIATION

Augustine signals his engagement with the actual reasons that the Stoics (proximately Seneca) offered for their rejection of compassion in two ways

---

[7] Note that the designation *adflictus* [*homo*], which Augustine uses in *civ. Dei* 9.5's "compassion with the afflicted in order to liberate him," can mean ethically base, ethically wretched. It is apparently in this sense that he uses it.

in *City of God* 9.5. First, he shows that he is responding to their account when he stipulates that it is good to commiserate (*contristari, conpati*) with one who is afflicted. This is a rather precise reference to a particular aspect of the Stoic theory. (We may take it as non-controversial that Augustine knew his intended audience – principally, the intellectual elites of the late Roman empire – would be familiar enough with Seneca to pick up this precise allusion.[8]) For Seneca does not actually disavow all mercy, but he does ban commiserating with the people whom we succor; by his choice of words, Augustine shows that his disagreement is directed specifically at this ban. Second, he alludes to Seneca's theory when he says that "this impulse [the *misericordia* that I am advocating] complies with right reason when shown in such a way that justice is preserved" (my translation). He alludes here to the virtue of mercy or "clemency" (*clementia*), which Seneca extols when begging the eighteen-year-old Nero to remain a merciful emperor. It is by definition a tendency to pardon from punishment in such a way as to preserve the principles of justice (see Seneca, *clem.* 1.18.1–2, 2.6.1).

Now this latter allusion that Augustine makes is particularly interesting. For it apparently means that the "compassion" he is advocating conforms to at least one of the criteria for Senecan clemency. (From now on, I will refer to Seneca's particular construal of mercy as "clemency," in order to avoid confusion.) It therefore behooves us to investigate exactly what those criteria are and how they play out in Seneca's picture.

Clemency, for Seneca, is an inclination to dispense with *rules* governing retribution, whenever circumstances indicate that the *principles* of justice have been satisfied – typically, that the guilty party has learned his or her lesson. Moral reform is the end of punishment, rather than simple retribution. This implies two things. First, it is acceptable to remit punishment if the end is attained before the sentence commences, or during its duration. Second, it is a lack of virtue to continue punishing after there is evidence that the guilty party has learned the lesson (see *clem.* 2.7.4, 1.2.2, 1.14.1, 1.17.1). Specifically, it would be acting from the passion of anger, a species of the passion of desire. (Anger is a desire for revenge in which inflicting suffering is erroneously conceived of as a good by the angry person.) So, clemency is a sensitivity which recognizes *reasons* for lightening a sentence: the perpetrator is old and frail, and so learns his lesson with a light punishment because he feels it more, or repentant, or young and

---

[8] On the intellectual audience of the *City of God*, see Brown 2000: 298ff.; on knowledge of more than a few works of Seneca as part of a respectable education, see Augustine's disappointment about Faustus in *conf.* 5.6.11.

inexperienced and thus was acting from only partial voluntariness and hence easily regrets the action (*clem.* 2.7.2, 1.1.4, 1.15.7). What the Stoics decry is mercy which acts from feelings of pity without regard for justice: sentimental people want to throw open the doors of prisons and let out the most harmful criminals if once they see them cry (*clem.* 2.4.1). This Seneca calls "compassion" (*misericordia*).

Now that the terms are defined this way, clemency looks more attractive than compassion, at least for anyone who, like Augustine, is committed to a "virtue ethics" in which deviations from justice are conceived of as harmful both to the person who is treated unjustly, and also to the (moral character of the) one who acts unjustly.

In fact, Augustine does uphold the criterion of justice in mercy, not only in *City of God* 9.5 but also in letters dealing with the punishment of criminals. When an amateur admirer of Stoicism writes to him expressing the opinion that criminals should not be subjected to beatings simply because the scars are always a fresh source of shame, he is presumably paraphrasing Seneca in one of his softer moments (*clem.* 1.17.3). (Book 1 of *On Clemency* contains Seneca's own opinions and pragmatic arguments in addition to the more doxographic Stoic material; this softness about the shameful scars is apparently one example.) Yet Augustine retorts along more orthodox Stoic lines that even though physical torture "is abhorrent to our way of thinking,"[9] this being why he did not want to press criminal charges against the suspected instigators of a church burning and looting in his diocese (who would have been subject to torture under interrogation), it is essential nonetheless that some punishment be meted out (*ep.* 104.17; cf. *ep.* 91.9). For known culprits, he advocates a heavy fine as punishment, instead of beating, because of "compassion." However, he presumably thinks that if this less severe punishment cannot be secured from the magistrate, the full force of the law is preferable to a simple pardon (see *ep.* 104.1, 104.5–7; cf. *ep.* 10*.4). Recall that this is how Augustine understood his own childhood beatings, which he compared to torture (*conf.* 1.9.14–16). Our ultimate criterion of compassion should not be what the perpetrator of crime finds desirable (*cupire*), he tells us, but his true, that is, moral, interests (*ep.* 104.8). The compassion (*misericordia*) that he advocates is therefore highly moralizing and subject to the demands of justice, as is Seneca's clemency.

---

[9] The translations and paragraph numbering used for these and other letters cited herein are from Atkins and Dodaro 2001. Seneca similarly associates the use of torture with the vice of cruelty: see *clem.* 1.13.2, 1.25.2, 2.4.2.

3 THE HEART OF AUGUSTINE'S CRITIQUE

Given Augustine's agreement with Seneca that mercy should be answerable to justice and aim at the moral correction of others, why does he insist on calling it "compassion" (*misericordia*), a term by which Seneca denoted an emotion that shows a lack of consideration for justice?

His disagreement with Seneca is primarily directed at his restricting of clemency to a *virtue*, a disposition toward external actions. The problem is that Senecan clemency is an officious set of deeds (Seneca: *facta, opera*), without affective involvement. It has the look of an efficient bureaucrat dispensing aid to anonymous recipients.

Augustine wants clemency to be defined as a feeling, a good emotion accompanying a tendency to do good works. He thinks that in this life the sage will be subject to "feelings of this kind even while performing morally appropriate actions" (*bona officia*; *civ. Dei* 9.5; my translation; cf. *s.* 259.3, 259.5). (Note that *officia* is Ciceronian Latin for Stoic *kathēkonta*, appropriate actions.) When he homes in on the idea of commiseration (*contristari, dolere, conpati*) and defines compassion (*compassio*) as "a kind of fellow-feeling in our hearts for the misery of another which compels us to help him if we can" (still 9.5; trans. Dyson), Seneca's notion of clemency is being supplemented, not rejected altogether.

Augustine uses the term *misericordia* to allude to a clement emotion because it is the only term that the Stoics have for an *affect* that is concerned with the ills of others. But his compassion is clement. Similarly to the case of the *pathē–eupatheiai* discussion in *City of God*, Book 14, Augustine is adhering to some elements of a conceptual distinction between two senses of mercy, while denying that one need stick to the technical Stoic names for particular affects.

When he says that it would have been "much more humane" (*longe humanius*) for the Stoics to have praised a feeling of compassion (*misericordia*), he is directly responding to Seneca. His point is that Seneca did not go far enough when he said that clemency is a particularly humane *virtue* (*ex omnibus virtutibus nulla humanior*; *clem.* 1.3.2).

4 STOIC INCONSISTENCY AND ISOLATIONISM

But why is it so important to Augustine that we sympathize with the people whom we help? First of all, he thinks, the Stoics offer no convincing reason for omitting an emotion of clemency from the set of *eupatheiai*, and so their position is not actually derived from the principles of Stoic virtue ethics – principles that Augustine himself generally likes.[10] Seneca's claim that feeling compassion is bad because it clouds the judgment (*clem.* 2.5.5, 2.6.1) looks to be a smokescreen; for if the Stoics really thought that feelings *necessarily* involve clouded judgment, they would not have the class of *eupatheiai* at all. This is Augustine's point when he says that sharing in the sadness of someone else can "comply with reason" (*civ. Dei* 9.5). The other Stoic argument, namely that affective clemency is impossible because this would be a kind of grief and the sage by definition can have no grief, since he never does anything morally wrong (*clem.* 2.5.4), is irrelevant to the question of grief over *others'* moral failures.

Similarly, Augustine implies, the Stoic prohibition on suffering with the sufferer conflicts with the ancient claim that virtue is to be valued for its own sake. As noted earlier, when he points out in *City of God* 9.5 that a concern for virtue as such will entail that the sage has emotional reactions to others' virtue or lack thereof, he implies that the sage *ought* to have concern for virtue as such – but that the Stoic sage does *not* actually have this. If the Stoic sage cared about virtue for its own sake, the matter of whether a virtue or vice were one's own or another's would not be a deal-breaker. If what distinguishes a good emotion (*eupatheia*) from a bad one (*pathos*) is that its object is a true (moral) good or evil rather than an indifferent, it is not clear what is grounding the stipulation that the good or evil must be a good or evil "of one's own." In the play *Medea*, for instance, when the chorus feels sorry for Medea that she is becoming morally worse by killing her own children, why could this not be a *eupatheia*?

Hence, the prohibition on grieving over another person's moral vice looks arbitrary. It is not derived from the distinction between moral value and everything else, which is supposed to be the basis for classifying emotions as good or bad. What, then, is motivating the Stoic proscription?

Augustine concludes that it must be the simple fact that grief is an interior pain, a suffering with the sufferer. He thinks that the Stoics reason as follows. Most people are morally bad, and their lives are messy because of their own wrongdoing and the vicious behaviors of others around them, which entice them to become worse. Consequently, a sage who opened herself up to being emotionally impacted by others' moral failures would potentially be continually upset. Continually being lacerated by such pains is not an enjoyable, healthy way to live (cf. the characterization of the Stoics in *s.* 348.3). So the sage's emotions should only be about her own moral states. This will reduce

---

[10] He does not like their claim, however, that we can (now, after the Fall) become virtuous without the aid of grace.

the amount of affective pain that the sage experiences to a negligible amount. The sage can fear the approach of moral evil, but it must be her own moral evil, and the real reason for this (unacknowledged by the Stoics yet nonetheless motivating them) is that since she is careful about her associates and the places she frequents, she will not often have to fear doing anything wrong. Similarly, it is *because*, being wise, she has no actual misdeeds and so never does grieve that the Stoics can allow that she could in principle be upset by a true evil (her own non-existent vice).

Now the Stoics, by their own eudaimonism, are not supposed to think that the avoidance of pain and attainment of pleasure are proper goals of ethical action; that would be Epicureanism. By refusing to make clemency a *eupatheia* the Stoics are (in fact though not officially) advocating a version of Epicurean freedom from the painful emotions of fear and grief (*ataraxia, aponia*).[11] They have thereby contradicted their own principles.

So Augustine thinks the Stoics are trying to avoid pain caused by involvement with others, and that their refusal to allow for clement grief is just one tell-tale example. Hence in *City of God* 9.5 he mentions grief at another's moral baseness alongside of frustration and fear provoked by others' actual or possible bad moral states – neither of which is pleasant. If Christian affective life is distinctive for unambiguously allowing that virtuous emotions can be elicited by others' lack of moral progress, then the reason this differentiates it from Stoicism is because the Stoics, in their desire to be rid of painful emotions, have adopted an all-out self-sufficiency. They have a fear of intimacy, because of the vulnerability to pain that it brings.

Augustine's reading of the Stoic allowance of suicide is another clue that we are right to think that this is the charge he wants to level against the Stoics in regard to compassion. Suicide is fleeing from pain, he thinks, as in the case of Cato, motivated by a desire to escape a painful feeling of embarrassment. It is because he thinks that this is a kind of weakness, a hedonistic motivation, that he makes Job a foil to Cato: "our opponents do not wish us to give preference over Cato to that holy man Job, who chose to endure... rather than to be rid of all his sufferings by putting himself to death" (*civ. Dei* 1.24).

By thus pinpointing Augustine's critique as a charge of pain-avoidance, we can make an important clarification of his excoriations of Stoic

---

[11] See Epicurus, *Key Doctrines* 10, Long and Sedley 1987: 21D; *Letter to Menoeceus* 127–32, Long and Sedley: 21B; and *DL* 10.136. Augustine knows the Epicurean position via Cicero; see, e.g., *Tusc.* 3.15.32–33, 3.6.12, 3.17.38.

"hardness" (*duritia*). He sometimes uses this term to designate their refusal to make clemency an emotion.[12] Commentators have often seen this, and his references to *apatheia* in *City of God* 14.9, as an accusation by Augustine that the Stoics advocate total insensibility.[13] The hardness Augustine has in mind, however, is more narrowly a reference to painful other-regarding emotions. When he mentions two senses of *apatheia* in *City of God* 14.9, namely, the Stoic sense of absence of morally bad emotions and the Cynic and Skeptic sense of total insensibility, he does not mistakenly identify the Stoic position with *apatheia* as insensibility. Moreover, as we have already seen above, he shows awareness of the Stoic *eupatheiai*, including painful fear, and he does not accuse the Stoics of withholding pleasant other-regarding emotions from the sage.

Notice that Augustine's charge of pain-avoidance also seems to gain some support from the Stoic list of species-*eupatheiai*, or morally appropriate emotions, a list which Augustine himself presumably did not know. These affects are simply named, but not elaborated upon, by Diogenes Laertius in his *Life of Zeno* (*DL* 7.116). Interestingly, some of these seem to be responses to others' good moral characters – "respect," "affection," "goodwill" (these must be references to the moral characters of others, since all *eupatheiai* are about true goods and evils, moral states). So the Stoics seem to allow fond feelings provoked by others' moral goodness, but deny the sage a painful feeling of grief over others' moral badness. Since even the morally good person is "external" to the sage's own moral character, the allowance of the former and the exclusion of the latter from the sage's affective life looks arbitrary, unless it is motivated by a desire to avoid pain, as Augustine implies.

The inconsistency whereby the Stoics fall into Epicureanism matters to Augustine not simply for reasons of logic. He cares about it because it also frustrates his effort to convert pagan intellectuals to Christianity – one of the main purposes of *City of God*. He regards the Stoics' aspiration for self-sufficiency (*sibi sufficere*) as their tragic flaw (*civ. Dei* 10.18), since it prevents them from accepting the idea that they need grace in order to be happy. But now we see that he thinks that their program of insulating the self from others is rooted in an aversion to affective pain. And an unwillingness to acknowledge that affective pain is a regular part of life, even for the sage, will

---

[12] *ep.* 104.17; *mor.* 1.27.54. In the latter text, his general point seems to be that just because compassion is a feeling, this does not indicate that it is necessarily evidence of moral *miseria*.

[13] O'Daly 1999b: 156 presents Augustine as only seeing one meaning of *apatheia*, viz. mental inhumanity and bodily insensitivity, and rejecting this supposedly Stoic view; cf. King 2009: 3.

prevent the Stoics from acknowledging that the world is fallen, which will again prevent them from accepting the need for a savior.[14]

It should be noted that there is an additional Stoic argument which is relevant here, though it is not mentioned in Seneca's treatise on clemency or addressed by Augustine. It is attested in Epictetus and mentioned in Seneca's *On Providence*, but without an explicit connection to the case of compassion (see, e.g., *ench*. 17, 30–31; *prov*. 5.7ff.). This argument would hold that compassion is wrong because to be upset about things over which we have no control – specifically the moral choices and voluntary states of others – is a kind of rebellion against providence. Had Augustine taken this up, he would have responded by saying that God merely allows other people to err morally (*ench*. 11); such things are merely known and tolerated by God, who does not actually make them happen.[15] So, grief or fear could be an appropriate emotion caused by the judgment that something ought not to have been done by someone else, or would not have happened in the ideal (pre-Fall) world. It need not be taken as tantamount to rebellion.

5 LESSER GOODS OR PREFERRED INDIFFERENTS?

But there is, of course, a second reason why Augustine disagrees with the Stoics about compassion, hinted at in *City of God* 9.4. While the charge of inconsistency applies to their handling of others' moral states as objects of emotion, Augustine goes farther than the Stoics would have gone had they been consistent. He wants to allow the physical and social hardships of others, and not merely their moral states, to be proper objects of compassionate clemency. This is anticipated in *City of God* 9.4, where he follows Cicero in arguing that the Stoics' "preferred indifferents" (*commoda*) are not merely indifferent to our happiness but are actually good ontologically and consequently can be good for us, that is, real contributors to human happiness.

Thinking back to the case of the looters and their possible torture cited in Section 2 above, we can add, then, that Augustine diverges from the Stoics in his underlying assumption that torture is truly bad for the one being

---

[14] As I argue elsewhere (Byers, forthcoming), this desire to emphasize the sage's experience of affective pain also seems to be the reason why in *City of God* 9 he uses technical words for Stoic passions (*perturbationes, passiones*) to refer to preliminary passions, distinguishing them from consensual emotions by placing them in the *animus* rather than the *mens*: he wishes to emphasize that in a preliminary passion, the sage is (without his own consent) subject to pain of the same quality as in a passion proper.

[15] Compare Wetzel's discussion (2001: 53) of "predestined" versus "merely foreknown" events.

tortured because of the harm done to the body and the accompanying physical pain – and not merely bad because it shows a moral defect in the torturer. It is thus something to be feared and sorrowful about, even if this is preferable to no punishment at all. (Again, this is similar to Augustine's understanding of his own childhood beatings.)

A parallel case of compassion-advocacy serves to confirm this reading of Augustine on torture. In the year 428, merchants were abducting free people from the African coast and selling them as slaves in other provinces. Augustine says he feels the urgency of working to free these people; if he and the other bishops do not have compassion on them, he worries, then no one else with enough clout to be effective will do so. And yet, compassion should extend to the slave traders themselves. He desires that the culprits should not face the possibility of punishment according to the applicable law, since it prescribes beating by whips tipped with lead. Instead he again advocates a fine (*ep.* 10*.3–4). He wants to use the law to *frighten* the traders into stopping the practice, but he wants as well to prevent the punishment of beating from being applied; the "abominable" culprits of illegal human trafficking, as well as perpetrators of sacrilege and theft, should also be shown compassion (*misericordia*; see *ep.* 10*.3–7, 104.6, 104.16–17).

The difference between Augustine and the Stoics very clearly lies in Augustine's statement that the trafficking of free people is a real "evil that has befallen Africa," one meriting grief: on hearing about the misfortunes of these people, "hardly one of us could restrain his tears." It also lies in his belief that the use of lead-tipped whips on criminals is an evil to be avoided because it can lead to death, the destruction of the body (*ep.* 10*.4). It is the Stoic refusal to call such things "bad" for the one who suffers them which prompts Augustine to say that Stoic ethics falls short in its failure to include *misericordia* (*ep.* 104.16–17).

6 HUMAN DIGNITY AND COMPASSION

If Augustine's claim that torture, beating, and kidnapping are to be feared and grieved over is not flowing from Stoic principles, what is its source? The answer surely lies in Augustine's account of human dignity. But here again, the question of precisely what differentiates Augustine's account from that of the Stoics will be complex.

Nussbaum has said that part of what motivated the Stoic repudiation of compassion was a respect for persons as dignified agents. Their view was strongly egalitarian and cosmopolitan, being rooted in a conviction that humanity has dignity by virtue of its power of choice (*prohairesis*).[16] According to this way of looking at things, compassion fails to give adequate attention to the natural dignity of the person, since it focuses on accidental features of the suffering person's life: on what has happened to someone, rather than on his or her rational capacity for moral choice.

It is true that in his account of clemency, Seneca implies that compassion devalues a human being. More precisely, the Stoic execration of compassion seems to be rooted in a refusal to identify a person with his or her bad fortune. Seneca speaks of self-congratulating pitiers who are averse to the people they pity. They shrink from contact with the handicapped, the elderly, and the destitute; they insultingly fling their alms while averting their glance. Apparently such people are repulsed because they make this false identification of "bad/repulsive circumstances" with "bad/repulsive human being." Perversely, they also *like* there to be needy people because it provides an opportunity for them to look compassionate and to feel proud of themselves for acting compassionately; they do not regard the recipients of their alms as equals, but inferiors (see *clem.* 2.6.2–3).

This Stoic point is insightful and again rather attractive, as was their earlier stipulation that compassion ought not violate justice. We might want to refuse to reduce a person to his or her bad fortune, just as we might want to resist the contemporary Anglo-American practice of identifying people with their accomplishments or lack thereof.

However, the viability of the Stoic attempt to articulate what *does* constitute human dignity is questionable. Here we must disagree somewhat with Nussbaum's interpretation. The whole emphasis of Stoicism implies that the dignity of a person resides in her acquired *moral character*. In Epictetus, the Stoic author who makes extensive use of the notion *prohairesis*, the term does name a rational power for making moral choices (that is, the power of assent used in the context of action, e.g., *disc.* 1.17.21). But it also not uncommonly names the dispositions acquired through the repeated use of this power; thus *prohairesis* has qualities – it is either morally beautiful or morally ugly (e.g., *disc.* 2.10.27–29, 3.1.40). More importantly, the power is valuable *as instrumental* for attaining the right kind of disposition, for becoming beautiful. What makes human beings preeminent in the scale of nature is not Kantian autonomy, but rather their ability to conform their choices to the order of things established by God (*disc.* 2.10.1–3). *Prohairesis* is valuable as a necessary condition for becoming "free" in the normative sense of freedom from vice and error, for forming a disposition by which we

---

[16] Nussbaum 2001: 357, 359, 364.

always choose in accord with right reason (e.g., *disc.* 1.4.18, 1.8.16, 1.12.10; *ench.* 30).[17] What inspires respect for the minds of others is their virtue. When the Stoics execrate compassion, then, they are not making a choice between identifying someone with her bad fortune and her rationality per se, but a choice between identifying someone with her bad fortune and the way she uses her rationality, that is, her moral character.

Now, if we are going to identify people with one or the other of these, the latter is obviously preferable as a basis for talking about human dignity. But of course the down side is that those with bad character will now be in a social position analogous to that of female or otherwise "defective" infants in Graeco-Roman societies, who could be taken out of the community and left to die by exposure. If you act contrary to virtue, the fact that your action was preceded by assent means that you acted from a failure to reason well, and also that you acted voluntarily; if you persist in making bad choices, you will certainly lack the (moral) identity which merits admiration. It is by no means clear from what the Stoic sources say that I still owe you "respect." It would, moreover, be irrational for me to have solicitude for your moral excellence, given that your state is voluntary. We are lacking a robust account of inalienable dignity that can unfailingly command respect for people simply as human and solicitude for their moral good, even when they have voluntarily made themselves bad. And so we are lacking an account of dignity that can adequately ground an *egalitarian* Stoic mercy, such as Nussbaum wants.

Seneca, it is true, does sometimes *seem* to verge on a theory of natural rights: human beings ought to love the whole human race as they love themselves, and even slaves should receive clemency (*humani generis comprendens ut sui amor; clem.* 1.18.1–2, 1.11.2). Notice, though, that he does not justify this "ought" by referencing the human power of assent. Instead, he implies or says two things. First, he implies that since society is universally morally corrupt and mired in error (e.g., *otio* 8, *ira* 2.10.3–4) everyone who does wrong is acting from partial ignorance and therefore deserves a lessening of their punishment, that is, clemency. Second, he appeals to our social nature, to the fact that the safety and well-being of the individual is tied up with that of the community (*clem.* 2.6.2, 1.3.2).

However, the normative force of this latter appeal to the common good, which looks *prima facie* as though it might foreground human rights, is attenuated because its foundation is unclear. In the same breath that Seneca says that slaves are due clemency, he indicates that people of higher social

---

[17] Cf. Gill 2006: 98.

rank (freed and free-born) and "honorable" people (*honesti*) are more worthy of clemency (*clem.* 1.18.1). (Similarly Cicero, working off Stoic material and seeming to lead up to the claim that all humans are equal in worth, in the same breath makes the relevant kind of equality the equality of friends equal in virtue; *leg.* 1.12.34.) Again, when Seneca explains how the good of the individual is supposed to be complemented by the good of the community, it turns out to be a mixture of pragmatism and Epicureanism. You ought to be clement because when you are clement toward inferiors, you are clement toward yourself: you ensure that they will not rise up against you. Thus can your life be pleasant, untroubled by disturbances (*clem.* 1.3.2, referencing Epicureanism; cf. *clem.* 1.5.1ff.). And running throughout Seneca's reasoning is the self-referential argument that if we do not act from clemency, we are likely to act from a desire for revenge, which is bad for our own moral character (see, e.g., *clem.* 2.6.2–3). That argument requires, and makes, no appeal to the dignity of the recipient of clemency.

In Augustine we find the same insight that we do in the Stoics, namely that there is a kind of feeling sorry for unfortunate people that is in fact demeaning and perversely desires the bad fortune of those whom it pities: "We should not wish people to be wretched so that we may be able to practice works of mercy ... If you render service to a wretched person, perhaps you desire to extol yourself before him and wish him to be subject to you, because you have benefitted him. He was in need, you bestowed; you seem to yourself greater, because you bestowed, than he on whom it was bestowed. Wish him [instead] to be your equal ..." (*ep. Jo.* 8.5).[18] The compassionate clemency that Augustine advocates therefore seeks to avoid this. But unlike the Stoics he grounds compassion in a robust account of human dignity.

It is at first tempting to think that this dignity is established by the importation of Christianity; after all, Augustine singles out compassion as a hallmark of the Christian approach to thinking about affectivity in ethics. But this is not quite accurate, if by "Christianity" we understand only biblical praise for clothing the naked, feeding the hungry, teaching the ignorant, visiting prisoners and so on (e.g., Matt 25:31–40). Augustine does not arrive at his concept of compassion simply by tacking divine commands onto Stoic ethics. Certainly such biblical injunctions are relevant to his way of thinking about the matter. But he actually thinks that such precepts are implications of the basic principles of natural law.[19] He also thinks that

---

[18] Trans. adapted from Browne and Myers 1888.
[19] See the discussion and texts in Byers, forthcoming.

God, who gives these divine commands, essentially is the immutable and intelligible standard of morality, along the lines of Plato's Forms. It follows from both of these facts that Christian ethics does not constitute a neat, separate category of ethical norms that Augustine need not defend, beyond saying that they are particular to his own religious preferences. According to the demands of his own theory, he must give a philosophical account of how biblical recommendations are compatible with classical virtues (such as justice), which are applications of stable standards or Forms that exist inside the mind of God (including Justice).

Augustine does this, of course, with an ontological account of the person that is deeply indebted to Plotinus. This account can explain why it is appropriate to fear or grieve when the goodness of the soul or body is threatened or damaged. The soul is a superior kind of substance (immaterial), and its intellect is an image of the mind of God, making it immortal. This ontological excellence justifies lamentation at the fact that people "defile" their souls with moral evil. Augustine says, for instance, that we should grieve over the dead souls of those who killed the African martyr Perpetua (*s.* 280.2). But that event was about two hundred years earlier; so the idea is apparently that even though it is useless to grieve, since the perpetrators cannot be saved from vice now, the self-inflicted damage to their souls is still worth lamenting. In Augustine's Plotinian account, the body also has "borrowed" dignity, given that the intellectual soul forms the body. So it is not irrational to grieve if someone is tortured, or their corpse is left to be eaten by birds – nor to fear that these things may happen, or get angry at people who want to do them. Relevant claims specific to Augustine's Christianity are amplifications of these ontological points. By the manner in which the incarnation was accomplished, God showed the goodness of both male and female bodies (see *s.* 51.3, on the incarnation of a male body through a female body); redemption itself was motivated by the beauty of the soul (*ep. Jo.* 8.10.2–3, 9.3.2, 9.9.2).

This goodness of the soul and therefore of the body, which is prior to and distinct from acquired moral character, allows Augustine to say that human beings deserve a certain protection and respect, regardless of what they have done – although he does not apply the principle as widely as we might like.[20] His wider concept of dignity thus overlaps somewhat with more recent discussions of respect in personalist schools born from

---

[20] See Rist 1994: 235–39 on Augustine's failure to say that we should work toward the abolition of institutionalized slavery and torture.

phenomenology (rooted in Kant),[21] although he justifies it differently. Compassion is compatible with and even demanded by the virtue of justice, because the ontological excellence of the person merits care and concern.

"Compassion in Christ," which Augustine thinks should supplant officious Senecan clemency (*ep.* 104.17), is therefore an empathetic attitude as well as an orientation toward clement action that preserves the principles of justice. Augustine's Christ is not Taylor's "non-Stoic" Christ; but neither does he operate from the "disengaged stance" which Taylor sees in the neo-Stoicism of early modernity,[22] and which Augustine saw in Senecan clemency. Christ looks like a Stoic sage, insofar as his feelings were according to right reason (*recta ratio*) and up to him: "His weakness derived from his power,"[23] since he had emotions only when he judged (*iudicare*) that they should be experienced. Yet Christ was sensitive, because he had perfect perception of how things ought to be, and of how they really are in the fallen world. He unambiguously had other-regarding emotions provoked by others' moral states – anger, fear, grief, and desire in reaction to others' potential and actual virtues and vices – and it pained him when others suffered from the physical effects of the Fall: death and other temporal afflictions (*civ. Dei* 14.9).

7 CONCLUSIONS AND IMPLICATIONS

Part of the appeal of Stoicism's cognitive psychology of the emotions is that it gives a relatively sophisticated ancient account of the relation between the emotional life of an individual and the good of others in society. If emotions are caused by voluntary assent to propositions, it is easier to hold someone responsible for the destructive societal effects of his rage, for instance, than it is if emotions are caused by non-rational psychological or bodily processes. Yet the Stoic proscription of painful other-regarding emotions such as compassion can be read as a reaction against the vulnerability that this link between the personal and the social entails. Rather than allowing ourselves to be saddened by the sadness of others, or made fearful by their fears, we should remember that other people are in the class of mere externals.

---

[21] Compare Spaemann's definition of forgiveness (2007: 232) as acknowledging that the person who has harmed us is more than this action of having harmed us; persons are not reducible to their moral actions or attributes.
[22] See Taylor 2007: 115–39.
[23] Here "weakness" refers to vulnerability to emotional impact from others.

In Augustine's schema, by contrast, the affectively healthy person ends up looking tougher than the Stoic sage, because more willing and able to bear affective pain. Clemency is not merely a disposition to do helpful things for others, but also to be sensibly affected by their suffering. Paradoxically, then, the toughness accompanies a general softness toward the condition of others. What prevents this softness from being mere sentimentality, as the Stoics feared, is the same thing that provides a more adequate justification for the "clement" actions of the sage than Seneca himself had provided. Augustine's ontological account of the human being as good, in which the body is an image of the soul and the soul is an image of God, gives him a way to speak of compassionate clemency as a proportionate, and thus just, response to bodily and moral afflictions.

The principle benefits of the Stoics' cognitive psychology can therefore be retained, despite the different ontological context in which judgments are carried out. In Augustine's system, the emotion of compassion is caused by an accurate judgment about the loss of real goods, although he will want to retain a distinction in magnitude between temporal goods and eternal goods (virtues). Hence accountability for emotions will still be possible, and the use of cognitive therapies will still be relevant.

CHAPTER 8

Augustine's rejection of eudaimonism

Nicholas Wolterstorff

Augustine's ethical thought in his late writings is commonly interpreted as a creative version of eudaimonism. To cite just one recent example: Martha Nussbaum, in *Upheavals of Thought*, says that Augustine developed a version of eudaimonism that is "a major philosophical achievement and a decisive progress beyond the Platonic accounts, because it situates ascent within humanity and renounces the wish to depart from our human condition."[1] In this essay I shall argue that in his late writings Augustine, rather than developing a distinct version of eudaimonism, broke with eudaimonism and constructed the outlines of an alternative.[2]

To prepare for this argument, I must explain what I take eudaimonism to be. I will have my eye on ancient versions of eudaimonism, since it is those that Augustine broke with. Whether my description fits all present-day ethical orientations described by their proponents as "eudaimonist" is an issue that I will not enter – though my impression is that it does.

There were two dominant versions of ancient eudaimonism, the Peripatetic (Aristotelian) and the Stoic. I intend my description to fit both. Though Augustine was acquainted with both, the version that dominated his milieu and that he most often explicitly engaged was the Stoic. Accordingly, after laying out what I take to be common to all ancient versions of eudaimonism, I will highlight some of the distinctives of the Stoic position.

My description of ancient eudaimonism will not be idiosyncratic; here and there I will quote reputable present-day scholars of ancient thought to show that it is not. The interpretation I offer is not, however, entirely non-controversial; I will flag what I judge to be its most controversial point.

---

[1] Nussbaum 2001: 547.
[2] I discussed Augustine's rejection of eudaimonism in chapter 8 of Wolterstorff 2008. There the discussion was part of a larger discussion aimed at showing that ancient eudaimonism did not and could not provide a framework for a theory of rights. In this present essay I will here and there take over a sentence from that earlier discussion.

My claim that Augustine rejected eudaimonism does not hang on whether or not I am right in attributing this "controversial" point to the ancient eudaimonists.[3]

I WHAT IS EUDAIMONISM?

Begin with the vexed question of what the ancient writers meant by the term *eudaimonia*. Though this is usually translated into English as "happiness," everybody who comments on the matter observes that the present-day meaning and connotations of "happiness" are quite different from those of the ancient Greek *eudaimonia*. In a previous writing of mine on these matters I said that "The ancient philosophers who wrote in Greek used the term '*eudaimonia*' for the well-lived life."[4] I now think I was mistaken about that.

In the *Nicomachean Ethics* (6.5; 1140a 25–28) Aristotle remarks: "It is thought to be a mark of a man of practical wisdom to be able to deliberate well about what is good and expedient for himself, not in some particular respect, e.g. about what sorts of things conduce to health or to strength, but about what sorts of things contribute to the good life in general." From the context in which this passage occurs we know that it's about the character of the *eudaimôn* life that the man of practical wisdom deliberates. Earlier in the *Ethics* (*eth. Nic.* 1.1; 1095a 17–20) Aristotle had taken note of disagreements concerning what constitutes *eudaimonia*. Those of "superior refinement" identify it with living well and faring well; others "think it is some plain and obvious thing, like pleasure, wealth, or honour."[5]

I think the most plausible interpretation of these remarks is that, in speaking of the *eudaimôn* life, ancient writers meant *the good life*. Concerning the overall character of the good life, those of "superior refinement" said that it was characterized by living well and doing well;[6] others said that it was characterized by pleasure, wealth, honor, and the like. If this interpretation is correct, then it was a mistake on my part to say that the ancient writers "used the term '*eudaimonia*' for the well-lived life." They used it for the good life. When it came to debating the overall character of the good life, those of "superior refinement" held that it is characterized by

---

[3] A fuller description of eudaimonism than I give here can be found in chapters 7 and 9 of Wolterstorff 2008.
[4] Wolterstorff 2008: 148.
[5] I am using the translation by Ross, revised by Urmson, in Barnes 1984.
[6] In Annas 1993: 44, Annas translates as "doing well" what Ross translates as "faring well." I think that Annas is right on this.

living well and doing well; others held different views. But it is not the case that *eudaimonia* just *meant* "living well." Had the term meant that, Aristotle could have dismissed those alternative views as abuses of the meaning of the term.

Though our term "the good life" seems to me better than "the happy life" for translating what the ancients had in mind by "the *eudaimôn* life," it too has irrelevant and distracting connotations. I judge that our term, "the estimable life," comes closer to what they had in mind. The *eudaimôn* life is the estimable life. Concerning the overall character of the estimable life, those of "superior refinement" held that it is characterized by living and doing well. Of course Aristotle counted himself among these; he himself was of the view that the estimable life is the life of living well and doing well. He was joined in this by all the other ancient writers that we nowadays classify as eudaimonists.

In order to elucidate the force of this thesis of the eudaimonists concerning the estimable life, I must make some comments about the concept of life-goods. Every ethical system, whether embedded in the practices of a society or articulated by some theorist, employs the idea of certain states and events in a person's life as good *for* that person. Likewise every ethical system employs the idea of certain actions and activities on the part of the person as good *for* that person. My being of good health is one of the states in my life that is good for me; my listening to a good performance of a Beethoven string quartet is one of the activities that is good for me. Let's add that if some state or event, some action or activity, in my life is a good *for me*, then it is a good *in my life*; it is one of my life-goods.

Some of the states and events in a person's life that are good for him or her are *intrinsically* good; some are *instrumentally* good. So too for the actions and activities that he or she performs. Something is an instrumental good for someone just in case it makes a causal contribution to something else that is a good for him or her; something is an intrinsic good for someone just in case it's being good for her does not consist at all, or not only, in its being an instrumental good for her. If getting bifocal glasses would be good for me, it would obviously not be an intrinsic but an instrumental good; its worth for me lies entirely in the fact that bifocals will bring about the intrinsic good for me of being able to see better.

The distinction between instrumental and intrinsic goods makes reference to causation. A parallel distinction can be made concerning the relation among intended actions within the action-plans of persons. A person may intend to do something because he judges that performing that action will be a means to something else that he wants to bring about. Alternatively, he may do it not at all, or not only as a means to something else, but for its own sake; in the latter case, it is an end in itself in the structure of his actions.

It is commonly assumed nowadays by writers on these matters that something is good *for* someone just in case it contributes positively to his or her wellbeing or welfare. This seems to me correct. When we say such things as "Exercising regularly would be good for you" and "It would be good for me to get bifocals," we mean that exercising regularly would contribute to your wellbeing, as would getting bifocal glasses to mine. So let me use the term "wellbeing-goods" for the states and events, the actions and activities in a person's life that are good for the person.

The ancient eudaimonists all shared what I shall call the *activity thesis* concerning the estimable life. They all held that the estimability of a person's life is determined solely by the actions and activities to be found in that person's life; the states and events to be found in his or her life play no role in determining its estimability. Describing ancient eudaimonism in general, Julia Annas has this to say: "Happiness is . . . thought of as active rather than passive, and as something that involves the agent's activity, and thus as being, commonsensically, up to the agent. This kind of consideration would rule out wealth, for example, right away. Happiness cannot just be a thing, however good, that someone might present you with. At the very least it involves what you *do* with wealth, the kind of *use* you put it to."[7] She quotes Arius' paraphrasing of Aristotle: "[Since the final good is not the fulfilment of bodily and external goods, but living according to virtue], therefore happiness is activity . . . Happiness is life, and life is the fulfilment of action. No bodily or external good is in itself an action or in general an activity."[8]

What the activity thesis implies is that the eudaimonists made a sharp cut within a person's life-goods, distinguishing between those (actions and activities) that contribute to determining the estimability of the person's life and those (states and events) that do not contribute. The Stoics

---

[7] Annas 1993: 45. Here is what Cooper says on the same point (Cooper 1985: 189): "According to Aristotle's account, [external goods] are needed as antecedently existing conditions that make possible the full exercise of the happy man's virtuous qualities of mind and character. In each case the value to the happy man consists in what the external goods make it possible for him, as a result of having them, to do. Any value goods other than virtuous action itself might have just for their own sakes is denied, or at least left out of account on this theory."

[8] The passage from Aristotle that Arius was paraphrasing is to be found in *Nicomachean Ethics* 1.7; 1098a 16–19: "Human good turns out to be activity of soul in conformity with excellence, and if there are more than one excellence, in conformity with the best and most complete. But we must add, 'in a complete life.' For one swallow does not make a summer, nor does one day; and so too one day, or a short time, does not make a man blessed and happy."

canonized the distinction by refusing to call the latter *goods*, reserving that term for the former. They called the latter *preferables*; and these, along with what one might call *dis-preferables*, they called *indifferents*.

Every ancient eudaimonist would have agreed with Aristotle's formula, that the happy or estimable life is the life lived in accord with excellence or virtue. What the Stoics called *preferables* and what the Peripatetics called *natural goods* are the "matter" on which the virtues do their work. The virtues are habituated skills in assessing priorities among the actual and potential preferables in one's life and acting accordingly. Here is how Annas makes the point: "The indifferents – conventional goods and evils – have value for happiness only in being the materials for and context within which the virtuous life is lived. On their own they neither add to the happiness of a life nor subtract from it."[9]

The Stoic distinction between *goods* and *preferables* has been a source of perplexity to commentators ancient and modern. Cicero and Augustine were of the view that it was a purely verbal distinction. In *City of God* Augustine remarks that "when [the Stoics] say that these things are not to be called goods but advantages (*commoda*), we are to regard this as a dispute over words, not as a genuine distinction between things" (*civ. Dei* 9.4).

Two pages earlier Augustine had himself cited the reason that the Stoics gave for their distinction: "The Stoics refuse to call bodily and external things 'goods' (*bona*). Rather, they call them 'advantages' (*commoda*), because they consider that there is no good for man except virtue, and that this is the art of living well, which exists only in the mind." (still 9.4). What Augustine then proceeds to argue is that, in refusing to call "bodily and external things" goods, instead calling them preferables or advantages, the Stoics were departing both from ordinary usage and from the usage of the Peripatetics: "in this question, the Stoics are only taking pleasure in a novel use of words." No doubt Augustine was right about that last point. But from the fact that the Stoics were departing both from ordinary speech and from the philosophical speech of the Peripatetics, it does not follow that they were not marking out a genuine distinction with their idiosyncratic use of terms. They were. It was – so I suggested above – the distinction between those life-goods (actions and activities) that contribute to determining the estimability of a person's life, and those life-goods (states and events) that do not.

The question to consider is why the eudaimonists held the activity thesis concerning the estimable life. Why did they hold that it's only what a person does that counts toward determining the estimability of his or her

[9] Annas 1999: 43.

life, not what happens to the person, not how he or she fares? Perhaps there are passages in which one or another ancient eudaimonist directly addressed this question in its full generality. In the passages I know, the author contents himself with arguing against specific versions of the alternative: being wealthy does not contribute to the estimability of one's life, having honors bestowed on one does not contribute to the estimability of one's life, and so on.

For you and me, reading the ancient eudaimonists today, it's worth noting that Kant held a thesis similar to that of the eudaimonists but concerning the estimability of *persons*; what determines the estimability of a person is what she does, not the states and events in her life, no matter how good (preferable) those may be. What Kant held for the estimability of persons, the ancient eudaimonists held for the estimability of a person's life.

Let's move on to a second thesis embraced by the ancient eudaimonists. All ethical systems, in addition to employing the idea of states and events, actions and activities, in a person's life that are good *for* him or her, also employ the idea of acting so as to enhance the wellbeing of someone or other. And implicitly or explicitly they all propose one or more rules specifying which wellbeing-goods of which persons one may or should seek to bring about as an end in itself, and under what conditions and in what manner. Different views concerning such rules constitute one of the most fundamental points of difference among such systems. So the question before us is this: what is the rule, or what are the rules, that the eudaimonists proposed?

Consider the rule embraced by philosophical egoism: the only wellbeing-goods one should seek to bring about as an end in itself are one's own; only as a means to the enhancement of one's own overall wellbeing should one seek to bring about some wellbeing-good of another person.

Eudaimonism is similar to egoism in that it too is agent-oriented. The eudaimonists insisted, however, that not only is enhancing the wellbeing of another sometimes a means to enhancing one's own wellbeing; promoting another person's wellbeing as an end in itself sometimes enhances one's own wellbeing. Promoting her wellbeing is then not a *means* to enhancing one's own wellbeing but a *component* therein, a *constituent*. The ancient eudaimonists often cited friendship as an example. Overall wellbeing requires friends. Friends do sometimes seek to enhance the wellbeing of the friend as a means to enhancing their own overall wellbeing. In true friendship, however, one goes beyond that and seeks to promote the wellbeing of one's friend as an end in itself. Promoting her wellbeing is a component within one's own wellbeing, not just a means to enhancing it.

These observations led the ancient eudaimonists to the position that one may seek to promote the wellbeing of anyone whatsoever as an end in itself – provided that doing so promises to enhance one's own overall wellbeing. Call this the *agent-wellbeing proviso*. The fact that such-and-such an action would enhance the wellbeing of some other person is incomplete as a reason for performing that action. To get a complete reason one has to add that it would be a means toward, or a constituent within, the enhancement of one's own wellbeing.[10] It makes no sense, said the eudaimonists, to promote the wellbeing of another, whether as a means or as an end in itself, if doing so does not promise to enhance one's own overall wellbeing. No wise person would do such a thing.

I mentioned that though my interpretation of the ancient eudaimonists would not be idiosyncratic, it would also not be entirely uncontested. My attribution to them of the agent-wellbeing proviso is probably the most contested part of my interpretation.[11] In discussions of these matters, some have argued that though the Stoics probably embraced this proviso, Aristotle did not.

It has to be conceded that the evidence in Aristotle for the proviso is less decisive than the evidence for the activity principle. I know of no plausible alternative interpretation of Aristotle, however, nor do I know of any passage in Aristotle that contradicts my interpretation. Further, it seems to me the plain sense of a passage already quoted (*eth. Nic.* 6.5): "It is thought to be a mark of a man of practical wisdom to be able to deliberate well about what is good and expedient for himself, not in some particular respect … but about what sorts of things conduce to the good life in general."

I mentioned above that every ethical system proposes one or more rules as to which wellbeing-goods of which persons one may or should seek to bring about as an end in itself, and under what circumstances and in what manner. To my formulation of their agent-wellbeing proviso, the ancient eudaimonists would all insist on adding a point about *the manner* in which one should seek to enhance one's own wellbeing and that of others insofar as theirs is intertwined with one's own: one should always do so in accord with virtue. Thus it is that we get Arius' apothegmatic paraphrase of Aristotle, quoted earlier (see *eth. Nic.* 1.7): happiness "is living in accord with virtue."

---

[10] Compare the following passage from MacIntyre, preeminent among our present-day eudaimonists (MacIntyre 1999: 86): "What constitutes a good reason for my doing this rather than that, for my acting from this particular desire rather than that, is that my doing this rather than that serves my good, will contribute to my flourishing *qua* human being."

[11] I develop and defend my interpretation more fully in chapter 7 of Wolterstorff 2008.

Living in accord with virtue is what Aristotle has in mind in a well-known passage in *Nicomachean Ethics* 9.8, where he asks "whether a man should love himself most, or some one else" (1168a 28). Aristotle's answer to this question is not that a man should not love himself most. His answer is that it all depends on what one takes true self-love to be. By "lovers of self" most people have in mind those "who assign to themselves the greater share of wealth, honours, and bodily pleasure" (1168a 15). If that were what constituted love of self, then one should not be a lover of self. But this is a mistaken understanding of self-love, says Aristotle; what such people desire for themselves is not what is in fact best for them. Those who have proper love for themselves are those who desire to act nobly, that is, virtuously. They "busy themselves in an exceptional degree with noble actions [that] all men approve and praise, and if *all* were to strive towards what is noble and strain every nerve to do the noblest deeds, everything would be as it should be for the common good, and every one would secure for himself the goods that are greatest, since excellence is the greatest of goods. Therefore the good man should be a lover of self" (1169a 5–11). The estimability of a person's life is determined by the extent to which he acts virtuously. The true lover of self is the one who loves most of all his own virtuousness.

Let me now add two principles characteristic of the Stoics that are worth taking note of because of Augustine's aggressive attack on them. The Peripatetics held similar views, and Augustine's attack on the Stoic principles implies the rejection of the Peripatetic alternatives. But rather than formulate those alternatives here, I will mention them when they become relevant in the discussion.

The Stoics were well known in antiquity for developing a highly articulate theory of the emotions and for holding sharply defined views as to the place of negative emotions in the estimable life. It was their view that in the truly estimable life there would be no negative emotions – no fear, no grief, no regret, no remorse, nothing of the sort. On their theory as to the nature of the emotions, the only way to eliminate such emotions from one's life is to divest oneself from all attachments to, and desires for, that which is not entirely within one's own control, no matter how much "worth" any of that may have. The only good that is entirely within one's own control is one's own virtuous activity. So it is to this and this alone that one should be attached; it is this and this alone that one should desire. Let's call this the Stoic *principle of emotional detachment*.

Last, it was the view of the Stoics that it is possible here in this life, by ardent effort and practice, to live a life that is fully in accord with virtue – to live a life that is in every respect estimable. The Stoics called the person who so lived a *sage*. It's possible to become a sage. Not easy, but possible. It is Augustine's aggressive attack on this *possibility of becoming a sage* that calls it to our attention; otherwise it might well have slipped by one's notice.

2 AUGUSTINE'S REJECTION OF THE AGENT-WELLBEING PROVISO AND OF THE STOIC PRINCIPLE OF EMOTIONAL DETACHMENT

Assume that the characterization I have given of ancient eudaimonism is correct. Let us now track the course of Augustine's rejection. It was indeed a course, a process, not a single episode. Augustine rejected the agent-wellbeing proviso and the Stoic principle of emotional detachment in his writings of the 390s: *Confessions*, *Of True Religion*, and *On Christian Instruction*. His rejection of the activity thesis came later, as did his emphatic rejection of the possibility of becoming a sage. In *City of God* his rejection is complete.

In *Confessions* 10.4.5 Augustine says this:

> Let all who are truly my brothers love in me what they know from your teaching to be worthy of their love, and let them sorrow to find in me what they know from your teaching to be occasion for remorse ... [M]y true brothers are those who rejoice for me in their hearts when they find good in me and grieve for me when they find sin. They are my true brothers because whether they see good in me or evil, they love me still. To such as these I shall reveal what I am. Let them breathe a sigh of joy for what is good in me and a sigh of grief for what is bad. The good I do is done by you and by your grace: the evil is my fault; it is the punishment you send me. Let my brothers draw their breath in joy for the one and sigh with relief for the other. Let hymns of thanksgiving and cries of sorrow rise together from their hearts.[12]

Augustine's rejection of the Stoic principle of emotional detachment could not be more emphatic. The Stoics held that we are each to be emotionally invested only in our own virtuous activity and lack thereof, and that whether or not we act virtuously is entirely in our own hands; for the sage this meant freedom from all negative emotions. Augustine says that we are each to be emotionally invested in the virtuous activity and lack thereof of our fellows; we are to grieve over their sins and rejoice over the good they do. He is assuming, obviously, that one is to do the same for oneself.

Augustine's objection to the Stoic principle of emotional detachment in the passage just quoted is an ethical objection: we *should not* conform to the

---

[12] I am using the translation by Pine-Coffin 1961.

Stoic principle. There are other passages in which his objection is rather that success in trying to achieve such detachment is impossible. In *City of God* (*civ. Dei* 9.4), he reports the story told by the author, Aulus Gellius, about "a distinguished Stoic philosopher" who, when a storm came up that threatened to capsize the boat on which he was traveling, "grew pale with fear." When the storm had calmed, his fellow passengers asked how his fear comported with his Stoic convictions. His reply referred to what was by then a standard part of Stoic doctrine. Certain mental images – *phantasiae* – are such that when they strike the soul it's not in one's power to inhibit a reaction. "When these images come about as a result of terrifying and awesome things, they of necessity move the soul even of the wise man." What a person need not do, however, is "consent" to this reaction. The Stoics held that emotions involve consent; emotions are cognitive phenomena, not bodily reactions.

Augustine charges that this is a purely verbal distinction. What the philosopher felt was fear, Augustine insists, whether we choose to call it that or not; and since the Stoics agree that it is impossible to eliminate one's response to such *phantasiae*, it follows that they do not really think that we can eliminate negative emotions from our lives. Their claim that we can rests on a purely verbal distinction.

I am not persuaded. Let me put what I take to have been the Stoic point in contemporary terms. Physiological reactions are not to be identified with emotions. They do not involve concerns and judgments in the way that emotions do. What the philosopher experienced was a physiological reaction, not an emotion. The fact that he reacted in the way he did does not prove that he feared death. We would all have reacted in the same way, whether or not we feared death. It was just his physiology doing its work.

It's not clear to me whether or not the philosopher's claim was correct, that what he experienced was a physiological reaction and not an emotion, and that his reaction does not show that he feared death. But *contra* Augustine, I do not think the distinction between physiological reaction and emotion is purely verbal. If one thinks the philosopher's claim was false, one will have to find some other reason.

Let's return to Augustine's ethical objection to the Stoic principle of emotional detachment. The Peripatetics differed from the Stoics in holding that virtuous activity on one's part is not entirely up to oneself; it can be hindered in various ways by "external circumstances."[13] And it is appropriate to react negatively toward such hindrances. But Augustine neither says

---

[13] I discuss their views concerning such hindrance in chapter 7 of Wolterstorff 2008.

nor suggests that one should grieve over the sin of one's fellow when his sin hinders one's own virtuous activity. We are to rejoice over the good they do and grieve over their sin whether or not those have any effect on our own virtuous activity. Augustine's objection holds as much against the Peripatetic version of the principle of emotional detachment as it does against the Stoic.

What was it that led Augustine to break from the eudaimonists on their principles for the regulation of emotions? From *City of God* it's clear that the behavior of various biblical characters played a role in his rejection. The "citizens of the City of God" (*civ. Dei* 14.9) behold St. Paul

> ... rejoicing with those who rejoice and weeping with those who weep, troubled by fightings without and fears within, desiring to depart and be with Christ. They behold him longing to see the Romans ... They behold him jealous for the Corinthians ... They behold him suffering great heaviness and continual sorrow in his heart for the Israelites ... They behold him as he declares not only his pain, but also his mourning for certain persons who had sinned already, and not repented.

And they behold Jesus displaying

> ... emotions in circumstances where He judged that they ought to be displayed. For human emotion was not feigned in him ... He was grieved and angry at the Jews' hardness of heart ... He even wept when He was about to raise Lazarus ... [A]s his passion drew nigh, His soul was grieved. Truly, He accepted these emotions into His human mind for the sake of His own assured purpose, and when He so willed.

The brief clause in the passage quoted a few pages back from *Confessions* 10.4, "they love me still," indicates that something else was motivating Augustine's rejection of the eudaimonist principles concerning the regulation of emotions than just the behavior of Jesus, Paul, and other biblical characters. What led Augustine to reject both the eudaimonist principles concerning the regulation of emotions and their agent-wellbeing proviso was his being confronted by Jesus' second love command – "Love your neighbor as yourself." Jesus attached no proviso to his command to love one's neighbor as oneself; in particular, he did not attach the proviso that we are to seek the wellbeing of our neighbors as an end in itself only if doing so promises to be a constituent in our own wellbeing.

In Book I of *Christian Instruction* (*doc. Chr.*), chapter 22 and following, we can witness Augustine's struggle to incorporate the second love command into his thought. At the beginning of chapter 22 he summarizes what he has argued for in the book thus far. God alone is to be enjoyed.

"The rest are for use, that we may be able to arrive at the full enjoyment" of God. It's a theme found in several of Augustine's previous writings, though the way he develops the theme here is somewhat idiosyncratic. Augustine then asks whether the formula he has arrived at also holds for human beings (*doc. Chr.* 1.22.20): "it becomes an important question, whether men ought to enjoy, or to use, themselves or to do both. For we are commanded to love one another ..."

Having introduced the love command into his discussion, what Augustine then proceeds to do is significant for our purposes. At no point does he try to interpret the command so as to make it compatible with the agent-wellbeing proviso. Instead he struggles to interpret it so that it is compatible with his prior conclusion that God alone is to be enjoyed. The thesis at which he arrives is that "all things are to be loved in reference to God" (*doc. Chr.* 1.27.28). A person is to love human beings in such a way that he "turns the whole current of his love both for himself and his neighbor into the channel of the love of God" (*doc. Chr.* 1.22.21).

Let me highlight a feature of Augustine's response to the second love command that is easily overlooked but that is in fact of fundamental importance. Augustine often makes the point that obedience to the command requires that we care about, and seek to promote, the religious and moral wellbeing of our neighbors. And when he makes this point, he often highlights the emotional implications: we are not just to *seek to promote* the religious and moral wellbeing of self and neighbor; we are to *grieve and rejoice* over their religious and moral wellbeing.[14] Sören Kierkegaard, in *Works of Love*, and Anders Nygren, in *Agape and Eros*, reflected at length on the second love command, far greater length than Augustine ever did. Neither has much to say about the implications of the command for our emotions. Augustine's highlighting of the emotional implications is part of what gives his thought on these matters its characteristic "Augustinian" quality.

In Book 3 of the *Confessions*, after reflecting on the fact that "friendly feelings well up in us like the waters of a spring," Augustine says (*conf.* 3.2.3) that though "everyone wants to be happy," nonetheless "we are not to arm ourselves against compassion. There are times when we must welcome sorrow on behalf of others." This sounds a new note. What we have so far

---

[14] The connection in Augustine's mind between the emotions, on the one hand, and the pursuit of someone's good, on the other, comes out in this passage (*civ. Dei* 14.6): "as a man's will is attracted or repelled by the variety of things which are pursued or avoided, so it changes and turns into emotions of one kind or the other." See also *civ. Dei* 19.13: "the loss of any good is a matter for grief rather than rejoicing: if, that is, the loss is not counteracted by the gain of a greater good."

heard Augustine saying is that we are to grieve and rejoice *over* the religious and moral condition of our fellows. Now we hear him saying that we are to feel compassion *with* our fellows. We are to grieve *along with them* when they grieve and rejoice *along with them* when they rejoice. This theme of compassion will loom large in *City of God*.

Without, so far as I know, anywhere arguing the point, Augustine appears to have taken the second love command as implying that we are not only to grieve *for* impairments in our neighbor's wellbeing but also to grieve *with* our neighbor in his grief (provided his grief is rightly ordered). Everybody in antiquity was aware that the Stoics were opposed to compassion. Augustine says that we should let compassion flow.

3 AUGUSTINE'S REJECTION OF THE ACTIVITY PRINCIPLE OF THE EUDAIMONISTS

In *City of God* 9.5, Augustine says the following:

We [who follow Scripture] do not so much ask whether a pious soul is angry as why he is angry; not whether he is sad but whence comes his sadness; not whether he is afraid, but what he fears. For I do not think that any right-minded person would condemn anger directed at a sinner in order to correct him; or sadness on behalf of one who is afflicted, in order to comfort him; or fear for one in peril, lest he perish. The Stoics, indeed, are wont to reproach even compassion. But … what is compassion but a kind of fellow feeling in our hearts for the misery of another which compels us to help him if we can? This impulse is the servant of right reason when compassion is displayed in such a way as to preserve righteousness, as when alms are distributed to the needy or forgiveness extended to the penitent.

Given what Augustine said in the *Confessions*, we are not surprised to find him speaking well of anger "directed at a sinner." We are surprised, however, to find him praising sadness "on behalf of one who is afflicted" and fear "for one in peril." So too, we are not surprised to find him saying in another place in *City of God* that those who love God will "feel pain for their [own] sins and gladness in their [own] good works" and will have the same feelings "on behalf of those whom they desire to see redeemed and fear to see perish" (*civ. Dei* 14.9). But we are surprised to hear him saying, with no hint of disapproval, that we are "anxious lest [our friends] be afflicted by famine, war, pestilence, or captivity, fearing that in slavery they may suffer evils beyond what we can conceive" (*civ. Dei* 19.8). We are not surprised to hear him say that a person "will take care to ensure that his neighbor also loves God" (*civ. Dei* 19.14). But we are surprised to hear him say, after he has called attention to the miseries produced by warfare, "Let everyone … who reflects with pain upon such great evils, upon such horror and cruelty, acknowledge that this is misery. And if anyone either endures them or thinks of them without anguish of soul, his condition is still more miserable: for he thinks himself happy only because he has lost all human feeling" (*civ. Dei* 19.7). Augustine rejects the view that we are to care only about the religious and moral wellbeing of our fellows; we are to care about their wellbeing in general.

The point comes through even more emphatically in the following passage (*civ. Dei* 19.8):

> The more friends we have, and the more places we have them in, the further and more widely do we fear that some evil may befall them out of all the mass of the evils of this world ... And when such things do happen (and the more numerous our friends the more often they happen) and the fact is brought to our knowledge, who, save one who has experienced the same thing, can understand the burning sorrow which then afflicts our hearts? Indeed, we would rather hear that our friends were dead; although this also we could not hear without pain: for if their life delighted us with the solace of friendship, how could it be that their death should not bring us grief? Anyone who forbids such grief must forbid, if he can, all friendly conversation: he must prohibit or extinguish affection; he must with ruthless disregard sever the ties of all human companionship, or else stipulate that such companionship must merely be made use of, without giving rise to any delight of soul. But if this can in no way be done, how can the death of one whose life has been sweet to us not bring us bitterness? For this is why the grief of a heart which is not inhuman is like a kind of wound or ulcer, healed by the application to it of our loving words of consolation. And though healing takes place all the more quickly and easily when the soul is well-conditioned, we must not suppose that there is nothing at all to heal in such a case.

I submit that the only way to interpret what Augustine is saying here is that he is rejecting the activity principle of the eudaimonists and rejecting, even more radically than he did before, the Stoic principle of emotional detachment. The estimability of a person's life is determined not only by what she *does* but by how she *fares*. The life of a righteous person living in misery is not a fully estimable (happy) life. The emotional corollary is that what's worth grieving and rejoicing over is not only what a person *does* but also what's *happening to* her in body and spirit.

There is a wonderful passage in *City of God* in which Augustine presses the point by mocking the Stoic ideal of the happy person, the sage (*civ. Dei* 19.4):

> They believe that their wise man – that is, he whom, in their amazing vanity, they describe as such – even if he becomes blind, deaf and dumb, even if he is enfeebled

in limb and tormented with pain, even if he falls victim to every other ill that can be described or imagined, even if he is compelled to put himself to death: that such a man would not shrink from calling such a life, beset with such ills, a happy one! O happy life, that seeks the aid of death to put an end to it! If this is happiness, let him remain in it; but if these ills compel him to flee from it, how is it happy? ... How senseless it is to call a life happy and at the same time persuade a man to flee from it! Is anyone so blind that he does not see that a happy life would not be one from which one would wish to flee?

What was it that led Augustine to his decisive break with the activity principle of the eudaimonists – apart from the patent implausibility of the principle in its Stoic form that he highlights in the passage just quoted? In part it was, once again, the influence of certain biblical passages (see especially *civ. Dei* 14.8, 14.9). But here too we can spy something deeper, something that Augustine sees as underlying what the biblical writers say about emotional investment.

It's obvious to everybody that we human beings tend to feel compassion for our fellows not only with respect to their religious and moral condition but also with respect to their condition generally. Augustine came to believe that this tendency is part of our created human nature; to stifle it and harden our hearts would be to go contrary to the will of the creator. In *Confessions* Augustine had already spoken up in favor of compassion. In *City of God* he expands its scope. Compassion "is a kind of fellow feeling in our hearts for the misery of another which compels us to help him if we can. This impulse is the servant of right reason when compassion is displayed in such a way as to preserve righteousness, as when alms are distributed to the needy or forgiveness extended to the penitent" (*civ. Dei* 9.5). We are to have compassion not only for the penitent but also for the needy!

In *True Religion*, after arguing that we should love only the souls of ourselves and our fellows and that we should love all souls equally, Augustine added (*vera rel.* 46.88): "Let no one think that is inhuman. It is more inhuman to love a man because he is your son and not because he is a man, that is, not to love that in him which belongs to God, but to love that which belongs to yourself."[15] Between *True Religion* and *City of God*, Augustine came to believe that it is in fact inhuman to care only about a person's soul and not about that person's condition generally.

Here is a sampling of passages from *City of God* in which he makes the point. (Some have already been quoted to make different points.) Rather

---

[15] I am using the translation by Burleigh 1953.

than joining the Stoics in rejecting compassion, it is "far better and more humane and more in keeping with the sensibility of the godly" to allow oneself to be open to compassion (*civ. Dei* 9.5). "If anyone either endures [the sufferings caused by warfare] or thinks of them without anguish of soul, his condition is still more miserable, for he thinks himself happy only because he has lost all human feeling" (*civ. Dei* 19.7). The person who tries to eliminate from his life all negative emotion "must with ruthless disregard sever the ties of human companionship." "The grief of a heart which is not inhuman is like a kind of wound or ulcer" (*civ. Dei* 19.9). "If we felt no [negative] emotions at all while subject to the infirmity of this life, we should then certainly not be living righteously. For the apostle condemned and denounced certain persons who, he said, were 'without natural affection.' The holy psalm also blames those of whom it says, 'I looked for some to take pity, but there was none.' Indeed, if, while in this place of misery, we were to be entirely free from pain, this, as one of this world's scholars [Cicero] has understood and said, 'would not be attained without a great price, savagery of mind, and stupor of body'" (*civ. Dei* 14.9).

"[W]hose eloquence is sufficient," Augustine asks (*civ. Dei* 19.4), "no matter how ready its flow, to depict all the miseries of this life? Is there any pain, the contrary of pleasure, any disquiet, the contrary of rest, that cannot befall [even] a wise man's body? Certainly the amputation or decay of his limbs undermines a man's soundness, deformity ruins his beauty, sickness destroys his health, weakness his strength, lassitude his vigour, torpor or lethargy his activity." Similar things can be said about what befalls a person's mind. When we survey this destruction of body and mind, "when we contemplate or see people in this condition, and when we consider their plight fully, we can hardly refrain from weeping, perhaps we cannot do so at all" (still 19.4). And we should not try. We are so created as to grieve over human misery, misery of body and soul, our own misery and that of others, members of our family, friends, even those to whom we have no attachments, the mere neighbor.

The point is not that anger, grief, fear, and the like are, as such, goods in one's life; they are not. They "belong to this life [but] not to the life to come for which we hope" (*civ. Dei* 14.9). In the life to come there will be nothing to be angry about, nothing to grieve over, nothing to fear. The Christian shares with the Stoic the conviction that in the truly estimable life there will be no negative emotions. He departs from the Stoic in his conviction that in this present age, with its "great mass of evils" (*civ. Dei* 19.8), it would be wrong to seek to eliminate negative emotions. "Human life is compelled to be miserable by all the great evils of this world" (*civ. Dei* 19.4).

Our emotions are not beyond critique, however. Though we do not ask "whether a pious soul is angry," we do ask "why he is angry"; not all anger is rightly ordered. Though we do not ask "whether he is sad," we do ask "whence comes his sadness"; not all sadness is appropriate. Though we do not ask "whether he is afraid," we do ask "what he fears"; sometimes the fearful person has to be corrected (*civ. Dei* 9.5). Christians "feel fear and desire, pain and gladness, but in a manner consistent with the Holy Scripture and wholesome doctrine; and because their love is righteous, all these emotions are righteous in them" (*civ. Dei* 14.9).

4 AUGUSTINE'S REJECTION OF THE POSSIBILITY OF BECOMING A SAGE

There remains one last component of Augustine's rejection of eudaimonism to be considered. The Stoics held that it is possible for any human being to become a sage – that is, to become fully virtuous and thereby to free oneself from all negative emotions and consistently to do the virtuous thing. The Peripatetics attached some qualifications. It's not possible, realistically speaking, for the person reared in a bad environment, to become fully virtuous. And being virtuous is not sufficient for doing the virtuous thing; circumstances may intervene to prevent one from achieving the virtuous thing one intended. To this may be added that the virtuous person living in straitened circumstances finds that some of her virtues she cannot exercise at all and that others she can exercise only in a very limited way.

Augustine considers the Stoic position and emphatically rejects it; the grounds of his rejection imply rejection of the Peripatetic principle as well. He asks, what is the task of virtue in this world? His answer is that its task is "to wage perpetual war against the vices. And these are ... not external vices but internal ones: not the vices of others, but clearly ours and only ours" (*civ. Dei* 19.4). This warfare of virtue against vice continues until there is "no vice in us for the spirit to lust against. We cannot manage to achieve this in our present life, no matter how much we may wish to ... Who has achieved such a degree of wisdom that he no longer has to maintain any struggle against his lusts?" The Stoics, "in their stupid pride, believe that the Final Good is to be found in this life, and that they can achieve happiness by their own effort" (still 19.4). It can't be done. We cannot by our own efforts overcome the power of sin in our lives; we await divine redemption. And even if we could, the happy life, the estimable life, requires not only that we be freed from the power of sin but also delivered from all the sorrows of body and spirit that befall us in our present existence.

5 IN SUMMARY

Augustine's rejection of Stoicism was more pointed and emphatic than his rejection of Peripatetic eudaimonism – understandably so, given the prominence of Stoicism in his intellectual environment. But there can be no doubt that the positions at which he arrived by the time he wrote *City of God* imply the rejection of the fundamental tenets of eudaimonism in general. The eudaimonists all held that the happiness or estimability of a person's life is determined entirely by what he or she does. Augustine found it preposterous to suppose that the life of someone such as the Old Testament character Job, righteous though he was, was happy, estimable. The eudaimonists all held that it is sometimes good to seek to promote the good of another as an end in itself, but only on the proviso that doing so promises to contribute to one's own wellbeing. Augustine understood Jesus' command to love one's neighbor as oneself to imply the rejection of that proviso. The Stoics held that it was possible for each of us to act consistently in accord with virtue, thereby to become a sage; the Peripatetics added the qualification that this was possible only if external circumstances cooperated. Augustine argued that it was impossible even if external circumstances did cooperate; it's the power of sin within that is the problem, and only God can deliver us from that. The Stoics held that we should invest ourselves emotionally only in our own virtuous activity; the sage, who has done this, is entirely free of negative emotion. The Peripatetics again attached a qualification: not only is it appropriate to invest oneself emotionally in one's own virtuous activity; it is also appropriate to react negatively to whatever circumstances hinder that activity. Augustine held that we are to invest ourselves emotionally not only in our own religious and moral condition but in that of our fellows, and not only in the religious and moral condition of oneself and others but in their wellbeing generally. We are to let the springs of our in-created compassion to flow. We are both to grieve *over* the "evils" in our lives and the lives of others and to grieve *with* those others in their grief; we are both to rejoice *over* the goods in our lives and theirs and to rejoice *with* them in their rejoicing. We are to be united with them in a solidarity of grieving and rejoicing – until that day for which we hope, when there is no longer anything to grieve over. This is what it is, here in this present age, to love one's neighbor as oneself. It is to be united to and with the neighbor in a solidarity of grieving and rejoicing.

CHAPTER 9

Augustine on the origin of evil: myth and metaphysics

James Wetzel

We know vividly from the *Confessions* that Augustine's struggle to conceive of the boundless reality of God turns on what he imagines evil to be. His considered view of the matter, that evil exists only as a "privation of the good" (*privatio boni*), a form of non-being, is a Neoplatonic commonplace.[1] But Augustine puts his own stamp on the bare metaphysics. He speaks in *City of God* of the split within the angelic ranks between the angels who fall into themselves and eternally darken their minds and those who hold steady to the deliverances of divine light; he speaks of Satan, the perverted light-bearer and father of lies, who shows up in Eden in a serpent's guise and seduces the woman into a fateful transgression; he speaks of Adam, her mate and the model of a human sinner, who sees through the serpent's deception but grievously underestimates the cost to him and his race of his obscurely motivated disobedience.

In *Confessions*, the privative nature of evil is intimated in Augustine's Adamic need to bring his flesh and spirit into some sort of sane conjunction. At a critical point in the Genesis story of creation and parting – a story of trouble in a garden paradise (Gen. 2:4b–3:24) – Adam finds himself having to choose between flesh and spirit (Gen. 3:6): his partner, the flesh of his flesh, has eaten fruit from the tree of knowledge; she offers him a taste of what his divine maker, the breath of his breath, has associated with death. Adam takes his taste, defies his God, and, by Augustine's reckoning, condemns all of his descendants to a mortal life and a life lived out of interior conflict: from now on there will be no easy choice of spirit over flesh. At the beginning of *Confessions* 8, the book where Augustine details his time of anguish in a garden retreat, he tells us that while he loved the

---

[1] Plotinus, the third-century Platonist whose writings were to revolutionize Augustine's conception of God, famously identifies evil with matter (see esp. *enn.* 1.8, 2.4), but the Plotinian notion of materiality is one of consummate deprivation: not solid stuff or indeed any kind of subject, but a beckoning, formless nullity, foreign to goodness. For an illuminating entry into the intricacies of this notion, consult Gerson 1994: 191–98. For a clear statement in Augustine of the *privatio* thesis, see *conf.* 3.7.12.

fleshless God of pure spirit, he still found himself tightly tied to his origins in a woman (*adhuc tenaciter conligabar ex femina*; *conf.* 8.1.2); he still wanted to embrace, with some part of himself, the life that takes in sex and death. The deprivation to which his recalcitrant desire attests has two aspects to it: like Adam before him, Augustine lacks the experience of what it means to be fully human and not feel compelled to make a choice between flesh and spirit; also like Adam before him, Augustine's deprivation is, in some way, his own choice. Augustine believes that all Adamic beings – or all human beings, that is, save Christ (who is Adamic only on his mother's side[2]) – have deprived themselves of a perfection that no human being, again save Christ, has ever experienced.

In *City of God* Augustine adds an angelic gloss to the Adamic plot. Before Adam ever makes his fateful choice of flesh over spirit, renegade angels abandon the heavenly chorus, fall into self-obsession, and make for hell, the infernal counterpart of God's celestial city. When the most self-obsessive of these renegades intrudes upon the earth and uses a serpent's tongue to tempt Eve into trading life for knowledge (or what she will see as greater life), he ends up playing two distinctive roles in Augustine's exegesis. On the one hand, Satan is a character in a story of human redemption. He begins the story by leading the original progenitors of humanity into sin and death; Christ, his antitype, will end the story by leading a number of their descendants (the number of angels lost) back to innocence, albeit this time an incorruptible one. On the other hand, Satan stands in for the absoluteness of sin itself, for the sin that exists prior to temptation and so makes the temptation to sin possible. Satan himself isn't tempted into sin; he needs no offer of flesh before he will act to corrupt his own spirit. His sin demonizes him, situates his self-corruption always in the "before" of any story of redemption. Not even Christ can alter the priority. And yet if, as Augustine will argue, it is the sin in Adam and Eve that leads them to fall into sin (see esp. *civ. Dei* 14.13), how are humanity's progenitors not demons themselves?

There is a heady mix of myth and metaphysics in the *City of God* account of evil's origination. I aim in this essay to sort things out and then revisit Augustine's commitment to the *privatio* thesis: his supposition that evil is an absence, only a shadow of something real, and so not a thing of its own

---

[2] From his mother, Mary, Christ inherits the mortality that comes of original sin but not the concupiscence. He is never truly tempted to subordinate his eternal spirit to the desires of his mortal flesh; throughout his life on earth, his holy father's will reigns supreme in him. It may have reigned similarly supreme in his mother, whose humanity Augustine finds only slightly less exceptional than Christ's; see *nat. et gr.* 36.42.

kind. Admittedly the specter of irretrievably fallen angels, working with Satan to sow misery into creation, suggests an evil that is by nature more than privative. An absence is not an agent, and still Augustine invites us to imagine perpetually unsettled beings who are always seeking to subvert the good: where does an absence get the legs for that? But I am not going to be arguing that Augustine tells a story about good and evil that just flatly contradicts his preferred metaphysics. The truth is more involved. His narrative ingenuity, much on display in *City of God*, sustains two subtly different readings of the *privatio* thesis. One I will call the "presumptive" reading; the other the "preemptive."

The presumption behind the presumptive reading is that God, being absolutely good, never acts to diminish goodness either in himself or in the beings whom he has created.[3] This is a presumption with complex and not always clear implications, but one implication it clearly cannot have for Augustine is that God never creates beings with less than absolute goodness. Such an implication would, in effect, drive a wedge between being perfectly good and being procreative, leaving God sublimely self-enclosed and alone. The alternative is to assume that the perfectly good God creates beings whose less than absolute goodness admits of a relative perfection. Neither angels nor human beings can, as creatures, have the perfection of their creator, but there are better and worse angels, better and worse human beings. The bad angels, having become demonic, are categorically bad; the bad human beings are all bad because of sin, but in the earthly plane of time and transformation, it is often hard to tell saints and sinners apart (*civ. Dei* 1.35).

There is also the calculation of the relative merits of angelic and human goodness, but that calculation does not play into Augustine's question of evil's first foothold. There the concern is with what makes relatively perfect beings imperfect. If the presumption is that God cannot be the answer, then that makes corruption the business of lesser creators. Some of the original angels have deprived themselves of their original goodness; they have created deprivation where before there was none. Analogously all human beings, by way of their solidarity with Adam, the paradigmatic sinner, have invented their own form of alienation from God. Self-corrupting human and demonic creators have together been corrupting the broader material order, translating internal deprivations into external forms of harm.

---

[3] I refer to Augustine's sublimely immaterial God as a "he" in recognition of Augustine's reverence for God as the eternal Father. I write the pronoun in the lowercase – "he" rather than "He" – in order to suggest what this form of reverence leaves unresolved.

I will set out the further terms of Augustine's presumptive reading of the *privatio* thesis in the section of my essay I call "metaphysics." I mean to signal by this designation a stark contrast with a more narrative rendering of evil's emergence, a myth or story of a character's loss of innocence. (And by "myth" I mean a peculiarly telling story, the story behind many stories, and not just a fanciful tale.) Augustine really has no story to tell about how a good angel goes bad; he has instead a metaphysical mystery that he tries to dress up as a story. The crux of the desired story, the transition from good to evil, turns out to be impossible to relate. For it is not out of goodness that an angel goes bad; it is not out of anything. It is out of nothing, in fact, or, more precisely, it is out of not being God. An angel, like any creature, is good being of God; is capable of having its goodness undone (*posse deficere*; *civ. Dei* 12.8) being other than God and of nothingness (*ex nihilo*). Satan is the angel who, failing to recognize his own beauty in the blinding divine light, seeks out the perspective of darkness, of decreation, where his ties to God and to all others will have come undone. But if the presumption behind the presumptive reading is right, no deprivation comes from God: Satan must have first rejected his gift of self-knowledge before chasing after an empty, illusory, and unsatisfying alternative.

When Augustine uses the angelic fall to frame the story of Adam, Eve, and the serpent, his disposition is to depict Satan as the paradigm of sin, human and demonic, and not simply as an agent of temptation. The assimilation of Adam's sin to Satan's brings out the chief liability of the presumptive reading: that it renders all sin irredeemable. Consider Satan's loss of grace, his demotion from being Lucifer, the light-bearer. His condition is irredeemable not because he is a uniquely horrific transgressor, but because he retains his capacity to reject whatever grace has been given him; he remains, as an independent contractor of deprivation, forever unstable in God. How would an Adam, sinning like a Satan, be any different?

In the section of my essay that I call "myth," I look carefully at the opportunity Augustine gives himself to tell a different story about Adam – one that differentiates human sin from its demonic parody. The bare narrative difference is obvious: Adam has a partner in sin, the woman, Eve, "the mother of all that lives" (Gen. 3:20); Satan sins unprompted by a demonic counterpart and without need of external encouragement. There is no woman, no lure of the flesh, in Satan's story – no solidarity in sin (hell being truly the antithesis of a city).

Augustine pays attention to the different roles that Adam and Eve play in bringing about the first human sin largely because of what Paul has to say about the matter in his first letter to Timothy (1 Tim. 2:13–14): "For Adam

Origin of evil

was formed first, then Eve; and Adam was not deceived, but the woman was and became a transgressor." In other words, Eve actually believes the serpent when he tells her that eating from the tree of knowledge is a good thing, a way to become more like a god, while Adam knows full well that the serpent is lying. But not wishing to abandon his partner to her folly, Adam joins Eve in her transgression. More so than in his two earlier forays into Genesis – the commentary against the Manichees (*Gn. adv. Man.*) and the great literal commentary (*Gn. litt.*)[4] – Augustine in *City of God* resolves to align his take on Adam's transgression with Paul's. The significance of this resolve is that Augustine's Adam acts out of a privation and does not only create one. Eve's transgression separates her not only from God but also from her human partner, and Adam feels his separation from her as a loss. He disobeys God and risks death in order to be with her again. Certainly it remains open to Augustine to refit his Pauline Adam to a Satanic mold, discount this Adam's love for Eve as a motive for his sin, and leave him nakedly God-defying. This tack returns Augustine to his presumptive reading of the *privatio* thesis, but it also distances him from Paul and his best chance of understanding the origin of evil in light of a story.

The "preemptive" reading of the *privatio* thesis avoids resolving myth into metaphysics. It sticks with a story, still in the making, about the transformation of human sin into the love of God. Adam chooses the flesh of his flesh over the breath of his breath – the woman over God – and his act of transgression, in keeping with both readings of it, preemptive and presumptive, remains inalienably his own. It is no part of the preemptive reading simply to move the onus of sin back to God and render Adam an innocent victim; Adam does lose his innocence, but his loss, freed from the framework of the presumptive reading, is no longer essentially damning.

Consider the inner life of his transgression, the question of Adam's motive. The presumptive reading presumes that at the end of the analysis, an Adam looking in on himself will have run out of reasons for his desire to transgress: he just sins, and that's it. The preemptive reading preempts this conclusion and leaves open the question of what Adam's sin finally means. When he chooses the woman over God, Adam transgresses, but he transgresses against the God whom he has conceived to be antithetical to his love of a beloved's flesh. Perhaps this is a naïve conception on his part, one he

---

[4] Some chronology: *Gn. adv. Man.* dates from 388; Augustine works on *Gn. litt.* over an extended period of time, from 401 to 415. He writes *civ. Dei*, Books 13 and 14, several years after the completion of *Gn. litt.*, likely between 418 and 420. For detailed chronological charts of Augustine's life, works, and historical context, see Brown 2000, the new edition.

needs to outgrow; he still knows too little about spirit to be assuming that his God is not also her son too, the mother of all that lives.⁵ On the preemptive reading, Adam acts to create a deprivation in his self-knowledge, but the deprivation is not his ultimate motive. He may discover, God willing, that he has been moved by God to seek God.

Augustine's angelology in *City of God* is too thin to sustain a preemptive reading of the angelic fall. He gives us far too little to conceive of the God that a fall of angels portends. The forgiveness of a Satan has to remain, then, inconceivable. But in the Adamic drama, it is relatively clear what God will have to have become to allow an Adam forgiveness: his mother's son. In the weighty matter of the origin of evil, my argument will be that we learn most from Augustine when we favor his Christology over his angelology and let *City of God* stand as testimony to the limits of presumption.

I METAPHYSICS

When Augustine speculates about human life in Eden prior to the first sin, he underscores its perfection (*civ. Dei* 14.10): Adam and Eve enjoy an untroubled love (*amor imperturbatus*) both for one another and for God; theirs is a fellowship lived out of trust and honesty (*fida et sincera societate*); they take great satisfaction from it, and it never ceases to be available to them (*non desistente quod amabatur*); consequently they have no trouble not giving in to sin – their avoidance of it is serene (*devitatio tranquilla peccati*). On the last point, Augustine further speculates that it cannot be fear of death that keeps Adam and Eve from eating from the forbidden tree of knowledge. Fear is not a tranquil emotion but a source of agitation, especially when mixed with curiosity and carnal desire, and Augustine insists that Adam and Eve are free from agitation of any kind. Indeed they have the sort of intelligent and inwardly stable happiness that worldly philosophers post Eden – the Stoics especially – try vainly to achieve.⁶

---

⁵ I am suggesting that Eve in the garden is both human and divine: the man's female counterpart, and so subject to Adamic anxieties about who God is and what God wants, but also the female image of God, or that aspect of divinity that is friendly to mortal life and its transformative possibilities. My suggestion is not Augustine's view of the matter – his Eve is a fallen woman and only that – but I submit that my suggestion is best in keeping with Augustine's sense of the redemptive power of incarnate spirit.

⁶ Augustine's discussion of Edenic life in *civ. Dei* 14.10 forms part of his broader reflection in Book 14 on the psychology of human happiness and its earthly limits. In his estimation, pagan philosophy, epitomized by Stoicism, promises more than it can possibly deliver: a virtual restoration of the original peace of mind that was lost after Eden. See Wetzel 1992: 98–111 for more on Augustine's polemical construct of Stoicism.

With their psychologies thus perfected, it becomes impossible to determine what would move an Adam or an Eve to sin. These two human originals have everything they need to be disposed to find steadfast obedience to God their heart's desire. But this is just Augustine's point. If they have everything they need – the internal resources especially – and they sin anyway, then nothing that God has withheld from them can possibly be the motive for their transgression. It is not because they feel deprived of the good of the fruit of knowing that they sin. The only good that this fruit represents, as Augustine tries to make clear (*civ. Dei* 14.17; *Gn. litt.* 8.6.12), is the good of never having disobeyed God. And this is a good that Adam and Eve have already been enjoying in abundance, being such richly endowed creatures. When they break trust with God, eat from the tree, and settle into a faithless self-awareness, something in them will have misconstrued what knowledge is and what knowledge has to do with life. That something comes from them and not from God, and, given the fullness of their lives, it is a something that amounts to little more than their sheer willingness to be deprived: it is little more, that is, than the nothingness towards which it tends.

The problem for Augustine's exegesis – putting aside for now the perplexity of an essentially deficient motive – is that he has a better candidate for the fruit of knowing than the ironical good of never having disobeyed. (Obeying God is a plausible enough good, but when its goodness is made out to be the fruit of knowing, the divine prohibition against eating makes for a blind and impoverished obedience.) The lure of the fruit of knowing is the lure of a divine life. The serpent tells the woman that she is "not doomed to die" if she eats, that she and her partner "will become as gods" and know good and evil as a god does; she in turn looks longingly at the tree, whose fruit has now become for her "good for eating" and a "lust to the eyes" – an erotic offering.[7] Augustine assumes in his exegesis that the serpent is lying and that Eve, having let her lust for life get the better of her judgment, falls for the lie. But even Augustine's undeceived Adam has a plausible motive for wanting to add more vitality to his life. Like his partner, he begins his existence in a body of clay. If he does not eat regularly from the tree of life, that clay body will age and die; in and of itself, it is mortal stuff (*civ. Dei* 13.23; cf. *Gn. litt.* 6.21.32). Adam's refined spiritual mind,

---

[7] It is also worth noting that when the serpent suggests to the woman that God (Yahweh) has forbidden her to eat from all the trees in Eden, she quickly identifies the tree "in the midst of the garden" as the only forbidden item (Gen. 3:1–3). She never mentions the tree by name. In Gen. 2:9, we are told that both trees, life and knowledge, are "in the midst of the garden." The implication of her ambiguous reference to the forbidden tree is that knowledge and life look the same to her. For my translation of Genesis, I am using Alter 1996.

unclouded by lust, will have told him that he is destined for a better incarnation, one that brings the source of his life's vitality more intimately into conjunction with his flesh. But Adam cannot simply give up on his flesh in order to abide more fully with spirit, for he is essentially an incarnate being: hence his dilemma when his partner, the flesh of his flesh, exchanges knowledge for life and bids him to do likewise.

Adam's mortality is a tricky subject. There is a clear sense for Augustine in which Adam is already mortal before he ever partakes of his partner's fruit and enters into the doom of death. He is mortal by virtue of his flesh. But Augustine also wants to insist that Adam's original mortality is somehow less doomed than the mortality that comes to him and his descendants when he joins with the woman and weakens the human condition.

Augustine cues his sense of the difference between the two mortalities to Paul's distinction in first Corinthians (1 Cor. 15: 44) between an animal body (*corpus animale*; *sôma psychikon*) and a spiritual one (*corpus spiritale*; *sôma pneumatikon*). Paul uses the distinction to mark the difference between the first Adam and Christ, the second, and also to suggest the miraculous transformation of an earth-born body into immortal, resurrected flesh. The spiritualized body of a resurrected saint has no need of physical sustenance; it is sustained by divine light, much as an immaterial angel in heaven is. But unlike the angels, the saints in heaven all begin in earth-sown bodies; and that kind of body, Paul says (1 Cor. 15: 35–36), has to die before anything spiritual can take its place. Augustine agrees, but he also wonders whether this was always so. Imagine an Adam who never sins. What becomes of this Adam's animal body? The answer is that he and his partner, the woman, here presumed sinless as well, both move tranquilly from animal to spiritual existence, without having to undergo a death – a violent sundering of soul from body.[8] Adam's animal body, according to Augustine, once had a miraculous capacity to morph directly into spirit (*civ. Dei* 14.10; *Gn. litt.* 6.23.34).

And so the big difference for Augustine between original mortality and what follows is that original mortality is provisional. Adam and Eve are of mortal clay, but as long as they have access to the tree of life, whose fruit is sacramental for them (*civ. Dei* 13.20), they not only do not die; they transform. They become spiritual beings, still embodied (albeit lightly),

---

[8] The sundering is violent because in an incarnate soul – which is what Adam or any human being is – the soul is incomplete apart from the body. Death violates the natural affinity between soul and body; it always counts, for Augustine, as an unnatural evil (see, e.g., *civ. Dei* 13.3, 13.6). For further explication of this seemingly anti-Platonic stance of his, see Cavadini 1999.

still dependent on a source of life, but no longer needing to make that source a part of themselves. Where before they had to eat; now they are free to contemplate. But when the still animal Adam and Eve violate the conditions of their provisional mortality and lose access to the tree of life, two things happens to the human experience of mortality: death becomes a necessity, and the difference between spirit and flesh becomes an antagonism (making for an especially confusing experience of sex). Death is necessary not because Adam's descendants have been denied a source of life, but because the source to which they do have access – Christ on a cross, a tree of human artifice – requires their death. It requires it because of the sheer depth of human resistance to transformation. We are the ones who turn difference into antagonism and put Christ upon the cross.

To read Augustine as claiming anything less radical than that is to miss the point of his two mortalities. Suppose, as did Pelagius and many of his sympathizers, that there is only one kind of mortality, that it is natural to the human condition, and that had Adam resisted temptation and kept to his virtues, he still would have died at some point of natural causes (cf. *Gn. litt.* 6.22.33). If the supposition is granted, then spiritualized flesh is no longer a human possibility, or at best it is an unnatural possibility that is less a boon to human advancement than a loss of natural beauty. Since the idea of a spiritual body is largely defined by the idea of what it is not – a body that eats and has sex, commingles and transforms – it can seem a curiously dispirited notion to interpreters who value a limited but, for that very reason, keenly felt life.[9]

Here it is important to understand that, for Augustine, a spiritual body is not a good whose deprivation we can experience or whose supplement to our happiness we can readily imagine, if at all. When Adam joins Eve in sin, he is unambiguously animal in his flesh; consequently he is in no position to lose by sinning a sublimity of body that he has yet to possess. It is not a spiritual body (or the idea of one), then, that can define for Adam his redemption (*Gn. litt.* 6.24.35). Adam loses his faith in Eden, not his spirit. At some point he ceases to trust in his maker's ability or perhaps willingness to lay hold of a human life, wrest it out of transgression, and refigure it into something new. It might have gone otherwise for Adam – hence the unnaturalness of his death. His descendants, by contrast, are born locked into an animal self-image. To break from it, they will need more than a

---

[9] Nightingale 2011 looks at Augustine's "transhuman" ideal of life first in Eden and then in heaven and basically concludes that his transhumanism is not human enough. See especially her epilogue on "mortal interindebtedness."

mediator who lives an exemplary life of virtue and dies a heroic death; they will need one who meets them in death, where no self-image can go.

Augustine finds himself committed both to the transformative possibilities of a graced humanity and to the original perfection of Edenic life. As I have been trying to suggest, this is not the easiest of conjunctions for him to sustain. How can Adam start off as a being who has it all and also be a being whose perfection awaits him? Augustine's exegetical hurdle is the apparent imperfection of Eden. When a sensual Eve offers Adam the forbidden fruit of knowing, she makes him vividly aware that he lacks the incarnation he is ideally meant to have: his spirit has yet to experience full communion with the flesh of his flesh, with her. In Augustine's Pauline terms: Adam has an animal body, not yet a spiritual one. Here is a lack that can be plausibly construed as the deprivation that moves Adam to sin. If Augustine wants to stick to the presumptive reading of sin's beginning – a reading that rules out divinely created imperfection – he needs to identify the original perfection that Adam has willfully abandoned. It will have to be a perfection that secures for Adam his essential humanity, in all of its fullness. The only plausible candidate for this is perfect faith in God's goodness. But what does it look like to have and lose that?

Augustine's attempt at an answer takes him into angelic speculation. At some point in the history of angels (though it is hard to say what time means here), "deserter angels" (*desertores angeli*; *civ. Dei* 13.24), Satan chief among them, turn from the light of God and enter into the darkness of their separate selves. Meanwhile the angels who do not desert maintain their faith in God's unwithholding goodness and secure their place as the first citizens of the heavenly city. It is in the contrast between the deserter angels and their steadfast counterparts that Augustine seeks his biggest clue to Adam's defection.

As Augustine reads Genesis, angels come to be, and then come to be split in their ranks, within the brief compass of two verses from the Priestly creation narrative. In the pause between "Let there be light" (Gen. 1:3) and "God divided the light from the darkness" (Gen. 1:4), he finds matter for an entire angelic epic (*civ. Dei* 11.9, 11.19–20, 11.33). It starts with a luminous creation, light from light, and quickly lapses into shadow and darkness. The deserter angels, having become loyal only to self, mix darkness into their original light, and God, with ruthless judgment, divides the light from the darkness and seals the antithesis between angels and demons. The former are the proven first citizens of heaven, the latter their airy spiritual parodies, left to languish and vent in the sublunary sky, the lowest part of heaven (*infimum caelum*).

The light at issue here is obviously not the physical effluence of celestial orbs (Gen. 1:14–19), not the light, that is, that makes for eyesight. Augustine's angels precede sunshine, moon-glow, and the cold light of the stars. Their light is divine wisdom itself, the second person of the Trinity; such wisdom is the bodiless intelligence that calls matter out of nothingness and into beauty and accords a created mind sufficient wit to get in on the act. The angels are not of the same essence as uncreated wisdom (or there would be no question of an angelic fall), but they are exquisitely attuned in their angelic nature to the logic of creation. They know, when they are mindful of God, that there is nothing to creation but love. Augustine likens such knowledge to the breaking of day, a "morning" knowing (*et fit mane*; *civ. Dei* 11.7); it contrasts with being more directly focused on the distinctiveness of creaturely life, a crepuscular mode of knowing that Augustine identifies with the first advent of evening (*facta est vespera*).

The intimacy between being morning and evening knowing is both fundamental and precarious. It is impossible to refer a creaturely love to God apart from some awareness that one is irreducibly a creature and not God. But too much focus on that distinction tends to distort the extent of creaturely independence and lends the false impression that the self, when rendered into an abstraction, is still a something. Evening yields to night, a loss of knowing. In Augustine's exegesis of the first six days of creation (Gen. 1:3–31), night is not God's doing; only evening is: "Night never falls," he writes, "while the Creator is not forsaken by the creature's love. Accordingly, when Scripture enumerates those days in order, it never includes the word 'night'" (*vocabulum noctis*; *civ. Dei* 11.7).[10] The angels who create night for themselves arrogate selfhood from God and end up becoming less self-aware than they were before. But this is not a nightfall that they are willing to see. They continue to cling to an empty center, all the while imagining that they embrace a self there; the tighter they cling, the more violent their passion for deprivation becomes.[11]

In their fallen condition, the deserter angels are more like storm-systems than organized selves. But before they ever begin to unravel psychically, they act out of the same God-given integrity that any other angel has.

---

[10] Augustine's claim is not that the word is never used in the narrative but that it is never used in the formula that announces the creation of each new day: "And it was evening and it was morning, [first through sixth] day." His exegesis puts a premium on the difference between *vespera* (evening) and *nox* (night). For a provocative reading of the significance of Augustine's exegetical strategy in *civ. Dei* 11.7, see Pranger 2006: 113–21; esp. 120–21.

[11] Augustine has more to say about demonic psychology in Book 9 of *City of God*, where he takes on Apuleius, a fellow African and a pagan Platonist, and tries to discount the polytheistic path to human wholeness. (The gods turn out to be fallen angels.) See *civ. Dei* 9.3, 9.5, 9.8–9.

Augustine briefly entertains the notion that there must be a difference here – perhaps the deserters were, from the start, more insecure – but he is inclined not to think so (*civ. Dei* 11.13): "It is hard to believe that the angels were not all created equal in felicity at the beginning, and remained so until those who are now evil fell away from the light of goodness by their own will." There is equal felicity among the angels, then, but apparently not equal enough. The nagging perplexity of the presumptive reading comes to the fore: what inclines some perfect beings, but not others, to break from God and seek their own self-generated light? Augustine will claim that pride (*superbia*) is the beginning of sin (*civ. Dei* 12.6, 14.13; cf. Ecclus. 10:13), but this is to define sin, not account for it. Let sin be defined as a form of illicit self-assertion. There is nothing present in the original psyche of one angel but not in another that can account for pride.

The most that Augustine will claim about the cause of an evil will – a will to sin – is that it is deficient (*deficiens*), not effective (*efficiens*). He neatly encapsulates what he means by this in the following passage (*civ. Dei* 12.7):

> For to defect from that which supremely is, to that which has a less perfect degree of being: this is what it is to begin to have an evil will. Now to seek the causes of these defections, which are, as I have said, not efficient causes, but deficient, is like wishing to see darkness or hear silence. Both of these are known to us, the former by means of the eye and the latter by the ear: not, however, by their appearance, but by their lack of appearance.

The imagery is both striking and misleading. The issue is not how we see darkness, but whether we cause the darkness that we know by not seeing. When it comes to sin, Augustine imagines us to have a spoiler's power, prototypical in the deserter angels, to defect from God and pursue imperfection. We move towards the nothingness in creation *ex nihilo*, trade in eternal perfectibility for endlessly diminishing returns, and model for God what is means to be God-bereft and wed to non-being. The moral for Augustine of all this ironic self-assertion is that we are solely culpable for our barren inventiveness; God, meanwhile, is free to judge.

The problem with the moral is what it seems to imply about the fracture in creaturely desire. If an angel or an Adam can come to love a nothingness that, as it were, predates creation, then there is no divine self-offering that can secure even an unfallen angel's desire, let alone the longing of one of Adam's conflicted heirs. Any offer of life will be dogged by a prior and perversely desirable deficiency.

The logic of deficient causality, fitted first to angels, perpetually threatens to undo a world of purely spiritual beings, where transparency is the rule.

Origin of evil 179

It poses the same kind of threat in an Adamic setting, where flesh veils spirit and makes a muddle of motive. The question that I intend to pursue now is not whether the logic can be rendered more solidifying in one or both of those contexts, but whether Augustine has, in his narrative musings, left himself some alternative to Adam's angelization.[12]

2 MYTH

When I refer to Adam's angelization, I refer to Augustine's tendency to assimilate Adam's spirit to that of a deserter angel: an angel able not to sin who sins anyway, and for no good reason. The assimilation is wholly in keeping with what I have been calling a presumptive reading of evil's origination. At heart this reading is a form of moralism. It aims to keep the moral fault lines between God and creaturely defectors from God absolutely clean. God is not the slightest bit responsible for defection and the misery and chaos it causes; the creaturely defectors are altogether culpable. Fundamentally for this form of moralism, defection is a turn away from the good and not a choice of a lesser good over a greater; thus the analysis of sin, whether angelic or human, must always come down to deficiencies. Deficiently motivated defectors choose deficiency; anything else is anathema. There is to be no bleed of goodness from God to the defectors, no good the desire for which can excuse or mitigate the guilt of defection.

It is when Augustine is most concerned to justify the damnation of sinners that he is most apt to absolutize sin and discount temptation. With sin so conceived, I am never led into sin; it is always my sin that leads me into temptation. In *City of God*, Augustine speaks of sin as a secret transgression; "It was in secret," he writes (*in occulto*; *civ. Dei* 14.3), "that Adam and Eve began to be evil." He means by this that before Adam is ever tempted to be with the woman and not with God, he secretly wills himself to be receptive to a God-bereft life. Similarly for Eve, before she is ever tempted to believe the serpent's lies, she secretly wills herself to be receptive to a God-bereft knowledge. All this willing is in secret, and necessarily so, because by the time we have something evident to notice – some dramatic realignment in a relationship – it is already too late to catch the moment of

---

[12] MacDonald 1999 makes a plausible general case for thinking of inattentiveness, as opposed to ignorance or weakness of will, as the deficient cause of a moral lapse. But in paradisiacal contexts (Eden, heaven), where inattention to God suggests something sinister – namely, a love of deprivation – the question of cause continues to nag.

sin's inception. The turn that counts comes prior to even a self's relationship with itself. And so although Augustine is somewhat notorious for his insistence on the sexual transmission of sin and the resultant "sin-heap" of infected souls (*massa peccati*; *Simpl.* 1.2.16), sin, by the logic of deficient causality, is the least catchable of contagions. I sin singularly within me, you sin singularly within you; there is no common sin for us to share. In that regard, there is really only ever one original sinner, and each of us is it.

But still Augustine has to preserve some role in his theology, in fact a large one, for temptation as it is more traditionally conceived. He needs to be able to speak sensibly of an Adam who is able, in the face of temptation, to preserve his innocence; otherwise, mere susceptibility to temptation is going to be evidence enough for an irredeemably corrupt disposition. The logic of deficient causality, when pressed into the service of a presumptive moralism, leaves Augustine with only one of two possibilities: either a world in which no one is tempted who is not already damned, or one in which everyone at all times lives untried. The one world is hell; the other is decreation, or God reduced to solitude. There is no foothold for a Christology in either possibility, no way to bring God down to earth.

Deficient causality should by now seem ill conceived to any hopeful heir of Adam. But can Augustine really do without it and still be able to account for creaturely responsibility for sin, the *sine qua non* of any theological moralism?

The great metaphysician of morals, Immanuel Kant, gives us reason to think that Augustine's dilemma may be both unavoidable and beyond resolution. In his late work, *Religion within the Boundaries of Mere Reason*, his defense of a theological moralism, Kant attempts to account for the possibility of moral personality. He tries to explain, that is, how it is possible for rectitude to be restored in a person who has willed contrary to the categorical demands of the moral law. Though not normally given to mixing biblical exegesis into his critical philosophy, Kant makes an exception in *Religion*. There he is keenly interested in how the Scriptures, if read to accord with a moral hermeneutic (e.g., the presumptive reading of evil), can suggest the appropriate limits of a critical analysis.

Take the case of the serpent in the garden. Kant underscores the abruptness of the serpent's insertion into the Genesis narrative, where before harmonies have been the rule: male and female, God and humanity, heaven and earth. The serpent connives to subvert these harmonies and turn them into antagonisms. He does this by tempting Adam (through Eve) to disobey God's command, here construed as the moral law. Kant's moral hermeneutic inclines him, like Augustine, not to make deception the cause of Adam's lapse; this means, for Kant (and for Augustine as well), that Adam retains his disposition to reason even as he gives into the temptation to subvert the rational order, the order of God's good creation.

The secret of a reasoner who reasons against reason is not amenable to further analysis, and this limit, thinks Kant, is precisely the point of the serpent's unprecedented appearance. It is Scripture's way of signaling an aporia. For no narrative that includes a first sin – an original turn from good to evil, plenitude to privation – can begin at the beginning. The first sin always shows up as an interjection, a disruption of narrative time. It is the sins to follow (if following makes any sense here) that speak to a struggle over time against temptation; they are the half-heartedly incarnate things that both fuel and frustrate a hope for redemptive closure. Here is Kant on the logic of sin's depiction:

> The absolutely *first* beginning of all evil is . . . represented as incomprehensible to us (for whence the evil in that spirit?); the human being, however, is represented as having lapsed into it only *through temptation*; hence not as corrupted *fundamentally* (in his very first predisposition to the good) but, on the contrary, as still capable of improvement, by contrast to a tempting *spirit*, i.e., one whom the temptation of the flesh cannot be accounted as a mitigation of guilt. And so for the human being, who despite a corrupted heart yet always possesses a good will, there still remains hope of a return to the good from which he has strayed.[13]

This is still the logic of deficient causality. Notice why it simply cannot be a logic of redemption. If the temptation of the flesh mitigates guilt, then there must first be guilt to mitigate. That guilt returns the "tempting *spirit*" to its human host, and once again Adam is hopeless.

I bring Kant to the discussion of Augustine principally for two reasons. Because Kant is so much more intent than Augustine is on a demythologized moralism, Kant's concessions to mythology powerfully suggest the limits of a metaphysical approach to evil. It turns out not to be philosophically otiose for an Augustine or a Kant to become preoccupied with the intricacies of the Genesis narrative. Our sense of the origin of evil may not, after all, be so independent of our inability to finish a story that has a doggedly obscure and perhaps irreducibly symbolic beginning. Once this is recognized, Kant's other offering stands out. Because his reluctantly mythologized moralism is still a moralism, Kant shows us what habits of exegesis tend to sustain moralism. One habit in particular does most of the work. Kant pays no attention to the different roles that Adam and Eve respectively play in framing the first sin. Eve disappears into his Adam, and Adam, the

---

[13] Kant 1793/1998: 65, original emphasis.

mysteriously self-subverting reasoner, directly violates the law of his own highest nature under a veil of temptation.

The closest analogue in Augustine to this Kantian exegetical practice is his decision in his early allegorical interpretation of Genesis, written against the flesh-hating Manichees, to relegate Eve to the unthinking senses (*Gn. adv. Man.* 2.14.51). He gives Adam the part of pure reason. Reasonable Adam is susceptible to unmanly overthrow by his sensual wife, but he is naturally and ideally in a position of rulership over her. When allegorical Adam and Eve get together, we get one individual: a well-functioning Adam.

In his later commentaries, where Augustine aims to be more literal and less allegorical, his Adam, who is as animal in his flesh as Eve is in hers, comes to have a sensuality of his own.[14] Adam no longer subsumes Eve; he relates to her. When she parts from him through transgression, he feels distress as well as longing. He cannot bear the thought of abandoning his partner to her separate fate. In Augustine's extended literal commentary, it is not lust or any ignoble feeling that moves Adam to rejoin with her, but "a kind of friendly benevolence" (*amicali quadam benevolentia*; *Gn. litt.* 11.42.59). This same Adam reappears in *City of God*, expecting from his maker, if not exoneration, at least some sympathy for the difficulty of his choice (*civ. Dei* 14.11).

The choice to dramatize Adam's choice, relative to *Eve's* transgression, is the exegetical practice of Augustine's that is least likely to sustain the moralism that he and Kant mostly share in common.[15] This is not to say that Augustine cannot fight against the drift of his choice and find his way back to moralism. Take, for example, his insistence in *City of God* on an "undeceived" Adam (*non seductus*; *civ. Dei* 14.11, cf. 1 Tim. 2:14). He does

---

[14] Unlike some readers of Augustine on Genesis, I do not believe that Augustine ever thought of Adam as having spiritualized flesh. Whether he is interpreting Genesis allegorically or literally, he consistently thinks of Adamic life in Eden as probationary: the man and the woman begin with unproven spiritual promise and some version of an animal body. The most that can be said of their somatic status in *Gn. adv. Man.* is that their animality is vaguely more ethereal than it is later on. Augustine criticizes himself (*retr.* 1.10.2) for having once been too delicate in his affirmation of Adam's original animality, but not for having entertained a quasi-Plotinian fall of an immaterial soul, undividedly male and female, into a man and woman of mortal flesh. For contrary readings of *Gn. adv. Man.*, see Teske 1991, who outfits Adam and Eve with celestial bodies, and O'Connell 1991, who combines their spirits within a single, archetypical, trans-historical soul.

[15] In his poignant "Letter to Augustine," Connolly 1991: 151–52 blithely dismisses the importance of Eve to Augustine's reading of the fall. In this, he shows himself to be one of the many modern interpreters who are prepared to overstress Augustine's moralism and assimilate him, in effect, to the Kant of *Religion*.

not mean absolutely undeceived. After having managed not to play the serpent's fool, Adam straightaway becomes his own; he deceives himself into thinking that his sin is venial and easily forgiven. Augustine says of this Adam that he is "unacquainted with the divine severity" (*inexpertus divinae severitatis*; *civ. Dei* 14.11). Bear in mind that Augustine's God is severe, not out of anger (as if God's feelings could be hurt), but out of the strict imperative of justice that expresses who God is. Adam cannot transgress against divine justice without having first separated himself (in secret) from the being that makes an order of the good possible. For an Adam already thus deprived, the choice of Eve over God is one of pure pretence. A choice of any good would have served as well – maybe Adam just likes the taste of apples – and no choice of good would have been forgivable. Undeceived Adam isn't seduced by Satan because he doesn't need to be: his lack of acquaintance with "the divine severity" is damning enough.

Moralism is always available to Augustine in his reading of Genesis. This is because it is not, strictly considered, a reading; it is the presumption of a reading. What if we suspend the presumption and allow Augustine's Adam the substance of his human motivation? The story might go something like this.

Part I: Adam does not wish to be separated from the flesh of his flesh. His animal flesh does not in fact dispose him to seek self-enclosure; Eve is distinctive to him, a separate beauty, and not merely a means to extend or sustain the sameness of himself. He is good with her, and otherwise bad, bereft (Gen. 2:18). He assumes that God, who knows the true meaning of good and bad, will understand, will forgive him for his choice.

Part II: It is also true that Adam, like an angel about to fall, cannot quite believe that trust in God's goodness is all that knowledge of God can possibly be. He takes his taste of knowledge out of trust, but also mistrust, and it is the mistrust that soon begins to show. He hides from God, fearing retribution and death. When God calls him out, Adam is evasive and self-veiling: "The woman whom you gave by me," he explains (Gen. 3:13), "she gave me from the tree, and I ate." Augustine readily sees the sin behind the veil (*civ. Dei* 14.11; *Gn. litt.* 11.35.47): Adam is giving over his responsibility to Eve and to God, the two sources of his life, and offering up his partner as sacrifice; he imagines that he is lessening his own punishment. Having tested his trust in his divine father in order to be with Eve, "the mother of all that lives" (Gen. 3:20), Adam has done anything but affirm his renewed partnership with her. Within the frame of his mistrust, his transgression looks shamefully naked. God soon drives Adam and the woman, still unrecognized (despite her being named), from the garden, to block their access to the tree of life.[16] One beginning is over.

The two parts of the proposed story are not neatly chronological. Adam's mistrust does not succeed his trust and take its place; it is superimposed upon it. The trust and the mistrust go together and seem to occupy the same psychic space, suggesting – falsely – that there have always been two stories to tell about him: one of damnation, the other of redemption. The truth is that there has only ever been one story to tell. The other story isn't even a story; its narrative ambitions disappear within a sinkhole of deficiency. But undoubtedly the redemptive turn in Adam's story is every bit as radical and hard to believe as Augustine and Paul have made it out to be, maybe even more so. Where a moralist sees in Adam a mistrust of perfection and an inexcusable loss of moral faith, a saint has to confront a more unsettling possibility: that Adam's mistrust is the face of his faith, revealed in darkness – like the sun in eclipse. The faith is still there, but dangerous to behold.

Consider original knowledge, good and evil. The God of pure spirit, as an object of human knowing, is always a withdrawal, an absence of presence, a second death. That is the evil part of knowing – the deprivation – and it is the part that Adam tastes first. But the good news is that he remains, while in the doom of death, wholly a part of the divine knowing. That is why not having a spiritual body has never been a source of deprivation in Eden. It does not suddenly become one when Adam sees darkness and suspends the generosity of his animal flesh. Outside the garden he will look not for new flesh but for a renewed knowledge, through her, the mother of generosity, of the sinless original – mortal and redemptive, Christ's flesh. Returning to the good part of knowledge is only a matter of time; indeed it is the very meaning of time.

In *City of God*, we find Augustine, the Genesis exegete, at his moralistic peak. He tries his level best to fold Adam and Eve within a single sin, whose paradigm is fleshless and Satanic. But ultimately the saint surpasses the moralist, and we are left less with the unforgiving logic of self-willed deficiencies and more with the shifts in relative goodness that make for a story of redemption. I say this not to sanctify Augustine – he hardly needs

---

[16] Scripture (Gen. 3:24) speaks of the expulsion from Eden of the *adam* – not, that is, Adam as the distinctively male part of the original human couple, but as the creature formed from earth (*adamah*) and enlivened with divine breath. Alter 1996 is a good source for the nuances of Biblical Hebrew; see, for example, p. 5, n. 26. I often use the name "Adam" to refer to the first man, but I am keenly aware of its primary denotation. Similarly I take "Eve" to refer to the first woman, the man's counterpart, and also to the mother of all that lives.

me for that — but in recognition of what may be a part of the logic of sanctification: that the saint shows up when the moralist begins to relearn the meaning of perfection.

3 PRIVATION

In my attempts both to interpret and extend Augustine's thinking about the nature and origin of evil, I have not abandoned the *privatio* thesis. I accept his acceptance of the broad thesis that evil is basically a privation of goodness, or, in theological language, an absence of God. The thesis holds true even for positively demonic agents of deprivation. Also I have not entirely abandoned the analysis of deficient causality that Augustine so tightly associates with the *privatio* thesis. But while I agree that it is not possible to give a good reason for a privation, apart from a prior privation, I have resisted Augustine's inclination to absolutize deficient agency. If the conditions are perfect for the flourishing of my best self, and I can still be moved to will my self-corruption, then I am not just a deficient agent; I am irredeemably deficient.

But if it were simply the case that responsible agents never will deficiently, then evil in a providential order would be an illusion. I am more inclined to think, in keeping with Augustine, that God makes a good use of sin. And so while we do sometimes will deficiently, we do not thereby have a special power of agency that is unique to us and sealed off from God. We are not literally in the deprivation business. Having to give over this last, rather pathetic, shred of autonomy leaves us perpetually open to self-revision, but such openness, all moralism aside, is itself a form of responsibility. In the face of evil, we are called to be better citizens of a *corpus permixtum*, an entangled body, and not archeologists of an abandoned perfection. This means no less than to venture compassion where explanation has failed. The more lies beyond my competence to envision.

CHAPTER 10

Hell and the dilemmas of intractable alienation
John Bowlin

The account of last things that Augustine develops in the concluding books of *City of God* assumes his treatment of first things in *civ. Dei* 11–14. Taken together, it's a story of beginnings and endings, of humanity's progress from creation and fall to judgment and mercy, and it puts the will front and center. Forty years earlier, in Book 1 of *On Free Will* (*lib. arb.*), the recently ordained Augustine regarded the will as a creature of theodicy and beatitude. Its potential for perversity provided for the hard facts of sin and thus guaranteed the goodness of God, the right order of creation, and the justice of punishment. At the same time, its mysterious self-sufficiency made eternal blessedness a temporal prospect and perfect virtue a sensible ambition. By these early lights, sin and beatitude were each had in the same way: through a simple turn of the will (*lib. arb.* 1.12.26). But here, in *City of God*, the will is largely a creature of biblical exegesis, of Genesis 3, Romans 7, and Matthew 25:31–46. It enables Augustine to begin and conclude the drama of salvation, to get Adam out of Eden, incontinence up and running, and sheep separated from goats.

This mature account of the will is clearly an improvement over the somewhat flat-footed earlier view, with its blithe confidence in our ability to will at will and its reduction of every sin to perverse pride, and yet traces of the impulse to theodicy remain. On the last day, we must be able to count God just in both judgment and mercy. The eternal misery of the damned must be deserved, and the grace that the blessed receive must confirm God's righteousness. To secure this outcome, Augustine makes two moves. First, he insists, as he did forty years earlier, that the will's perverse loves are not only possible but free. They are not only an actual feature of our relationship to the good, but they are also done knowingly, with sin's consent. Because they are possible, hell's eternal alienation from the good is imaginable. Because they are free, hell's torments are deserved. Second, he insists that the love bestowed upon the blessed is entirely gracious, that God's pardon comes entirely as gift. Put negatively, grace comes to sinners who have no ties of kinship or debt to the one who gives. Without those ties, it cannot be owed; its absence cannot be arbitrary or cruel.

In what follows, I recount the story of last things that Augustine tells in *City of God*, and I consider the role he asks the will to play in the drama of salvation, in its tragic beginnings and comic endings. Along the way, I consider whether the impulse to theodicy that remains in his treatment of judgment and mercy runs afoul of other aspects of his thought. My hunch is that it does on at least two counts. As we shall see, his insistence on the free character of Adam's fall conflicts with the treatment of voluntary agency that he assumes in his account of perversity. The will's loves can be either perverse or voluntary but not both, and he needs them to be both only as he hopes to guarantee the justice of God's response to Adam's sin. So too, we will find that his account of grace sits uncomfortably with his treatment of creation, kinship, and Christology. Once again, he can have one or the other but not both, and he needs both only as he hopes to secure the righteousness of God's mercy.

I DISOBEDIENT UNTO DEATH

Getting Adam out of Eden and at least some of his progeny into hell poses "great and difficult questions" (*civ. Dei* 15.1), and for Augustine the difficulty comes in two parts. On the one hand, it's not exactly clear how to account for sin in paradise when, as Augustine sees it, every reason that might explain its origin has been discounted, every cause dismissed. On the other, it's not exactly clear how eternal torment can count as a fitting response to that sin. Wouldn't something less than an eternity in duration be more proportionate to Adam's crime however it is imagined? Wouldn't something less horrific in substance be more compatible with God's mercy and love? Yet Augustine persists, as he must, given the claims of Genesis 3 and the predictions of Matthew 25, and his replies come with an elegant symmetry and a relentless logic. The only sin that can be imagined in paradise is precisely the sort that can justify intractable alienation from God as punishment, or so Augustine thinks. The eternal death experienced by the sons of Adam turns out to be a fitting conclusion to their father's sin, or so Augustine assumes.

Sin is difficult to imagine in Eden because its ordinary sources, simple incontinence and habitual malice, cannot be found in its gardens. The reason is straightforward. God "created man righteous," without vice in the soul or disorder in the passions (*civ. Dei* 13.14). Our natural ability to know the human good, judge and rank its various instantiations, and love in accord with that judgment was, in Adam, perfected by divine grace (*civ. Dei* 13.13). His judgments were always right and his will always loved in accord with what he had judged. He was, as a result, always able to treat the various persons and goods that he confronted justly, giving to each the love that each is due by right given the kind of thing that each is. Because of that same grace, his passionate responses to the world "did not...exist in their present vicious form. For they were not then moved to do anything contrary to a righteous will" (*civ. Dei* 14.19). They could not fix his attention on goods of lesser rank, distort his judgment about their relative merit, and compel him to love what in a cool hour he would otherwise resist. Add the pleasant conditions of Eden's gardens, where Adam lived without want for food, drink, or life, without anxiety or sorrow, and it's easy to conclude that "he enjoyed supreme health in body, and entire tranquility of soul." Without division or conflict in his loves, he responded in perfect obedience to God, whose command he obeyed with ease and whose presence he enjoyed in gratitude. Unable to render false judgment or deny each person or thing its just due, he shared a "faithful fellowship of honest love" with other human beings. Without clash or quarrel between the coolness of judgment and the "excitement of passion," he lived in perfect concord with his body (*civ. Dei* 14.26, here and above), its movements and members always subject to the command of his will.[1]

Given this grace-perfected soul and these happy external conditions, neither incontinence nor malice can account for Adam's sin. His judgments were not corrupted by passion; his loves were not fractured by habit. Without compulsion or struggle, he acted with easy obedience to God, the source of all goodness, and his obedience was nothing more than his untroubled desire for the good that he judged best in every circumstance that he confronted. In every instance, his soul obeyed God, and his body and its passions obeyed his soul. Indeed, as Augustine readily admits, the story of Adam's fall cannot be a drama of temptation, of initial resistance and eventual lapse (*civ. Dei* 14.10, 14.13), for this assumes a divided soul that his original righteousness rules out. Rather, "in this state of blessedness, there would have been the certain assurance that no one would sin and no one would die" (*civ. Dei* 14.10). How then does Adam fall into each?

The answer that Augustine develops in Book 14 goes roughly like this. While we can offer no reason for Adam's sin, no explanation that would make it intelligible, we can locate its source in his will, prideful and perverse.

---

[1] Traces of this lost control remain in the freakish, willful control that some of us have over some portion of the body. See *civ. Dei* 14.24.

No reason can be offered for his disobedience because a reason would refer to a disordered judgment about the relevant goods at stake as potential ends of Adam's action, and Augustine has ruled out all possible sources of disorder. Had Adam judged the good that is eternal fellowship with God as somehow less than best and the good that comes as that fellowship is forsaken as somehow better, then we would have an explanation for his sin in the sources and substance of that false judgment. But of course God's grace and Adam's virtue discount all such sources, which means that only one answer remains. Insofar as Adam chose to forsake fellowship with God willingly, the source of his sin must be located in his will, in its ability to refuse the good that he has judged aright and, in full knowledge, love something less than best.[2]

Augustine calls this ability, this love, *amore perverso* (*civ. Dei* 12.8). It is done "contrary to nature" and thus perverts our humanity (*civ. Dei* 14.1). Human beings were made to know and love the good, to rank its various instantiations best to worst, and to refer to those rankings when we justify and explain what we say and do.[3] What's more, we were made to count the immutable good best and to love that good above all. As this good is none other than the God who creates but is not created, Augustine can confess that we were made by God for fellowship with God. He can assert that the peace we all desire, the beatitude for which we yearn, comes only as we rest in Him (*civ. Dei* 19.12; *conf.* 1.1.1). But this means that the person who willingly refuses the good that he knows to be best, indeed the good that has no peer, not only departs from reason for no reason, but in so doing, he "falls away" from his own nature. He lapses (*deficit*). He decays. He defects from his humanity. Like an enzyme, his sin denatures his soul and leaves him less than he was, less than the human being that God made him to be (*civ. Dei* 14.13).

Augustine calls this perverse defection from nature an act of pride, of willful disobedience. *Initium ... omnis peccati superbia. Quid est autem superbia nisi perversae celsitudinis appetitus?* Pride is the beginning of all sin precisely because sin has its origin in Adam's "appetite for a perverse kind of elevation," one that "forsakes the foundation upon which the mind should

---

[2] This is precisely what it means for the will to be a deficient cause of Adam's sin: it is source but not explanation. Hoping to find in this source a cause that explains is equivalent to "wishing to see darkness or hear silence" (*civ. Dei* 12.7).

[3] Throughout my interpretation of Augustine's treatment of will and agency, I make explicit what he often leaves implied: that "approbation must always be a part of our recognition of the good," that our desire for it and delight in it always assumes our cognitive appraisal of it, our positive judgment about its merit. See Wetzel 1992: 201.

rest" (*civ. Dei* 14.13). Had he remained humble, Adam would have conceded his status as creature. He would have recognized that his happiness depends upon a good that transcends him and all other creatures, a good that must be judged truthfully and loved justly. In a sense, Adam's perversity amounts to nothing more than a failure of this humility, an assertion of this independence. By turning away from a good that he knows to be best and without fear or self-deception fixing his love on something less, he asserts himself against the God who transcends him, whose goodness should be recognized, obeyed, and received as blessing (*civ. Dei* 14.12).

The consequences of Adam's sin follow from its origin in his will's perversity. Some are immediate effects of the act itself; others come from God as punishment for disobedience. Both plunge Adam and his progeny into death, first in foretaste and then in full measure. If human beings are created by God to know and love God and to find life and fulfillment in that knowing and loving, then a will that "falls away from Him Who has no superior" tilts toward death (*civ. Dei* 14.13). It is as if Adam wills his own demise, the decay of his own nature, and in that very act receives a portion of what he desires. Augustine adds the relevant caveats: "To be sure, man did not fall away from his nature so completely as to lose all being. When he turned toward himself, however, his being became less complete than when he clung to Him Who exists supremely. Thus, to forsake God and to exist in oneself – that is to be pleased with oneself – is not immediately to lose all being; but it is to come closer to nothingness" (*civ. Dei* 14.13). It is not exactly to die, but to live in death, to allow the end of life to afflict its every moment (*civ. Dei* 13.10).[4]

God's response to Adam's sin concedes Adam's desire for independence and confirms the adage that urges caution about wishing. "He who, in his pride, has pleased himself, was now, by God's justice, handed over to himself" (*civ. Dei* 14.15). The grace that had once perfected Adam's soul and sustained his life is now withdrawn (*civ. Dei* 13.13), and, on his own, Adam tilts toward death evermore. The difference is that here, east of Eden, his perversity has passed and thus death arrives unwelcome. Once "disobedient unto death," Adam now laments the death that comes as punishment for his disobedience. In foretaste, it comes in "the conflict between lust and will" (*civ. Dei* 14.23), between his body's passions and his loves that conform to his better judgments. In full measure, it comes in the fact that he is

---

[4] Commenting on Is. 66:22ff. Augustine finds a link between falling and dying in the way we speak about each (*civ. Dei* 20.21): "For who does not see that corpses (*cadavera*) are so called from their falling (*cadendo*)?"

Hell and alienation 191

"doomed against his will to die in body also" (*civ. Dei* 14.15). In each instance, Adam is "divided against himself" (*civ. Dei* 14.15). Though his will commands, his flesh rebels and threatens his self with loss, a threat made good in the body's death and that he knows even now in his own fractured agency, his own loss of self-control.[5] For Augustine, it's a punishment that fits the crime. "To state it briefly then: in the punishment of that sin, what is the retribution for disobedience if not disobedience itself? For what is man's misery if not simply his own disobedience to himself, so that, because he would not do what he could, he now cannot do what he would? ... For who can count the many things that a man wishes to do but cannot? For he is disobedient to himself: that is, his very mind, and even his lower part, his flesh, do not obey his will" (*civ. Dei* 14.15).

This conceptual connection between disobedience and death finds its full expression in the eternal misery of the damned. If the incontinent and the afflicted are like the dying in their inability to control themselves, if their unwelcome passions and pains bear witness to their mortality that comes *contra voluntatem*, and if the conflicts that divide their souls generate disagreements between friends and within households, discord in communities, and deadly wars among nations (*civ. Dei* 15.4–5, 19.5–7), then the second death that comes as punishment to all who are not "chosen by grace" for membership in the "City of the Saints" (*civ. Dei* 15.1) arrives as endless incontinence, pain, and strife. In that state, "men will not be before death or after death, but always in death, and, for that reason, never living, never dead, but endlessly dying" (*civ. Dei* 13.11). And this endless dying will be nothing but an eternal conflict between will and passion, just as its yield will be nothing but war without end among hell's inhabitants. Of this bellicose second death (*secunda mors*) Augustine writes (*civ. Dei* 19.28): "What war, then, can be imagined more grievous and bitter than one in which the will is so much at odds with the passions, and the passions with the will, that their hostility cannot be ended by the victory of either: a war such that the force of pain is in such conflict with the body's nature that neither can yield to the other?"

It is a logic as stunning in consistency as it is relentless in inference. Adam's perverse disobedience must be imagined in order to get sin into

---

[5] Thus Brown (1988: 405, 408) can write: "Death always remained for Augustine the most bitter sign of human frailty. For death frustrated the soul's deepest wish, which was to live at peace with its beloved, the body. Death could never be welcomed as a freeing of the soul from a body to which it had been joined by accident. It was an unnatural occurrence." The body's unruly passions, its sexual urges above all, offer "a miniature shadow" of this unnatural frustration. "Like death, the onset and culmination of sexual sensation mocked the will."

paradise, and hell's eternal dying becomes imaginable precisely because perversity is. Get sin into paradise, without saving grace, and hell's horrors come as consequence. Since Satan falls according to the same logic (*civ. Dei* 12.6–9), Adam "resembles the devil" when his will defects from God (*civ. Dei* 14.4). Indeed, as Augustine sees it, a will "so darkened and chilled" (*tenebresceret et frigesceret*; *civ. Dei* 14.13) by sin as Adam's deserves the devil's company for eternity (*civ. Dei* 15.1). Even now, "the miseries and ills...to which the human race is subject" as punishment for Adam's sin land us squarely on hell's doorstep. For human life is so full of pains and sorrows, so rife with the cruelty and injustice that "comes forth from that root of error and perverse love" (*erroris et perversi amoris radice venientia*), that it is "like a hell on earth (*quasi quibusdam inferis vitae*); and there is no escape from it other than through the grace of Christ, our Savior, God and Lord" (*civ. Dei* 22.22).

2 JUST IN MERCY AND JUDGMENT

Indeed, it is a "misery common to us all" (*civ. Dei* 22.22). Adam chooses perversely and deadly consequences follow, a punishment that all receive, even as grace redeems but a few (*civ. Dei* 21.12). Taken together, these two declarations about divine judgment and mercy must not only account for the relevant biblical texts and our vexed life in time – we do indeed die, sin incontinently, and act virtuously only with struggle – but they must also guarantee the justice of God's response to sin, both Adam's and our own. Whether in punishment or pardon, we are addressed "by God's justice" (*civ. Dei* 14.15, 14.26–27), or so Augustine assumes, and once again it is the will that guarantees the assumption, or so he thinks.

Augustine develops four claims that create this linkage between justice, theodicy, and last things. First, Adam sins freely. His perverse defection from God is his own. It's a human action and it can be assigned to him. "Where the will becomes evil, this evil would not arise in it if the will itself were unwilling; and its defects are therefore justly punished, because they are not necessary but voluntary" (*non necessarios, sed voluntarios*; *civ. Dei* 12.8). Even in paradise, while it was not within Adam's power "to live well without God's help, ...it was within his power to live ill." Exercise that power and "his blessedness would not endure and a most just punishment would ensue" (*civ. Dei* 14.27). The claim is fundamental. If Augustine is to guarantee the justice of God's response to Adam's sin, then Adam's sin must be voluntary. "For no one suffers punishment for faults of nature, but [only] for vices of the will" (*civ. Dei* 12.3).

Second, the magnitude of the first transgression, both in act and consequence, corresponds to God's response. Yes, "eternal punishment seems harsh and unjust (*dura et iniusta*) to human senses," but we must "understand what great a crime was committed in the first transgression" (*civ. Dei* 21.12). Augustine calls it an act of utmost impiety, which is exactly right. Recall that Adam's sin was hardly ordinary. His defection from God was not the consequence of a false judgment about the relative merit of the goods at stake. He did not choose a good other than God because he had, in that instance, judged it best and loved it because of that judgment. Indeed, had he sinned in this ordinary way, we might call him unjust for his failure to respond to God's goodness as he should, with the recognition that it deserves, but we would not count him among the willfully perverse. His judgment would have been false and his action contrary to the right, but an ordinary sinner he would have been. But not so the real Adam. Made right by grace in judgment and passion, his defection from God was done, not only willfully, but knowingly. He had already found enjoyment in God's presence, and he understood what he was forsaking as he turned from the immutable good to something less. Given this experience and knowledge, he had no *reason* to turn, and yet he turned nevertheless. But this means that his impiety was of an altogether different kind. It did not follow from his failure to recognize God's goodness, but indeed, it emerged from that very recognition (*civ. Dei* 21.12)!

In this way, Augustine addresses what Ted Sider calls the vagueness problem that afflicts most (perhaps all) attempts to count eternal punishment proportionate to the crime it addresses.[6] The problem goes roughly like this. Given the fact that hell is a very bad place, where alienation from the good for which we were made is permanent and where "bodies burn without being consumed, and suffer without dying" (*civ. Dei* 21.9), its defenders must be certain that its punishments fit Adam's crime. Those punishments must be proportionate to what he has done, and what he has done must single him out for these unique torments. But this means that Adam could not commit just any crime. Why? Because the severity of punishment must in some way conform to the wickedness of the crime. But hell's eternal anguish is utterly distinct in severity, and thus every attempt to set aside those ordinary crimes that deserve *this* punishment from those that do not will resort to an arbitrary criterion. Such a judgment will regard moral matters of degree, of vague differences across similar cases, and yet in the end a line will have to be drawn. On one side will be crimes that receive

---

[6] Sider 2002.

grim hell as punishment, on the other, crimes that receive punishment of some sort but not *this*! Since crimes come in degrees of wickedness, the criterion used to draw this line will invariably treat very similar crimes very differently. Some sinners will find themselves in hell while their near neighbors, morally speaking, will not. But this violates the demands of proportional justice, which prohibits very unequal treatment of very similar crimes. As Sider points out, "such a cutoff would be monstrous."[7]

The vagueness that afflicts our moral judgments runs afoul of the distinct character of hell's punishments. What's needed, then, is a crime as different in kind from all others as hell's punishments are from the cellblocks of Sing-Sing. Combine the perverse character of Adam's sin with the intimacy with God that he forsakes and you get a crime of precisely this sort. Adam's sin admits of no comparison, no assessment by degree, precisely because it lands nowhere on our ordinary spectrum of moral agency. To refuse the good that you know to be best, to do so without self-deception, ignorance, or passion-charged confusion, and to love instead a good that you know will do little to quiet your heart's restless yearning for beatitude – *this* is no ordinary sin. Choosing a lesser good or ignoring a divine command is one thing, but to act as Adam does – to choose and ignore without (even temporarily) regarding those actions and ends as somehow better than their alternatives – *this* is another thing altogether. It creates a "gap" between perversity and ordinary sin that does indeed warrant an altogether distinct response.[8]

Of course, one might accept this solution to the vagueness problem, admit that Adam's impiety is an altogether different sort of sin, and yet still consider eternal punishment disproportionate. Yes, Adam knowingly and willfully disobeyed God's goodness and refused his own happiness. Yes, the mysterious perversity of this act makes it sufficiently distinct from ordinary sin to justify an altogether different response. But why does this deliberate slight against God's immutable goodness warrant eternal alienation from that good? How can *this* punishment be a just response to *this* crime?

Augustine replies: God's judgment is just because Adam's disregard for the good threatens to undermine his humanity. Adam was made to know, love, and take delight in the good, to obey its claim upon him, and to regard the changeless good as best. This is the nature he was given and that he refuses in his willful disregard for the blessings of God's company. In this deliberate denial of the good for which he was made, he expresses a nihilistic self-hatred

---

[7] Sider 2002: 61.
[8] Sider 2002: 60. Sider's argument comes down to this: in a world without moral gaps of this kind, hell is unjust, obscene.

and in that expression succeeds in diminishing himself (*civ. Dei* 14.13). God's response simply leaves things where Adam left them. The creature who can neither bring himself into being nor flourish on his own refuses each, both existence and flourishing, and thus embraces their opposites, both death and misery. Since humanity enters the torrent of history only as Adam makes these refusals and leaves the garden, there is a sense in which this drama of creation and decreation takes place in an eternal frame.[9] Eternal death and misery merely confirm that frame. If the just recognize things for what they are and respond in accord with that recognition, then, as Augustine sees it, nothing could be more just than the response to Adam's sin – its substance and consequence – that God in fact provides.[10]

But of course, it's not just Adam who receives this sentence. *He* sins and yet *all* are punished; all live "a life under condemnation" (*civ. Dei* 22.24). "For he who first gave admission to sin has been punished together with those who were in him as a root, so that no one may escape this just and deserved punishment unless redeemed by mercy and undeserved grace" (*civ. Dei* 21.12). If this is to be a just punishment, then all must somehow share in Adam's sin, in both its perverse beginnings and its penal incontinence.

This is the third claim that Augustine develops, and here the matter regards the manner of our creation, a manner that distinguishes us from both angels and beasts. Angels neither reproduce nor die, and thus they were created en masse on the first day (*civ. Dei* 11.9). Beasts do die and they do reproduce, and so it was unnecessary to create all of them all at once. Nor did "God produce these from a single individual" (*non ex singulis propagavit*; *civ. Dei* 12.22). Rather, on the fifth and sixth days of creation God commanded that several individuals of each species come into being, knowing full well that each would reproduce itself from these. Human beings, by contrast, were created one and alone from a single individual. The aim was not that Adam might remain alone, "bereft of human society, but that by this means, the unity of society and the bond of concord might be commended to him more forcefully, mankind being bound together

---

[9] As expressed in Markus 1970: 10: "The creation is the beginning of all things. Time itself only came into being with the creation of the temporal things. In a strict sense, however, man's condition between the creation and Adam's fall, though temporal, can be described as not fully historical. But for man's primal sin and fall from the condition of grace there would have been no need for God's saving work. Nor would man's existence in that state, had he continued in it, have been fully historical."

[10] Augustine concludes with a challenge that brings together the first two claims (*civ. Dei* 14.15): "Anyone who deems this measure of condemnation to be excessive or unjust certainly does not know how to measure the greatness of the iniquity in the sinning where it would have been easy not to sin."

not only by similarity of nature, but by the affection of kinship" (*cognationis affectu*). It was for this reason that Eve was created, not entirely anew but from Adam, "so that the human race might derive entirely from one man" (*civ. Dei* 12.22; cf. *civ. Dei* 14.1).

For Augustine, two consequences follow from our common origin in Adam's flesh. Together, they confirm what we know of human sinfulness and bear witness to the justice of God. On the one hand, we share Adam's propensity for perversity. He fell, and so can we. While we do not live in God's company as he did and cannot, therefore, defect from so great a good, we can refuse what we know to be best in this or that circumstance of choice, and, in full knowledge, will something of lesser worth. We can also love an action that we know to be evil (*conf.* 2.4.9) and take sadistic delight in the evil that others endure (*conf.* 3.1.1). In this respect at least, we share in Adam's original sin.

But we also share in his subsequent sins. Adam turned from God, and God turned from Adam. Left to himself, without the assistance of God's grace, Adam became "disobedient to himself" so that "his very mind, and even his lower part, his flesh, do not obey his will" (*civ. Dei* 14.15). Sins of weakness followed willy-nilly. As we come from Adam's flesh, we share Adam's fate. As Adam's nature changed when grace was withdrawn, it's that changed nature that we inherit. As God would not have created us disobedient to ourselves and thus prone to moral weakness, this inheritance must come as punishment for the sins of Adam that we share as kin, first in origin and now in consequence.[11]

For now, this punishment is penal, but on the last day it will become eternal also (*civ. Dei* 13.2). This life of dying will become our permanent abode. But not for all. While all are guilty and deserve punishment, forgiveness comes to some as gift, as pardon, as redemption from the second death that all deserve. Some have been "predestined by grace and chosen by grace" for this mercy; some have not (*civ. Dei* 15.1). Both have been treated justly, the latter because they receive the punishment that fits their crime, the former because they receive a gift "freely given" (*gratuita*; *civ. Dei* 14.26).

---

[11] See *civ. Dei* 13.3: "For nothing could be born of them which was not what they themselves had been. Their nature was changed for the worse in proportion to the condemnation attaching the magnitude of their sin, so that what arose as a punishment in the first human beings who sinned also follows as a natural consequence in the rest who are born of them ... But man the parent is the same thing as man the offspring. In the first man, therefore, there existed the whole human race which was to pass through the woman into her progeny when that conjugal pair received that divine sentence of its own damnation. And what man became, not when he was created, but when he sinned and was punished: this he propagated, so far as the origin of sin and death are concerned."

This is the fourth claim that Augustine makes in defense of God's righteousness, and it turns on the logic of punishment and mercy, justice and gift. As all deserve punishment and none are owed mercy, none can complain of injustice when some are singled out for redemption (cf. *Simpl.* 1.2.16). God does not choose the redeemed for their merits, but by grace, and in this "He shows his bounty" (*largiatur ostendens*) to both redeemed and damned alike (*civ. Dei* 14.26). Of course, "if punishment had indeed been visited upon all men, no one could justly have complained of the justice of Him who avenges" (*civ. Dei* 21.12) or deny the good bestowed by this just act. But in his wisdom and mercy, God has redeemed some, and thus "we have reason to give most heartfelt thanks to our Redeemer for His free gift in delivering so many" (*civ. Dei* 21.12). On that last day, all will recognize that the redeemed have been rescued by a goodness not deserved but freely given and that the damned are not denied what they are due (*civ. Dei* 14.26).[12]

3 NATURAL AND NECESSARY, IRRATIONAL AND UNNATURAL

Critics of Augustine's account of sin and damnation tend to concentrate on the third claim. How can it be just for Adam's progeny to receive punishment for a sin they did not commit? How can they deserve a life of weakness and death in time followed by an eternity of anguish and pain when the crime singled out for punishment belongs to another? For most, Augustine's talk of common perversity and shared flesh does little to quiet these worries.

For my part, I'm inclined to think that the more pressing problems come both earlier and later in the *City of God's* drama of sin and salvation. It's not the condemnation that comes to Adam's progeny that should give us pause, at least not at the start. Rather, we should ask whether Adam himself deserves punishment for that first crime, and it's not exactly clear that he does. And of course, if he doesn't, then, given the logic of kinship, nor do we. By the same token, it's not exactly clear that we should rest content with Augustine's insistence that grace will be in short supply on the last day. At the very least, we should wonder whether the kinship we share with Adam, and that Augustine defends in order to guarantee divine justice in punishment, in fact jeopardizes divine justice in mercy.

---

[12] Augustine concedes the obvious. In just punishment, the good bestowed is mediated through loss, and thus the punishment itself counts as evil (*civ. Dei* 12.24).

In this section, I consider whether Adam's perverse refusal of God is sufficiently voluntary to warrant punishment of any sort, whether hell's grim torments or something altogether less horrific. I will argue that it is not. In the section that follows, I consider whether Augustine's treatment of our shared kinship, first in Adam and then in Christ, casts doubt on his desire to yoke justice to grace. I will argue that it does. In each instance, I pit one aspect of Augustine's thought against another, all in the hope of separating kernel from chaff.

Two problems confound Augustine's treatment of Adam's perversity as *human* agency, and they do so in opposite ways. The first makes Adam's sin natural and thus necessary. The second makes it irrational and thus unnatural. Two different senses of the natural are at work here, and yet taken together they threaten the voluntariness of Adam's sin and the justice of God's response.

In the first sense, Adam's defection from the good was natural because it was unavoidable and unavoidable because Adam was made. He is creature, not Creator. But this means that his existence is, strictly speaking, unnecessary. Only God is necessary being and thus God alone is fundamentally changeless. All others – all creatures – have a certain measure of mutability built into their very being insofar as they have made the transition that God never does, from not being to being, from nothing to something. Notice what follows. If Adam is, like all creatures, a contingent being, then he was disposed by his nature – by the fundamental contingency that comes from being created – to fall out of existence. Since Adam exists as a human being only insofar as he knows the human good and loves in accord with what he knows, this disposition to fall away from his humanity finds expression in his willful defection from the good. Thus Augustine can write: "though the existence of the will as a nature is due to its creation by God, its falling away from its nature is due to its creation out of nothing" (*civ. Dei* 14.13).[13] Indeed, created things will always defect from their nature, they will always decay and die and return to nothing. They will fall away because they were made, and they will do so necessarily unless they are sustained in being by the One who made them (*civ. Dei* 14.11).[14]

The inference should be obvious. If, given his status as creature, Adam's defection from the good was bound to happen, then it's not at all clear that

---

[13] Note the contrast with necessary being (*civ. Dei* 12.8): "God cannot ever, anywhere or in any way, be defective, whereas natures made out of nothing can be."

[14] It's the account of creation, contingency, and perversity that he developed many years earlier in the *Confessions* (see *conf.* 7.10.16ff.).

he should be responsible for that defection. If the propensity for perversity is built into his created humanity, if it's a necessity that he cannot avoid, then how can he be held to account when he acts as he was made and turns from God to something he knows to be less than best? How can he be liable for the decay that afflicts all creatures?

To this complaint Augustine would no doubt reply that Adam's defection, though inevitable, was nevertheless willed, and, as such, it is an action that we can assign to him and hold him responsible for. He could have chosen to remain in God's company and retain his humanity, but he didn't. He was offered eternity. It was his for the taking, but he refused. Indeed, "it would have been so easy not to sin," and yet sin he did (*civ. Dei* 14.15). As this "betrayal occurs by an act of free will," we can certainly assign it to him and count God's response just in both judgment and punishment (*civ. Dei* 14.13).

But the problem with this reply is that it's difficult to conclude that Augustine accepts the account of the voluntary that it assumes. In *that* account, Adam sinned freely because his defection from the good was willful, and it was willful because we can find no other explanation for what he did. But the fact that the will wills is, by itself, insufficient evidence for the freedom of its act. By itself, the subjective state of willing does not guarantee the voluntariness of that state. What's needed, in addition, is attention to the object willed and to the agent's cognitive relation to it. More to the point, we need to know whether the agent's apprehension of the object's goodness provides a reason for the subjective state, for the fact that the will fixes its love on this object and not that. If the goodness of the object as apprehended by the agent cannot provide that reason, then we will be hard pressed to count that subjective state free and to hold the agent responsible for the actions that follow from it.

Augustine himself agrees. Indeed, he *must* agree in order to get his account of Adam's sin up and running. Recall, Adam's defection from God was perverse because it was unnatural, and it was unnatural because we were made by God to know and love the good, to judge some goods better than others, and to regard the changeless good as best. To will in accord with that regard is not only to be fully human, fully rational, but "truly free," and perfection of this kind comes only to those who are not enslaved to "vices and sins" (*civ. Dei* 14.11). Made right by God's grace, this was certainly Adam's condition. The only power that could threaten his virtue and thus diminish his freedom was his will, his capacity to resist judgment and to love a good that he knows to be less than best. Exercise that capacity as Adam did, and it's not human agency that follows, rational and free, but something more akin to barking madness.

The best way to see the insanity in this sin is to recall that it is God – the perfect good that has already provided perfect delight – whom Adam knowingly, willfully, and thus perversely refuses. And he refuses while recognizing the misery that will follow from his choice of a lesser good. As with the gourmet who rejects a five-star meal and, for no apparent reason, eats something vile and disgusting instead, we can give no account of Adam's refusal, no reason for his choice, and we are as a result prevented from assigning the act to him. No matter how willful that action might be, its irrationality undercuts both its status *as an action* and its rank among the voluntary.

Indeed, in Adam's refusal of God's goodness it's not just agency and freedom that depart but humanity. The person who "acts" proceeds as one in bondage to a power, in this case the power of death, a power that he cannot forsake and that finds expression in his will's choice. But this means that he is more an instrument of that power, more a thing compelled, than a human being who judges, wills, and acts of his own accord. Had Adam refused to will as he did and instead remained as he was, fixed in love for God, he would have retained his agency and humanity, his rationality and freedom.[15]

Notice the competing character of these necessities and the shared logic of freedom and perversity. Adam is most free, not when he exercises his power of choice, but rather when he is bound by his own judgment to will what he cannot forsake. By the same logic, his freedom is most threatened when he is bound by his creaturely propensity to decay in being and choose a good that he knows to be less than best. In the first instance, there is freedom but no choice, in the second, choice but no freedom. In each, necessity is at work, but the first bears witness to the voluntary character of his agency, the second to its undoing. The first follows from the fact that we were made to love the good that we know, the second from the fact that we were made. If we can't help but judge some good best, then our love for that good follows willy-nilly, with an unavoidable and yet welcome necessity. Judgments about the best generate loves of this sort, and these loves remain free precisely because they follow from *our* judgment. By contrast, our tendency to forsake our judgment and will what we know to be unworthy of our love, while unavoidable given the fact that we were made, is not a necessity *for which* we were made. It is, rather, a feature of our life that

---

[15] Put plainly, choice adds nothing to freedom, not to Adam's, not to ours, not to the perfect freedom of the blessed. Unlike Adam and ourselves, these latter cannot sin. For them, it is an impossibility that follows from their gracious participation in God's sinless life. And, like God, their inability to choose sinful courses of action is an expression of their perfect freedom (*civ. Dei* 22.30).

follows from the fact that we are not God. It is an accidental consequence of the fact that we are creatures, not the substance of our created nature.

If this conclusion is sound, if, in order to account for the perversity of Adam's sin Augustine must assume an account of human agency that undermines the voluntary character of what Adam has done, then he will be hard pressed to count God's response just and hell's torments fitting. Because it is perverse, Adam's sin lands off the ordinary spectrum of moral agency and assessment. This might address the vagueness problem, but once it lands there, doubt is cast on its status as human action, as something that can be assigned to Adam and for which he can be justly punished. Mercy might be a fitting response to this sin, and so too rescue from the conditions that make it possible, but not judgment.

4 SONS OF FLESH, SONS OF PROMISE

Given the desire for symmetry and resemblance that governs Augustine's treatment of sin and punishment, we might think that mercy would not only be a fitting response, but also a *likely* one. Adam tilts toward death, and his progeny receive a life of dying in return. He disobeys God's goodness, and they become disobedient to themselves. He asserts his independence, and we gain a life of exile. By this logic, Adam's perversity should yield God's grace to us all, precisely because the action that most resembles Adam's sin is God's mercy. Both are done for no apparent reason, and thus the former is a kind of shadow and prophetic image of the latter (*civ. Dei* 15.2).

Yet, as we have seen, Augustine resists this logic and insists instead that the last day will bring condemnation to most of us, not mercy, and that however God responds to our sin, justice will be done. In order to reach this conclusion he tells a story that speaks not only of judgment and grace, but also of kinship and sacrifice, and the question is whether these two parts make a coherent whole. My hunch is that they do not, that Augustine's efforts here fall to pieces. He tries to preserve the justice of God's judgment in both punishment and mercy, but this effort runs afoul of his assumptions about kinship, human and divine. He limits the scope of God's love and counts this limit just when in fact the kinship he assumes we share with Adam strikes against this limit and challenges this claim.

In brief, the kinship story goes like this. Adam sins and all are condemned to die, first at the close of this life and then after the resurrection of the body, when all deserve to be "driven headlong, as their due punishment, into that second death to which there is no end" (*civ. Dei* 14.1). United in kinship through Adam's flesh, we are all "sons of Adam" insofar as we share his fallen nature (*civ. Dei* 21.15), and thus "the whole race of... men" is slated to share his misery (*civ. Dei* 20.1). The sins we commit across our days only confirm God's judgment and compound the punishments that we receive, some in this life, some in the next. Yet God is gracious and though all are due punishment some are predestined for mercy. These are "called to adoption by His grace" (*civ. Dei* 12.23), clipped from humanity's "vitiated root" (*vitiata radice*; *civ. Dei* 14.26) and grafted onto a new family tree. They become "sons of God" and receive even now a pledge of their "new inheritance in the world to come" (*civ. Dei* 21.15).

It's the tale of a father's love for a prodigal son, and yet the imagery is largely Pauline and draws on the kinship Christology of Romans 5 and 8. Like Paul, Augustine specifies the mechanism of this grace that redeems, this adoption that saves, in terms of Christ's own descending and dying (*civ. Dei* 21.15):

For there is only one Son of God by nature, Who in his compassion became the Son of man for our sakes, that we, being by nature sons of men, might become sons of God by grace through Him. For He, abiding unchangeable, took our nature upon Himself so that, through that nature, He might take us to Himself. Even while holding fast to His own divinity, He became a partaker in our infirmity, that we, being changed for the better, might, by participating in His immortality and righteousness, lose our condition of sin and mortality, and preserve whatever good quality He had implanted in our nature, now made perfect by the supreme good which is the goodness of His nature. For just as we have fallen into this condition of great evil through one man who sinned, so through the justification of the one Man Who is also God shall we come to a condition of sublime goodness.

By these lights, Christ's incarnation generates the benefit, while his sacrifice mediates its bestowal. God became man so that we might "be conformed to the image of His Son, that He might be the firstborn of many brethren" (*civ. Dei* 13.23), and that we might find a place in this lineage, this household. God took on our infirmity and made Himself subject to the death of the cross so that we might receive this grace, this regeneration.

That sacrifice generates kinship and mediates grace is only implied in this remark from Book 21, but matters are spelled out in Book 10 of the *Confessions*, in the sacramental conclusion (*conf.* 10.43.69):

For us he was victorious before you and victor because he was a victim. For us before you he is priest and sacrifice, and priest because he is sacrifice. Before you he makes us sons instead of servants by being born of you and being servant to us.[16]

---

[16] For a comparative study of sacrifice as a medium of kinship, see Jay 1992.

The sons of promise are adopted into God's family through Christ's sacrifice and receive redemption as their inheritance. The sons of the flesh remain in Adam's family and receive the second death they deserve. The discrimination at work here follows the logic of gifts, and yet it preserves the righteousness of the giver only as Augustine assumes what he cannot, that all involved are strangers.

Give a stranger a gift on a deserted street and, all things being equal, no injustice is done to those nameless and unknown who do not receive. But meet two strangers who are bound together as friends or kin and who are equals in their fellowship, and a gift to one does injustice to the other. It takes no notice of the tie between the two, of the life they share and the equality that abides between them. Of course, the giver might claim invincible ignorance of these ties that bind, but the case that Augustine imagines discounts this defense. If we are all kin, all sons and daughters of Adam, all sinners in need of punishment, and if, despite these ties, God adopts and forgives some, refuses and punishes others, then it's difficult to defend the justice of this grace. Imagine the prodigal had a brother who tagged along. Both break ties with the family. Both need rescue from a wanton past and a punishment deserved. Then imagine a savior who knows of their plight and common kinship, who could sacrifice his honor and adopt and forgive both, but who nevertheless and for no reason chooses only one. Augustine's God is like this.

5 CONCLUSION: A STORY REWRITTEN

If all are united in one flesh, one kinship, one household, and if this union is specified in order to justify the condemnation of all, then all must receive grace according to that same kinship. In one lump we must remain. All must be punished or all adopted. The father must either condemn all to eternal exile or elect all to eternal fellowship, and it's hard to imagine a just and loving God who chooses the first. It's a conclusion that Augustine resists, despite its possible Pauline warrants. He notes the apostle's words (1 Cor. 15:21–22): "Since by man came death, by Man came also the resurrection of the dead. For as in Adam all die, even so in Christ all shall be made alive." And he immediately replies: "This is not to say that all who die in Adam are to become members in Christ; for by far the greater number of them will be stricken with the second death, which is eternal. Rather, the apostle uses the word 'all' in both clauses because, just as no one dies in an animal body except in Adam, so no one is made alive in a spiritual body except in Christ" (*civ. Dei* 13.23).

It's a strained interpretation, one that preserves the prospect of eternal alienation only as it constrains God's grace and resists the logic of kinship in Paul's Christology, a logic that otherwise governs Augustine's tale of sin and salvation. Forsake that resistance and abandon those constraints, and the rewritten tale would accent mercy and rescue, not judgment and hell. If all things made tend toward death, if creatures like us mysteriously turn from the good that we know and for which we were made, and if we are, in addition, troubled by weakness and bound by habit, then it might be punishment that we deserve but it is surely rescue that we need. If we are brothers and sisters of Adam's flesh, then a just and loving God will adopt us all into His eternal lineage through Christ's sacrifice. Our perverse and prodigal lives might merit punishments that fall short of eternal torment, but if we are Adam's kin, then so are we Christ's.

CHAPTER 11

On the nature and worth of Christian philosophy: evidence from the City of God

John Rist

I PRELIMINARIES: THE CASE FOR ADVANCED PHILOSOPHY

Philosophy is a matter of argument, scrutiny, and construction, and is often said to be dependent on reason alone. That cannot be true as stated, for we have to get the data on which we philosophize from somewhere, whether from measuring and evaluating the external world or from introspection or from apparently self-evident beliefs, as the law of contradiction. Any philosophy starts, that is, with certain assumptions, but it is often assumed that these assumptions should not be religious assumptions, even if they eventually point to some sort of religious conclusion. As for Augustine, as soon as he was inspired by Cicero's *Hortensius* to think philosophically (*conf.* 3.4.7), he too tried to look for truth through the use of reason alone – so we can certainly recognize his ensuing mental activity as philosophical. But that activity predates those of his writings we actually possess, though in his earlier books Augustine seems to want to think by reason alone as far as possible. Yet almost immediately he also makes claims about his intellectual activity that make it sound far from our conventional view of philosophy. He tells us for the first time in *The Teacher* (*mag.* 11.37) that he is concerned, in the words of Isaiah 7:9 (in the Latin version of the Septuagint) to understand his faith; for "unless you believe, you will not understand";[1] you will only understand if you believe. The difficulty with that, of course, is this: what should you believe and why should you believe it? Even before his conversion to Catholic Christianity, Augustine began to think that with belief would come a greater understanding both of what philosophy had so far taught him, and also much of what he could not yet understand at all. What I want to show, therefore, are his two different versions of

---

[1] The text remains a *leitmotiv* through his subsequent career: e.g., *lib. arb.* 1.2.4, 2.2.6; *f. et symb.* 1.1; *s.* 91.7.9, 118.1, 126.1.1; *ep.* 120.1.3; *Trin.*7.6.12, 15.2.2; *Jo. ev. tr.* 29.6, 45.7; *c. Faust.* 1.46.

philosophical activity – as he came to see them when he held that at least for some philosophical questions, belief is an essential weapon in the thinker's armory.

In the first place it was not faith that led Augustine to philosophy. Cicero's *Hortensius* encouraged him to believe that through philosophy, more or less as we often understand it, that is by the use of reason alone, he could attain the truth. I shall refer to this type of philosophizing as General Philosophy and distinguish it from philosophy dependent on a faith that it intends to justify and understand. That I shall call Advanced Philosophy. Some would prefer to say "Theology," but the difference in terminology would (perhaps rightly) matter little to Augustine. As we shall see, it was his discovery in General Philosophy of two inadequacies inherent in its own methodology that led Augustine to recommend progressing to Advanced Philosophy. The paradox is that if Augustine himself had not philosophized "generally," he would not have recognized that Advanced Philosophy is the method that philosophically – not merely in terms of the acceptance of true beliefs – can secure the greater understanding.

The same problem can be presented in other terms: General Philosophy was Augustine's original order of limited discovery, while Advanced Philosophy became his preferred method of exposition of what he had learned to understand better. Yet without going through the procedures of General Philosophy it may be difficult if not impossible to give an account of why the truths revealed by Advanced Philosophy are ultimately true, for they can easily but unwisely be presented with no accompanying explanation of why General Philosophy must bring the thinker into a cul-de-sac from which only Advanced Philosophy can release him. In that case the professor of Advanced Philosophy can reasonably be accused of encouraging not Catholic philosophy but Catholic fideism or blind faith, which should have disturbed an Augustine who already tells us in *Against the Skeptics* (*c. Acad.* 3.20.43) – his first book after his conversion – that he wants not just belief but understanding. Yet, despite his personal history and deepest beliefs, it probably did not disturb him enough.

On Augustine's own account his conversion to Manicheism was encouraged by the claim of the Manichees that although they were a Christian group, they relied not on authority but on reason alone to support their teachings (*b. vita* 1.4). They differed from the superstitious Catholics, they said, in that they never pressed anyone to convert unless their beliefs had been fully discussed and clarified as rational (*util. cred.* 1.2, 9.21, 11.25; *vera rel.* 1.4; *conf.* 3.6.10). It was the very failure of such pretensions to rationalism, not least in Manichean acceptance of astrology, which weakened and then helped destroy Augustine's confidence in the sect.[2] The Manichees had failed in General Philosophy.

So Augustine, disillusioned, returned to his starting point,[3] in Cicero and his skepticism, and he followed the version of skepticism that Cicero (perhaps wrongly) attributed to Carneades,[4] namely a "global" skepticism that argued (dogmatically) that assent to philosophical propositions should always be withheld. To this, however, he added the strange claim, of uncertain origin, that Carneades himself was really a dogmatist who adopted a skeptical posture to protect a genuinely Platonic metaphysic from the philosophically illiterate (*c. Acad.* 3.17.37–39). We need not concern ourselves with that. What is immediately important is how Augustine, by purely philosophical arguments, without appeal to authority, thought that global skepticism could be defeated. In the first place he believed that truth must, somehow, be within reach of the human mind.

Yet if positive truth could not be identified by General Philosophy, perhaps some other approach might be necessary. Thus, in *util. cred.* 8.20, Augustine writes: "Often it seemed to me that truth could not be found, . . . but often again, as I reflected to the best of my ability how lively was the human mind, how wise, how penetrating, I could not believe that the truth must be undetected. Possibly the manner of seeking truth might be hidden and would have to be accepted from some divine authority." Thus begins the search for some reliable guide – which would eventually lead Augustine to Advanced Philosophy. Before identifying the results of that search, however, let us see what he still thinks can be discovered by General Philosophy alone.

The arguments of the Skeptics, as presented by Cicero, were originally aimed at the Stoic claim that there are some propositions to which we must assent; in Stoic language we are virtually dragged to assent. Of course, it matters how we define "assent," and Augustine's account, at least eventually, is different from that of the Stoics.[5] In any case, Augustine came to believe that "global" skepticism could be refuted, without reference to religious belief, and not least by arguments that will assure me of the fact of my own existence as a living being. The most famous of these arguments

---

[2] See *conf.* 4.3.6, where Augustine mentions the skepticism of his philosophical friends Vindicianus and Nebridius; also 5.10.19. Cf. *retr.* 1.1.1, and generally Van Fleteren 1973, Kretzmann 1990, and Rist 2001.
[3] For disillusion, see *conf.* 6.4.6. For the caution it engendered, see already *ord.* 2.5.17.
[4] For discussion, see Frede 1984.
[5] See Rist 2001: 38, though the account of *voluntas* in that essay needs to be supplemented by the work of Byers, esp. Byers 2006. There she rightly ties *voluntas* not only to (Platonizing) "love" but also closely to the Stoic "impulse" (*horme*).

("If I am deceived, therefore I exist") does not appear in his specifically anti-Skeptical treatise (*c. Acad.*), and we cannot be sure when Augustine first formulated it precisely, but something of the same approach is visible both in this book (*c. Acad.* 3.9.19: "It is absurd to suppose that the wise man does not know that he is living") and in a number of other early texts. In *On the Happy Life* (*b. vita* 2.7), it is assumed by Augustine's brother that he is alive; in the *Soliloquies* (*sol.* 2.1.1), Augustine asserts that he knows that he exists (without being able to explain the source of his knowledge). In *On Free Will* (*lib. arb.* 2.3.7), he rejects the possibility of doubting his own existence (linking this with an argument for the existence of God), while in *City of God* (*civ. Dei* 11.26) we eventually meet the most famous and most quoted version ("If I am mistaken, I exist"; *si enim fallor, sum*). Finally and again fairly late in his life – indicating that he is still happy with some of the methods of General Philosophy – Augustine offers two similar arguments in *The Trinity*: "Who would doubt that he lives and remembers and understands, and wills and thinks and knows and judges? Since even if he doubts, he lives" (*Trin.* 10.10.14); "Perhaps you are dreaming? Or insane? But even so you know that you are alive" (*Trin.* 15.12.21).

So it is by a type of self-referential argument that Augustine believed, and continued to believe, that global Skepticism could be defeated. And there are other areas too where General Philosophy, undefended by appeals to authority, can still be profitable. Already in *Against the Skeptics* Augustine is clear that by reason alone we can have knowledge of logical and mathematical truths (*c. Acad.* 3.11.25):[6] "There is one world or there is not"; "Three time three is nine." And by unaided reason we can also grasp "subjective truths" about how we "feel" as a result of the activities of our senses (*c. Acad.* 3.11.26):[7] "When a man tastes something, he can swear in good faith that this is sweet to his palate ... and no Greek sophism can deprive him of that knowledge." Yet these three types of knowledge do not get us very far in philosophy. If, however, this is all that General Philosophy can provide, how is it that the Platonists are able to make substantively true claims in metaphysics, not least in talking about an intelligible world, and indeed about the existence of some sort of transcendent God? Must not these claims too, since made by those without benefit of Christian belief, be within the range of reason alone, unsupported by faith and authority? The challenge is clearly visible in *On Free Will* (*lib. arb.*) when Augustine argues from our knowledge of the existence of our own minds to the existence of what can be called God.

---

[6] See Matthews 2001: 172.   [7] See Kirwan 1989: 24.

Augustine's argument is essentially that if we can find something higher than our own minds we should reasonably call it God (*lib. arb.* 2.6.14). We can indeed find "Platonic" Forms (2.16.44) and in particular Truth – and this Truth is indeed "higher and more excellent than *our* minds" (2.12.34). Augustine then goes on to identify Truth as Christ (2.13.37), but that is not immediately relevant to our enquiry. What he believes he has shown, by reason alone, is the existence of God: what he does not claim to have shown by such means is that truth (as Christ) is God. Here then we have a dividing line between General and Advanced Philosophy. In General Philosophy we can follow the Neoplatonists (and Plotinus in particular) in arguing that if truth exists independently of the human mind, it must exist in a divine mind (see also *vera rel.* 31.57), but more about the nature of that divine mind General Philosophy cannot tell us. Thus by implication what it tells us are its own limits, unless reason is somehow supplemented with historically revealed information.

More generally, unaided reason cannot give us a historical *knowledge* but only belief; indeed it is especially ineffectual, as we shall see, in generating knowledge about acts of God only revealed in Scripture and the traditions of the Church. So that if we hope to advance beyond the metaphysics of the Neoplatonists, and indeed if we want ultimately to validate those metaphysical claims themselves, we must move from General Philosophy to some sort of Advanced Philosophy.

It looks as though the faith that reason tries to understand is a combination of metaphysical knowledge and historical truth, so to proceed further we must consider a text in which Augustine most clearly and provocatively spells out the limits of knowledge (now identified as the subject matter of General Philosophy) and the nature of our understanding of historical events. That text is *On the Advantage of Believing* (*util. cred.*).

Although there are some kinds of religious belief which are entirely inaccessible to the human mind without divine revelation – Augustine mentions the Resurrection and the Day of Judgment (*vera rel.* 8.14, cf. *Trin.* 4.16.21) – he also wants to argue that much religious belief (and hence religious faith) is not different in kind from other sorts of beliefs, especially those which relate to historical events. In all such cases, whether the historical event is of a religious character or merely secular, we have to rely on authorities, and it is one of the important tasks of reason to identify which authorities are reliable. For authority is an unavoidable substitute for the first-hand experience necessary for any kind of *knowledge* other than that deriving from self-referential arguments or more generally arguments within the spheres of logic and mathematics. Thus it is necessary for any possible understanding of places I have never seen or of events in the past, whether these are in the public domain or in the more private sphere. We only believe (rightly) that Cicero executed the Catilinarian conspirators in 63 BC because reliable historians and others (including Cicero himself) tell us so (*vera rel.* 11.25; cf. *div. qu.* 48; *ep.* 147), and we "know" who our parents are on the authority of our mother (who – even before DNA – will identify the father) or of various other persons (like midwives) who were present at our birth (*vera rel.* 12.26, 14.31; cf. *civ. Dei* 11.3). "Unless we take these things on trust we should accomplish nothing in this life" (*conf.* 6.5.7). Certainly such beliefs are strictly neither knowledge nor understanding, but they may put us in the way of understanding. In particular religious belief about specific historical events may provide the necessary groundwork for more advanced theological and philosophical claims. Augustine himself said that he would not have believed the Gospels had he not accepted the authority of the Church (*c. ep. Man.* 5.6). He knew about the Gospels (*cogitare*) but did not understand them (*intellegere*). And belief in the Day of Judgment and the General Resurrection can only follow upon more basic historical claims, as about the life, death, and resurrection of Jesus. For those more advanced "theological" beliefs divine illumination is required over and above the basic faith – itself for the mature Augustine a gift of God who prepares our "will" to accept it[8] – which is its precondition. Thus when we try to understand the Trinity, we are trying to make sense of our basic religious beliefs; then indeed faith is seeking understanding, and we are in the world of Advanced Philosophy in seeking not just for knowledge or faith but also for wisdom (*sapientia*).[9] But for that understanding we need illumination: Augustine recalls a time when he could read the Scriptures without any grasp of their content (*Trin.* 11.8.15). Heretics too can read the Scriptures, though they fail to understand them (*ep.* 20.3.13).

Let us pursue the pure reason of the Neoplatonists a little further. Augustine tells us in *conf.* 7.20.26 that with hindsight he was glad that he discovered Neoplatonism before he was converted to Catholic Christianity because otherwise he might have opted for "presumption" rather than "confession": that is, he might have attempted to fill out the remaining inadequacies of his metaphysical and theological understanding by resorting to some form of pagan cult – he calls it theurgy – instead of recognizing the necessity of Christian humility as an antidote to intellectual pride and overconfidence. He might have tried to avoid moving from General to Advanced Philosophy by a pathetic appeal no longer to reason but to

---

[8] See esp. Sage 1964. [9] For further discussion, see esp. Gilson 1960: 115–26.

irrationality. But he has avoided this fate by learning "never to abandon the authority of Christ" (*c. Acad.* 3.20.43).

In Augustine's view there are two obstacles to the advance of students of General Philosophy beyond what has been achieved by the Neoplatonists. The first is the limitations of the human mind, the second the lack of data on which to speculate in the absence of truth revealed in the Church and the Scriptures. It is not clear how much further Augustine supposes that Adam could have advanced by reason alone before the fall, and in his earliest writings he offers little explanation of human mental inadequacy. But for most of his life he believed that the weakness and inadequacy of our understanding are to be explained as effects of the fall. We suffer not only directly from "weakness" and "ignorance" but also indirectly in that our loves and desires have become perverted: we normally do not even want to know "inconvenient" truths. In the *Confessions*, Augustine tells us that he did not want to know too much about chastity, lest he be impelled to it (*conf.* 8.7.17).[10]

Since our weakness, combined with our lack of data, should tell us that there are recognizable limits to General Philosophy – roughly speaking Plotinus has reached those limits – there seem to be three primary pursuits to which as thinkers in General Philosophy we should be committed. We need to pursue what in that discipline is within our grasp and, when we reach the limits of our capacity, to recognize those limits and admit our failure to proceed further on our own. Then (hopefully) we should recognize Christian revelation as providing both the further data we need and the god-given strength to resume our advance. That further advance will be the pursuit of an understanding of what we have come to recognize we should believe, following the proper authorities, while they in turn will enable us to recognize the essentially Christian doctrine that the virtues by which we should try to live are not modes of reason (as the Stoics in particular were wont to claim) but modes of love, and that such love of them as we have is only fueled by God's love (*mor.* 1.25.47–1.30.62). In our fallen state we would, unaided, almost inevitably love the wrong things for the wrong reasons (not least to satisfy our pride and desire for absolute autonomy).

But how would an appeal to authority achieve such results? Augustine never answers this question directly, but it seems that his preferred mode of procedure, as the *Confessions* in particular makes clear, is that we admit our weakness and then look for alternative ways of thinking which will allow

---

[10] Contemporary students are often concerned not to listen too much to Augustine, lest he be right. See Rist 2007: 287–300.

us – without forgetting our own inadequacies – to make further philosophical progress. In the end proposing the "Christian hypothesis" will be philosophically and morally fruitful in so many different ways that we shall be obliged to assent to it; it would be irrational to do otherwise.

What then is it to which we assent? The answer is to the authority of Christ, to the Incarnation as an historical event with reference to which we can both advance in metaphysics and find the strength (otherwise lacking) at least to progress in the moral and spiritual life. In metaphysics we shall understand what the Platonists can only infer, and we can understand it because we can identify the Platonic intelligible world, of which first-hand experience is possible "philosophically," with beliefs about the historical figure of Jesus who is to be identified, as we have seen, with Truth. Thus Platonic "abstract" or impersonal Forms (at least those of the virtues) can be identified as what we should call divine attributes, that is, as attributes of a living being present in history as well as in heaven.

We can now pass from our activities in General Philosophy to what we can achieve in Advanced Philosophy. As I have already observed, the practices of General Philosophy are available to believers and non-believers alike; in that sense there is as yet no specifically Christian philosophy. But when we recognize the limitations of General Philosophy and the need, once converted, for Advanced Philosophy, we are doing the sort of philosophy only possible for Christians (or people hypothesizing themselves as Christians). And this is true not only in that the Advanced student is aided by God in overcoming his mental inadequacies and given new historical material about which he can philosophize, but by clear implication in that he is now capable of doing more advanced philosophical work; he can, for example, in Augustine's opinion, advance in understanding the nature of evil, the providence of God, and the ultimate justification of moral and aesthetic judgments. All these areas, in Augustine's view, must be studied without success by non-Christian philosophers – not least because although such thinkers may talk about God and the virtues, they cannot be aware of what such talk entails by first-hand experience. Thus we can see some of the advantages, from Augustine's point of view, of his claim that pagan or heretical virtues are not genuine virtues at all.[11] Since the nature of virtue depends on the nature of God, it cannot be understood except through the specific light and illumination which Christians obtain through baptism and thus from working in an ecclesial context. Through the sacraments the Christian can have a first-hand experience of God of a kind which is not

---

[11] For further discussion, see Rist 1994: 168–73.

available to the non-believer, and it is that kind of first-hand experience which enables the Christian philosopher to convert his faith into understanding.

To do that, however, is not only difficult but also obligatory. Our reason is given by God, and we have an obligation to apply it (philosophically) to our Christian beliefs. About the year 410, in an exchange of letters with a certain Consentius (*ep.* 119, 120), the now elderly bishop Augustine tells his correspondent unambiguously that we do not have the luxury of relying on faith without recourse to reason, let alone rather than reason. Fideism is not appropriate for Christians: God forbid that he should hate in us that faculty by which he made us superior to all other living beings.

So for the student of Advanced Philosophy faith will seek understanding. But what is faith itself, properly understood? In answering this question we shall find ourselves on the familiar ground of the right kind of love (*amor*), the right kind of will (*voluntas*). Augustine's clearest definition of faith or belief is that it is nothing other than "thinking with assent" (*praed. sanct.* 3.5), and elsewhere he says that "to yield our consent ... or to withhold it is the function of our *voluntas*." And our *voluntas* is the reflection of our loves and hates; hence for Augustine it is controlled by our love of God or lack of it.[12] For whereas the Stoics, from whom much of Augustine's account of assent derives, treated assent simply as assent to propositions (and certainly not to a personal authority), Augustine wants to emphasize that whether it is given or withheld may well depend on the state of our loves and hates. In other words we may refuse to assent to self-evident propositions, not least moral propositions, because we do not want to know about them, as I noted earlier. A good modern parallel would be a holocaust-denier. He refuses assent to the truth simply because he does not want to acknowledge it.

We are now in a position to turn more explicitly to the question of history and the mixture of historical and metaphysical truth that forms the core of Augustine's theology. Our faith in the Incarnation depends on the authority of its original witnesses, Mary for the birth of Christ (as our mother for our own father) and his disciples and evangelists (as accepted by the Church) for his life, death, and resurrection. And if philosophy is to involve itself with the particularities of history as well as with metaphysics, we should expect Augustine to provide us with philosophical comment on the nature of history itself. The obvious, though not the only, place to look for such material, and to search for a blend of historical and metaphysical questions is in *City of*

---

[12] See Rist 2001: 35.

God,[13] a book not primarily about politics but about the difference between godly and ungodly living in this life and society and in the next.[14]

2 EVIDENCE FROM THE *CITY OF GOD*

The subject of ordinary historical enquiry is the *saeculum*, the society constructed by human beings on earth, and the historical time in which the construction takes place. Within the Augustinian *saeculum* we find the "Two Cities" (*civ. Dei* 1.35), one of which is the city of God, formed by the love of God, yet simultaneously transcending the *saeculum* itself, the other being a strictly earthly city formed by human self-love. Christian and pagan literature sum up the different mentalities. James, in his Epistle, talks of God resisting the proud and giving grace to the humble (James 4:6); Virgil, preaching to the Roman pagans, tells them to act like God: "To spare the humble and subdue the proud" (*Aen.* 6.853; *civ. Dei* pref.). Thus it is human society as a whole, with its divine and diabolical associations, which is the subject matter of *City of God*. As Augustine himself says in his prefatory remarks to Marcellinus, a Roman official and a Christian with whom he had exchanged letters on the question of the superiority of the Christian God to his pagan rivals (cf. *ep.* 136–38), he will now fulfill his promise to write more extensively on the matter – and he begins by observing that the eternal city of God exists in the *saeculum* as a pilgrim in time. Yet the *City of God* is no mere book of history in the ordinary sense; indeed our present project is to examine whether it may, among other things (such as a radical repudiation of the nostalgic pagan culture of Roman literary aristocrats), be identified as somehow a work of philosophy; a strange but Christian philosophy of history. Augustine's readers are aware that it is a lengthy and rambling text packed with diverse material and long digressions, and they may be pardoned if, despite the signposts Augustine sets up as he proceeds, they seem to lose sight of its overarching theme. Or perhaps the relationship of that overarching theme to the separate sections of the book has been indicated but only sketchily worked out?[15]

---

[13] The problem of history goes back to Augustine's earliest writings against the Manichees, to the time when he recognized with increasing clarity that if he could not defend the historical (as well as the symbolic or allegorical) sense of both Testaments, he could neither explain (as distinct from explain away) the apparent immoralities of Old Testament heroes nor the historicity of Christ's birth and resurrection against Manichean docetism: the thesis that Jesus only appeared to be born and suffer in a "carnal" body. For the importance of Augustine's anti-docetism in his understanding of the special position of the Jews (and of the need for the protection of their religion), see Fredriksen 2008.

[14] For a precursor, see *vera rel.* 27.50.

[15] For a concise account of the structure of *City of God*, Guy 1961 is still very helpful.

Though there are hints of more, the *City of God* begins with an apparently limited objective to which Augustine is still prepared to refer at the end of his life (*retr.* 2.43), if perhaps only as the trigger which sparked the bigger project already in his mind: the bigger project was to discuss the heavenly and earthly cities – Jerusalem and Babylon; the smaller was the repudiation of the pagan claim that Rome (the latest representative of Babylon) had been sacked by Alaric and his Goths because the Romans had abandoned the old religion, itself a revised version of the old canard against Christians that they provoked the anger of the traditional gods. So Augustine's first task is to show that under the old regime too appalling disasters had occurred. The pagan gods had not protected the city, nor had they encouraged decent living. It was not just in the decadent period of the late Republic, as recorded by Sallust, that the Romans had committed atrocities against their own people as well as in their dealings with their neighbors; such evil behavior, echoing in its own way the practices of pagan religion, had characterized Roman society from the time of Romulus the murderer and rapist (*civ. Dei* 3.6; cf. 2.17). In contrast to the virtues of the Christians, who are steered by the humility of Christ and act in accordance with the wishes of a benevolent providence, the Romans had always longed for earthly glory, for an ultimately self-seeking and arrogant fame – impelled as they were by cruel and obscene demons. Their empire, like that of others, not least Alexander the Great, can be compared to piracy on a grand scale (*civ. Dei* 4.4).

In Book 5 Augustine explains that the immediate success of the Roman people is due neither to chance nor to astrological determinism but to the will of God (*civ. Dei* 5.12), and that, however morally vacuous love of fame may be, it served the Romans at least as a mechanism for controlling other more blatant vices – until they had destroyed all foreign rivals – and God rewarded their limited virtue, imperfect and delusory though it is (5.19), with temporal rewards (5.51), themselves as nothing compared with the rewards of true religion. For certainly the desire for glory is superior to the lust for power to which it may easily descend (5.19), and when Constantine converted to Christianity, abandoning the worship of demons, he was even more plentifully rewarded. Best so far, however, is Theodosius (5.26), who "rejoiced more in being a member of the Church than in being a ruler of the world" and in that spirit suppressed the practice of pagan worship.

In Books 6–7 Augustine widens his theme, turning to those who think that no earthly success but eternal life is the goal of true religion, and such persons, Augustine believes, can be discussed via Varro's distinction between mythical, natural and civil religion (*civ. Dei* 6.5). So he proceeds to argue not only with respect to the Roman context from which his examples largely come, but at least by implication more generally, that "mythical" religion is cruel and obscene, depicting immoral gods whose worship can only encourage vice, and that "civic" religion, the religion of the state, is in practice no better (6.7). So we have now moved in *City of God* from discussing the immediate charge that Christianity has failed to protect the Roman people, via an analysis of the failures and absurdities of Roman popular and civic religion, to a wider treatment of the inadequacies of traditional "mythical" and "civic" worship in general. And when we move on to Book 8 we find that our theme has broadened still further. Now, as we look at "natural" religion, we can investigate what the best of the metaphysicians, namely the Platonists, have to offer in "theology." That discussion had already been foreshadowed in Book 1 (*civ. Dei* 1.36), where Augustine had spoken of the need to refute the most illustrious of the philosophers, those who in many ways think as Christians on the immortality of the soul, on God as creator and on his providence.

Augustine now reverts to this wider theme. Plato and his followers (they are not always clearly distinguished as moderns would wish, and that has its disadvantages for the coherence of Augustine's account) have recognized that God is the cause of existence, the basis of our understanding of the world and a pattern in accordance with which we may achieve the good life (*civ. Dei* 8.4). Such ideas summarize certain central doctrines of Plato himself, most of which can be found in the *Republic*, especially in Books 6 and 10, with which Augustine was familiar not directly but through the writings of Plato's "successors," such as Cicero (in his role as reporter of past philosophies) and the Neoplatonists Plotinus and Porphyry. In any case Augustine now wants to challenge the "best of the philosophers," but, as we shall see, his real aims are unexpected and – at first sight – more limited.

Augustine's immediate objection to the claims of the Platonists is that although they accept a single First Cause, they offer worship and blasphemous sacrifice to lesser created gods, instead of treating such intelligent beings in the Christian spirit as angels who themselves accept no worship but devote themselves to the worship of God. Thus Platonists compromise their monotheism. As we have seen, Augustine is inclined to lump all his opponents together with regard to their attitude towards what the philosophers called *daimones*, where he himself preferred "demons," though he admits that the Platonists do distinguish between good and evil specimens. Nevertheless, he takes his fellow African Apuleius and Porphyry as typical members of the school as a whole, neglecting the more skeptical Plotinus[16] whom he mentions only in passing in this connection (*civ. Dei* 8.12, 9.10, 9.17). His more fundamental charge, however, is that all the Platonists, in misunderstanding Plato's comment in the *Symposium* (203a, cf. *civ. Dei* 8.18, 8.20) that there is no direct contact between gods and men, and in their consequent worship of "demons," have failed to recognize the need for a genuine historical Mediator between man and God, who can only be the God–man Jesus Christ (*civ. Dei* 10.20). Despite their confused recognition of the need for some kind of mediation, they have compromised with popular mythology as to the place where such mediation can be found. Hence they have been led, in their intellectual arrogance, to blasphemous and confused conclusions and have latterly resorted to theurgy, a crude attempt to manipulate the gods themselves.[17]

Augustine is emphatic that it is arrogance, for which Christian humility is the only remedy (*civ. Dei* 10.28), that has led the Neoplatonists to betray their own metaphysics; hence in the latter part of Book 10 he rehearses a further and more traditional Christian objection to its effects: that the Platonists, though not, thinks Augustine, Plato himself (10.31), believe the soul to be naturally immortal and thus excessively godlike. With immortality of this sort comes the transmigration of the soul from human body to human body and – in the view of many, including Plato himself and Plotinus (10.30) – even into animal bodies.

The Platonists grasp neither the truth about the divine Mediator nor the correct relationship between the soul and the divine nature. That is not least because they fail to recognize the evidence of sacred history, as revealed in both the Old and New Testaments (*civ. Dei* 10.32). The broader implication of this is that metaphysics can indeed reveal God's *existence* but that the Platonists have necessarily made a pig's ear of theology, not least in their version of the Trinity (10.23, 10.28), since they cannot recognize God's *nature* and his utter transcendence over his creation. Nor do they grasp the full significance of creation from nothing – and long before Augustine Christians were saying that without such understanding it is impossible to recognize the nature of God's transcendence.[18] So Platonic metaphysics, though impressive, is incomplete (and in its unacknowledged

---

[16] Porphyry records that he and others were disconcerted when Plotinus, invited by his pupil Amelius, now grown fond of sacrifice, to participate in various religious festivals, replied, "They ought to come to me, not I to them" (trans. Armstrong 1966: 35).

[17] Augustine oversimplifies the nature of theurgy, which is more a kind of pagan sacramentalism than he wants to admit. For the associated third-century crisis in Neoplatonism about human moral strength, see Rist 1992.

[18] For the development of Christian ideas of creation from nothing, see esp. May 1994.

incompleteness a source of pride). It needs to be supplemented by data which only revelation can provide and which Christian thinking can make even more intelligible. Ultimately the failure of the Platonists is a moral failing, from which only the acceptance of Christ's humility can save them. Our knowledge of such humility derives not from metaphysics, however, but from God's historical testimony – and with that, at the end of Book 10 and the analysis of the weaknesses of the best form of non-Christian thinking, the more strictly "destructive" part of *City of God* comes to an end.

Book 11 opens the next major section of *City of God* with a return to the two cities; their origin will be discussed in four books – to be followed by four more on their progress through human history and a further four on their eschatological prospects. But that does not mean that Augustine has abandoned what we should label philosophical questions; indeed he moves quickly to basic problems such as the nature of space and time, reaffirming that the Platonists are the most successful of the pagan thinkers (*civ. Dei* 11.5). But his approach is now exegetical – we need to use Biblical data to make progress in these areas – and thus, in Augustine's view, historical. We should recall that he had now completed a vast "literal" commentary on Genesis in which Adam and Eve are above all historical figures. In *City of God* (esp. *civ. Dei* 11.13–14) he has us attend carefully and first of all to an even earlier historical event, that of the fall of the angels, which already in the opinion of Origen provides the key by which we may unlock the problem of evil (*c. Cels.* 4.62–70).

Origen himself, however, is *too* Platonist for Augustine; he fails to recognize the goodness of the human body as created by God and believes that souls are sent into bodies as a punishment.[19] This indicates his confusion on the nature of the human "person" – Augustine had begun to use the word *persona* in discussing the soul–body complex as of *ep.* 137[20] – and thus is Origen led into heresy (*civ. Dei* 11.23). And yet he was right to emphasize the fall, not least the fall of the angels, for it is with the fall of the angels that we can first recognize the two cities. Augustine concludes Book 11 with the comment that in the distinction between the good and bad angels lies the origin of the two sets of human beings: those, as we shall see, devoted to the love of God, to the Trinity in whose image they have been created (11.28), and those devoted to love of themselves.

---

[19] Plotinus' pupil Amelius, who apparently thought highly of the opening of John's Gospel, seems to have read John's comments in accordance with some sort of "Origenist" interpretation whereby souls fall into bodies. For references, see Rist 1969.

[20] Cf. *ep.* 169.8 along with Rist 1994: 100, and now more generally Burnell 2005.

Christian philosophy

The fall of the angels "explains" or fails to explain, the origin of evil – which pushes the problem behind Adam and Eve but leaves similar problems in its wake.[21] God created the angels entirely good, but some failed to persevere and were not prompted to do so by God (*civ. Dei* 12.9): the fault lay in their wills and cannot be traced further back (12.3). It is to be associated with the necessary fact that they are created *ex nihilo* (12.6) – as were we humans (*civ. Dei* 14.11, 14.13) – but it is not clear why this affected some of them adversely and others not; apparently that random fact, though foreseen by God, could not be prevented (*civ. Dei* 11.13, 12.9). Such evil possibilities are inevitable if freedom of the will is to be possible. It should be noted, however, that despite Augustine's apparent intention, the pushing back of the problem of evil to the wills of angels rather than those of Adam and Eve may make it even more difficult to understand. For perhaps the human race needs to learn the hard way of its utter dependence on God, while for the angels such learning is impossible: if they fall, there is no return. Be that as it may, the cause of the trouble, as with human beings, is pride and the desire to be autonomous, that is, self-creating (*civ. Dei* 11.3, 12.8). With the human race there is a further factor: the devil's envy has promoted such perversity.

Augustine now turns to the fall of man, that fatal choice of Adam and Eve that infected the "genes" of their descendants (*civ. Dei* 13.14). For from one man our sinful selves (even Eve's sinful self) derive (*civ. Dei* 12.22): a standard Augustinian reading of scripture. Here again pagan philosophers and their Christian disciples (such as Origen) are mistaken: the bodily death which guilty Adam and his descendants have incurred neither marks the body as peculiarly evil – evil rather lies in the "will" (cf. *civ. Dei* 14.6), in false loves, in pride and self-worship resulting in disobedience (14.12) – nor does it even mark its end, for where there are human beings there are bodies, and thus bodily resurrection must be associated with the immortality of the soul. It is only the "fallen" body in its "second" nature, not its original form, which ends in what we call physical death. Nevertheless, only the grace of God prevents all the children of Adam from second death, namely the damnation of the soul (*civ. Dei* 14.1), and in the separation of the elect from the rest we see again the inhabitants of the two cities, each desiring its own kind of peace: peace in earthly life for the damned and peace in the eternity

---

[21] There may be good reason to believe that Christian inability to explain the fall of the "free" angels was a major factor in explaining the late medieval shift from thinking of free choice as the ability only to choose the good to the more modern notion that for the will to be free it must be autonomous, able to choose either good or evil. But that is another story.

of the spirit for those who "persevere." So after detailing the nature of sexual relations before and after the fall – significant because it indicates the conflict of body and will which disturbs the fallen – Augustine closes this section of *City of God* with a text which has been treated as the classic exposition of his position (*civ. Dei* 14.28):

> Two cities have been created by two loves: that is, the earthly by love of self extending even to contempt of God, and the heavenly by love of God extending to contempt of self.

Having detailed the origins of the two cities Augustine proceeds in the following four books to detail their history in human society after the fall of Adam. That history develops in four movements: from Adam to Noah, from Noah to Abraham, from Abraham to David, and from David to Christ. Much emphasis is placed on the representation of Old Testament figures and events as symbols of Christ and his Church. The two cities are founded on the first sons of Adam and Eve, namely Cain, the murderous founder of the earthly city, and Abel, slain not least because he was good – for, as Augustine believes, the evil hate and envy the good simply because they are good.

It is noted that the fratricidal Cain has his analogue in the founder of Rome, who killed his brother Remus (*civ. Dei* 15.5). Yet in the whole of this section non-Biblical history is discussed only with reference to its Biblical counterpart, for Augustine's overriding purpose is to show how God reveals the separateness of the two cities. But this limited attitude to secular history needs further inspection.

Literalism is an essential part of Augustine's account of the whole Bible. He maintains that the Old Testament stories cannot be deprived of their historical content by allegorization. Both historical and allegorical interpretations are appropriate (e.g., *civ. Dei* 13.21, on Eden; 15.27, on the Flood), but the modern reader cannot but find that history read in this way is often impossible to accept – which threatens the viability of Augustine's project. Thus although Augustine admits he does not know the age of the universe (*civ. Dei* 12.17), he is happy to insist that by adding up the recorded ages of Old Testament figures we can be certain that men have inhabited the earth for less than 6000 years (*civ. Dei* 12.11, 18.40). And the history also has to be "moralized." Thus the patriarchs have to be impeccable by "Christian" standards: there was no sexual lust or irregular behavior (*civ. Dei* 16.19, 16.25),[22] and even in the sacrifice of Isaac, the intended murder at God's

---

[22] See Hunter 2002.

command is permissible because Abraham, the man of faith, knew that his son would be brought back to life (16.32) and that God never delights in human sacrifice. Instead of seeing Old Testament history as the record of the growing awareness of God's nature by the Hebrews, Augustine thinks of it as literal truth dictated, as it were, by God – and yet he is also credulous about non-religious accounts of the earlier days of the human race!

While Augustine continually asserts the superiority of Christian revelation to the stumbling efforts of the breed of philosophers who have appeared comparatively recently in human history (*civ. Dei* 18.37, 18.41), the fact that he keeps referring to them indicates a degree of uncertainty (or an insufficiently direct analysis) not only about the precise significance of pagan philosophy but also about pagan history more generally. Augustine's ambivalence about pagan "virtues," which are really vices, is thus echoed by his attitude to the best pagan philosophers, who, though failures, are yet somehow admirable. At least the Platonists do a fairly good job of General Philosophy, though Augustine is now unwilling to acknowledge them as what they were, not least for himself: namely, a preparation for the Gospel. Philosophers, as was traditionally claimed by ancient Christians, stand condemned by their diversities, yet when speaking of heretics and indeed of anti-Christians more generally, Augustine also comments that if they can inflict actual bodily harm they train Christians to be patient, while if only their beliefs are damaging they aid the development of greater Christian wisdom.

In the last four books of *City of God* Augustine turns to the final destiny of the two cities. In the details of this reckless and often brutal theological speculation there is little immediately relevant to our present discussion, but the overall presentation is informative about Augustine's view of history itself. The "end-times" mark the last act of a drama that began with the fall of the angels. Yet notice that even near the very end of his "huge" work Augustine returns to the Platonists, and specifically to disagreements between Plato and Porphyry (*civ. Dei* 22.26) about proper attitudes to the body. If the two philosophers had been able to communicate, he continues (22.27), they might have become Christians: an over-optimistic comment in view of the fact that he has earlier noted that the most important difference between the Christian and the Platonist approach – a difference which agreement about the body could not of itself resolve – concerns the necessity of thinking historically as well as metaphysically if philosophical progress is to be made on the "big problems." For it is the fact of the historical particularity of the Christian revelation, which only the authority of Jewish and Christian history can confirm, which ensures that the

Platonists will ultimately fail: not least, as we have seen, in their search for a link between God and man, that is, for a Mediator.

But if history is so important for human understanding, we should pursue further the question of why Augustine limits his constructive use of it to immediately "religious" history in its Judaeo-Christian form. Why, though he cannot avoid giving a certain credit to the philosophers, and to the Platonists in particular, does he not see Graeco-Roman society as some sort of preparation for the Gospel, not least because he himself had been liberated by the Platonists in general, and Plotinus in particular, from materialism? We cannot be sure of the answer, and perhaps in a book written in part to condemn the religious practices of the pagan world as diabolical in their inspiration and dire in their effects we should not expect too much. As I have suggested, the account of the end-times is the last act of a terrible drama, which Jewish and Christian history has set before us. That history has a final cause, complete with a beginning, a middle, and an end, while secular history is one damn thing after another, a monotonously futile search for earthly peace in an intrinsically unstable world (*civ. Dei* 20.3). Such history, unlike its religious counterpart, is going nowhere; it is merely endlessly repeating itself. Which in detail is not entirely true, and the variations might be spiritually enlightening. For just as the Stoics thought that all sins are equal *qua* sins, though some deserve more punishment than others, so Augustine himself is prepared to admit that some vicious societies are, humanly speaking, "better" than others. Is nothing important to be learned from that?

Perhaps there is a more immediate thought in Augustine's mind. He has become increasingly skeptical about the thesis – already visible in Origen (*c. Cels.* 2.30) and adopted by his successor, the historian Eusebius, and by others, not least Ambrose, his own father in faith – that Christianity has taken over a pagan world already politically prepared for it, and that the theological significance of this takeover can be seen in the role of the now Christian Emperors. Before Augustine began to write *City of God* – in the wake of the anti-pagan legislation of Theodosius and the suppression of African paganism by his son Honorius in 399 – he had been attracted by the triumphalism of that sort of vision of "Christian times."[23] But he became more cautious. There are tribes to be Christianized beyond the Roman Empire (*ep.* 199.12.46–47; cf. *civ. Dei* 18.32); that empire, like its predecessors, will pass away without loss to the city of God. Its Christianization

---

[23] For good discussion of the theme, see Madec 1975. The classical discussion is still Markus 1970: 32–44.

Christian philosophy

marks no new phase in the story of the descendants of Adam from Christ till the Last Judgment.

In Augustine's view (as in Origen's) all non-Christian philosophy must ultimately fail, and that failure will afflict Christians too if they persist in a limited and merely pagan approach to the subject. Constructive philosophy must move from General Philosophy to Advanced Philosophy, and that involves using historical data supplied by Revelation. That is Augustine's thesis, and he supports it by trying to show how by adding history to Platonic metaphysics we can offer intelligible solutions to many of the unresolved problems of philosophy. Does that mean that philosophy has to turn into exegesis? Certainly Augustine is tempted to that conclusion – not least by his limited interest in "secular" history and in virtue of his failure to understand God's "inscrutable judgments"[24] – but his respect for the better pagan thinkers and for thinking itself restrains him. Certainly the philosopher moving beyond General Philosophy needs exegesis and cannot do without it. The difficulty – inadequately noticed – is the nature of the exegesis required. Augustine has too limited a notion of the sort of "history" that the Old Testament offers. *We* need to see what the Old Testament offers. We need to see the Old Testament not as the literal word of God (like the Koran) but as the continuing revelation of God's nature through history to the Jewish people. We need to emphasize not so much that God hates human sacrifice but that the Jewish people have recorded in the Old Testament their growing realization that God hates human sacrifice.

Augustine has rejected, too prematurely, the idea that politically the Roman Empire was a providential structure paving the way for Christianity – perhaps because he has confused such preparation with the distinct "Eusebian" claim that the conversion of Constantine shows that the now sacred Empire itself is a continuing part of the divine plan. And perhaps more importantly, he gives too little weight to the fact that intellectually the philosophy of the pagans had prepared many, not least himself, to advance towards the faith. In that regard he seems almost to forget his own account of the educational value of General Philosophy. But if his understanding of historical writing can be thus broadened (which is certainly possible without sacrificing the special nature of the story of the old and the new Israel), as well as enriched by inspection of the histories – more varied than he admits – of non-Jewish and non-Christian societies, then his critique of the limitations of General Philosophy and his wish to

---

[24] For recent comment (not least on how such inscrutable judgments affected his "theology" of Jews and Judaism), see Fredriksen 2008: esp. 133–39 and on the debate with Faustus.

complete it with Advanced Philosophy can better be sustained. For all his polemical discussion of Roman history, he fails to recognize that Rome is indeed a special case, quite different for example from the history of the historical Babylon. That is because in the special example of an "earthly city" which is pre-Constantinian Rome, there is already a mix of the few saved (that is, various elect Christians) and the mass of the reprobate, whereas in many other societies there are no baptized and therefore no possibly saved individuals at all.[25] Rome should provide him with an opportunity to study the mix of the heavenly and the earthly cities in a unique historical setting.

But these are details. Augustine's more basic claim is that a blend of historical and metaphysical enquiry offers the hope of intelligible solutions to longstanding philosophical puzzles, as well as enabling the Christian philosopher to think not only about *kinds* of events and peoples but about the nature and destiny of personal individuals: those individuals and persons of whom Aristotle said we have no definition and who were thus, as such, outside philosophical enquiry. Such an ambitious project is certainly what Augustine has in mind when speaking of an understanding of faith. Indeed he had already written his own metaphysical and personal history in the *Confessions* to promote such an understanding.

---

[25] For an introduction to other problems caused for Augustine by his "literalist" theory of baptism, see Rist 1994: 280–81 and Rist 2008: 120–21, 130–31.

CHAPTER 12

Reinventing Augustine's ethics: the afterlife of City of God

Bonnie Kent

People who dislike sharp dichotomies will probably dislike *City of God*. Augustine divides the entire human race into two groups, with different values and different destinies. The most concise statement of his position, in Book 14, claims that two loves created two cities: the earthly city, destined for eternal misery, and the heavenly city, destined for eternal happiness. Everyone belongs to either one city or the other. Those belonging to the first city love their own strength and seek glory from men. Those belonging to the second city love God above all, glory in him, and rely on his strength. In describing them Augustine quotes Psalms 17:2: "I will love Thee, O Lord, my strength" (*civ. Dei* 14.28). The Latin word *virtus*, here translated as "strength," can also mean virtue. Thus the passage from Psalms helps lay the ground for Augustine's definition of virtue in Book 15. "A brief and true definition of virtue," he says there (*civ. Dei* 15.22), "is rightly ordered love" – the *ordo amoris* or, more literally, the order of love.

Augustine declares that the two cities are at present intermingled and will remain so until the last judgment, when God separates them (*civ. Dei* 1.35). As some people currently within the church will end up in hell, so some currently outside the church will end up in heaven. In acknowledging the intermingling Augustine is not positing some middle-ground inhabited by partly virtuous people destined for a partly happy eternity. All he means is that we cannot be sure to which city any given individual belongs. We can only know how the two cities differ. Indeed, Augustine devotes the second part of *City of God* mainly to detailing their different origins, development, and ends. The extended critique of pagan virtue beginning in Book 1 grows even stronger in the second part of the work. It culminates in Book 19 with Augustine's argument that even the best ancient philosophers gave an irremediably flawed account of ethics. What they praised as virtues are actually vices (*civ. Dei* 19.25):

Thus, the virtues which the mind seems to possess, and by which it governs the body and the vices so that it may obtain whatever it desires, are really themselves vices, and not virtues at all, if they do not have reference to God. Some, indeed, suppose that the virtues are true and honourable when they have reference only to themselves and are sought for no other end. Then, however, they are puffed up and proud, and so are to be adjudged vices rather than virtues.

Modern readers often recoil at Augustine's sharp division between people with genuine virtues, destined for heaven, and everybody else. Most prefer the ethics of Aquinas's *Summa theologiae*, which now shares with *City of God* a secure place in the Western canon. Granted, the *Summa* itself comes packed with citations from Augustine's works. Aquinas himself holds that the only perfect and unqualified virtues are gifts of grace rooted in the God-given virtue of charity. By today's standards, he can hardly be hailed as a model of religious pluralism, let alone secularism. On the other hand, the *Summa* also comes packed with citations from philosophical works, and Aquinas expressly claims that virtues any human can acquire through her own natural resources are indeed true virtues. They cannot be perfect virtues because they do not make us good as members of God's city, nor are they rewarded with eternal happiness. But because they do make us good as human beings and citizens of the earthly city, they are genuine virtues, helping us to attain the imperfect happiness possible here and now (*ST* 2a2ae 23.7).

Does the *Summa* reject *City of God*'s account of virtue, support it, or revise it in ways that Augustine himself might well have endorsed? The battle among interpreters already under way in the fourteenth century escalated in the sixteenth and continues to this day. Some try to prove Aquinas closer to Augustine than he looks at first glance; others try to prove Augustine closer to Aquinas than he looks at first glance. Those who concede that there are indeed big differences between these two great books themselves divide, with some praising and others deploring Aquinas's divergence from Augustine. On only one point do all interpreters seem to agree: the differences between the two, whether deep or superficial, result mainly from the rediscovery of the Aristotelian corpus in the Latin West and its influence on Aquinas.

Aquinas's ethics surely was influenced by his reading of Aristotle and his commentators. Augustine knew very little about the Aristotelian corpus, whereas Aquinas studied virtually all of it. He even produced commentaries on eleven of Aristotle's works, including the *Nicomachean Ethics* and the *Politics*. Aquinas's engagement with Aristotle's works holds so much philosophical interest that historians have paid enormous attention to it. Alas, relatively few have given serious consideration to how well he knew *Augustine's* works. Noting how often Aquinas cites Augustine in his *Summa theologiae*, one author claims that he wrote it "in an uninterrupted dialogue with Augustine." In the same vein, he expresses certainty that Aquinas at least read Augustine's "main works." Admitting that Aquinas might not always have had Augustine's works at hand when he was composing the *Summa* (1271–1273), the author dismisses this as a trifling problem, because Aquinas "could rely on his fabulous memory" for references.[1] Most historians stop well short of casting the *Summa* as an uninterrupted dialogue with Augustine. Yet they share the assumption that Aquinas knew Augustine's main works, including *City of God*, probably at least as well as most scholars today do.

In this essay I argue, to the contrary, that most medieval theologians read *City of God* selectively, if at all. Aquinas was no exception. The evidence suggests that he read some parts of it but not a good many others. Different works by Augustine, seldom studied today, did more to shape the ethics of Aquinas and other leading thinkers of the Middle Ages. Equally important, the notion that Aquinas and his contemporaries *should* have studied this great book is doubly anachronistic. Not only does it assume that they had no trouble getting access to it; it assumes that they regarded it as a great book. Again, the evidence suggests otherwise. Only in the fourteenth century did *City of God* attain something approximating the status it has now, and it did so for reasons unrelated to the moral and theological positions it defends.

I AUGUSTINE IN THE MIDDLE AGES

Some problems that Augustine posed for medieval scholars are plainly ones that we share. He wrote so much that it would take an enormous amount of time to read all of his works. Just reading *City of God* consumes so much time that few people today resist the temptation to skip some chapters, even entire books. Augustine was also a practical and tempestuous writer, well schooled in Latin literature and rhetoric. Many of his works engage in polemic against intellectual adversaries. He chose his words with the sensibility of a poet and a preacher, deliberately preserving multiple meanings he considered worth preserving, and modifying both the substance and style to suit the occasion. As a result, people may struggle to resolve apparent inconsistencies even in the relatively small subset of Augustine's works

---

[1] Elders 1987: 166 and 1997: 343.

that they read. Is the difference only one of emphasis, or did he change his mind? We normally resolve the problem by focusing on only those parts of the Augustinian corpus we happen to find interesting, useful for our own authorial purposes, or both.

Of course, there is nothing new about scholars' extracting only those parts of an author's works that they like or can use while ignoring the rest. From the outset Augustine was one the authors most subject to such treatment, with good reason. He produced so many works that even Possidius, his friend and biographer, complained that nobody could possibly read them all.[2] We find his complaint echoed in seventh-century verses supposedly composed by Isidore of Seville and posted over the shelves of Augustine's works in his library. Because Isidore's protest was more pointed, history books are far more likely to mention it. Where Possidius complained that nobody could read all of Augustine's works, Isidore declared that anyone claiming to have read them all is *lying*.

Today's busy readers, feeling aggrieved that the Augustinian corpus is too vast to master in a single lifetime, chuckle at the thought that even a seventh-century bishop felt the same. In reality, though, the verse attributed to Isidore expresses a different grievance to this hugely prolific Church Father (*PL* 83, 1109):

> He lies who claims that he has read all of you.
> What reader can even have all of your works?

As Isidore saw it, the problem lay less in finding time to read Augustine's works than in getting copies of them. Now, when we can get so many things just by logging on to the internet, we have trouble imagining a time when someone would make a months-long journey just to read some work by Augustine he had never seen. If he wanted a copy of the work for his own library, he would need a scribe to do the copying or have to copy it himself. Hence many of the quotations from Augustine in medieval texts come from summaries (*epitomes*) that people had compiled of his teachings, and especially from *florilegia*: collections of excerpts from his writings or from his writings along with those of other "authorities." The sheer length of *City of God* made it an especially onerous work to copy. When we find a medieval author quoting this text, we accordingly have good reason to wonder whether he had actually read it.

The florilegia themselves were a mixed bag. Even when they included nothing but extracts from authentic works of Augustine, the extracts might

---

[2] *v. Aug.*, c. 18 (*PL* 32, 49).

be quite short – conclusions without supporting arguments, on a par with "soundbites" – and of course they always reflected the compiler's own interests. His interests might lie mainly in scriptural exegesis, in specific theological issues of concern in his own day, or in timeless advice about living the religious life. Never did they lie in finding what modern scholars would consider the most important passages, for our own judgments usually reflect our interest in understanding how Augustine's views agree or disagree with those of the ancient thinkers who preceded him and the medieval and modern thinkers who followed.

Our medieval counterparts faced yet another obstacle to understanding Augustine that we ourselves do not. Various works attributed to him were fakes. Peter Lombard's *Sentences* cites several of these pseudo-Augustinian works; Aquinas's *Summa theologiae* does, too. Their number grew as time passed. The large pseudo-Augustinian corpus created headaches for sixteenth-century editors struggling to produce a printed edition of Augustine's complete works. Of the 187 early printed books (*incunabula*) that listed Augustine as their author, roughly two-thirds were spurious.[3]

What evidence do we actually have that Aquinas read *City of God* before writing the *Summa theologiae*? None of Augustine's works were included in the curriculum of medieval universities, and Aquinas never wrote a commentary on any of them. The only evidence we have that Aquinas read *City of God* before (or while) writing the *Summa* are his citations from it. Citations, however, are flimsy evidence that any medieval author has actually read the text from which he quotes.

Consider, for example, Augustine's "brief and true definition of virtue" as the *ordo amoris* – all the more memorable in a work where he often looks incapable of saying anything briefly. When Aquinas mentions this definition in his commentary on the *Sentences*, he refers to it vaguely, as something Augustine says. Later, in the *Summa theologiae*, Aquinas refers to it more specifically as something Augustine says in his treatise *On the Catholic Way of Life* (*mor.*).[4] Aquinas's citation is incorrect. Augustine never defines virtue as the *ordo amoris* in this treatise. Only one text in all of Aquinas's extant works – q. 11, a. 1 of his *Disputed Questions on Evil* – correctly attributes Augustine's definition of virtue as the *ordo amoris* to *City of God*. This citation of *City of God*, however, comes after Aquinas's usual citation of *On the Catholic Way of Life*. Does it come from Aquinas himself, or was it added later, by someone else? We cannot be sure. All extant manuscripts of his *Disputed Questions on Evil* derive from a single

---

[3] Visser 2008: 81.   [4] See *ST* 1a2ae 55.1, 62.2; 2a2ae 23.4.

manuscript which editors of the critical edition had trouble restoring, because the text was defective.

Aquinas's erroneous citations would hold little interest if Augustine gave substantially the same account of virtue in *City of God* that he did in his early treatise *On the Catholic Way of Life*. In fact, there is a significant difference between the two, though I can find no evidence in Aquinas's works that he was aware it. In his early treatise Augustine defines virtue as "the highest love of God," then argues that we should love God with "full charity." Towards the end of his life he regretted this perfectionist turn of phrase. He called attention to it in his *Retractations*, suggesting that "sincere charity" would have been better (*mor.* 15.25; *retr.* 1.6). Augustine expressed no regrets about *City of God*, where nothing he said about virtue could have been used as ammunition by contemporaries arguing that we can, and hence should, achieve moral perfection in our earthly lives.

Now Thomists might object that Aquinas actually had read Book 15 of *City of God*, including Augustine's pithy definition of virtue. His attribution of the definition to a different work was just a slip of the pen when he was busy composing his own magnum opus and sometimes relying on memory. Two facts weigh heavily against this objection. First, Aquinas demonstrates far more interest in some books of *City of God* than in others. In the *Summa theologiae* he cites Book 14 well over 60 times, two other books 30–40 times apiece, two 20–30 times, and ten no more than 5 times. Book 15 belongs to this last group. Second, there is nothing original about Aquinas's misattribution of Augustine's pithy definition to *On the Catholic Way of Life*, as there would be if it came from his own imperfect memory or a mistake in notes he himself had made on *City of God*. The same misattribution appears in works composed earlier in the thirteenth century by other theologians at Paris, including Philip the Chancellor, Albert the Great, and Bonaventure.

All things considered, I think it more likely than not that Aquinas never read Book 15 of *City of God*. He probably got the short quotations from it that he used in the *Summa theologiae* secondhand. (I suspect that the same holds for at least several other books of *City of God*, such as Books 2–4, which hold much greater interest for classicists than they do for philosophers or theologians.) Today this would be evidence of rather shabby scholarship. In the Middle Ages it was such a common practice that it would be astonishing if Aquinas had declined to participate in it. Those who deny that he did seem eager to acquit him of what nobody regarded as a failing at the time.

We must also avoid the anachronistic assumption that *City of God* was among the great books that Aquinas must surely have studied before composing his own great book, the *Summa theologiae*. If what we mean by a great book is a "must-read" for any serious student of Western thought, neither *City of God* nor the *Summa theologiae* attained this exalted status during the Middle Ages. They have it now partly because they figure in a sweeping historical narrative, constructed after the Middle Ages, about the development of Western moral thought. The narrative begins with ancient Greek accounts of naturally acquired virtues, shifts to Augustine's attack on ancient philosophical ethics in Book 19 of *City of God*, then skips ahead to the section on natural law in the *Summa theologiae*, to show how Aquinas rehabilitated ancient philosophical ethics. The conflict between these two great books adds drama to the story.

Medieval thinkers would have found our story puzzling. Although many noticed conflicts between the teachings of Aquinas and Augustine, even debated whether the differences were deep or merely superficial, only centuries later were those conflicts recast as conflicts between the *Summa theologiae* and *City of God*. Neither of these works had the importance in the medieval period that they later acquired. It was Peter Lombard's *Sentences*, not Aquinas's *Summa theologiae*, that medieval universities used as a theology textbook. Even Aquinas's own religious order, the Dominicans, largely continued to favor the *Sentences* over the *Summa theologiae*. As for Augustine's magnum opus, *City of God* was "magnum" chiefly in its length, and medieval students could hear an entire course of lectures on the *Sentences* without hearing much at all about it.

2 PETER LOMBARD'S *SENTENCES*

In composing his *Sentences* (c. 1155–1158), Peter Lombard deliberately kept his own theorizing to a minimum. Dismayed by contemporary theologians eager to demonstrate their own ingenuity, he made it his goal to compile a volume "from the witnesses of truth established for all eternity" (*sent.*, prologue). In practice this meant including a great many quotations from patristic writings. The overwhelming majority of them, a total of 680, come from Augustine's works. But one should not leap to the conclusion that Peter had made a thorough study of the Augustinian corpus. Research by Ignatius Brady has established that, when writing his *Sentences*, Peter had direct access to only four works by Augustine: *On Christian Instruction* (*doc. Chr.*), the *Enchiridion* (*ench.*), *On 83 Different Questions* (*div. qu.*), and *Retractations* (*retr.*). He knew other works by Augustine only secondhand.[5]

---

[5] For evidence see Brady 1971: 1 118*–122*.

Peter's need for secondhand sources did not deter him from quoting extensively from works he fancied, such as Augustine's *On the Trinity* (*Trin.*) and *Tractates on the Gospel of John* (*Jo. ev. tr.*) Since he quotes *City of God* fewer than twenty times, I think it safe to conclude that it was not among his personal favorites. About two-thirds of Peter's citations come from Books 20–22, where Augustine discusses the last judgment, hell, and heaven. Only one citation comes from Book 19, the book now considered most important. Peter never cites Book 14, where Augustine links the earthly and heavenly cities to two different kinds of love, nor does he cite the definition of virtue in Book 15. What he knew of *City of God* evidently struck him as less important for ethics than eschatology.

Peter Abelard, among the twelfth-century masters famed for his dialectical prowess, found *City of God* more useful than Peter Lombard did. He included more quotations from it in his *Sic et non* than Peter Lombard does in his *Sentences*, even though *Sic et non*, composed some thirty years earlier, is a much shorter work. Abelard's extensive quotations from Book 1 of *City of God* make it clear that he himself had direct access to at least this particular book. He found it valuable on three moral questions: whether sin is physical or strictly mental, whether it is permissible to kill oneself, and whether it is permissible to kill anyone else (*Sic et non*, qq. 143, 155, 157). But unlike the *Sentences, Sic et non* does not attempt to resolve the questions it raises. On the contrary, Abelard highlights conflicts between various passages in patristic writings in order to prove that theologians need some rational method for resolving them. He quotes Augustine's discussion of Lucretia's suicide (*civ. Dei* 1.19–20) to suggest that sin lies strictly in mental acts, and again to suggest that suicide is always a sin. Suicide was a touchy issue precisely because of a disagreement between the Fathers. Jerome generally denounced suicide as a sin but made an exception for women in danger of being raped and unable to preserve their chastity in any other way. Augustine argued forcefully on the opposite side, using the Romans' admiration for Lucretia's suicide as one more exhibit in his own case against ancient conceptions of virtue.

While *City of God* contributes little to Peter Lombard's *Sentences*, other works by Augustine contribute a good deal. Consider, for example, the definition of virtue. Instead of reporting some definition given by Augustine Peter fabricates one from remarks in the chapter of the *Retractations* where Augustine discusses his dialogue *On Free Choice* (*lib. arb.*; *retr.* 1.8). The chapter distinguishes between three kinds of goods: the lowest goods, such as physical beauty, which we do not need in order to live righteously; the intermediate goods, such as free choice, which we need for a righteous life but can use badly; and the highest goods, such as virtues, which we need for a righteous life and cannot use badly. The reason why virtues cannot be used badly is that the very work (or function: *opus*) of virtue is the good use of free choice. In other words, the claim that virtues cannot be badly used is a conceptual point, not the empirical assertion that someone having virtues is psychologically determined to act well. But even with the inclusion of free choice, Augustine's account of virtue might still sound close to the Stoics', who made much of the idea that virtues, unlike other supposed goods, cannot be badly used. Thus he emphasizes that all of these goods are given by God on the basis of no antecedent merit. Far from being a human achievement, as it is for the Stoics and other ancient philosophers, virtue is a gift of grace.

Peter Lombard sees in this chapter of the *Retractations* all the ingredients he needs for a definition of virtue true to the spirit of Augustine. First, however, he takes pains to address two issues that contemporaries had raised. One is various "Augustinian" remarks suggesting that people can do some good things through the power of free choice unaided by any special grace from God. Sometimes these remarks come from the pseudo-Augustinian *Hypognosticon*; sometimes they come from Prosper of Aquitaine's collection of extracts from Augustine's teachings; but at times they come directly from Augustine's own works. If God-given virtue is necessary for the good use of free choice, how can anyone do something good without it? Peter resolves the problem by distinguishing between doing something good, such as cultivating fields, and performing an act with *merit*. Through free choice alone nobody can do what has merit in God's eyes. Only works of virtue have merit (*sent.* 2.26.7–9). The other issue Peter addresses is an ambiguity in the notion of the good use of free choice as "the work of virtue." This might be taken to mean that virtue simply *is* the good use of free choice, hence a kind of mental activity: something the mind does, not something it has. Peter accordingly urges readers to distinguish between virtue itself and a work or act of virtue (*sent.* 2.26.11).

Having tried to ward off possible confusions, Peter proceeds to define virtue as "a good quality of the mind, by which we live righteously, of which no one makes bad use, which God alone works in us" (*sent.* 2.27.1). The last clause was soon modified, probably by Peter's follower, Peter of Poitiers, to read "which God works in us without us." (The addition of "without us" makes it clear that God's gift of virtue does not require the agent's consent, an act of free choice impossible for people too young to have the use of free choice.) From the early thirteenth century all the way to the sixteenth, the modified version was the definition of virtue taught in universities and discussed by theologians. What many saw as a weakness of it was just the vague word "quality." Even mental qualities range from dispositions (*habitus*), through conditions, which easily change, all the way to affections or passions. Various thirteenth-century theologians accordingly suggested that "quality" be replaced with "disposition." Since Aristotle defines moral virtue as "a disposition concerning choice," a slight change in Peter Lombard's definition would enable ethical theorists to place all virtues, whether naturally acquired or infused by God's grace, in the same ontological category. It would make both kinds of virtues the same sort of "thing." Thus at least some groundwork would be laid for a synthesis of Augustine's teachings and Aristotle's. Classifying God-given virtues as dispositions would push Augustine's ethics closer to Aristotle's – or would it?

3 ONTOLOGY, EQUALITY, AND SACRAMENTAL THEOLOGY

Historians commonly assume that theologians began treating God-given virtues as dispositions because of Aristotle's influence on Christian ethics during the Middle Ages. This view, already found in the writings of Martin Luther, arises from inadequate knowledge of both Augustine's works and twelfth-century theological texts. Peter Lombard himself regarded God-given virtues as dispositions. I suspect that he used the word "quality" in his definition of virtue mainly because Abelard, who argued that dispositions can only be produced over time, through an individual's own efforts, had skewed "disposition" in the direction of ancient ethics, thereby helping to make it a loaded word. Peter and his contemporaries, including Abelard, knew that Augustine treated virtues as dispositions given by God, not produced by human actions, and more, as dispositions that might never in the course of an individual's lifetime be manifest in her actions. If the occasion for exercising some particular virtue never arose, the disposition would remain hidden in her soul, unrecognized by humans and known only to God.

How did Peter and other twelfth-century scholars, with such limited access to Augustine's works, know that he had this conception of virtue? The answer, in brief, is that they paid close attention to passages from Augustine's *On the Good of Marriage* (*b. conjug.*), a short treatise that scholars from the sixteenth century all the way to the twenty-first have largely ignored. It drew plenty of attention in the twelfth century thanks to a decision by the second Lateran Council to annul all marriages of priests, monks, and nuns, including any contracts that clerics might have with concubines. Until 1123 the Church recognized clerics' marriages as valid but forbade them (vainly) to have sexual relations with their partners. The new ban on clerical marriage not only had major practical repercussions; it might also be taken to imply that even conjugal sex is bad – a view that Augustine's treatise on marriage strongly opposes. For this reason Abelard included long quotations from it in q. 130 of *Sic et non*, about whether any sexual intercourse, including conjugal intercourse, can be without sin.

Augustine does not venture to argue that conjugal chastity (i.e., having sex exclusively with one's spouse) is just as good as virginity or celibacy. *On the Good of Marriage* argues instead for a more subtle position, intended to discourage celibate Christians from feeling superior to married ones: that someone who has the virtue of virginity or celibacy only "in disposition" can be equal in merit to someone who has it both in disposition and "in action" or "in use." He takes Abraham, who married and sired children, as representative of someone with celibacy in disposition but not in action or use. Augustine argues that Abraham would have refrained from sex if it had been appropriate for him to do so, but at the time it was not. God wanted Abraham to increase the children of Israel. Augustine uses Abraham as just one example in order to teach the more general lesson that people may have virtuous dispositions which they never have an occasion to use. An individual might have the patience of Job or the fortitude of the Christian martyrs but never display these virtues in action because, the way her life happens to go, she never faces the trials of Job or the martyrs. Virtuous dispositions, given by God, may therefore go forever unrecognized by human beings.

Peter Lombard quotes from *On the Good of Marriage* in Book 4 of his *Sentences* (4.33.2), using Augustine's distinction between virtue in disposition and virtue in action to discuss whether the virginity of John the Baptist was better than the conjugal chastity of Abraham.[6] He again invokes Augustine's distinction in Book 3, when addressing wider problems regarding the connection of the virtues. The main problem arises from tension between Augustine and Jerome on a long-standing issue of ethical theory: whether the virtues can be separated. Jerome proclaimed that whoever has one virtue has them all – a thesis Augustine accepted, though he worried that people associated it with the all-or-nothing moral perfectionism of Stoicism and such disturbing Stoic paradoxes as the claim that all faults

---

[6] Peter copied the passage from Hugh of St. Victor's *On the Sacraments of the Christian Faith* – unfortunately, together with the misattribution of it to Augustine's treatise on virginity.

(or sins: *peccata*) are equal. In his reply to Jerome, Augustine argued that anyone with the God-given virtue of charity does indeed have all the virtues. Nevertheless, the virtues exist in different individuals in different degrees and always in earthly life come combined with vices (*ep.* 167).

Augustine's reply to Jerome on this issue was well known to twelfth-century theologians. In an effort to explain Augustine's position Peter Lombard distinguishes between virtue in disposition and virtue in action (*sent.* 3.36.2):

> Here it seems to be implied that someone can be said to have one virtue more than another because, through charity, he is more affected in the act of one virtue than another, ... although he has all of them at the same time and has them equally as regards the disposition of the mind or the essence of each. But in action he has one more and another less and even does not have some other virtue at all, as the just man making use of marriage does not have celibacy in action, which he nevertheless does have in disposition.

Peter's explanation clearly rests on the passage from *On the Good of Marriage* that he quotes in Book 4. I suppose that he declines to cite the treatise on marriage in this context because Augustine's reply to Jerome concerning the connection of the virtues does not invoke the distinction between virtue in disposition and virtue in action or use. So Peter is making a modest interpretative leap in suggesting that this distinction is implied.

Peter exercises even greater caution in discussing the effects of infant baptism – with good reason, because Augustine has nothing to say about this topic in *On the Good of Marriage*, and his remarks in other works leave his position unclear. On the one hand, he held that baptism is necessary for the remission of original sin, and the remission of original sin is necessary for salvation. Augustine insisted, contrary to the Pelagians, that unbaptized babies would not be saved. On the other hand, he was far less specific about the precise effects of infant baptism. Are baptized babies saved because God's gift of the virtue of faith makes them believers "in disposition," or are they made "believers" only in the social sense, through the faith of adult sponsors bringing them into the community of believers? Twelfth-century theologians engaged in heated debate on this question. Since each faction could quote passages from Augustine to support its own position, neither could prevail. As a result, Pope Innocent III refused to take sides. In a letter written in 1201 he simply reported both positions – that infants receive virtues in disposition but not in use through the grace of baptism, and that baptism effects the remission of original sin in infants without producing virtues – and declared them both acceptable. Thus the controversy about whether baptism does or does not give infants virtues in disposition would continue throughout the thirteenth century. There was no heated battle about whether the virtues God gives adults are dispositions, because the vast majority of theologians already agreed that they are.

Ironically, the group of theologians most eager to attribute virtuous dispositions to infants was the very one least influenced by ancient ethics: Peter Lombard and his followers, who regarded all true virtues as gifts of grace. Peter of Poitiers was especially forceful in defending the attribution of virtuous dispositions to infants. He argued that infants could have virtues in disposition but be unable to use them, just as a mute adult could know how to debate but be unable to display his knowledge in action.[7] The view of infancy as a temporary physical handicap, preventing someone from using virtuous dispositions but not from having them, would later be defended by Aquinas.

4 AQUINAS'S REINVENTION OF AUGUSTINE'S TWO CITIES

As Aristotle's works became available in Latin, tensions increased in the universities. Rebellious masters of arts used the new material to cast doubt on entrenched views about ethics. Masters of theology usually supported Augustine's teachings, but they often had trouble discerning what they were and proceeded to lock horns. Augustine lived in a different world, even farther removed in time from the world of thirteenth-century university teachers than their world is from our own. What he said in one work often diverged from what he said in another. Spurious works compounded the confusion.

The definition of virtue is a case in point. Philip the Chancellor reported eleven different definitions in his *Summa on the Good* (*c.* 1225–1228), then struggled mightily to reconcile them. Even the first six, all of which he attributed to Augustine, varied considerably:

[1] Augustine says in the book *On Free Choice*, 'Virtue is a good quality of the mind, by which we live righteously, of which no one makes bad use, which God works in us without us.' Furthermore, [2] he says in the book *On Spirit and Soul*, 'Virtue is a disposition of the well composed mind.' Furthermore, [3] he says in the book of *Soliloquies*, 'Virtue is right reason arriving at its end.' Furthermore, [4] he says in the book *On the Greatness of the Soul*, 'Virtue is an equality of life in harmony with or consenting to reason on every side.' Furthermore, [5] he says in the book *On the*

---

[7] *Sententiae libri quinque* V.6 (*PL* 211, 1232).

City of God, 'Virtue is good will.' Furthermore, [6] he says in the book *On the Catholic Way of Life*, 'Virtue is the order of love.'[8]

With such a wide range of competing definitions, medieval theologians might have wished that Augustine had said much less. In fact, he had. Definition 1 comes from the revised version of Peter Lombard's *Sentences*, not from a text written by Augustine. Definition 4 comes from *On Spirit and Soul*, a pseudo-Augustinian work composed only a few decades earlier. Definition 5 is found nowhere in *City of God* or any of Augustine's other extant works. The other three definitions are roughly correct, although Augustine uses definition 3 to characterize *perfect* virtue, and as we know, "Virtue is the order of love" comes from *City of God*, not *On the Catholic Way of Life*.

However defective, the list of "Augustinian" definitions recited by Philip had staying power. Albert the Great used the same list in his treatise *On the Nature of the Good* in the 1240s. Bonaventure used it in his own commentary on the *Sentences* in the 1250s. To his credit, Aquinas recognized that *On Spirit and Soul* was not Augustine's work and declared that it had no authority (*ST* 1a 77.8 ad1). Aquinas also described the textbook definition of virtue more accurately than most of his predecessors – as one that Peter Lombard compiled from Augustine's words, not as one that Augustine himself formulated (*ST* 1a2ae 55.5).

Thirteenth-century theologians evinced much greater interest in formal definitions than their predecessors had. As theology evolved into an academic discipline practiced by highly trained professionals, the language of theology became at once more precise and more technical. The definition of virtue was especially important to Aquinas, for a large percentage of his *Summa theologiae* goes to discussing virtues of one kind or another. Thus it may come as a surprise that he develops no truly new definition. Instead he chooses to modify the definition in the *Sentences*. Aquinas recommends only two revisions: that "quality" be replaced with "disposition" in order to make the definition more exact, and that "which God works in us without us" be omitted in order to make it general enough to encompass naturally acquired virtues. Aquinas devotes far more space to discussing dispositions than he does to defining virtue. What accounts for this decision?

Even the most conservative theologians of the time already agreed that God-given virtues are dispositions. Aristotle, too, taught that virtues are dispositions, albeit ones that people acquire by natural means. There were,

---

[8] *Summa de bono* 2.1 (Wicki 1985: II 535).

however, more than minor differences between Augustine's concept of a disposition and the various concepts found in works by Aristotle and his commentators. The intellectual challenge lay in developing some concept wide and thin enough to resolve, or at least sidestep, the conflicts between Augustine and the new Aristotelian corpus. Equally important, there was no work where Augustine, the most revered Father of the Latin Church, himself defined virtue as a disposition. Although he spoke of virtue as a disposition in *On the Good of Marriage*, neither there nor in any other work did he actually define it as a disposition. The only works where he appeared to do so were the pseudo-Augustinian *On Spirit and Soul* and texts where Augustine was discussing Cicero's definition of virtue, not his own.

Having already dismissed *on Spirit and Soul* as spurious, Aquinas could hardly use it to justify including "disposition" in the definition of virtue. He chose instead to make the concept of a disposition more Augustinian, even while paying close attention to various points raised by Aristotle and his commentators. Indeed, Aquinas pays so much attention to their views that one scholar complains about his constructing an Aristotelian notion of a disposition, then needing to rework it when he turns to the definition of virtue.[9] It would be more reasonable to protest that the *Summa*'s treatise on dispositions tends to mislead (*ST* 1a2ae 49–54). While Aquinas comments at length on various Aristotelian claims, he works mainly to recast dispositions along more Augustinian lines.

Three examples of Aquinas's Augustinian spin on dispositions must suffice. First, from the very beginning of his career he insisted that infants receive virtuous dispositions through the grace of baptism. He continues to defend this wholly un-Aristotelian position in the *Summa* (*ST* 3a 69.6), and nothing in his treatise on dispositions contradicts it. Second, Aquinas draws directly on the account of dispositions in *On the Good of Marriage* in order to weaken the link between disposition and action (*ST* 1a2ae 49.3). His claim that a disposition "implies a relation to action" does not entail that some disposition an individual possesses will at some point be manifested in action. If he defended this position, he would be contradicting not only Augustine's treatise on marriage but also his own view about the virtuous dispositions of infants. All Aquinas means is that dispositions are tendencies to do something or other, at least in the mental sense of "do." They are never merely tendencies to brute reactions, such as flinching at a sudden movement. Third, Aquinas argues that the very concept of a disposition entails that it is principally related to the will. Hence humans and angels can

---

[9] Jordan 1993: 238.

have dispositions properly so-called, but animals cannot (*ST* 1a2ae 49.3, 50.5–6). This link between dispositions and the will fits nicely with Augustine's link between virtuous dispositions and the free choice of the will. Careful readers will notice that Aquinas develops a concept of dispositions designed specifically for service in ethical theory. Conceived along the lines he suggests, dispositions can play no significant role in biology.

To be sure, Aquinas's support for Augustine's ethics has its limits. The present essay began by noting the most obvious conflict. *City of God* argues that virtues which people appear to possess, if acquired through their own natural resources, are actually vices. The *Summa theologiae* grants that some naturally acquired virtues are really vices in disguise, but Aquinas denies that this holds for all of them (2a2ae 23.7):

> Just as the end is twofold, one ultimate and the other proximate, so too is the good twofold, one ultimate and the other proximate and particular. A human being's ultimate and principal good is the enjoyment of God ..., to which a person is directed by charity. On the other hand, a human being's secondary and quasi-particular good can be twofold: one that is truly good inasmuch as it is, by its very nature, capable of being directed to the principal good that is the ultimate end; the other an apparent but not a true good, because it leads one away from the final good ... If virtue is understood in relation to some particular end, something can be called a virtue without [God-given] charity, insofar as it is directed to some particular good ... If that particular good is a true good, such as the preservation of the city or the like, it will indeed be a true virtue, but imperfect, unless it is referred to the final and perfect good.

Had Augustine been able to reply, he might have objected that Aquinas's reasoning proves only that some of people's naturally acquired "virtues" can *become* true virtues if directed to the ultimate end by God's grace. Thus it proves, at most, that they are potentially true virtues, not actually true ones.

As Aquinas argues that naturally acquired virtues can be true virtues, so he argues that humans belong both to the earthly city and to the heavenly city. He envisions precisely the kind of dual citizenship that *City of God* refuses to allow. Although he supports this position in the *Summa theologiae*, his clearest, most concise statement of it comes from a disputation dating from the same period (*Disp. qu. de virtutibus*, a.9):

> A human being is not only a citizen of the earthly city but also a member of the heavenly city of Jerusalem, which is ruled by the Lord and has as its citizens angels and all the saints, whether they are reigning in glory and at rest in their homeland or still pilgrims on earth ... Now it is clear that those virtues which belong to a human being insofar as he is a member of this [heavenly] city cannot be acquired by him through his own natural resources, which is why that they are not caused by our

actions but must be infused in us through divine gift. On the other hand, the virtues of a human being insofar as he is human, or a member of the earthly city, do not exceed the capacity of human nature, which is why a human being can acquire them through his own natural resources, from his own actions.

Was Aquinas aware that Augustine rejects the very position he himself is pressing? I am confident that he was. Although he never quotes the passage from Book 19 of *City of God*, which declares that virtues having no reference to God are actually vices, he quotes a sufficient number of other passages from Book 19 to suggest that he had read it. Besides, he quotes passages from Augustine's treatise *Against Julian* (*c. Jul.*) that defend the same position. Aquinas did not go out of his way to advertise his disagreement, but he did indeed disagree.

Many authors have already detailed Aquinas's reasons for rejecting a crucial aspect of Augustine's mature ethical theory. The only original contribution I can think to offer has to do with the circumstances in which he developed his views. Aquinas lived during a time of bitter opposition by some of the secular clergy to members of the new mendicant orders, the Dominicans and Franciscans. Seculars fought tooth and nail to prevent mendicants from joining the ranks of masters at the University of Paris. To modern eyes, this looks like nothing more than academic infighting of the worst kind. With the number of positions capped by university statutes, any gain by the newcomers would come as a loss to the entrenched faction. Maybe the ensuing battle actually was nothing but academic infighting. Nevertheless, it came combined with fierce apocalyptic rhetoric.

The best example is *On the Dangers of the Last Times*, a diatribe penned by William of Saint-Amour, the leader of the anti-mendicant wing at Paris. William saw nothing wrong with secular clergy like himself, who sometimes taught in universities; nor did he see anything wrong with members of monastic orders, who largely remained in their monasteries. In contrast, the new mendicant orders – friars without monasteries, dedicated to preaching and social work in the wider world – struck him as both a monstrous violation of the proper order of things and a sign of the coming End. William did not rest content with arguing that mendicants should be banned from teaching at Paris. He cast them as forerunners of the Antichrist, salting his treatise with plenty of quotations from Paul's Epistles and Augustine's later works.

Aquinas experienced first-hand the effects of this ugly hybrid between Augustine's sharp dichotomies and thirteenth-century apocalypticism. A contemporary report says that when he gave his inaugural lecture at Paris, the king's archers had to be there to protect him and his listeners.[10] Undaunted, Aquinas produced a treatise later that year defending the mendicants, especially against William's inflammatory treatise *On the Dangers of the Last Times*. He challenged both William's interpretation of scripture and his interpretation of Augustine's teachings. At the same time, Aquinas presented cool, philosophical objections to the thesis that the same person cannot belong to two associations. This is clearly possible, he argued, when one association is a part of the other, as a household is part of a city. It is equally possible when one association is public and perpetual and the other, whether public or private, is temporary. As an individual who belongs to some civil society may also belong to a military regiment, so he may also associate with others at an inn. Using Augustine's terminology, he concluded that "one and the same person can be a citizen of two cities" (*Contra impugnantes* 2.2).

Aquinas's citations from *City of God* in the *Summa theologiae* confirm what one might expect from his youthful battle with William and the antimendicant faction. Books 20–22, the very ones that Peter Lombard cited the most, rank among those that Aquinas cites the least. By far Aquinas's favorite book of *City of God* is Book 14, but less because of the opening chapters, where Augustine discusses the sins of Adam and Eve, than because of chapters 7 and 9, where he discusses moral psychology.

5 THE BIRTH OF A GREAT BOOK

The fourteenth century witnessed a couple of developments that helped to win *City of God* the status it now enjoys. One was a far more careful, critical approach to the Augustinian corpus. Earlier medieval thinkers knew most of Augustine's works secondhand, were fairly casual about quoting them, and often naïvely accepted as authentic virtually any texts that carried his name. The new breed of scholars tried hard to obtain copies of the texts themselves, to establish their authenticity, to quote them exactly, and to quote them at sufficient length to convey Augustine's reasoning, instead of using only "soundbites." Virtually all of them belonged to either the Augustinian Canons or the Augustinian Hermits. The first was a monastic order, the second a mendicant order. Both traced their lineage to the original order founded by Augustine himself.

How could one prove that a particular text was truly Augustine's work? The easiest way was to consult Augustine's own catalog of his major works

[10] Torrell 1996: 79.

in the *Retractations*. If the work matched his description of it, this constituted at least some evidence for its authenticity. The *Retractations* also revealed various ways in which Augustine's thinking had developed over the course of his life. This might have given Augustinians a tendency to prefer his later works, including *City of God*, to his earlier ones. Some also had a doctrinal reason to prefer his later works. They were waging a campaign against what struck them as a new Pelagianism. By the turn of the fourteenth century various theologians had moved beyond Aquinas's ethics to arguing that people can even acquire perfect moral virtues through their own natural resources, with no special grace from God.

The most influential adversary of what appeared a new Pelagianism was Gregory of Rimini (d. 1358), an Augustinian Hermit. He labored to revive Augustine's doctrine that only God-given moral virtues can even be true virtues, let alone perfect ones. He drew heavily on Augustine's later works in arguing his case, quoting the key passage from Book 19, chapter 25 of *City of God*, along with parallel passages in Augustine's treatise *Against Julian* and other polemical works aimed at the original Pelagians.[11] So many later medieval thinkers followed Gregory's teachings that by the sixteenth century – when his fellow Hermit, Martin Luther, was a student – "the way of Gregory" (*via Gregorii*) was a recognized approach to teaching theology. Alas, his anti-Pelagian campaign represented only a modest victory for *City of God*. Gregory himself preferred shorter works with a tighter focus to Augustine's sprawling magnum opus, where Augustine's erudition was on full display.

The other fourteenth-century development, representing a clear victory for *City of God*, was growing appreciation of Augustine's excellent writing and his impressive knowledge of Roman history, literature, religion, and philosophy. Nicholas Trevet and Thomas Waleys, English members of the Dominican Order who wrote the first commentaries on *City of God*, loved it precisely because of their interest in classical studies. Glossing over Augustine's sustained polemic against the pagans, they concentrated on what the polemic taught them about antiquity.[12] Waleys' interest in this aspect of the work is all the more evident because of his decision to comment on only the first ten books, where Augustine gives plenty of information about ancient Roman history and culture.

In 1333, around the time Waleys finished his commentary, *City of God* was also winning admirers in Italy. The famous scholar Petrarch included it in a short list of his own favorite books. The list began with several moral

---

[11] Trapp and Marcolino 1980: esp. 31. [12] Smalley 1960: 58–65, 88–108.

treatises by Cicero and Seneca. *City of God*, the sole work on his list by a Christian, won a place owing to Petrarch's appreciation of Augustine's vast learning and fine Latin style. Later Renaissance humanists praised it for the same reasons. Thanks to them, *City of God* became one of the first printed books. They admired Augustine's *Confessions* even more, in part because the style was more personal, in part because they saw it as a tribute to the contemplative life, and in part because it included less theology.[13] But at least *City of God* was well on the road to joining the Western canon, albeit for reasons that would have been a source of dismay to Augustine himself. I imagine that he would have looked with greater approval on the highly selective presentation of his magnum opus by Peter Lombard, who had never read it.

---

[13] For a helpful study of how humanists received Augustine's works, see Gill 2005.

Bibliography

Alici, Luigi. 1994. Storia e salvezza nel *De civitate Dei*. In Naldini. 85–100.
Alter, Robert. 1996. *Genesis: Translation and Commentary*. New York: W.W. Norton & Company.
Ando, Clifford. 2006. Religion and *Jus Publicum*. In Ando and Rüpke. 126–45.
Ando, Clifford, and Jörg Rüpke, eds. 2006. *Religion and Law in Classical and Christian Rome*. Stuttgart: Steiner.
Annas, Julia. 1993. *The Morality of Happiness*. Oxford University Press.
  1999. *Platonic Ethics: Old and New*. Ithaca, NY: Cornell University Press.
Armstrong, A. H., trans. 1966 *Plotinus: Enneads*, vol. 1 2nd edn. Cambridge, MA: Harvard University Press.
Assmann, Aleida. 2008. Canon and Archive. In Erll and Nünning. 97–107.
Atkins, E. M., and R. J. Dodaro, eds. 2001. *Augustine: Political Writings*. Cambridge University Press.
Backus, Irena, ed. 1997. *The Reception of the Church Fathers in the West*, vol. 1. Leiden: E.J. Brill.
Barnes, Jonathan, ed. 1984. *The Complete Works of Aristotle*. Princeton University Press.
Blanchard, Alain, ed. 1989. *Les débuts du codex: Actes de la journée d'étude organisée à Paris les 3 et 4 juillet 1985*. Turnhout: Brepols.
Blowers, P., A. Christman, D. Hunter, and R. Young, eds. 2002. *In Dominico Eloquio / In Lordly Eloquence: Essays in Patristic Exegesis in Honor of Robert Louis Wilken*. Grand Rapids, MI: Eerdmans.
Bochet, Isabelle. 2010. The Role of Scripture in Augustine's Controversy with Porphyry. *Augustinian Studies* 41: 7–54.
Bouchard, Donald, and Sherry Simon, eds. and trans. 1977. *Michel Foucault: Language, Counter-Memory, Practice – Selected Essays and Interviews*. Ithaca, NY: Cornell University Press.
Boulding, Maria, O.S.B., trans. 1997. *Saint Augustine: Confessions*. Hyde Park, NY: New City Press.
Bowersock, G. W. 1995. *Martyrdom and Rome*. Cambridge University Press.
Brady, Ignatius C. 1971. Prolegomena to Peter Lombard. *Sententiae in IV libris distinctae*, vol. 1: 8*–129*. Grottaferrata: Collegium S. Bonaventurae ad Claras Aquas.

Brown, Peter. 1981. *The Cult of the Saints: Its Rise and Function in Latin Christianity.* University of Chicago Press.
  1988. *The Body and Society: Men, Women, and Sexual Renunciation in Early Christianity.* New York: Columbia University Press.
  2000. *Augustine of Hippo: A Biography*, new edn. Berkeley, CA: University of California Press.
Browne, H., and Joseph H. Myers, trans. 1888. *Augustine: Homilies on the First Epistle of John.* Edinburgh: T. & T. Clark.
Burgess, R. W. 2002. Jerome Explained: An Introduction to His *Chronicle* and a Guide to Its Use. *American Historical Bulletin* 16: 1–32.
Burleigh, John H. S. trans. 1953. *Augustine: Earlier Writings.* Philadelphia: Westminster Press.
Burnell, Peter. 2005. *The Augustinian Person.* Washington, DC: Catholic University of America Press.
Byers, Sarah. 2006. The Meaning of *Voluntas* in Augustine. *Augustinian Studies* 37: 171–89.
  2003. Augustine and the Cognitive Cause of Stoic Preliminary Passions (*Propatheiai*). *Journal of the History of Philosophy* 41/4: 433–48.
  Forthcoming. *Perception, Sensibility, and Moral Motivation in Augustine.* Cambridge University Press.
Castelli, Elizabeth. 2004. *Martyrdom and Memory: Early Christian Culture Making.* New York: Columbia University Press.
Cavadini, John C. 1999. Ambrose and Augustine *de bono mortis.* In Klingshirn and Vessey. 232–249.
  2004. Simplifying Augustine. In Van Engen. 63–84.
  2008. The Sacramentality of Marriage in the Fathers. *Pro Ecclesia* 17/4: 442–63.
Cheney, Patrick, and Frederick A. de Armas, eds. 2002. *European Literary Careers: The Author from Antiquity to the Renaissance.* University of Toronto Press.
Clark, Gillian. 2007. City of Books: Augustine and the World as Text. In Klingshirn and Safran. 117–38.
Connolly, William E. 1991. *Identity/Difference: Democratic Negotiations of Political Paradox.* Minneapolis, MN: University of Minnesota Press.
Cooper, John. 1985. Aristotle on the Goods of Fortune. *Philosophical Review* 94/2: 173–96.
Curbelié, Philippe. 2004. *La justice dans la Cité de Dieu.* Paris: Institut d'Études Augustiniennes.
Damasio, Antonio. 1999. *The Feeling of What Happens: Body and Emotion in the Making of Consciousness.* New York: Harcourt, Brace.
Delage, Pascal-Grégoire, ed. 2006. *Les Pères de l'Église et la voix des pauvres.* Grenoble: Association Histoire et Culture.
De Vries, Hent, and Lawrence Sullivan, eds. 2006. *Political Theologies: Public Religions in a Post-Secular World.* New York: Fordham University Press.
Dodaro, Robert. 2004. *Christ and the Just Society in the Thought of Augustine.* Cambridge University Press.

Dolbeau, François. 1996. *Augustine D'Hippone: Vingt-Six Sermons au Peuple D'Afrique*. Paris: Institut d'Études Augustiniennes.
Dyson, Robert W., trans. 1998. *Augustine: The City of God Against the Pagans*. Cambridge University Press. [Quotations from *City of God* are all taken from here, occasionally with emendation.]
  2005. *St Augustine of Hippo: The Christian Transformation of Political Thought*. London: Continuum.
Elders, Leo J. 1987. Les citations de saint Augustin dans la *Somme theologique* de saint Thomas d'Aquin. *Doctor communis* 40: 115–67.
  1997. Thomas Aquinas and the Fathers of the Church. In Backus. 337–66.
Erll, Astrid, and Ansgar Nünning, eds. 2008. *Cultural Memory Studies: An International Interdisciplinary Handbook*. Berlin: W. de Gruyter.
Feeney, Dennis. 2007. *Caesar's Calendar: Ancient Time and the Beginnings of History*. Berkeley, CA: University of California Press.
Fitzgerald, Allan D., O.S.A., ed. 1999. *Augustine through the Ages: An Encyclopedia*. Grand Rapids, MI: Eerdmans.
Fitzgerald, Allan D., O.S.A., Karla Pollmann, and Mark Vessey, eds. 1999. *History, Apocalypse, and the Secular Imagination: New Essays on Augustine's* City of God. Bowling Green, OH: Philosophy Documentation Center.
Flint, Thomas P., ed. 1990. *Christian Philosophy*. University of Notre Dame Press.
Foucault, Michel. 1971; trans. 1977. Nietzsche, Genealogy, History. In Bouchard and Simon. 139–64.
Frede, Michael. 1984. The Skeptic's Two Kinds of Assent and the Question of the Possibility of Knowledge. In Rorty, Schneewind, and Skinner. 255–278.
Fredriksen, Paula. 2008. *Augustine and the Jews: A Christian Defense of Jews and Judaism*. New York: Doubleday.
Frend, W. H. C. 1985. *The Donatist Church: A Movement of Protest in Roman North Africa*. Oxford University Press.
Frye, Northrop. 1957. *Anatomy of Criticism: Four Essays*. Princeton University Press.
Gaddis, Michael. 2005. *There is No Crime for Those Who Have Christ: Religious Violence in the Christian Roman Empire*. Berkeley, CA: University of California Press.
Gerson, Lloyd P. 1994. *Plotinus*. London: Routledge.
Gill, Christopher. 2006. *The Structured Self in Hellenistic and Roman Thought*. Oxford University Press.
Gill, Meredith Jane. 2005. *Augustine in the Italian Renaissance*. Cambridge University Press.
Gilson, Etienne. 1960. *The Christian Philosophy of Saint Augustine*, trans. L. Lynch. New York: Random House.
Glancy, Jennifer. 2002. *Slavery in Early Christianity*. New York: Oxford University Press.
Goldie, Peter, ed. 2009. *The Oxford Handbook of Philosophy of Emotion*. Oxford University Press.

Grafton, Anthony, and Megan Williams. 2006. *Christianity and the Transformation of the Book: Origen, Eusebius, and the Library of Caesarea.* Cambridge, MA: Harvard University Press.

Gregory, Eric. 2008. *Politics and the Order of Love: An Augustinian Ethic of Democratic Citizenship.* University of Chicago Press.

Griffiths, Paul. 2009. The Quietus of Political Interest. *Common Knowledge* 15/1: 7–22.

Griswold, Charles. 1981. The Ideas and the Criticism of Poetry in Plato's Republic, Book 10. *Journal of the History of Philosophy* 19/2: 135–50.

Guy, Jean-Claude. 1961. *Unité et structure logique de la Cité de Dieu.* Paris: Institut d'Études Augustiniennes.

Halliwell, Stephen. 2002. *The Aesthetics of Mimesis: Ancient Texts and Modern Problems.* Princeton University Press.

Hamilton, Edith, and Huntington Cairns, trans. 1961. *Plato: The Collected Dialogues.* Princeton University Press.

Harding, Brian. 2008. *Augustine and Roman Virtue.* London: Continuum.

Heather, Peter. 2006. *The Fall of the Roman Empire: A New History of Rome and the Barbarians.* New York: Oxford University Press.

Helm, Rudolf, ed. 1984. *Die Chronik des Hieronymus.* Die griechischen christlichen Schriftsteller der ersten drei Jahrhunderte 47. Berlin: Akademie-Verlag.

Hill, Edmund, trans. 1991. *Sermons 51–94A, The Works of Saint Augustine,* vol. III.3. Brooklyn, NY: New City Press.

 trans. 1994. *Sermons 273–305A, The Works of Saint Augustine,* vol. III.8. Brooklyn, NY: New City Press.

Holtz, Louis. 1989. Les mots latins désignant le livre au temps d'Augustin. In Blanchard. 105–13.

Horn, Christoph. 2007. Politische Gerechtigkeit bei Cicero und Augustinus. *Etica e politica* 9: 46–70.

Hunt, Mary E. 2001. Just Good Sex: Feminist Catholicism and Human Rights. In Jung, Hunt, and Balakrishnan. 158–73.

Hunter, David. 2002. Reclaiming Biblical Morality: Sex and Salvation History in Augustine's Treatment of the Hebrew Saints. In Blowers, Christman, Hunter, and Young. 317–35.

Hurtado, Larry W. 2006. *The Earliest Christian Artifacts: Manuscripts and Christian Origins.* Grand Rapids, MI: Eerdmans.

Inglebert, Hervé, ed. 2003. *Idéologies et valeurs civiques dans le monde romaine.* Paris: Picard.

Jager, Eric. 2000. *The Book of the Heart.* University of Chicago Press.

Janaway, Christopher. 1995. *Images of Excellence: Plato's Critique of the Arts.* Oxford: Clarendon Press.

Jay, Nancy. 1992. *Throughout Your Generations Forever: Sacrifice, Religion, and Paternity.* University of Chicago Press.

Jordan, Mark D. 1993. Theology and Philosophy. In Kretzmann and Stump. 232–51.

Jung, Patricia Beattie, Mary E. Hunt, and Radhika Balakrishnan, eds. 2001. *Good Sex: Feminist Perspectives from the World's Religions*. New Brunswick, NJ: Rutgers University Press.
Kant, Immanuel. 1793/1998. *Religion within the Boundaries of Mere Reason*, trans. George di Giovanni. Cambridge University Press.
Karras, Valarie A. 2006. Sex/Gender in Gregory of Nyssa's Eschatology: Irrelevant or Non-Existent? *Studia Patristica* 41: 363–69.
Kaufman, Peter Iver. 2003. Augustine, Macedonius, and the Courts. *Augustinian Studies* 34: 67–81.
　2007. *Incorrectly Political: Augustine and Thomas More*. University of Notre Dame Press.
King, Peter. 2009. Emotions in Medieval Thought. In Goldie. 167–88.
Kirwan, Christopher. 1989. *Augustine*. London: Routledge.
Klingshirn, William, and Linda Safran, eds. 2007. *The Early Christian Book*. Washington, DC: Catholic University of America Press.
Klingshirn, William, and Mark Vessey, eds. 1999. *The Limits of Ancient Christianity: Essays on Late Antique Thought and Culture in Honor of R. A. Markus*. Ann Arbor, MI: University of Michigan Press.
Kretzmann, Norman. 1990. Faith Seeks, Understanding Finds: Augustine's Charter for Christian Philosophy. In Flint. 1–36.
Kretzmann, Norman, and Eleonore Stump, eds. 1993. *The Cambridge Companion to Aquinas*. Cambridge University Press.
　eds. 2001, *The Cambridge Companion to Augustine*. Cambridge University Press.
Kristeva, Julia. 1982. *Powers of Horror: An Essay on Abjection*. New York: Columbia University Press.
Lancel, Serge. 2002. *Saint Augustine*. London: SCM Press.
Lepelley, Claude. 1987. Un aspect de la conversion d'Augustin: La rupture avec ambitions sociales et politiques. *Bulletin de litterature écclesiastiques* 88: 229–46.
　2001. *Aspects de l'Afrique romaines: Les cités, la vie rurale, le Christianisme*. Bari: Edipulglia.
　2003. Le lieu des valeurs communes: le cité terrain neuter entre païens et chrétiens dans l'Afrique romaine tardive. In Inglebert. 271–85.
　2006. Saint Augustin et la voix des pauvres: Observations sur son action sociale en faveur des déshérités dans la région d'Hippone. In Delage. 203–15.
Leyerle, Blake. 1993. John Chrysostom on the Gaze. *Journal of Early Christian Studies* 1: 159–74.
Long, Anthony, and David Sedley. 1987. *The Hellenistic Philosophers*, 2 vols. Translation and Commentary. Cambridge University Press.
Loseby, S. T. 2009. Mediterranean Cities. In Rousseau. 139–55.
MacDonald, Scott. 1999. Primal Sin. In Matthews. 110–39.
MacIntyre, Alasdair. 1999. *Dependent Rational Animals*. Chicago: Open Court.
MacMullen, Ramsay. 1990. *Changes in the Roman Empire: Essays in the Ordinary*. Princeton University Press.

Madec, Goulven. 1975. *Tempora Christiana*: Expression du triumphalisme chrétien ou recrimination paienne? In Mayer and Eckermann. 112–36.
Markus, Robert A. 1970/rev. edn 1988. *Saeculum: History and Society in the Theology of St Augustine*. Cambridge University Press.
  2006. *Christianity and the Secular*. University of Notre Dame Press.
Marrou, Henri-Irénée. 1938. *Saint Augustin et la fin de la culture antique*. Paris: E. de Boccard.
  1949. 'Retractatio' *Saint Augustin et la fin de la culture antique*. Paris: E. de Boccard (issued with original edition, pagination continuous).
  1950. *L'ambivalence du temps de l'histoire chez saint Augustin*. Montréal: Institut d'Études Médiévales.
Mathewes, Charles. 2007. *A Theology of Public Life*. Cambridge University Press.
Matthews, Gareth, ed. 1999. *The Augustinian Tradition*. Berkeley, CA: University of California Press.
  2001. Knowledge and Illumination. In Kretzmann and Stump. 171–85.
  2005. *Augustine*. Oxford: Blackwell.
May, Gerhard. 1994. *Creatio ex Nihilo: The Doctrine of Creation Out of Nothing in Early Christian Thought*, trans. A. S. Worrall. Edinburgh: T. & T. Clark.
Mayer, P., and W. Eckermann, eds. 1975. *Scientia Augustiniana: Studien über Augustinus, den Augustinismus, und den Augustiner Orden*. Würzburg: Augustinus-Verlag.
McGill, Scott, Cristiana Sogno, and Edward Watts, eds. 2010. *From the Tetrarchs to the Theodosians: Later Roman History and Culture 284–450 CE*. Cambridge University Press.
Milbank, John. 1990/rev. edn 2006. *Theology and Social Theory: Beyond Secular Reason*. Oxford: Blackwell.
  2009. *The Future of Love: Essays in Political Theology*. Eugene, OR: Cascade.
Miles, Margaret R. 2005. Sex and the City (of God): Is Sex Forfeited or Fulfilled in Augustine's Resurrection of the Body? *Journal of the American Academy of Religion* 73/2: 307–27.
  2007. *Facie ad Faciem*: Visuality, Desire, and the Discourse of the Other. *Journal of Religion* 87/1: 43–58.
Morrison, Karl F. 1982. *The Mimetic Tradition of Reform in the West*. Princeton University Press.
Naldini, Mario, ed. 1994. *La fine dei tempi: storia e escatologia*. Fiesole: Nardini.
Nightingale, Andrea. 2011. *Once Out of Nature: Augustine on Time and the Body*. University of Chicago Press.
Nussbaum, Martha. 2001. *Upheavals of Thought: The Intelligence of Emotions*. Cambridge University Press.
O'Connell, Robert J. 1991. *Saint Augustine on Genesis*: A Review of Roland J. Teske. *Augustinian Studies* 22: 223–30.
O'Daly, Gerard. 1999a. *Augustine's 'City of God': A Reader's Guide*. Oxford: Clarendon Press.
  1999b. *Augustine's Philosophy of Mind*. London: Duckworth.

O'Donnell, James J. 1992. *Augustine: Confessions – Text and Commentary*, 3 vols. Oxford: Clarendon Press.
  1999. Bible. In Fitzgerald. 99–103.
O'Donovan, Oliver. 2004. The Political Thought of *City of God* 19. In O'Donovan and Lockwood. 48–72.
O'Donovan, Oliver, and Joan Lockwood. 2004. *Bonds of Imperfection: Christian Politics, Past and Present*. Grand Rapids, MI: Eerdmans.
Parsons, Sister Wilfrid, trans. 1953. *Saint Augustine: Letters*, vol. II. Washington, DC: Catholic University of America Press.
Parrish, John. 2007. *Paradoxes of Political Ethics: From Dirty Hands to the Invisible Hand*. Cambridge University Press.
Petitmengin, Pierre. 1986–1994. Codex. *Augustinus Lexikon* 1: 1022–37.
Pine-Coffin, R. S., trans. 1961. *Saint Augustine: Confessions*. New York: Penguin.
Pollmann, Karla. 1996. *Doctrina Christiana: Untersuchungen zu den Anfängen der christlichen Hermeneutik unter besonderer Berücksichtigung von Augustinus,* De doctrina christiana. Freiburg, Switzerland: Universitätsverlag.
Pollmann, Karla, and Mark Vessey, eds. 2005. *Augustine and the Disciplines: From* Cassiciacum *to* Confessions. Oxford University Press.
Porphyry. 1966. On the Life of Plotinus and the Order of His Books. In Armstrong. 1–87.
Potter, David. 1993. Martyrdom as Spectacle. In Scodel. 53–88.
Pranger, M. B. 2006. Politics and Finitude: The Temporal Status of Augustine's *Civitas Permixta*. In De Vries and Sullivan. 113–21.
Raikas, Kauko. 1997. *Audientia Episcopalis*: Problematik zwischen Staat und Kirche bei Augustin. *Augustinianum* 37: 459–81.
Rawls, John. 1993. *Political Liberalism*. New York: Columbia University Press.
Rist, John M. 1969. St John and Amelius. *Journal of Theological Studies* 20: 230–31.
  1992. Ps-Dionysius, Neoplatonism, and the Problem of Spiritual Weakness. In Westra. 135–61.
  1994. *Augustine: Ancient Thought Baptized*. Cambridge University Press.
  2001. Faith and Reason. In Kretzmann and Stump. 26–39.
  2007. Augustine's Spirituality in the Twenty-First Century. In Van Bavel and Bruning. 287–300.
  2008. *What Is Truth?* Cambridge University Press.
Rohrbacher, David. 2002. *The Historians of Late Antiquity*. London: Routledge.
Rorty, Richard, J. B. Schneewind, and Quentin Skinner, eds. 1984. *Philosophy in History: Essays on the Historiography of Philosophy*. Cambridge University Press.
Rousseau, Philip, ed. 2009. *A Companion to Late Antiquity*. Oxford: Wiley-Blackwell.
Runia, David. 1993. *Philo in Early Christian Literature*. Assen: Van Orcum.
  1995. *Philo and the Church Fathers*. Leiden: E. J. Brill.
Sage, Athanase. 1964. Praeparatur voluntas a Deo. *Revue des études augustiniennes* 10: 1–20.
Salamito, Jean-Marie. 2005. *Les virtuoses et la multitude: Aspects sociaux de la controverse entre Augustin et les pélagiens*. Grenoble: Millons.

Salvian of Marseilles. 1930. *On the Government of God*, trans. Eva M. Sanford. New York: Columbia University Press.
Sanday, Peggy Reeves. 1981. *Female Power and Male Dominance: On the Origin of Sexual Inequality*. New York: Cambridge University Press.
Scodel, Ruth, ed. 1993. *Theater and Society in the Classical World*. Ann Arbor, MI: University of Michigan Press.
Shanzer, Danuta. 2005. Augustine's Disciplines: *Silent diutius Musae Varronis?* In Pollmann and Vessey. 69–112.
Sheed, F. J., trans. 1993. *Augustine: Confessions*. Indianapolis, IN: Hackett.
Sheets-Johnstone, Maxine. 1994. *The Roots of Power: Animate Form and Gendered Bodies*. Chicago: Open Court.
   2009. *The Corporeal Turn: An Interdisciplinary Reader*. Exeter, UK: Imprint Academic.
Sider, Ted. 2002. Hell and Vagueness. *Faith and Philosophy* 19: 58–68.
Smalley, Beryl. 1960. *English Friars and Antiquity in the Early Fourteenth Century*. New York: Barnes and Noble.
Spaemann, Robert. 2007. *Persons: The Difference Between 'Someone' and 'Something,'* trans. Oliver O'Donovan. Oxford University Press.
Stock, Brian. 1996. *Augustine the Reader: Meditation, Self-Knowledge, and the Ethics of Interpretation*. Cambridge, MA: Harvard University Press.
Taylor, Charles. 2007. *A Secular Age*. Cambridge, MA: Belknap Press.
Teske, Roland. 1991. St. Augustine's View of the Original Human Condition in *De Genesi contra Manichaeos*. *Augustinian Studies* 22: 141–55.
Tornau, Christian. 2006. *Zwischen Rhetorik und Philosophie: Augustins Argumentationstechnik in* De civitate Dei *und ihr bildungsgeschichtlicher Hintergrund*. Berlin: W. de Gruyter.
Torrell, Jean-Pierre. 1996. *Saint Thomas Aquinas: The Person and his Work*, vol. 1, trans. R. Royal. Washington, DC: Catholic University of America Press.
Trapp, A. D., and Marcolino, V., eds. 1980. *Gregory of Rimini: Lectura super primum et secundum Sententiarum, In 2 Sent. dist. 26–28, q. 1*. Berlin: W. de Gruyter.
Uhalde, Kevin. 2007. *Expectations of Justice in the Age of Augustine*. Philadelphia, PA: University of Pennsylvania Press.
Van Bavel, T. J., and Bernard Bruning, eds. 2007. *Saint Augustine*. Brussels: Mercatorfonds.
Van Engen, John, ed. 2004. *Educating People of Faith: Exploring the History of Jewish and Christian Communities*. Grand Rapids, MI: Eerdmans.
Van Fleteren, Frederick. 1973. Authority and Reason, Faith and Understanding in the Thought of Augustine. *Augustinian Studies* 4: 33–71.
Van Oort, Johannes. 1990. *Jerusalem and Babylon: A Study into Augustine's* City of God *and the Sources of his Doctrine of the Two Cities*. Leiden: E. J. Brill.
Vessey, Mark. 1997. Opus imperfectum: Augustine and His Readers, 426–435 A.D. *Vigiliae Christianae* 52: 264–85. Repr. in *Latin Christian Writers in Late Antiquity and Their Texts*. Aldershot: Ashgate, 2005.
   1999. Introduction. In Fitzgerald, Pollmann, and Vessey. 1–16, 21–26.

2002. From *Cursus* to *Ductus*: Figures of Writing in Western Late Antiquity. In Cheney and De Armas. 47–103.

2010. Reinventing History: Jerome's *Chronicle* and the Writing of the Post-Roman West. In McGill, Sogno, and Watts. 265–89.

Visser, Arnoud. 2008. Reading Augustine through Erasmus's Eyes: Humanist Scholarship and Paratextual Guidance in the Wake of the Reformation. *Erasmus of Rotterdam Society Yearbook* 28: 67–90.

Von Heyking, John. 2001. *Augustine and Politics as Longing in the World*. Columbia, MO: University of Missouri Press.

Westra, Haijo, ed. 1992. *From Athens to Chartres: Neoplatonism and Medieval Thought*. Leiden: E. J. Brill.

Wetzel, James. 1992. *Augustine and the Limits of Virtue*. Cambridge University Press.

2001. Predestination, Pelagianism, and Foreknowledge. In Kretzmann and Stump. 49–58.

2007. Review of Markus 2006. In *Church History* 76/2: 395–97.

Wicki, Nickolaus, ed. 1985. *Philippi Cancellarii Summa de bono*, 2 vols. Berne: Francke.

Williams, Rowan. 1987. Politics and the Soul: A Reading of *City of God*. *Milltown Studies* 19/20: 55–72.

Wolterstorff, Nicholas. 2008. *Justice: Rights and Wrongs*. Princeton University Press.

Wu, Tianyue. 2007. Shame in the Context of Sin: Augustine on the Feeling of Shame in *De civitate Dei*. *Recherches de théologie et philosophie médiévales* 74: 1–32.

Index

Abel 220
Abelard, Peter 232, 234
Abraham 221, 235–36
activity principle 161–65
activity thesis 152–54, 157
Acton, Lord 62–63
Adam
  defection from God 197–201
  descendants of 219–20
  and fall of man 219–20
  as historical figure 218
  and kinship 201–3
  perversity of 197–201
  sins of 10–12, 16–17, 167–85, 186–97
Advanced Philosophy 12, 206, 207, 210, 212–14, 223–24
advantages (*commoda*) 152–54
Aeneas 35
affectivity, Stoicism and theory of 130
Against Julian 241, 243
Against the Skeptics 208
Agape and Eros 160
agent-wellbeing proviso 155, 157–61
Alaric 75–76, 215
Albert the Great 238
Alexander the Great 215
Alici, Luigi 65, 70
Alypius 121
Ambrose 19, 80, 222–23
amore perverso 189–90
Ando, Clifford 66
angels 167–85, 195–96, 216, 218, 219, 221, *see also* deserter angels
anger 135
Annas, Julia 152
Antiquitates 23, 30
apatheia 9
apathy 62
Apuleius 132, 216
Aquinas, Thomas 13, 226–27, 229–31, 237–42

Aristotelian (Peripatetic) eudaimonism 149, 150
Aristotle
  and agent-wellbeing proviso 155
  influence on Aquinas 226–27
  on moral virtue 234
  on virtues as dispositions 238–39
Arius 155
arrogance
  and humility 217
  in perfectionism 70
assent 213
Assyria/Babylon 24
Athens 25
Attic Nights 8
Augustine
  and activity principle 161–65
  and activity thesis 157
  and agent-wellbeing proviso 157–61
  as arbitrator 64–65
  authentication of 242–43
  conversion to Catholic Christianity 205–6, 210–11
  conversion to Manicheism 206–7
  critique of Seneca 137
  and emotional detachment 157–61
  in Middle Ages 227–31
  rhetorical virtuosity 120
  scholarly studies of 227–31
  use of history 222
  on virtues as dispositions 238–39
  works seen as Pelagian 242–43
Augustinian Canons/Hermits 242–43
Aulus Gellius 131, 134, 158
authority 16–18

Babylon/Rome 44–45, 46–51
baptism 236–37
beatitude and will 186–87
belief 205–6
  and divine revelation 209–10

254

Index

bishops
  authority of 74
  in courts 63–64, 72–73
blandimenta (charms) of the world 70
blasphemy 2
bliss 95–96
Bonaventure 238
Book of Rules 17, 18
Bowersock, G. W. 121–22
Bowlin, John 11–12
Bradbury, Ray 58
Brady, Ignatius 231
Brave New World 58
Brown, Peter 73
Bull of Phalaris 79
Byers, Sarah 8–9

Cain 68, 220
calamities in *saeculo maligno* 65
canon-formation 25
Carneades 207
Cato 123, 124, 125–27
Cavadini, John 6–7, 120
celibacy 235
charity 236
chastity
  Augustine on 211
  pride in 81–82
Christ 34, 159, 166
  and humility 120
  incarnation 202
  and lost angels 167–72
  as mediator 217
  perfect maturity of 98–100
  resurrection of 97
  sacrifice of 103–4, 202–3
  and truth 212
Christian canonical writings 26
  as *scripturae* 15
Christian Instruction 159–60
Christian love, as surpassing pagan love 123
Christian magistrates, responsibilities of 68–69
Christian martyrdom 50–51
  as spectacle 112, 114
Christian philosophy 12, 205–24
Christian politics 6
Christian self-control 63
Christian soldier, responsibilities of 68–69
Christian/Jewish scriptures 26–27
Christian/pagan conversion 3, 140, 215, 223–24
Christian/pagan rulers 36
Christianity
  and human dignity 145–46
  and leadership 57
  and political culture 55–56
  Roman contribution to 223–24
  as taking over pagan world 222–23
Christians
  in hoc saeculo 51–52
  in mimesis of God 127–28
Chronicle (of Eusebius) 24, 25, 31–32
Church, as congregation and fellowship 104–5
Cicero 22–23, 72–73, 96, 126, 132, 205, 206, 209–10, 216, 243–44
citizenship 38–40
city
  as *res publica* 40–41
  as society 38–40
city of gaud 6, 74
City of God
  and Aquinas 229–31, 237–42
  as Augustine's greatest work 5, 6
  authentication of 242–43
  comparative literature 24–27
  examined 131–34
  and history 27–32
  length of 227–31
  status of 226–27
  as variously described by Augustine 1
civic religion 215–16
civitas Dei (city of God) 42–43, 44–45
civitas term 38, 42
civitas terrena (earthly city) 42–43, 44–45
Clark, Gillian 28
clemency (*clementia*) 130, 134–36, 137, 138, 141, 143, 144–45, 147–48
clerical marriage 234–35
codex book technology (codicology) 28, 29, 30–32
commiseration 137
commonwealth
  Roman 71
  term 40
compassion 102–4, 137, 141–42
  in Christ 147
  and clemency 135
  and fiction 114–17
  and grief 160–61
  and human dignity 142–47
  and human nature 163
  psychology of 130–48
  Stoics' reproach of 161
concupiscence *see* lust
Confessions 14, 18–19, 28, 29, 31–32, 211, 224, 243–44
conjugal chastity 235
Consentius 213
consolations 56–57, 58–59
Constantine 215, 223–24
constructive philosophy 223

corruption 59–61
courts
    Augustine as arbitrator 64–65
    avoidance by Christians 63
    and order 61–62
    pilgrims in 65–66
    presided over by bishops 63–64
creation
    manner of 195–96
    story of in Genesis 167–79
cultural memory 18

daimones 216
    of Apuleius 132
damnation 44, 186–87, 191
damnatorum solacia (consolations for those condemned to live) 56–57
Day of Judgment 209–10
De cultu deorum (On the Worship of the Gods) 20
De doctrina Christiana (On Christian Instruction) 17, 18
De Genesi as litteram (On the Literal Sense of Genesis) 29
De republica 96
De Trinitate (On the Trinity) 29
death
    as an evil 98, 174
    of Christ 100, 175, 202
    and disobedience 190–91
    and martyrdom 50–51, 112, 114, 120, 121–22
    as punishment 167, 187, 190, 191
    and reproduction 87
    second 191, 203, 219
    see also resurrection; suicide
demons *see daimones*
Descartes 88–89
deserter angels 176, 177, 179, 180
Deus creator omnium 19
Dido 114–17
Diogenes Laertius 140
dis-preferables 152–54, *see also* Stoicism
disciples (of Christ) 213–14
Disputed Questions on Evil 229
distentio see suspense
divine scripture compared to literary sources 22
divine severity 183
Dodaro, Robert 123, 124, 128
domination, love of *see libido dominandi*
Dominicans 241, 243–44
Donatists 71
dual citizenship (of cities) 240–41
dystopia 6, 74
    correctness of term 58–64
dystopian fiction 58

Eden, garden of 167–85, 186–92
egoism, and eudaimonism 154–55
emotional detachment 157–61
emotions, and Stoics 131–33, 156–61
Enchiridion 231
end times, of two cities 221, *see also* eschatology
Epictetus 141
Epicureanism 139, 140–41, 144–45
eschatology 3, 4, 5, 6, 42, 43, 45, 51–54
eternal life, as goal of true religion 215–16
ethics, flawed view of 225–26
eudaimonia, ancient meaning of 150–51
eudaimonism 9–10, 139, 149–66
    activity principle 161–65
eupatheia 131–33, 137, 138, 139–41
Eusebius 24, 25, 31–32, 222–23
Eve
    and fall of man 219–20
    as historical figure 218
    and sin 167–85, 186–87, 196
evil
    origin of 167–85, 219
    as privation of goodness 185

Fahrenheit 451 58
faith 205–6, 213
faith-invested philosophy 12
false gods 46–47
female body
    Augustine's interest in 77
    as normative body 7
    in resurrection 77, 87–88, 99–100, 146
fictional suffering 114–17
fideism 213
Final Good *see summum bonum*
Firmus 27, 29
First Cause 216
first-person body 91
fornication by the soul 116–17
forsaking God 190
France, Anatole 58
Franciscans 241
freedom, love of 125–26
friendly feelings 160–61
friends, and grief 162

genera humanae distinctions 47–48
General Philosophy 12, 206, 207–12, 221, 223–24
Genesis 187
glorification of God 101
glory
    pagan/Roman 125–28, 215
    and possessions 72
God
    ability to see 93–94

forsaking of 190
justice of response to sin 192–97
response to Adam's sin 190–91
gods, sins of 114–15
good life and *eudaimonia* term 150–51
goods (bona) 152–54
Gospels, belief in 210
Goths 75–76, 215
government and disharmony 69–70
grace 128
Grafton, Anthony 31–32
Gregory, Eric 62–63
Gregory of Rimini 243
grief 138–39, 160–61, 163–64
and friends 162
Griffiths, Paul 5–6

happiness 160–61
and *eudaimonia* term 150–51
Hebrew culture 25
Hebrew prophets 26
hell 186–87, 193–94
Herdt, Jennifer 8
higher goods 69–70
historical enquiry 16
history 16–18
Augustine's use of 222
and *City of God* 27–32
and human understanding 222
and literalism 220–21
Old Testament 223
and truth 213–14
holy spectacles 121–22
Homer 25
Honorius 222–23
Horace 125–26
Hortensius 205, 206
human dignity 142–47
human experience of life 19
human mind, limitations of 211
human ontogeny 17
human phylogeny 17
human trafficking 141–42
humanity, perversion of 189–90
humility 78, 120–22, 123, 217
and rape 82
Huxley, Aldous 58
hypocrisy 71–72
Hypognosticon 233

idolatry 46–47
impotence 84
incarnate life 6–7
incarnation 7, 146
and faith 213–14

indifferents 152–54, *see also* Stoicism
inestirpabile insediamente (ineradicable parasite),
and creation 70
infant baptism 236–37
infants, virtuous disposition of 236–37
Innocent III, Pope 236
instrumental goods 151–52
intelligent body 91
interpretation issues 226
intrinsic goods 151–52
Io, daughter of Inachus (aka Isis) 26
Isidore of Seville 228
Isis 26
Israel/Church 44–45, 46–51

Jager, Eric 31
James, Epistle of 214
Jerome 24, 25, 26–27, 31–32, 75, 232, 235–36
Jesus *see* Christ
Jewish scriptures, supreme importance of 21
Jewish/Christian scriptures 26–27
John the Baptist 235–36
justice
in government 72–73
in mercy 136

Kant, Immanuel 154, 180–82
Kaufman, Peter 5–6
Kent, Bonnie 12–13
Kierkegaard, Søren 160
killing, commandment against 81
kinship and sin 56, 197, 201–4
Kristeva, Julia 84

Lateran Council, marriage annulments 234–35
leadership and Christianity 57
Lepelley, Claude 62–63, 67–68
Liber regularum 17–18
liberty, love of 125–26
libido dominandi (lust for mastery) 48–49, 78, 85, 125–26
Libri disciplinarum 22
life under condemnation 195
Life of Zeno 140
life-goods 151–52
literalism 220–21
liturgy, theatrical character of 120
Livy 71–72
Lombard, Peter 229, 230, 231–37, 238, 242, 243–44
love command 160–61
love, of souls 163–64
Lucretia 81, 123, 232

lust 83–84, 99–100
  as punishment for sin 87
Luther, Martin 234–37, 243

magistrates
  in Africa 67–68
  responsibilities of 66–67, 69
Manicheism 16, 17, 206–7
Marcellinus 28, 214
Markus, Robert 3–4, 5, 6, 86
marriage, among priests/nuns/monks 234–35
Marrou, Henri-Irénée 14
martyrdom 50–51, 112, 114, 120, 121–22
Mary (mother of Christ) 213–14
Matthew 25 187
Medea 138
Mediator 221
medieval scholars of Augustine 227–31
mendicant orders 241
mental images (*phantasiae*) 158
mental qualities 234
mercy 102–4, 134–36, 137, 201, *see also* clemency
metaphysics 167–72, 212, 215–16, 217, 223
metaphysics of the will 10–12
Milbank, John 67
Miles, Margaret R. 6–7
mingled cities 4, 5
misericordia see compassion
Monica 93
moral personality 180–82
moral virtue 234
moralism
  Augustine and Kant 182
  in Genesis 183–84
morality 138–39
mortalities 174–75
Moses 16–17
myth, and origin of evil 179–85
mythical religion 215–16

natural goods 152–54
natural religion 215–16
natural rights (Seneca) 144
Nectarius 67–68
  correspondence with Augustine 71
Neoplatonists 209, 210–11, 217
Nicomachean Ethics 150, 156
1984 58
North Africa, news from 55–57
Numa Pompilius 20–24
Nussbaum, Martha 130, 142, 143, 149
Nygren, Anders 160

Old Testament history 223
ombudsmen 61–62

On 83 Different Questions 231
On the Advantage of Believing 209
On the Catholic Way of Life 229–30, 238
On Christian Instruction 231
On Clemency 130, 134–36
On the Dangers of the Last Times 241–42
On Free Choice 232, 237–38
On Free Will 186–87, 208
On the Good of Marriage 234, 235–36, 239
On the Greatness of the Soul 237–38
On the Happy Life 208
On the Nature of the Good 238
On Providence 141
On Spirit and Soul 237–38
On the Trinity 208, 232
On True Religion 163–64
order of love 225–26
Origen 114, 218, 219, 222–23
origin of evil 167–85
original sin (Genesis) 10–12, 16–17, 167–85
Orosius 75–76
Orwell, George 58

pagan philosophy 221
pagan spectacle 112–14, 121–22
pagan virtue 7–10, 123–25, 128–29, 207–12, 221, 225–26
pagan worship 111, 112, 113
pagan/Christian conversion 3, 140, 215, 223–24
pagan/Christian rulers 36
paganism
  African 222–23
  as demonic perversion 3
  as lust for mastery 2
  pillars of 73
pain, and Stoicism 139
parental sins 56, 197, 201–3
Parrish, John 62–63
passiones martyrum (martyrdom) 50–51
pathos 132, 133
Paul, Saint 16–17, 159, 170–71, 174–75, 202
peace and tranquility 53–54
Pelagius 175
Penguin Island 58
peregrinatio 52–53
Peripatetic (Aristotelian) eudaimonism 149, 166
Peripatetic principles 156, 158, 166
Perpetua 146
persons, as components 88–92
perversion of humanity 189–90
perversity of Adam's sin 197–201
Peter of Poitiers 233, 237
Philip the Chancellor 237–38
philosophers, and imagination 95–96

philosophical egoism 154–55
philosophy, non-Christian 223
pilgrimage 1
pillage *see* rape
pineal gland 88
pity 143
Plato 216–18
    and Porphyry 221
Platonists 7, 212, 223
    and body/soul link 108
    and complacency 109–10
    and ideology of empire 106
    and Incarnation 106–7
    and mimesis 117–19
    as pagan thinkers 218
    and polytheism 107, 216–18
    and pridefulness 119
    and resurrection 95, 96–98
    and worship/glorification of God 101
Plotinus 146, 211, 216, 222
political perfectionism 52
politics, secular 51–54
Porphyry 16, 101, 105–6, 107, 118, 216, 221
possessions 68
Possidius 14, 228
power of choice 142, 143–44
prayer 67
preferables 152–54
preferred indifferents 141
pride
    in chastity 81–82
    and Platonic mimesis 117–19
    and sin 177
    as worldly desire 102
principle of emotional detachment 156–57
procreation, lust-free 84
prodigal son 202
prohairesis see power of choice
prophetic authority 94
prophetic revelation, and salvation 105–6
prophetic scripture 95
providence 5, 15, 21, 97, 141, 212, 215, 216
Psalms as inspiration 20
Ptolemy Philadelphus 26–27
public service 71
punishment 136, 141–42, 190–91, 193–94, 196–97, 203–4, 218
    and kinship 56, 197, 201–03

rape 76, 77–83
ratiocinatio, as distortion of reason 95
reason
    and knowledge 209
    and truth 208
Regulus 123, 124–25, 126–27

Religion within the Boundaries of Mere Reason 180–82
remota justitia (justice removed/remote) 59
Remus 220
Republic 72–73
res populi 40–41
res publica 40–41
resurrection 6–7, 209–10
    of bodies 88–92
    of Christ 97, 99–100
    Ephesians passage 98–99
    of female body 77, 87–88, 99–100
    and nature 96
    and Platonists 95, 96–98
    and reasoning 94–101
    and virginity 80
    and vision of God 93–94
Retractations 1, 28, 29, 32, 230, 231, 232, 233, 242–43
Revelations (as book of life) 31
revenge 135
righteousness of man as created 187–88
Rist, John 12, 123
Rome
    atrocities, on own people 215
    Christianization of 222–23
    decline of 55–57, 75–76
    epics 14
    moral corruption 112
    as paving way for Christianity 223–24
    sack of 2, 75–76, 78–79, 215
    spectacle 112–14, 121–22
    stagnation of 108–09
    success and will of God 215
Romulus 26, 220
Runia 131

saeculum 4, 6, 19, 214
    hoc saeculum 33, 34, 45
    meanings of 33–34
    political constitution of 38–46
    saeculum futurum 33, 38
    and the secular 35–38
sage
    possibility of becoming 165
    Stoics' use of term 157
saints, eternal life of 93–94
Salamito, Jean-Marie 62–63
Sallust 71–72, 125–26, 215
Salvian of Marseilles 60
sanctuary 76
Satan 167–85, 192
scriptores historiae 26
second death 191
secular cities story 35

secular clergy, and mendicant orders 241
secularity
  Augustinian 51–54
  and the *saeculum* 35–38
select gods 21
self-glorification 48–49, 102, 103
Seneca 130, 134–36, 137, 141, 143, 144, 243–44
Sentences 229, 231–34, 235–36, 238
Septuagint 26–27
serene fear 62
servitium in caritate (service in loving kindness) 49
Seven Sages 25, 26
sexual activity (lust) 83–84
Sheets-Johnstone, Maxine 80, 91
Sibylline prophecies 26
Sic et non 232
Sider, Ted 193–94
sin
  Adam's *see* Adam
  equality of 222
  original 10–12, 16–17, 167–85
  in paradise 187–92
  perversity of 197–201
  and pride 177
  punishment of Adam 190–91
  punishment for parents' 197
  sexual transmission of 179, 180
  and will 186–87
Skepticism 207–08
slavery 65–66, 83
social order 85–86
societal norms/laws 37–38
societates hominum (human societies) 38–40, 43–45
solidarity 7
solidarity-in-transformation 103
Soliloquies 208
sollertia (integrity/ingenuity) 62
Solomon 65
sorrow 160–61
soul/body mixture 89
souls
  fornication by 116–17
  love of 163–64
  punishment of 218
spectacles *see* holy spectacles; pagan spectacle; stage plays
spiritual reconnaissance 65
spurious works 237
stage plays 114–17
state, term 41
Stoic eudaimonism 149
Stoicism 8–9, 130–48, 147–48
  and activity thesis 152–54
  and assent 213
  Augustine's rejection of 166

characteristics of Stoics 156–57
and clemency 139, 143
dis-preferables 152–54
emotional detachment principle 157–61
and Epicureanism 139, 140–41
and equality of sins 222
and Final Good 165
goods and preferables 152–54
inconsistency of 137–41
indifferents 152–54
and isolationism 137–41
pain avoidance 139–41
preferred indifferents 141
principle of emotional detachment 156–57
and punishment 222
and suffering 138
and suicide 139–41
and theory of affectivity 130
sub specie aeternitatis 43
suffering, as permitted by God 81
suicide 49–50
  by pagan heroes 125
  Cato's 126–27
  denounced by Jerome 232
  and rape 80–81
  and Stoicism 139–41
Summa on the Good 237–38
Summa theologiae 226–27, 229–31
summum bonum 165
suspense (distentio) 20
Symposium 217

Taylor, Charles 147
The Teacher 205–06
Tertullian 114, 121–22, 127
The Theater of the Virtues 8
theatrical fiction 117–19
theodicy and will 186–87
Theodosius 222–23
theologia 20
theurgy 118, 210
tomology 30
torture 136, 141–42
Tractates on the Gospel of John 232
tragic drama 114–17
tranquillitas ordinis 37
Trevet, Nicholas 243–44
true reason 94
true religion, eternal life as goal of 215–16
true worship of God 101–02
truth 209
  and history 213–14
  inconvenient 211
Tusculan Disputations 132

two-cities distinction 1–4
two-loves ethic 12–13
Tyconius 17–18

Upheavals of Thought 149

vagueness problem, and punishment 193–94
Valerius Pinianus 60–61
Varro 20–24, 26, 30–32, 34, 215
Vessey, Mark 5, 13
via Gregorii 243
Virgil 28, 35, 125–26, 214
virginity 235
    and resurrection 80
virtue 134, 138, 233
    as dispositions 234–37, 238–39
    and free choice 233
    as good will 237–38
    as highest love of God 230
    Latin definition 225–26
    living with 156
    moral 234
    as *ordo amoris* 229–30
    as rightly ordered love 225–26
    in *Summa theologiae* 226–27
    as vice 225–26, 240

virtue ethics 136, 137
virtues
    multiple definitions of 237–38
    naturally acquired 240–41
    pagan 7–10, 123–25, 128–29, 207–12, 221, 225–26
    separability of 235–36
virtuous dispositions 235
    of infants 236–37
Visigoths 2, 75–76
vision of God 93–94

Waleys, Thomas 243–44
wellbeing-goods 151–52
Wetzel, James 10–11, 128
wicked world, as seen by Augustine 58–59
will 186–87
    to sin 178
William of Saint-Amour 241–42
Wolterstorff, Nicholas 9–10, 62
Works of Love 160
world
    beauty of 100–01
    as a land of lies 70

Zeno of Citium 132

Printed in the United States
By Bookmasters